These Things We Tried

A Five-Year Experiment in Community Development
Initiated and Carried out
by the
Extension Division
of the
University of Virginia

Ogden, Jean (Carter)

Jean and Jess Ogden

Foreword by

George Baskerville Zehmer

University of Virginia Extension

Vol. XXV, No. 6   October 15, 1947

Published monthly in August, November, December, March, April and
semi-monthly in September, October, January, February, at
University, Virginia

UNIVERSITY OF VIRGINIA EXTENSION DIVISION
SPECIAL PROJECTS IN ADULT EDUCATION

Special Projects Staff

JOHN LLOYD NEWCOMB, President of the University

GEORGE BASKERVILLE ZEHMER, Director

JESSE SWITZER OGDEN, Associate Director

JEAN CARTER OGDEN, Associate Director

JOHN CHENEY, Librarian, January, 1941-December 31, 1942

ANNE IRVIN FAULKNER, Field Work Assistant. March, 1943-June, 1944 (half time)

MARGARET SNYDER, Special Assistant in Resource Use Education Materials. September 1, 1945-

THOMAS HOWARD CORDLE, Secretary. January 1, 1941-February 15, 1942[1]

JENNY CHRISTOFFERSEN FERNBACH, Secretary. February 15, 1942-September 15, 1944

BESSIE LEE DESPER, Secretary. September 15, 1944-

SPECIAL ASSISTANTS FOR SUMMER PROGRAMS AND LOCAL WORKSHOPS

WAYLAND JACKSON HAYES, Professor of Sociology, Vanderbilt University
Summer Workshops, 1943, 1944, 1945
Local Workshops, January, 1945-August, 1945

WILLIAM BUNYAN JONES, Professor of Sociology, University of Tennessee
Local Workshops, September 1, 1945-December 31, 1945

MORRIS RANDOLPH MITCHELL, Macedonia Cooperative Community
Summer Workshops, 1943, 1944

WILLIAM RICHARD SAVAGE, Principal Holland High School
Summer Program, 1941-1942

MEMBERS OF EXTENSION DIVISION WHO HAVE ASSISTED

JOHN ALEXANDER RORER, Associate Director of the Extension Division

JOHN NORVILLE GIBSON FINLEY, Associate Director of the Extension Division[2]

---

[1]Left for service with armed forces, February, 1942
[2]Left for service with armed forces, April, 1943

FOREWORD

Acknowledging contributions to a cause in which one is deeply interested is a pleasing experience. Giving credit to those who have assisted Special Projects in Adult Education is a duty as well, for the facts concerning the numerous contributions, whether they consisted of money, ideas, or services, are an important part of the story of the initiation of Special Projects and of their development.

Acknowledgments are not easy to record because many persons have contributed in many different ways, on many different occasions, and under many different circumstances. Furthermore, everyone associated with Special Projects was so absorbed in the program, and the *esprit de corps* was so high that no one seemed concerned whether he received credit personally for whatever contribution he made. As one looks back over the experiences of the past five years it is difficult, if not impossible, in most instances to say who contributed the idea or service which led to some noteworthy development. The spirit of cooperation that characterizes the successful community activities described in this report prevailed also among those who initiated and conducted this experimental program. However, while realizing the difficulty in telling the full story, I wish to make some acknowledgments.

In the years when I was exploring the possibility of a regional program in adult education, the following gave generously of their time and ideas and offered many words of encouragement: President Frank P. Graham of the University of North Carolina; President Oliver C. Carmichael of Vanderbilt University; Dr. Arthur Howe, then President of Hampton Institute; Dr. A. F. Kuhlman, Librarian of Vanderbilt University; and Dr. Morse A. Cartwright, Director of the American Association for Adult Education. Valuable suggestions and encouragement came also from many Southern leaders in adult education too numerous to mention here. In several instances these leaders traveled many miles at their personal expense to lend support to the proposal.

iii

When the idea of a regional program failed to develop into reality, no person contributed so much to the initiation of the Virginia experiment as William A. Smith. He was most active in raising funds necessary for starting Special Projects. Equally important were his enthusiasm—even zeal—for the undertaking and his many valuable suggestions for its establishment and conduct.

Mr. Smith's interest in discovering new and more effective ways for helping people to help themselves was born of conviction. As director for Virginia, first of Federal Emergency Relief Administration and then of Works Progress Administration, he had seen clearly the necessity of direct government aid to individuals and communities during the depression years; but he was convinced that he saw in such aid dangers both for individuals and communities affected thereby. He observed evidence of willingness on the part of individuals and communities to let the state and federal governments assume responsibility which in a democracy belongs to the individuals themselves or to the neighborhoods and communities of which they are a part. He felt that the movement toward state and federal responsibility in government was too rapid and that in some areas it had already gone too far. He wanted to keep the people conscious of their rights and responsibilities as citizens and to see that they helped build the communities in which they were to live. Furthermore, he was aware of the fact that in periods both of prosperity and depression the communities of Virginia and of the South were not conserving and using intelligently their resources—natural, human, and institutional. He saw the necessity for a thorough-going study and analysis of all these and related factors and for a new, vigorous, and perhaps unorthodox approach to the problem.

Fortunately, many of Mr. Smith's ideas about the experiment were put down in rather voluminous notes. He was in the process of reorganizing and editing these notes at the time of his death. They have been carefully studied and have been a source of inspiration and help throughout the experiment. They are affectionately referred to by the staff as the "William

iv

A. Smith Bible." This "Bible" and the project itself constitute a monument to the man—a monument which he himself helped build out of his fervent desire to serve his state and nation.

President Newcomb's interest, his advice on questions of policy and procedures, and his assistance on budgetary matters have been invaluable, both during the formative years and throughout the program.

Dr. Rowland A. Egger, Director of the University Bureau of Public Administration, who at the time was Director of the Budget for the State of Virginia, was most helpful also in initiating Special Projects and in obtaining the original appropriations with which to finance the program.

The project was fortunate in having in the early days of the experiment the counsel of a number of experienced men of affiairs who were kind enough to serve as consultants. Some of these consultants traveled at their own expense to the University to spend a day or more in conferences. Their fruitful suggestions contributed to the pool of ideas from which the program emerged. The following served in this capacity: Dr. George S. Mitchell, Farm Security Administration, Washington, D. C.; Dr. Floyd Nelson House, Professor of Sociology, University of Virginia; Mr. Robert West, formerly Director of the Bureau of Industrial Research, University of Virginia; Dr. Robert House, Dean of Administration, University of North Carolina; Dr. Dabney S. Lancaster, State Superintendent of Public Instruction; Dr. Lorin A. Thompson, Director, University Bureau of Population and Economic Research (formerly the Bureau of Industrial Research); Mr. R. S. Hummel, then State Administrator of WPA; and Mr. Hugh R. Pomeroy, then Director of the Virginia State Planning Board.

Immediately preceding this acknowledgment will be found the names of the members of the Special Projects staff, also the names of members of the Extension Division staff who made special contributions to the program. Not only did I receive the heartiest cooperation from each member of the official family, but I observed unusual devotion on their part to the project and to the purposes it was established to serve. It is

v

important to point out also that many members of the Extension Division staff and of the faculty who have not been mentioned by name made valuable contributions by way of suggestions or encouragement. These often came in conversations, or in the form of notes or memoranda written in longhand and left on my desk or that of another staff member. None of these suggestions or words of encouragement has gone unnoticed or unheeded.

Acknowledgment should be made of the assistance received from many, many individuals in the experimental centers in which Special Projects helped conduct programs and in the communities visited in search of *New Dominion Series* stories or other information. As pointed out in the report, first association with individuals in the field frequently revealed little more than skepticism mingled with courtesy toward the University's demonstrating an interest in community affairs. From this not unexpected beginning there developed general interest and, in many instances, most enthusiastic cooperation. Cooperation meant sharing of ideas as well as of labors. Out of these associations have grown warm and lasting friendships based on common interests. Nothing would give me and the other members of the Special Projects staff more pleasure, and nothing would be more in the interest of the truth concerning the whole program than to record the names of those in the field who have contributed so generously to the program. But it is literally true that such a list would require many pages; furthermore, it would be difficult indeed to prepare a list that would not omit the names of many who should be included. However, failure to recognize the contributions of citizens—lay and professional, old and young, white and colored, rich and poor—would result in an inaccurate picture of the manner in which the program developed and functioned.

Neither should "fan mail" go unrecognized nor should its importance be overlooked. Immediately following the distribution of the first number in the *New Dominion Series*, letters began to arrive. As other *New Dominion Series* were released and as word about the project as a whole spread, letters increased in numbers. They came from every state in the nation and from several foreign countries. They came from laymen as well as professional workers. Most frequently they asked to be placed on the mailing list for *New Dominion Series* and other releases or announcements about the program. But often they extended words of encouragement also and sometimes offered excellent suggestions, asked for additional information, and called attention to good community self-help programs. In fact, studying and answering "fan mail" could have become an important and almost full-time job for a person well versed in the project's purposes and program.

While it is true that many individuals contributed ideas or services, or both, which in the aggregate make up the story of Special Projects, a word should be said about the role that Mr. and Mrs. Ogden played in this little drama. With the exception of the director, they have been members of the Special Projects staff longer than any others. They have devoted all their time to developing the program. "All" means almost literally all, for they worked all hours of the day and night, and frequently Sundays and holidays, as well as week-days. For nearly five years they have not had what could properly be called a vacation! But they contributed more than time and effort. They gave generously of ideas and suggestions. They exhibited in a noteworthy degree other qualities so essential to the conduct of an experiment of the character described: sympathy with and faith in people; human understanding; tact; organizing ability; perseverance to follow through with a program to its conclusion, successful or otherwise; mastery of techniques and flexibility in applying them to situations. Throughout, they have been originators as well as doers. In all sincerity I can say that in many ways I have been at school to the Ogdens. Special Projects owes much to them.

Members of the staff and of the workshops held at the University will approve, I feel sure, my recognition of Mrs. Zehmer's contributions in sympathy and interest as well as in more tangible ways. A cool drink or a plate dinner prepared frequently without the assistance of servants and served on our lawn after a hot day on the road or during summer workshop conferences did not hinder the development among staff and workers of the spirit of *camaraderie* and fellowship to which I have already referred.

Not only did ideas and suggestions come from many different sources, but financial contributions were shared widely also. Through Mr. Smith's interest and effort and through Dr. Egger's understanding and assistance, the sum of $42,800 was assigned to Special Projects from balances in FERA funds when that agency was liquidated. Later, from an anonymous source, $7,700 was added to the original appropriation. The American Association for Adult Education through the interest of its director, Morse A. Cartwright, contributed $7,500 to help finance the *New Dominion Series*. The General Education Board made several grants to the projects or closely related activities: one of $7,500 to the local workshops in community study and development; another of $3,300 to the summer programs with high school principals; a third of $8,000 to activities dealing specifically with the conservation and use of community resources. The Peoples National Bank and the National Bank and Trust Company of Charlottesville jointly contributed $2,000 for the purchase of motion pictures on community resources and their conservation and use. Communities helped meet the costs of the community workshops and other local projects undertaken cooperatively. (The services of members of the Special Projects staff or those of members of the Extension Division staff represented the only contributions, with two exceptions, that were made to localities. The fact that Special Projects could not finance local programs was explained clearly and forcibly whenever and wherever such programs were initiated.) Institutional agencies, such as the Virginia Federation of Women's Clubs and Ruritan National, contributed to special programs in which they cooperated. Two state departments made financial contributions toward programs in which they were especially interested. The University of Virginia assisted through general Extension

Division appropriations and through appropriations to Special Projects. In round numbers, $71,500 was actually spent on the more experimental and exploratory phases of Special Projects up to June 30, 1945. Since that date the University, through appropriations to the Extension Division, is carrying most of the cost of the program which we hope is now on a permanent basis.

A final note of caution seems in order. There is danger that readers of the report on Special Projects may conclude from the emphasis placed on the spirit of cooperation among staff members, from the statements concerning the qualifications of the Ogdens for the role which they played in the experiment, and from the smoothness with which the story unfolds, that an indefinable something approaching magic was largely responsible for the successes reported. Such a conclusion would indeed be erroneous. If I had to summarize briefly those factors contributing to the success of this experiment in community development, they would include the following: a sound and integrated philosophy which includes faith in people and in the democratic way of life; extensive training and experience in working with people; mastery of techniques without slavish adherence to patterns of procedure; a willingness and ability to learn from others and from new experiences; almost unlimited patience when people and communities do not move as fast as you would have them or in the direction in which you would like them to go; and last, but not least, hard work. There is no substitute for hard work—and that work at times when the people are conscious of the need for assistance, rather than at hours or seasons determined by the program of an institution or the convenience of an individual.

—GEORGE BASKERVILLE ZEHMER, *Director*
Extension Division, University of
Virginia.

April, 1946

CONTENTS

INTRODUCTION

The Virginia Program In Brief Review

As these words are being written, the world is waiting for confirmation of the report that the war in the Pacific has ended. The past week has been one of the most momentous in history. It has seen the use by man of atomic energy which can—and will for better or for worse—revolutionize the physical world. Its first use has been for destruction—an unavoidable destruction, we hopefully assure ourselves, that is to clear the way for building a brave new world.

The suffering and sacrifice of the years just past can be justified by nothing less than the finest world of which the mind of man can dream. With the war ended, we must turn our energies to waging a total peace. which will make that dream reality. Are we ready for the task? Ready or not, it is ours to attempt. And in the quality of the attempt lies the significance of the victory.

The experimental program which is the subject of this report could not end at a time better fitted to test the validity of its findings. It has had for its purpose discovering techniques whereby communities can help themselves. It has been based on the assumption that democracy begins in the community. It has proceeded with the conviction that "each individual affected must come better to understand his problems, his proper relationship and responsibility to the economic, social, and political orders. He must have an individual part in evolving and executing simple, understandable plans for the solution of those problems and the establishment of those relationships. Only in this way can he be expected to assume his rightful part and full share of responsibility as a citizen."[1] Only as he assumes that part and that responsibility can the dream of democracy be realized.

The problems to be met on the home front are so urgent and so immediate that one hesitates, at this moment, to use

---

[1]William A. Smith, "How People Can Educate Themselves to Help Themselves." 1940. Typed. 60 pages.

precious time for writing a report. On the other hand, questions come daily from other communities, from other states, from other countries that likewise are groping for ways of working more deftly and more effectively at the grass roots. It is to offer our experience in partial answer to these questions, as well as to rally our own forces for fresh attack, that we pause for summary and evaluation.

THE PROGRAM IN SUMMARY

In the next few pages an attempt is made to present the general plans for and procedure in a program, each part of which is analyzed in detail in subsequent sections of the report. With this introductory background, the reader, it is hoped, can use any one or more sections in which he is especially interested and see them in relation to the whole.

Special Projects in Adult Education Begin

In January, 1941, the Extension Division of the University of Virginia began actual work on an experimental and exploratory program called *Special Projects in Adult Education*. This beginning was the culmination in Virginia of several years of thinking and planning that had been directed toward the economic, social, and cultural advancement of the Southern region. That this phase of the program began as it did at the University of Virginia at this time was, in large part, the result of a plan made by Mr. William A. Smith and of funds made available through his efforts. The background of the program and its relation to regional plans are discussed in the section of the report entitled "Evolution of the Virginia Approach."

Purpose, Range, Philosophy, and Approach

Reduced to its simplest terms, the purpose of the Virginia program was: *to find ways of helping communities to help themselves through the efforts of their own citizens.*

Its range included all phases of living—social, economic, and cultural. To find ways to stimulate communities to raise their standards in any of these areas and then to help them to implement their programs, drawing on whatever resources—

local, state, or federal—were available, was the assignment of the staff of the Extension Division and of the Special Projects in Adult Education.

The philosophy on which the program was based was an honest belief in the democratic way of life. Democracy, it was assumed, *exists* where everyone has the *opportunity for choice*. If it is to do more than exist, everyone *must desire to use his opportunity for choice*. Assuming that our constitutional government gives us the framework which makes possible the realization of such a goal, the general aim of the program was to help individuals and communities learn to choose their ways of living and, having made the choice, to achieve the desired results.

The specific objective of the staff was *to discover ways*: (1) of arousing interest, or disturbing inertia, or creating a divine discontent; (2) of broadening horizons in social thinking with reference to the potentialities of community life; (3) of achieving community goals *considered desirable by those whose lives were to be affected*, through the combined thinking and effort of those same persons.

Though tangible results were to be sought as evidence of the soundness of a special approach or method, *the primary concern was with method rather than with results*. For the sake of this experiment, results were to be the by-products, and validated generalizations about procedures were the main objective.

The approach to the problem was from two directions: (1) finding and disseminating information about ways that have worked—or are working—in various communities; (2) experimenting in selected areas with ways that might work.

Emphasis in both cases was on *finding methods that make people increasingly able to help themselves*.

Steps in Exploration

In connection with what was already being done successfully in many communities in certain areas of living, the first step was to discover, collect, and evaluate printed materials and unpublished reports of various agencies and groups concerned with community betterment. The second step was to visit community programs that were already under way and to talk with persons responsible for them. The third was to work out effective ways of making the information thus collected available to citizens and of helping them to relate it to their own problems and programs. Tangible results of this exploratory program are:

(1) Pamphlet Files and Kits

Printed pamphlets, unpublished reports, clippings, and mimeographed material on many aspects of community life have been classified for easy use by staff and students. Selected materials have been put together in kits available through the Extension Division to individuals, local study groups or workshops, and community councils. Special kits are assembled by the staff to meet special requests.

(2) The *New Dominion Series*

A series of 72 success stories has been published and distributed by the Extension Division. Each story describes a successful community program with emphasis always on *how* and *by whom* rather than on what. The stories have been written for the ordinary citizen, though professional workers, teachers, and students have not been excluded from the mailing list. This series has been mailed eighteen times a year to upward of 4,000 persons in all walks of life in the hope of inspiring some communities to action and of helping others implement the programs already under way.

Procedures used in the three steps of this exploratory program are described in detail and evaluated on the basis of our experience and observation in the sections of the report entitled "Looking at Others" and "Ways That Have Worked —or Have Not."

Setup for Experimentation

For the experimental part of the program, it was decided to select three different kinds of rural communities in Virginia, each typical of areas found throughout the Southeast.

One was a mountain county made up largely of marginal

and submarginal farms, typical of the Southern Appalachian area.

The second was a central Virginia piedmont county of moderate prosperity in which agriculture and timber were the chief resources and in which the small farmer rather than the tenant composed the bulk of the population.

The third was in the tidewater area. It had large farms and many tenants and extremes of wealth and poverty. It also presented the complex problems faced by rural dwellers who earn their living in a nearby industrial area.

A different approach was made in each county. It was determined to a small degree by the interests of the staff; and in large part, by the nature of the community, by the patterns of living and attitudes of the people, and by already existing programs and leadership, both lay and professional.

In the mountain county (Greene) an approach was made through getting well acquainted with the people in the various communities in an attempt to have them gain an understanding of neighborhood problems and to work out toward the development of a countywide program. Two staff members lived in the county for several months and have continued to identify themselves with activities there. No attempt was made to set up a new agency but every effort was made to supplement and strengthen programs already in operation.

In the piedmont county (Louisa) the method was to invite prominent citizens to meet with members of the Extension Division staff for discussion of county problems, and through a citizens' council to attempt solution of these problems. Staff members, after a number of preliminary informal visits, have gone into this county primarily to work with the council or its committees and to cooperate with other organizations when especially invited.

In the tidewater county (Nansemond) an attempt was made to encourage the development of a program in one section of the county, the Holy Neck District, under the direction of the principal of the consolidated high school. Here the Extension Division acted in an advisory capacity and paid the principal to devote his summers entirely to community work.

Extension of Experimental Program

Partly as a result of the experience in Nansemond, and partly in response to interest expressed by school people, in the spring of 1943 a plan was made in cooperation with the State Board of Education for extending the experimental community program through the employment of selected high school principals on a twelve-month basis with the understanding that the summer months would be devoted largely to community work.

It was decided to begin the summer program with a three-week workshop in community development at the University conducted by the staff of the Special Projects assisted by a sociologist and numerous guest specialists. The seven principals selected formed the nucleus of the group. The State Department of Public Welfare selected and sent three county superintendents. An elementary school principal made the eleventh member of the workshop.

The extension staff continued to work in an advisory capacity to members of this group in their local community programs throughout the following year. In two of the counties represented, the principals who had attended the summer workshop asked that staff members come to their communities throughout the winter to conduct local workshops in order that more people might have an understanding of the possibilities and procedures in community programs. This plan worked so well that the number of requests increased more rapidly than they could be met by the limited staff.

Second and third summer workshops at the University in 1944 and 1945 included not only more counties but also, on recommendation of the first group, many interests and agencies other than school principals and welfare workers. Vocational agriculture teachers, ministers, representatives of women's clubs and service clubs, county officials, and public health workers were among those who attended.

It was necessary to add a special member to the year-round staff in 1944-45 to help conduct local workshops organized as a result of the interest of participants in the summer workshops. Thus by the end of 1945, twenty-two counties in the state had become a part of the extended experimental program of the Special Projects in Adult Education.

A detailed analysis and evaluation of the experimental work is given in the section of the report entitled "Trying Things Ourselves."

Special Techniques

Just as it was decided to try a different approach in each community, so it was determined to try in all communities a variety of adult education "techniques." These included: (1) experiments with the printed word, such as books specially selected for a particular group, kits of pamphlet materials, reading lists accompanied by the offer to supply the material referred to, bulletins specially prepared by local groups for local consumption, and the *New Dominion Series* already referred to; (2) use of motion pictures with groups on various levels of socialization and education; (3) study groups and workshops—in neighborhoods, on a countywide basis, with professional workers from a district of the state, at the University Summer School, and on wheels.

Reports of these "techniques" logically belong with "Trying Things Ourselves." They are referred to in the various community programs discussed in that section. A detailed report on each, however, would blur the main story there. In order to answer the many questions we have received about specific techniques and, at the same time, to avoid hiding the woods by the trees, we have devoted a separate section to their discussion. A chapter on each technique is included in the part entitled "Ways That Have Worked—or Have Not."

The Geographical Area and Its Implications

The geographical areas of both experimentation and first-hand exploration were, of necessity, restricted. The experimental program involved only Virginia communities; the exploratory included for visit and evaluation communities in Virginia, Maryland, North Carolina, South Carolina, Tennessee, Kentucky, Georgia, and Alabama. For the collection of materials about programs, communities throughout the United States and in other countries were drawn upon. A study of

these shows certain fundamental problems and methods of attack whether the community be in Virginia or Ohio, in South
India or southern United States. We have found much in
the exploration of communities in other states and regions
that has been of help in those communities in which we were
especially interested. In like manner, we believe that what
we have learned by experimenting in Virginia and by exploring the Southeast has more than local application and significance.

The Usefulness of This Report

This report does not offer any formula or pattern—except
possibly the formula that each community must work out its
own pattern. It does offer, we believe, some indication of direction and some ways in which citizens may find that direction and may move steadily along toward the goal of the good
community.

As the Virginia program has evolved, staff members have
steadfastly sought to isolate and define more clearly those
ways of working that would make individuals and their communities increasingly able to help themselves. More spectacular immediate results might have been achieved in other
ways, but, we reiterate, *the process rather than the product
has been our concern.*

Only as individuals and communities become adept in the
process of self-development can we have anything more than
sporadic and isolated movements toward the kind of world
that is both desirable and possible of attainment. Adult education must be concerned with giving the persons involved
mastery of the tools of social progress. The Special Projects
in Adult Education sponsored by the Extension Division of
the University of Virginia have tried to do that in the areas
they have touched.

All members of the staff have had that same faith in people and in democratic processes that motivated those whose
vision was responsible for setting up such a program within a
state university. They have sought ways of stimulating and
guiding and of making information available to individuals,
neighborhoods, and larger communities. They have retained

an experimental attitude and flexibility in adapting themselves to the needs of each community. Only as this faith exists and this flexibility is observed will the approaches and techniques described in the following sections of this report have any validity for others.

Part One

EVOLUTION OF THE VIRGINIA APPROACH

CHAPTER 1

Southern Educators Seek Solutions

The experiment in community development which has been conducted by the Extension Division of the University of Virginia is only one expression of the ferment that is at work in the South. Although this report must deal primarily with that experiment, it must be considered in relation to the total picture rather than as an unrelated bit of practical research.

During the late Thirties there was considerable discussion of the need for a regional program of adult education that would prepare the South to utilize its natural and human resources in such a way as to assure a more abundant life for all. What was beginning to happen in those areas touched by the TVA stirred the imagination of many an educator and socially minded citizen. Among those who were deeply concerned with regional planning in the South was George B. Zehmer, Director of Extension at the University of Virginia.

Southern Readings Project

For a period of more than two years, he took the initiative in conferring with educational leaders throughout the Southeast and in national organizations concerned with problems of adult education. Numerous interviews and voluminous correspondence resulted in a plan for stimulating thinking on all educational levels through a Southern Readings Project to be undertaken cooperatively by colleges and universities and other adult education agencies in the several Southern states. The thinking of two years culminated in two conferences in the spring of 1939, the first in Columbia, South Carolina, and the second in Greenville.

The need for reading materials better adapted to those persons with little formal education and no reading habit had received continuous emphasis during these conferences. Hence thinking moved from ways of getting available books into the hands of people who wanted them, to the more difficult problem of making people want books and information especially in the areas that concern "the health and the social, economic, and cultural life of the people of this region."[1]

As discussions progressed, the problem was even more clearly defined: Getting books to people was important, but relatively simple; getting people to want the information to be gained from books was even more urgent; preparing printed materials in certain fields important to the development of the South must be considered if those of limited reading ability, or habit, were to be reached; and, finally, other possible techniques for "telling the people" must be explored. All concerned recognized the need for money to launch such a program. Foundation grants were under consideration.

A Man with a Plan for Virginia

It was at the close of the Greenville conference that Mr. Zehmer was approached by another Virginian hitherto unknown to him. This man was William A. Smith. He had listened quietly but very thoughtfully to the discussion. He saw a direct relationship between all that was being said and the problems he had faced as the first state director of the Federal Emergency Relief Administration. He knew that what had happened before and during the depression years must not happen again. He was convinced that it could be prevented only if people—*all the people*—"educated themselves to help themselves." To find ways of stimulating and preparing them to take advantage of the opportunity for choice guaranteed by democracy was merely another facet of the problem of utilization of natural and human resources.

Mr. Smith thought he saw a way of attacking the problem in Virginia. Grants for the proposed regional program failed to materialize. Mr. Zehmer was not only interested in Mr. Smith's plan but also was convinced that what might be learned in Virginia could be applied to other areas in the Southeast.

In June, 1940, Mr. Smith formally requested the University of Virginia to accept a fund he had made available to

---

[1]From a report of findings of the conferences, prepared by George B. Zehmer for the American Association for Adult Education.

carry out an experimental program, the nature of which he described in a sixty-page typed booklet entitled "How People Can Educate Themselves to Help Themselves." In his subtitle he stated that this was a "program of action to stimulate and develop individual initiative for the economic and social betterment of individuals, neighborhoods, and communities."

The University Considers the Plan

Dr. John Lloyd Newcomb, President of the University, took the matter under consideration. He felt that the implications of such a program must be carefully weighed. Its relation to the University and of the University to other agencies already engaged in community work on either state or local levels must be analyzed. The sociological and economic aspects of the proposed program were clear. The educational procedures involved would have to be highly experimental. President Newcomb asked Mr. Zehmer to investigate the proposal that the University undertake, in cooperation with the Works Progress Administration in Virginia, some experimental studies in adult education as outlined by Mr. Smith.

After consultation with many persons in Virginia, in other Southern states, and in national agencies interested in certain aspects of such a program, Mr. Zehmer reported to the president in August, 1940, as follows: "With reference to the reaction to Mr. Smith's proposal, I wish to report that it was the unanimous opinion of those consulted that, while the purpose of the project is broad, general, and idealistic, it is a laudable one and one vital to the welfare of this country. . . . Furthermore, it was the almost unanimous opinion of those consulted that, while the problem is a difficult one, with the proper approaches it might be solved in part at least, and that the University of Virginia should accept the responsibility proposed by Mr. Smith and undertake to discover practical and effective means for meeting it."

In the meantime, between the submitting of his proposals in the booklet in June, 1940, and the report by Mr. Zehmer to the president in August, Mr. Smith had died. The fact that he would not be able to give advice and guidance as the program evolved was reason for further delay in final decisions.

Extension Division Named Administrative Agency

An advisory committee was invited to meet with the president. It included representatives of the Governor, of the Works Progress Administration, of the Bureau of Public Administration, and of the Extension Division of the University. Plans for administration and control were clarified. Formal approval of the program was given on December 18, 1940, with the University assuming complete responsibility and control and naming the Extension Division as the administrative agency.

Guiding Principles

In the foreword to his memorandum of June, 1940, Mr. Smith expressed the basic philosophy from which the program must develop.[2]

World unrest as it exists today forces upon the American people social, economic, and political problems of tremendous import. . . . . These result increasingly in a growing confusion of mind. Thus it is well for us to take stock, think simply, and evolve simple, understandable plans for the re-establishment of the well-being of our whole people and for the preservation of our sacred democratic institutions.

Our nation was developed and achieved its greatness through individual initiative, through individual acceptance of the challenge of the difficult, and through cooperation in meeting and overcoming obstacles and dangers. Thus by the application of the same principles, its institutions of freedom must be preserved.

This can be done only as the individual can have his rightful share and assume his proper responsibility in efforts to obtain the objective. . . . . But, as confusion and bewilderment prevail even among some of our best thinkers, so even greater confusion and bewilderment exist in the minds of the common people. . . . . Each individual must be enabled to assume his rightful part and full share of responsibility as a citizen.

[Therein is suggested a program] through which confusion may be reduced and understanding of problems increased, and through which individual efforts toward greater individual, community, and national well-being may be stimulated and encouraged.

It proposes *no quick panacea.* Instead it proposes a long-time concerted program of helping people to learn to help themselves. From such a program our national fiber and unity may be strengthened, our understanding and belief in the democratic processes and institutions made more firm. . . . .

It proposes no new organization, no diversion of attention or

------

[2]William A. Smith, "How People Can Educate Themselves to Help Themselves." 1940. Typed. 60 pages.

energy from existing regular programs, nor great expenditure of funds. Instead, it contemplates the cultivation of a more complete, effective, and intensive use of existing facilities, services, and resources in every community. . . . .

Although designed primarily for the development of opportunities for people in rural and semi-rural areas . . . . the methods and principles may be applied to urban areas as techniques improve from experience in rural areas. . . . . Out of it will come a greater self-sufficiency. . . . .

To attain this ultimate goal, Mr. Smith insisted the proposed program must achieve the following objectives:

(1) Reduce the confusion and bewilderment to the minimum possible in the minds of individuals and their families, among neighborhood groups and communities, among our governing authorities—local, state, and national;

(2) Develop and utilize local resources—human, natural, agricultural, social (including religious and spiritual as well as educational)—in a manner to provide an adequate and well-rounded living for all;

(3) Implement in fact our economic, social, and political systems to satisfy at least the essential needs for the well-being of our entire population;

(4) Provide a positive reaffirmation of what life is and can be, expressed in the personal experience, in the individual's rather than the nation's room to grow, in the unlocking of human powers and human opportunities, and in the building in a democracy of a kind of life that shall seem to all men desirable.

Such a program, Mr. Smith reiterates, must not be institutionalized. It must remain flexible. It must be developed as a program *of the people, by the people, and for the people.* It must recognize that "real individual progress can be made *only to the extent the individual participates in the formulation of a plan affecting him, and applies his energies and intelligence in its execution.*"

He states again and again his "inherent faith in the ability of the common man to improve his condition and environment if helped to help himself." To achieve this end, individuals and communities must be helped to discover and analyze their problems and to evolve a plan. They must be guided in effectuating plans and programs in solution of their problems. People, he insists, *can learn if given opportunity and will learn if given encouragement and stimulation.* Whatever is done "must be done in the democratic way—plan and work from the bottom up, not from the top down."

His general plan concludes with the statement:[3]

The last territorial frontiers and geographical areas and depleted natural resources which challenged the adventurous and offered opportunities for exploitation and wealth must be replaced by the opening of equally challenging frontiers in every community—the trails of which have been, or are being, blazed by science and research and are now awaiting the exploration and exploitation by the adventurous and inquisitive through the acquisition and intelligent, practical, and energetic application of knowledge.

Specific suggestions for procedure are offered. They include such things as neighborhood study groups, surveys by the people, community councils, and coordinating committees.

Need for Open-Mindedness and Flexibility

In his letter to President Newcomb recommending that the University accept the responsibility proposed by Mr. Smith and undertake to discover practical and effective means for meeting it, Mr. Zehmer stresses the need for open-mindedness and flexibility in the matter of exact procedures:[4]

While these approaches to the problem appear to me as being practical, they must be considered tentative and they must be clarified and modified in the light of further suggestions and study. Furthermore, even if they are undertaken, they should be altered, in the light of experience, as they are carried forward.

Progress in any of these undertakings would suggest other possible approaches to the general undertaking of helping individuals and communities to help themselves in the solution of their economic, social, and cultural problems. Each new suggestion should be examined carefully and critically . . . . .

Again and again the point was emphasized [in conferences with others] that, in so far as possible, the University should work with and through present organizations or agencies functioning in the communities which we might select as experimental centers. Care should be taken to avoid duplication and overlapping of effort. Furthermore, the dominating motive in all University effort should be to get individuals and communities to help themselves in the solution of their problems. That would mean strengthening in selected communities the agencies that are now working effectively or helping build up locally some organization or organizations that will function in the local communities. In a very genuine sense the aim of the University

3*Ibid.*
4Letter from G. B. Zehmer to President Newcomb, Aug. 28, 1940.

in the undertaking should be to make its own effort less and less
necessary and desirable. Individual and community self-help must
be the ultimate goal.

As the program developed, it moved steadily forward toward the ultimate goals as set up by Mr. Smith and Mr. Zehmer. At the same time the precautions suggested in the above
quotation were continuously kept in mind. Flexibility in approach; sensitivity to each community's assets, problems, and
folkways; and sincere interest in strengthening existing
agencies through more widespread understanding and participation by citizens were cardinal principles on which the program was based.

CHAPTER 2

Virginia Starts an Experiment

The Extension Division of the University of Virginia began actual work on its exploratory and experimental program in adult education in January, 1941. The time had come to implement the ideas that had evolved during the regional discussions of the preceding years and to make concrete the general and highly idealistic suggestions of Mr. William A. Smith.

Responsibility for achieving this purpose—for covering the bare skeleton of theory with the flesh and blood of practical application—rested with the director of the Extension Division and members of his staff.

While the regular staff gave what time they could to making the transition from planning to action, attention was turned to selecting a special staff that could give full time to developing the Special Projects. This part of the program was given the same thoughtful consideration that had characterized the growth of the idea up to this time. The plan was Mr. Smith's. His death placed on others complete responsibility for its execution. To carry it through successfully, staff members must have the same interest in people and the same faith in democratic processes that he stressed so urgently throughout his memorandum, "How People Can Educate Themselves to Help Themselves."

It was the opinion of Mr. Zehmer and his advisers that a large staff would not be necessary nor, perhaps, even desirable. This opinion was based on the assumption that "much of the work in selected communities can be accomplished more effectively by those residing and working in those communities. . . . Since the chief aim is to help individuals and communities to help themselves, emphasis should be on getting local residents to do as much of the work as possible without thought of remuneration . . . ."[1]

_____

[1]Letter from George B. Zehmer to President Newcomb, August 28. 1940.

In the same letter Mr. Zehmer stressed the importance of "selecting those whose interests, sympathies, and, above all, tact and common sense combine to give them the necessary qualifications for working effectively along the lines indicated with rural people."

In January, 1941, a secretary and librarian were engaged. They began work immediately under the supervision of the Extension Division. The extension staff also continued to visit Virginia communities and to talk with citizens concerning the program, in an attempt to narrow down the selection of experimental centers. Later in the spring two field workers were employed. In addition to the exploratory work already started, it was then possible to begin actual experimentation in selected areas. For this the two field workers assumed chief responsibility. The entire staff continued to act as consultants and to assist whenever called upon.

The librarian had worked in the TVA. In addition to his skills as a librarian concerned with collecting, classifying and circulating reading matter, he had a genuine interest in people and a desire to find the right materials in terms of their ability and needs. He was willing to double as operator of the movie projector, to print posters announcing meetings, to serve as secretary of a community meeting, to attend picnics or church suppers, or to assist in any other way that gave him opportunity to know better the people his library files were to serve.

The two field workers had a wide variety of adult education experience behind them, much of it of the informal or opportunistic nature required by the Special Projects. They had worked with both rural and urban programs. They liked people. They had faith in the efficacy of planning by those whose lives are affected, and they believed in the effectiveness of democratic processes. They were primarily interested in the Virginia approach because it was set up *not to push people into a preconceived program, but to shape programs to meet people's needs.*

The secretary, a University of Virginia alumnus, had to withdraw before the end of the first year to enter the navy.

His successor played an important part in the development of the project for three years, and her successor has valiantly met the challenge of drawing together the various parts of the program during the last experimental year. The librarian continued with the project during its first two years while materials were being collected and classified. The two field workers have given uninterrupted service throughout the program.

There have been additional part-time staff. The principal of the consolidated high school in one of three experimental areas devoted his summers for two years to the development of the program there and received remuneration for this work from the Extension Division. He had been active in community work for several years and was well qualified to assist in carrying the experiment in that center.

The director of the Extension Division's Drama Bureau gave half time to the program for more than a year, assisting with community meetings, movie programs, and leadership training especially in recreation and dramatics.

Summer workshops, as they developed in 1943, 1944, and 1945, required additional personnel to supplement the field workers who, for the duration of each workshop, devoted full time to its program. The sociologist who assisted in the summer workshops was the logical person to help with local workshops when it was possible in January, 1945, to add someone to the staff for this purpose. He and his successor were granted leaves from their regular college positions and served with the Special Projects for eight and four months respectively.

The most recent member was added to the staff in September, 1945, under a special grant for work with local groups in preparing materials especially in the field of resources. She brought to the project long experience both in writing and in working with people in communities.

The staff of the Special Projects worked under the direction of Mr. Zehmer and in consultation with him and other members of the Extension Division. Plans and programs were worked out in staff conferences which were long and

frequent. Also, during the first year, a series of staff conferences were held with guest specialists from other departments
or other universities. These included such persons as members of the Virginia State Planning Board, representatives of
the Agricultural Extension Service, professors of sociology.

The advisory committee met occasionally with the staff
during those first months when clarification of aims and policy was of primary importance. Individuals on the committee
continued to be available for consultation. Those who had
worked with Mr. William A. Smith were especially helpful in
interpreting his ideas to members of the staff who had not
had the privilege of knowing him. With the coming of the
war and the demise of WPA, most of the original members of
the advisory committee were called to other states or other
countries and the committee ceased to have an active part in
the program.

There were, of necessity, departures from specific proposals of Mr. Smith as the program developed. His emphasis,
for example, on the Scandinavian study group plan and the
community council suggested too rigid a pattern. It did not
fit the communities selected for experimentation. Some were
not yet ready, and preliminary socializing needed to be done.
Others already had machinery set up, and ways had to be
found to make it run more effectively. Local patterns were
always kept in mind.

Likewise it did not seem expedient to start each community with a survey and "scoring" program. In many cases, in
fact, there was evidence that surveys had been ends in themselves and that there was greater need for implementing surveys than for making them. In other instances, meeting an
immediate and obvious need was the logical starting place.
Working on this frequently led naturally to the next step,
and anything like a formal survey never entered the picture.

Perhaps the most radical departure from his planning
was in the *tempo* of the program. His estimate of the time
required "to educate people to help themselves" was more optimistic than realistic. The program, as originally outlined,
was for a two-year period. This did not allow for "reaction

time" of the people involved. Members of the staff felt sure of this in the beginning, but were willing to do as much as was humanly possible in the period provided for. By careful planning and by adding to the original fund small grants from various sources for special purposes, a five-year experimental program was possible. This allowed for germination, growth, and ripening of products from seed sown in the beginning. At the end of a two-year period much of this seed had scarcely sprouted. It was impossible at that time to do more than guess at whether or not it had fallen on fertile ground. Some seed is undoubtedly going to yield a rich harvest at a still later time—but, at any rate, there is considerably more tangible evidence of progress now than could have been mustered at the end of two years.

Throughout the program, however, there was no departure from Mr. Smith's basic assumptions. There was complete acceptance of his hypothesis that if you "set a people to doing great things, they will develop great leaders." In fact, it was assumed and, we believe, proved that *if you set people to doing things important to their own and their community's welfare, they will develop that realization of their own importance essential to self-development.*

It may even be unfair to say the program departed at all, except in time of accomplishment, from Mr. Smith's plan, if one accepts the implications of his statement that the ideas "for implementing the program are suggestive only and intended to be neither inclusive nor restrictive."

The exigencies of war necessitated even greater flexibility and adaptability than had been anticipated when the program was conceived. Training young persons in their communities, for example, and using graduate students at the University for field work could not be worked out on the scale that had been hoped for. Young people were busily engaged elsewhere, and it was the job of the project to help the older people on the home front plan for the kind of community to which the young people would want to return. The extent to which this has been achieved is one of the important tests of the program in helping people to help themselves.

Part Two

LOOKING AT OTHERS

CHAPTER 3

Printed Materials and Unpublished Reports

In starting its experimental program for discovering techniques whereby communities might help themselves, the Extension Division of the University of Virginia recognized the fact that considerable information bearing on the subject already existed. Therefore one of the first staff members to be engaged was Mr. John T. Cheney, a librarian. He was asked to locate, procure, and classify printed materials and unpublished reports concerned with community programs.

Purpose of Collection

The purpose of the collection was threefold: (1) for use of the staff in setting up experimental programs; (2) for use of study groups or councils within the communities selected or of individuals in any community, requesting information in relation to programs they were developing; (3) for use in leadership training programs for students or for community leaders wishing to learn to work effectively with adults in planning and carrying out community programs.

Problems of the Collector

Material bearing on community development is to be found in divers forms and places. Because so often it is useful today and outdated tomorrow, much of it never acquires the dignity of print. Some that does get into print is too ephemeral in nature to be put between the covers of a book. It varies in form from the one-page flier or oversized poster, to the pamphlet, series of pamphlets, or unbound booklet. Usually it is published by the agency responsible for its preparation and, as a result, receives little publicity.

During recent years, commercial publishers have been putting out more and more books of value to those interested in making democracy work in the community. In fact, Eduard C. Lindeman points out that, whereas sociologists used to furnish material for writers, now writers give information to sociologists. The books, however, do not constitute a problem for the collector other than the necessity of his keeping informed about them and asking the library to order and catalogue them.

It is the first two groups of materials that present many problems. Yet they contain much of the most pertinent and timely information. They include typed reports of individuals, study groups, or communities; mimeographed reports or news releases; copies of speeches; magazine articles; and newspaper clippings or even entire special issues of a paper. Discovering some of them requires ingenuity. Collecting involves many hours of patient and not-too-interesting work. Selecting demands unusual foresight and superhuman judgment compounded with endless scanning of things that obviously do not apply and almost endless reading of things that may apply.

But it is in classifying and storing them in such manner as to make them simply and readily accessible that the real job lies. This becomes even more difficult when the ultimate consumer is the citizen in the community rather than the teacher, professor, or graduate student trained in hunting for his specific needle in the general haystack of volumes grouped by chronology, periodical, or agency, and bound inexorably together by the library bindery.

The job of the Special Projects in Adult Education was to educate adults in their communities. Materials must be discovered, selected, classified, and assembled with their needs and abilities in mind. The organization of these materials must be kept flexible, permitting of new groupings to meet new situations. The result of the attempt of Special Projects to achieve this end is designated by those who work with it as the "pamphlet files"—though many items are not pamphlets and the system which evolved has little resemblance to any orthodox file. But the collection is good and the grouping usable and flexible.

Exploration and Discovery

In the beginning the librarian wrote to agencies regularly working with some aspect of community life. He asked for whatever materials might be of use in a program designed "to help communities to help themselves." These included both public and private agencies such as the Department of Agriculture, the Public Health Service, Cooperative League of the U.S.A., and National Recreation Association. Since not all materials were available from national headquarters, inquiries had to be sent to the institutions or agencies in each state responsible for the local administration of a program.

Many persons responded not only with their own materials but with lists that had been compiled by field workers, supervisors, professors, or graduate students. Such lists were checked, and seemingly pertinent materials were sent for. Much came that was useful, together with much that appeared to have no immediate bearing on the matter at hand. Hasty decisions as to usefulness, however, were not made since the program was definitely exploratory and experimental, and no one involved felt qualified to prognosticate more than the direction of its development.

Classifying for Use and Flexibility

By May, 1941, an extensive file of materials published by recognized agencies had been collected. Then the entire staff began to work on a usable system of classification. Here, too, indefiniteness as to exact procedures and needs that might emerge in various communities made for slow progress. Sometimes what had been agreed upon had to be discarded a few months later as unwieldy or admitting of too much overlapping. But none of the effort was wasteful. In struggling to classify for future usefulness, the staff educated itself in existing programs and materials.

Following Clues to More Material

As the evolution of a system of classification went on, the librarian continued to collect. He explored materials produced by WPA programs in many states and in varied fields of interest. He read theses from colleges and universities, made summaries of their contents, and noted their sources for inclusion in the file so that they might be borrowed again if needed. He scanned current lists of pamphlet materials, current and not-so-current *Readers' Guide to Periodical Liter-*

ature. He and other members of the staff clipped newspaper and current periodical references to any project that sounded promising. *Life, Look, Readers' Digest, Newsweek, Better Homes and Gardens, Southern Agriculturist,* and similar publications yielded clues. Following up the clues consumed time and frequently led to blind ends. On the other hand, a few real discoveries justified the time expended.

Tried in the Laboratory of Community

For two years, this process of collecting, selecting, eliminating, classifying, and reclassifying went on. As the work in communities developed, needs were clarified. The librarian, as has been noted before, went into communities whenever possible in order to learn at first hand just what people needed and could use. Every specific request facilitated the process of selection and classification. One community was in process of organizing a council. It wanted sample constitutions. Another was setting up a recreation commission. Another was interested in a freezer-locker plant and needed to know whether cooperatives or privately owned plants were rendering more efficient and more economical service. Usually in the beginning either the librarian or a field worker took what material was available to the persons asking for it. This afforded a personal check on its usability. Almost always, staff members came back from such a field trip scurrying about to find more pertinent material; to make more definitive selection; and to set up a new classification in the file for future usefulness.

Filing by agencies or organizations did not serve the purpose. Breaking down the materials into subject classifications presented problems because so often an agency or writer had attempted to cover the earth in one pamphlet. Cross-references helped, but eventually tended to become crisscrossed and confusing. Since the aim was to work out a file that anyone could use to find material on any aspect of community development, increasing simplicity was continuously sought.

Put to the Test of Workshop Use

At the end of the two years for which the librarian had been engaged, an impressive array of materials had been as-

sembled. They were still stored in open-end folders in file
drawers. Irregularity in size and shape of pamphlets made
for problems. Folders had a way of sliding down and out of
sight at the moment there was the least time available for a
search. Still members of the staff could manage. They were
zealous in their search and eventually found what was needed.

With the advent of the first resident workshop the following summer (1943), everyone admitted that the file-drawer
system was not good for popular consumption. The drawers
were heavy. The lower ones required the searcher to squat,
or kneel, or lie on his stomach, while he fumbled through
countless folders to find what he wanted. Usually he did not
want it enough to warrant that effort. The hazard to silk
stockings discouraged the ladies so that they confined their
interests to those letters of the alphabet that got into the up-
per drawers of the file. Sometimes these failed to coincide
with their real needs. A folder once removed from the drawer
seldom got back in the right place. A pamphlet removed from
the folder almost invariably was replaced in a neighboring one
and was more or less permanently lost.

Yet the materials in the files were found useful. An assistant in the workshop, at the request of members, worked
out a general list of sources of file materials they found pertinent to their work in Virginia communities. Some of them
had hopes of assembling collections in their own schools or
communities. Their later experience, however, indicated that
their time for community work was too limited to make this
generally practicable. Hence they recommended that the
Special Projects procure duplicate copies of the most useful
materials and lend them, separately or in kits, on request.
Nevertheless the work on the list by people with the community point of view was a valuable step toward classification for
use.

From Folders to Boxes

It was during the 1943 summer workshop that the box-
file system began to evolve. Materials on subjects of special
interest to the group were taken from the file drawers, and
put together in boxes. These boxes were clearly labeled and

stood up like books on shelves in order to save time, patience, and energy on hot July days.

The following winter, necessity pushed the development of the box system still further. Local workshops required that file materials be carried to distant parts of the state. Boxes were assembled not in the logical order of the file—but in response to the stern logic of immediate need. The perversity of each community in needing information on different subjects speeded up the process. By the time the 1944 summer workshop met, the most generally used materials were in boxes on the shelves. The file drawers were still available to those whose community curiosity took them off the trails blazed by previous students. The process of shifting to boxes continued through four more local workshops and the summer workshop of 1945.

To be sure, the right kind of box had become a wartime scarcity. Old open-backed boxes were salvaged from the library, and the dust endured until closed boxes could be found. Empty typewriting-paper boxes were pressed into service as they could be gathered together. They are now being replaced by the more convenient and sturdy hinged boxes which are again available.

Out of continuous use of materials in workshops, both resident and local, for three years, has grown a simple classification system which works, and which does not require too much time for filing new material as it appears. Perfection has not yet been attained—and probably never will be. But, in this case, usability was the goal and that has been reached.

Filer's Work Is Never Done

The job has required the skills of a librarian plus a working knowledge of communities and people. It still requires eternal vigilance to add what is new and to discard what is no longer pertinent, or what experience has proved is too technical, too detailed, or too unattractive to be useful to the layman. The busy citizen concerned with community problems in his always insufficient leisure time, has not the patience to select from an unassorted mass. The current nature of current events and the fact that tomorrow with its new ideas is

upon us before we have digested those of today preclude the
possibility of taking any time out. He who struggles with the
problem of classifying and storing pamphlet material for the
everyday use of laymen rather than for the occasional research of students finds that, like the Red Queen, he must run
as fast as he can to keep in the same place.

From Collector to Consumer

As soon as the collection and classification had reached
proportions that warranted publicity, the staff gave attention
to letting people know about it. There were notices in county
papers describing the material and urging anyone interested
in pursuing a certain subject to get in touch with the Extension Division or the librarian of Special Projects. In articles
or speeches about the whole experimental program, the files
and their availability were always stressed. Annotated lists
of pamphlets on specific subjects were prepared and enclosed
in letters going out from the Extension Division.

Supplements to New Dominion Series

The *New Dominion Series* was then being mailed to some
2,500 persons in the state and was, if we could judge from "fan
mail," being read. So we tried enclosing suggested reading
supplements with each issue from June through September,
1942. Each one suggested more materials dealing with the
subject matter of the New Dominion story. "Adventures in
Joint Ownership" (August 1, 1942), for example, carried the
supplement which is reproduced on the following page.

Supplement   August 1, 1942

Extension Division Publication

NEW DOMINION SERIES

COMMUNITIES TACKLING THEIR PROBLEMS

THE WHEAT COMMUNITY, by J. H. McLeod

What the people of a rural community have done in three years of working together to solve their economic and social problems.

Land Policy Review, September-October 1939. Bureau of Agricultural Economics, U. S. Department of Agriculture, Washington, D. C.   5c

REMEMBERING THE SABBATH LED TO ORGANIZATION FOR COMMUNITY FARM HOME IMPROVEMENT

What the men's Sunday School class of Hurricane Creek did as the result of meeting during the week to talk over their common problems.

Agriculture Extension Service, University of Tennessee, Knoxville, Tennessee.   Free

BIRCHWOOD WASN'T LICKED, by Fred Schneider

What three highland communities did to build up the poorer parts of their farms and save their schools and churches.

Chattanooga Evening Times, April 23, 1941. Chattanooga Times, Chattanooga, Tennessee.   10c

UNITED THEY ADVANCE . . . by Joe A. Elliott.

What 20 community organizations did to develop additional sources of farm income in Claiborne County, Tennessee.

Agriculture Extension Service, University of Tennessee, Knoxville, Tennessee.   Free

These pamphlets may be secured from the sources indicated above, or they may be borrowed for 3c postage from the

UNIVERSITY OF VIRGINIA EXTENSION DIVISION

Box 1487, University Station

CHARLOTTESVILLE

Though "Adventures in Joint Ownership" was one of the most popular of the New Dominion stories and brought hundreds of requests for copies both for individual use and for conferences and meetings of agricultural agencies, the material listed on the supplement was asked for by no one. Of course we had no way of knowing whether requests may have gone to the publishers of the leaflets and reports. We only know that no one asked to borrow from our files.

Other supplements included suggestions on such subjects as *Community Councils in Action* and *Health for Rural Communities* with appropriate issues of the *Series*. One list headed *For Further Information* was printed not on a separate sheet enclosed in the bulletin, but on the last page of the story itself. Each time a list was prepared, kits of the suggested readings were put together by the librarian and duplicate copies were procured. We were prepared to meet a rush of business that never materialized.

Pamphlets at Movies

Another attempt at stimulating interest in the printed word was made in connection with the movie programs described in Chapter 13. We selected what seemed to us the best pamphlets on nutrition, or canning, or school lunches, or home improvement, or health, or any other subject in which the audience might be interested as a result of the movie. When we had posters or pictorial charts in colors that we could give away, they were seized upon eagerly to be used for decorative purposes in home, school, or store. Likewise when we had enough copies of an attractive looking leaflet for general distribution, the pile disappeared. Whether they were ever read we do not know. But when we had library copies that we offered to lend to anyone who wanted to do some reading on the subject, there were no takers. The professional workers with whom we were cooperating in holding the meetings with movies were almost the only borrowers of the printed materials we had spent considerable time in selecting and displaying for each meeting.

In one community a few young people borrowed books of a light-reading kind but not enough interest was shown to warrant the time and energy the staff spent getting them there. In another community, in which the teacher cooperated in a film forum on historical and current events movies, there was real interest in the books which we were able to leave in the community for several months. But even here our pamphlet material made no converts.

Personal Service Required

During the first two years of the program less than a score of requests for materials dealing with community development were filled. Most of these came not as a result of any publicity on the files nor in response to lists sent out, but as a result of a staff member's saying to an individual, "We have some pamphlets on that subject which our librarian will send you. Drop him a card." Always we tried to make the person send in the request rather than to bring it in ourselves, hoping to give him the habit. The word-of-mouth suggestion brought better results than other attempts. This fact in itself shook our faith in the printed word as an effective stimulator.

Each time there was a request for material, we found that ready-made kits did not serve the purpose. Material had to be selected in terms of the particular situation—and the more we knew about the situation, the more difficult it was to find just the right stuff in print. The librarian indicated page numbers and marked special sections in pamphlets dealing with more general subjects but having something on the one asked for. Usually long letters of explanation and suggestions for use accompanied the packets that went out. Individuals were encouraged to come in to talk things over or, when possible, the librarian or another staff member visited the community.

Study Groups Lead to Use, Evaluation, and Rewriting

It was not until the end of the second year of the program, when community council and local workshop committees began to bite into their special problems, that the materials of the files became really useful outside the University. It then occurred to us when we carried a boxful of pamphlets on soil conservation, frozen food lockers, recreation, or public health

to a committee member to ask him to mark those that he
thought really useful for more widespread distribution. We
got some excellent advice in this way. Also we had furnished
an additional motivation for reading. One young farmer remarked with a smile when he returned a box he had borrowed, "You didn't fool me any. I knew you were just trying to
get me to read them. But anyway I marked them like you
said."

Our hope had been that once the materials on community
development had been selected and classified, the files could
be turned over to the general library and that a member of
the library staff could classify new materials and answer requests. As time went on, experience indicated that this hope
had been unrealistic. The need, we discovered, was not for a
custodian and dispenser of books and pamphlets but for someone at work in the community who could suggest and supply
material in relation to specific needs as they arose. There was
also an even greater need for someone who could rewrite research reports in terms meaningful to the people who must
use them.

Rediscovery of Southern Readings Project's Conclusions

That people who have no reading habit should not be
eager for books and pamphlets did not surprise us. Neither
did the fact that the people with whom we were working had
no reading habit when we realized that 72.3 per cent of Virginia's rural population has no library service. But, in retrospect, it seems as if we had to try for ourselves before we
could really comprehend the significance of the findings of the
group interested in the late Thirties in establishing a Southern
Readings Project. They had concluded that "getting books to
people was important but relatively simple; getting people to
want the information to be gained from books was even more
urgent; preparing printed material in certain fields important
to the development of the South must be considered if those
of limited reading ability, or habit, were to be reached; and,
finally, other techniques for *telling the people* must be explored."

It is a commentary on the person conditioned by formal

education that, though our program was concerned largely with finding "other techniques," we persisted at first in leaning heavily on getting people to read what had been written.

It was only when one community group with which we were working decided to experiment with selecting and rewriting in terms of their own needs that we really went to work on translating materials of research into usable form for the non-readers who must be stimulated. We were reminded of the old adage, "A wise man can learn from the experience of others; a fool from his own." We pass it on hoping to find wisdom among our readers!

CHAPTER 4

Finding and Telling Success Stories

The *New Dominion Series* has received more general attention than any one aspect of the Extension Division's program to help communities to help themselves. The reason for this is that eighteen times a year for four years it has been mailed to about 1,200 persons who, in our opinion, should receive it and about 2,500 who have especially asked to be placed on the mailing list. Thus, in its very nature, it has had a kind of publicizing that other aspects of the program could not have.

The *Series* grew out of the same conviction that resulted in the accumulation of materials about other programs. Good things were being accomplished by people in many communities. The people concerned in them must, consciously or unconsciously, have learned something about ways of working. We could learn from them. Perhaps we could even interpret the best programs we found in such a way as to interest and inspire to action persons in other communities. Thus the *New Dominion Series* came into existence in September, 1941, with the stated purpose of "describing experimental approaches to democratic living that are being tried effectively in various communities."

Definition of Terms

Our definition of terms was simple. *Experimental* we interpreted as something that was being tried. A program did not have to be entirely novel or at all radical to meet this specification. *Democratic* was also freely interpreted for our purposes. A program to qualify must afford opportunity for participation in planning as well as in execution by those whose lives it affected. In the stories reported, there is to be found a wide range in the degrees of "experimentalness" and of democracy involved.

Our definition of *community* provided for an equally wide range. Sociologists could undoubtedly quarrel with it. The term was used to designate groups of persons bound together by a common interest and working for a common purpose. In one story the community is made up of half a dozen neighbors who belong to no specific geographical subdivision; in another it is a school or the area served by a school; in another it is a town or a county; in two stories the entire state has been considered as a community.

Finding the Programs

No scientific procedures for finding programs were followed. There was no attempt to compile a complete list of community projects and make a judicious and balanced sampling therefrom. Those included were discovered through keeping an ear to the ground and following up any lead; through answering requests for help that have come to the Extension Division from some communities; through following up references in magazine articles, news-letters, and other published material; through conversations or correspondence with individuals; and, occasionally, quite by chance when staff members have been on the trail of some different matter. There is no claim that the *best* programs have been found, but all that have been described are *good*.

Although suggestions from readers have been invited from time to time, only five have come in this way. Only one of these suggested a project for which the reader had some personal responsibility. Modesty does not seem to be entirely to blame for this. Frequently it has been found that persons who are busy in a flourishing community program are not aware of doing anything unusual. Implications for other communities are seldom seen by the ordinary citizen who has felt a need in his own community and helped make plans for meeting it.

We looked about us for programs that had enriched community life in any of its many aspects—social, cultural, economic, or civic. We then attempted to find what made those programs work. We were concerned more with *method of achievement* than with achievement itself. The *why* and *how* rather than the *what* became the central characters in the stories. The *what* merely furnished the background.

Justification of "Success" Approach

The *Series* is a collection of success stories. Each story shows democracy grappling successfully with some community problem or dealing effectively with some phase of community life. The stories present an impressive bit of evidence of democracy triumphant. Each story is true. Yet added together they do not add up to The Truth.

Each community described is but a small part of this great land of ours; and in many cases the phase of its life depicted is but a fraction of the whole. The picture is admittedly fragmentary and one-sided. What, then, is the justification for its presentation? The answer lies in our conviction that *we learn from our successes.*

We did not close our eyes to the existence of programs that were not good. Nor did we sidestep the job of analyzing what was wrong with them. A general summary of these programs is given in the next chapter. But we did not include them in the *New Dominion Series.* There we reported only those that seemed to say, in no uncertain terms, *"It can be done."*

For this was an experiment in the effectiveness of success stories—of emphasis on the positive and the constructive. Four years of such experimentation have yielded considerable evidence that to "accentuate the positive" is an educational device that has some validity. This evidence is summarized in Chapter 15, "Experiment in Pamphleteering."

During these years the world has continued to furnish an increasing number of examples of the undemocratic, the bureaucratic, the superimposed, and the destructive forces at work in communities everywhere. There was little danger, we were convinced, that our success stories would create an undue optimism. We hoped they might relieve the weight of pessimism enough to encourage a few more "experimental approaches to democratic living."

Criteria for Inclusion

Criteria for deciding whether a story should be included in the *Series* were purely subjective. Since our purpose was to stimulate and inspire other communities, the first prerequisites of a program must be its general usefulness, its workability, and its adaptability to other situations. Further requirements were local initiation and financing; local, and preferably widespread, leadership and participation; development of indigenous leadership; utilizing of community resources; and carefully planned use of state, federal, or private agencies or funds to carry out a program set up by the community. That is, we tried to find programs in which the direction of delegation was *up* rather than *down*. A community must know its needs, understand available resources and draw upon them rather than accept, more or less blindly, what might be offered by a state department, a federal agency, or a private institution interested in doing good. This accounts for the omission of stories of notable achievements such as splendid housing, hospitals, schools, and other important assets to good living. *We were less concerned with the material gains than with the intellectual and spiritual growth of the community resulting from the process of acquiring the gains.*

There was no attempt to represent in fair proportion all agencies concerned with community betterment. Our interest was in the story that showed a community "lifting itself by its own bootstraps." *We considered all regularly constituted agencies legitimate servants of the community in such a process and therefore not especially deserving of credit for having helped in the jobs they were set up to do.* As a matter of fact, in many of the best programs both agencies and individual leaders had recognized the wisdom of merging their identity with that of the whole community. A few programs were found that, though good, had failed of full realization of their potentialities because agencies, institutions, or individuals responsible for starting them had been too tenacious of credit. These stories were not included in the *Series*.

Getting the Story

The investigation, evaluation, and reports of all programs have been made by two members of the staff of the Special Projects. Getting a story has never involved a formal survey. It has, however, in all cases included visits to the communities and discussion with as many persons as possible who partici-

pated in the programs or had opportunity of observing their
development. An effort was always made to get the point
of view of laymen in the community and of professional
workers, such as teachers, ministers, or public officials. Whenever records of any kind had been kept, they were carefully
read. In most cases, however, there was surprisingly little in
writing. One must go to the human sources for information.
Because every project and every community was so different
from every other, it was not possible to use any formal questionnaire or consistent method of approach. A deep and sincere interest in community programs and an eagerness to
know just how the thing was done have probably been the
two most important factors in getting at the essence of the
story. Ability to listen and to ask the right questions at the
right time likewise has been of paramount importance. In order to be sure of getting a complete picture, certain questions were kept in mind, though frequently they were answered without being asked. Nevertheless they served as a kind
of check list for the investigators: Who started it? Why?
Where did the money come from? How did people get interested? What means were used to disseminate the necessary
information in the community? What were the exact steps
in the development of the program? What difficulties had to
be met and how was this done? Was an effort made to draw
in all persons or agencies concerned? Was the program dom-
inated by one person or group? Did individual or organizational jealousies hinder the program? Is there evidence that
the community is better off as a result of the program? Have
individuals become more responsible citizens because of their
participation? Would the withdrawal of a particular person or
agency mean the collapse of the program or has leadership
been developed in such a way as to assure its continuance?

Frequently the persons participating in an excellent program had never analyzed what had been done. The process
became clear to them only as they tried to satisfy the curiosity
of the investigators. Important links in the chain of events
appeared often, not in answer to direct questions that should
have brought them out, but in the informal reminiscing that

got under way as the exciting or discouraging beginnings were recalled.

No, a community leader would tell us, they had no "educational program." They just got together a dozen men who were interested and each of them went to see ten of his neighbors and explained "what the facts were." Or they just found out "what the facts were" and called a meeting to tell people about them and make a plan. Or they took the report of a survey made by the health department and published the facts in the paper. "The facts" always seemed to be important to the instigator of a project, but that getting facts to citizens in such a way as to make them act had any relation to an *educational* program or campaign had seldom occurred to him. Likewise local people would tell us they had done nothing about "developing leadership." But in the course of the conversation we discovered that one person had been given a job to do and that someone else had been given another job, and that they now carried complete responsibility for those parts of the program. "I don't even know what they are doing about those things now, but they are being taken care of," the original leader would report. Yet he had no idea of having "developed leaders."

One of the most important by-products of the *Series*, if one can trust "fan mail" and personal remarks, is the new life that a program frequently has taken on as a result of the analysis to which the participants subjected it in attempting to tell their story. The fact that the bulletin would be distributed locally always made for an extremely thoughtful and carefully accurate report.

Writing the Story

After discussion by the two staff members who had visited the project, one of them assumed responsibility for writing the story, keeping in mind the desirability of simplicity, brevity, informality, and vividness. The manuscript was submitted to one or more of the local persons interviewed for a check on accuracy of facts and interpretation, and to all staff members of the Extension Division for comments and suggestions. A final revision was then made, and the story went to print.

Care was always taken to say nothing that might affect the program adversely in its own community. This sometimes meant not calling attention to what might be one of its most progressive features. In one community, for example, where both white people and Negroes were using facilities they had provided for themselves through cooperative effort, we asked about its interracial nature. The leader questioned was at first surprised. Then he asked us not to call attention to this aspect of the program lest local people be made self-conscious about what was happening naturally and become fearful of criticism.

Geographical Area Covered

The fact that all the stories are about communities in the Southeast does not indicate that more is happening there than in other parts of the country. Our primary purpose was to stimulate programs in Virginia. At the same time we were trying to get intimately acquainted with as many Virginia communities as possible. So we began at home. The first ten stories (September, 1941—February, 1942) reported Virginia programs. The eleventh was about a South Carolina community. Later there were added programs from Alabama, Georgia, Maryland, North Carolina, and Tennessee, with still the largest proportion coming from Virginia as indicated in the following table:

TABLE 1. DISTRIBUTION BY STATES OF *NEW DOMINION SERIES* STORIES

Alabama	1
Georgia	5
Maryland	2
North Carolina	4
South Carolina	1
Tennessee	5
Virginia	46
Techniques	6
(with examples from previous stories)	
Reports on revisits	2
Total	72

The area covered was determined in large part by our location and the exigencies of travel in wartime. The period of publication of the *Series* included in this report began three months before Pearl Harbor and ended less than one month after V-J Day. Good programs in many other communities including all the states in the Southeast came to our attention during that time. They were not included because we were unable to visit them, and all the stories are first-hand reports. The relative number of stories from the several states is in no sense indicative of the relative progressiveness of those states. Problems and programs described are typical of communities to be found in all these states and, for that matter, in all sections of the country. The ideas involved are, we believe, fundamental to democracy and, therefore, universal in their application to American communities.

Scope of the Series

Subjects have ranged from the very simple story of getting together books for a rural school library to that of a public health program adequately serving three counties; from joint ownership of washing machines and grain drills to a poultry cooperative which ships 13,000,000 pounds of poultry a year from the community it serves. An annotated list of titles of four years of publication appears in the Appendix.

All aspects of community life are included—economic, cultural, recreational, health, welfare. An attempt has been made to include all ages, both sexes, and both races. Stories also show a wide range of agencies and organizations initiating or participating in community programs with emphasis usually on coordination of efforts. Analysis of the first 72 stories appears in the tables that follow.

TABLE 2. CLASSIFICATION OF PROGRAMS AS TO PRIMARY EMPHASIS

Economic	17
Health and welfare	15
Civic	12
Cultural and recreational	13
Total community planning	7
Techniques*	6
Revisits*	2
Total	72

*The eight bulletins dealing with techniques and revisits are not included in the tables that follow; hence the total of 64 rather than 72.

TABLE 3. CLASSIFICATION OF PROGRAMS BY AGE GROUPS

For youth	14
By youth	2
By adults	10
By both	2
For adults by adults	19
For total community	31
By youth	3
By adults	19
By both	9
Total	64

TABLE 4. CLASSIFICATION OF PROGRAMS BY RACE

White	34
Negro	5
Mixed*	25
By white for Negro	0
By white for both	19
By both for Negro	4
By both for both	2
Total	64

*It should be noted that though this number is large, it is explained by the fact that 19 of the 25 listed as "mixed" are "by white for both," whereas only 2 are "by both for both."

TABLE 5. AGENCIES SPONSORING PROGRAMS REPORTED IN *NEW DOMINION SERIES*

Schools		18
Public	16	
Private	2	
Churches		6
Civic organizations		6
Community council or committee		16
Individual citizen		2
Business or industry		2
Federal agency		3
FSA	2	
REA	1	
Farmers' organization		1
Agricultural extension service		4
General extension		1
State department		2
Health	1	
Education	1	
Local public agency		3
Public welfare	1	
Recreation commission	1	
Health unit	1	
Total		64

TABLE 6. PERSONS INITIATING PROGRAMS IN *NEW DOMINION SERIES*

Professional worker as part of his job	24
Professional worker as citizen	20
Laymen in the community	20
Total	64

TABLE 7. PRINCIPAL SOURCE OF LEADERSHIP AFTER PROGRAM WAS STARTED

Professional worker as part of his job		26
Same as initiator	12	
Employed by initiators	10	
Accepting delegation from initiators	4	
Professional worker as citizen		12
Laymen in community		26
Total		64

Distinctions in the above tables are not always clear-cut. It is not possible, for example, to say exactly where a minister's, teacher's, or county agent's job ends and his role as a citizen begins. In general, however, "as part of his job" means that which he is paid to do. The 24 professional workers in Table 6 above are by no means all included in Table 7. For example, 10 programs initiated by citizens or professional workers developed to the point of having paid leadership and 4 others had volunteer leaders to whom the job was delegated by the initiators. These include such programs as the Rockingham Poultry Cooperative, the Tri-county health program, the Radford recreation program, the Montgomery County Area Library. In all cases citizens continued to work with the employed or delegated leader in advisory or planning capacity, working out satisfactory relationships between citizens' committees and professional workers.

Twelve professional workers of the original 24 did not succeed in placing chief responsibility elsewhere although at least 3 of these developed active supporting committees.

The "professional workers as citizens" who initiated programs, in 16 cases withdrew from active leadership and in 4 cases retained it. On the other hand, 8 "professional workers as citizens" became leaders in programs they did not initiate.

Laymen initiating programs in 14 cases turned the active leadership over to professional workers. In 6 cases they continued to furnish leadership in programs they initiated. In 20 cases they assumed leadership for programs started by professional workers.

Such changes in responsibility might be interpreted by the casual observer as part of the process commonly known as "passing the buck." Thoughtful study of the cases involved shows something much more hopeful for democracy. Leadership is fluid, rather than fixed as it is in authoritarian societies. Professional workers and sponsoring agencies are not always concerned with credit. They frequently encourage community groups to take over what they have started. Bureaucracy does not appear to be a serious threat. *Citizens are tending to reverse the direction of delegation by planning programs to be carried out by the professional workers who are their public servants.*

Keeping in Touch

At the end of the first year of publication, it was possible for the staff to make a personal check on each of the eighteen programs described up to that time. Their progress was reported in No. 19 of the *Series*, "Communities Carry On."

It should be remembered that Pearl Harbor came three months after the beginning of publication. The relation of peacetime programs to wartime needs was therefore naturally the approach in that first summary, September, 1942. The introductory paragraphs state:

In normal times a year would bring changes to community projects, but the nature of the change would be determined usually by factors over which a project would have some control. In the year just ending, both the kind and degree of change have been determined, or at least largely influenced, by an emergency situation beyond the control of the community but vitally affecting its welfare.

Since December 7, we of the United States have been personally involved in a great crisis of civilization feeling that all we hold dear is at stake. A war must be won; a peace must be created. Each individual must examine the contribution he is making by doing his regular job in comparison with the contribution he might make by doing something else. Guidance is available but responsibility for the decision in most cases rests with the individual. Organizations and community projects, like individuals, must face this issue.

The report of what happened to each program is followed by this conclusion:

In only two instances have war efforts made it seem desirable to suspend a program that was under way. In most cases the projects have seemed as important in planning a total war as they seemed before with, at most, a shift of emphasis. Likewise in most cases the projects have been stimulated to greater activity by the emergency. The increased emphasis on recreation is significant. Communities are discovering and utilizing their own resources in a way that they would not have thought possible a year ago. The enforced trend toward smaller neighborhood groups for both recreational and educational activities invites speculation. If this means an increase in the participation of individuals and in the acceptance of community responsibility, it may serve to strengthen democracy at home while we defend it abroad. At any rate, this limited survey seems to indicate that in general the soundly established and functioning community project finds it possible to make an important contribution in time of war as in time of peace.

During the war years that followed, we found nothing to change the conclusions drawn at that time. In fact, continued observation of these first projects and those subsequently studied strengthened our conviction that war was not accepted as an excuse for marking time on the home front.

Projects Revisited

Need to limit travel during the war years, increasing pressure of the experimental aspects of the program, as well as the increase in number of projects described in the *Series* which continued to appear eighteen times a year, made it impossible to visit again all the communities included. We did keep in touch by correspondence and by personal visits whenever business took us to a community whose program had been reported. Hence an up-to-date file has been kept on each project.

At the end of the third year of publication, No. 55 of the *Series* (September, 1944) was devoted to "Programs Revisited." It reported in some detail the Jordan Area (*New Dominion Series,* No. 11) which had had three years of growth since our first visit; the Rockingham Poultry Cooperative, first visited two years earlier; the Rabun County Maternity Center and Carroll County cooperatives visited the preceding year. All these continued to flourish. The Raleigh Teen-age Club had fallen by the wayside, and the reasons for its failure were analyzed.

This bulletin concluded with the statement:

Each differs in purpose and pattern. In all, there is one common characteristic. Though activities deal with the present, plans look forward toward the postwar world. One cannot feel entirely pessimistic about that world with so many local groups seriously considering their responsibility toward it.

Follow-up by Questionnaire

Toward the end of the four years of experimental publication of the *Series,* a questionnaire was sent to a leader in each of the 64 programs described up to that time. Their replies are summarized in some detail because of the numerous inquiries from readers as to growth or failure of a program subsequent to the publication of its story in the *Series.*

Of the 64 programs described, 58 were reported as continuing. Of these, 32 reported rapid growth with new activities developing out of those already under way. The other 26 indicated little change. Half a dozen of these, of course, had been too recently reported to have had many changes take place.

With reference to leadership, 30 reported no important changes; 19 reported normal changes due to willingness of other persons in the communities to accept responsibility; and 15 reported complete leadership turnover due, in most cases, to the war. Of this last group 12 reported that the program had lost no ground as a result of the change, 2 reported that they had survived but had lost momentum, and 1 indicated complete cessation of activity.

TABLE 8. PRESENT STATUS OF PROGRAMS AS REPORTED IN
QUESTIONNAIRE

Expanding activity	32
Continuing with little change	26
Discontinued	6
Total	64

TABLE 9. LEADERSHIP CHANGES AS REPORTED IN
QUESTIONNAIRE

No important change	30
Normal change	19
Complete turnover	15
Total	64

Programs Discontinued

Of the programs that had been discontinued, three gave the war as the chief reason. Each of these was dependent on use of automobiles or school busses. A fourth gave as the sole reason the withdrawal of the sponsoring agency which had failed to teach the people to carry on by themselves. A fifth blamed the community which failed to understand and hence to support the program. Misunderstanding, workers felt, had resulted from over-zealous publicity in national magazines which gave the wrong emphasis to the purpose of the program. In the sixth instance, removal of professional workers to other communities was the reason assigned.

A brief explanation of each of these six programs which are no longer going forward follows. Information and opinions about changes are based on correspondence, rather than on personal observations as in the case of the original stories. Usually more than one person has been consulted.

The Albemarle County Forums (*New Dominion Series,* No. 1, September, 1941) were discontinued immediately following Pearl Harbor. School busses had been used to bring patrons and children to the local schools for discussion with county officials. Restrictions on transportation and preoccupation of citizens with wartime activities made it seem unwise to continue. In September, 1942, the chairman of the forum committee was of the opinion that civilian defense activities and Red Cross classes were easier to organize as a result of the forums. He also felt that, with the coming of peace, the forums would be resumed. Since that time the chairman has died. The superintendent of schools now reports that some schools and communities are conducting their own forums as a direct outgrowth of the previous program. He does not know whether an attempt ever will be made to revive the countywide program with transportation provided.

Both programs described in "Supplementing Farm Income" (*New Dominion Series,* No. 9, January, 1942) have been discontinued. The *Old Dominion Home Industries* depended entirely on tourist trade for its market. This decreased, even on U. S. Highway No. 1, to a degree that cut into sales pretty seriously. At the same time, production declined because of increased employment until there were too few products to supply even the decreased demand. When the land where the shop stood was bought by the government for camp purposes, it semed unwise to start again in a new location. Sponsors are of the opinion that the program will be revived as defense workers and men and women from the armed forces return to their communities thus relieving many craftsmen of other duties they had to assume during the war period. The number of requests for this bulletin and similar material that are now coming in (October, 1945) indicates that many communities anticipate a postwar need for handcrafts or small industries.

The program at the Shenandoah Homesteads, described in the same issue, has a somewhat different story. What had started as a local craft program was absorbed by Shenandoah Crafts, Inc., which worked under government employed teachers. The program was planned without reference to the interests and skills of the people concerned. At the same time, marketability of products was not considered. Large orders were disregarded while unwanted products piled up in the shop. The objection offered to producing for market was that people should be allowed to "produce beauty for beauty's sake." Yet the producers had no feeling that what they were producing was beautiful. They were paid by the hour to make whatever they were told to make. They ceased to regard themselves as craftsmen and became "day laborers in what was theoretically their own shop." When the FSA program went out, teachers were withdrawn, the equipment was sold to repay the government loan, and the shop was boarded up.

One observer who helped finance the small local cooperative with which the program began, and who was repaid from earnings as it developed, claims that the people were making real progress in a venture which was their own and which was planned on a scale they could comprehend and manage. Then came the large government subsidy with well meaning but impractical plans, and, according to our informant, this is what happened:

. . . . I watched the cooperative die and the people work as day laborers with no understanding of what became of the goods and no real pride in making products any better than absolutely necessary to get their pay. . . . . Everyone had good intentions, but there was no practical plan, and no attempt to help the people learn to run their own business.

There should be clear understanding in such an undertaking as to whether the group is to produce handcrafts or machine-made novelties. Handcraft methods and scale of production for the chainstore type of product are impractical.

If a subsidy is desirable in the beginning, the people must be
taught to do without it as quickly as possible so that when it is withdrawn, they will be able to carry on

It is my belief that such programs should start small enough for
the people who participate in them to understand them. They should
grow out of the people's desire for opportunity and not out of a pattern
imposed by large-scale planners with no feeling for local attitudes and
interests.

Sensitivity to market is as important as sensitivity to local interests.
Unless there is sufficient surplus to take care of large unsold stock, it
should not be allowed to accumulate. In fact, there was no excuse for
such accumulation. The demand for articles such as the homesteaders
had been making (baskets, wood-carvings, weaving, etc.) far exceeded the supply. There was no demand for the poor imitations of fac-
tory-made novelties they were taught to produce.

The people themselves must be willing to accept losses as well as
successes. They will accept them and learn from them *if the mistakes
are their own*. They cannot learn from them if they do not understand
what is happening. There is no reason for them to learn if the losses are
taken care of by a subsidy.

There are a few good things that came from the program. The
basket-maker found better markets and has bought and almost paid
for his home. One woman who learned to make hooked rugs still sells
all she can make. Several who learned to finish furniture have used
that skill to advantage in their own homes, and some do work of
this kind for their neighbors. One woman made draperies for her new
home and will probably weave for sale again when materials become
plentiful.

There may even be another cooperative when peacetime leisure
returns to rural areas. But it will be the people's. They have learned
enough not to be talked into an impractical plan again. At least they
know *what not to do*.

The Halifax Council of Community Organizations (*New
Dominion Series*, No. 18, August, 1942) was another casualty
of the war. Long distances in a completely rural area made
countywide meetings impractical during gas rationing. The
former chairman reports that resumption of activity is among
their peacetime aspirations.

No word has come from the Raleigh Teen-age Club since
the report of its demise in "Programs Revisited," September,
1944. We quote from that report:

The Teen-age Club of Raleigh, N.C., in which readers were keenly
interested, (No. 45—"By the Youngsters") has closed its doors. There
are plans under way, community leaders say, for a "bigger and better
organization." Yet it seems worthwhile to point out what it was that
the young people in this club found most discouraging to their really
fine program.

Because theirs was one of the first teen-age clubs, it attracted nationwide attention. It was started by boys and girls who wanted sociability for themselves. It pre-dated the frenzied movement for "recreation to prevent juvenile delinquency." Yet it was caught up in this movement and was held up as a glowing example of just such a program. The members resented this. They did not consider themselves as delinquents nor prospective delinquents. Neither did the community so consider them until national magazines began to label them. The club suffered from the reaction on the local people. If it were a place for juvenile-delinquents-in-the-making, parents felt it was not the place for their boys and girls. This reacted unfavorably on membership. The budget was dependent on dues. The problems became too difficult for the Junior Board.

Their advice to other communities would be to establish recreation for recreation's sake—and juvenile delinquency will take care of itself. Keep the approach a positive one.

The fine school-community program in the Cold Springs School, Bremen, Alabama, (*New Dominion Series, No. 46,* February, 1944) is reported as marking time at present. The new principal writes that the former principal has gone to work with the extension division of the state university, and that not a single teacher we met in August, 1943, is now in the school. This program, however, survived the death of the man who started it in 1936 and flourished under new leadership. We feel that unless something most unusual has happened, it is quiescent rather than dead. We suspend judgment until we can visit the community again.

Returned to Life

A program that received the death sentence from the community but refused to die is the one described in "From Gangs to Boys' Club" (*New Dominion Series, No. 8,* December, 1941). The club had lost its meeting place when its story was written. It was in an area already congested with wartime expansion. Finding a new meeting place seemed impossible. Yet the need for such a club was increasing every day with the growth of the community. The New Dominion story ended with the following paragraph:

The Boys' Club has been a veritable Pied Piper calling the boys from their street-corner and back-alley gangs. Its beginning was accidental, its leadership inspired and devoted. Its rapid and continuous growth proves that it met a very real need. The need still exists and will increase in an area which is growing rapidly around new industries. It has influenced directly some 2,000 boys in the nine years of its life and indirectly the welfare of the community and even of the nation. It points the way to further development that should be neither accidental nor dependent on voluntary leadership. "Foy Aust's boys" are his only by adoption. They are here, as elsewhere, the inescapable responsibility of the community.

The opinion in the last sentence was corroborated by newspaper editorials on the story and in letters to the editors of several papers. The Richmond *Times-Dispatch* pointed out that the "adults must gang up" in such a way as to promote the boys' club idea if the state and the nation were to be saved from a wave of juvenile delinquency during the war years. "Pulaski is almost certain to solve its problem," the editorial stated, because it had citizens and agencies interested in solving it. Yet, in spite of a nine-year demonstration, Pulaski moved slowly in a period when emergency needs demanded no delay. In September, 1942, *New Dominion Series* No. 19 reported:

> The Pulaski Boys' Club is still without a home—but not without hope, nor entirely without a recreation program. Since the publication of "From Gangs to Boys' Club," the Pulaski Recreation Commission has come into existence. With $1,000 from the Community Chest and several WPA workers, a very fine summer program has been carried on. There are three playgrounds, each open and supervised six hours a day six days a week.
> "The program," the supervisor says, "is not for a so-called under-privileged group. It is for everybody. We are all very much under-privileged from a recreational viewpoint due to the necessary restrictions on travel, and we will undoubtedly continue to be for the duration of the war. It is recreation for everyone, and everyone needs it whether in a strenuous form such as athletics or in a quiet way such as reading and handicraft, or as mere spectators."

But time proved that this general program did not meet the specialized need of gang-age boys. Rather pessimistic reports kept coming to us from local social workers. There were desultory discussions from time to time among service clubs of reviving the boys' club but nothing was done about it until the fall of 1945.

Now with a "clubhouse" again available, with a cash donation for equipment from several local business men, with the active interest and direction *of a young man formerly in the boys' club,* it begins to look as if the present and future crops of teen-age boys in Pulaski will have their gang energy directed into useful and wholesome channels after a four-year interim—a long enough period for some of the "old boys" to grow up and insist that their younger brothers have the opportunity they had.

The dramatics group of the Weavers' Guild in Gatlinburg, Tennessee, (*New Dominion Series,* No. 34, July, 1943) finally had to give up productions for the duration. The reason given was that most of the actors had gone into the army or into defense work. Now revival of the group looks hopeful. Next summer's visitors to Gatlinburg may again see presented in dramatic form the customs and the lore of the mountain folk by some of those same folk who are unwilling to have their heritage entirely submerged in the new ways of the "fotched-on" folk who have come in such great numbers during recent years.

Leadership Strengthened in Many Areas

Among the developments reported, about twenty claimed that progress had been made in strengthening local or lay leadership. The person who reported the Carroll County, Georgia, program said that the professsional worker responsible for the widespread development of small cooperatives in that area had left, but that the program was going forward. The people know how to handle their organizations, but "Ed's enthusiasm is missed greatly."

This situation affords a test case for our evaluation of his type of leadership as stated in *New Dominion Series,* No. 40:

As director of the community activities of the student-teachers, Mr. Yeomans has apparently succeeded in giving them an understanding of his own type of leadership. His—and their—skills and knowledge are put at the disposal of the communities. Opportunities for community meetings are provided. The actual plan and active leadership for every program, however, come from the citizens of the community concerned. Local leaders grow quickly in proficiency through the experience of working together toward tangible goals. The school principal, the teachers, the secretary of the cooperative league, take their rightful places as members of a community interested along with other citizens in the common welfare. Such leadership is at present as rare as it is essential to true community-rooted democracy.

We shall watch the cooperative program in Carroll County with interest during the next few years.

Extension of Activities

A gratifying number of programs reported addition to or extension of activities. The Gerow Community House (*New Dominion Series*, No. 7) has added a community cannery and is planning locker refrigeration. Its program of recreation and sociability continues for the community and has been extended to include servicemen from nearby camps. The same property committee continues to function but committees working on programs change annually.

In Prince Edward County adventures in joint ownership are progressing (*New Dominion Series*, No. 17). Four new joint-ownership services have been added and none have been dropped. In three years they have begun to show results in increased production and better living. "Lime spreaders and drills have increased quality and quantity of production. Haymowers, rakes, sorghum mills assure harvesting and processing of crops."

The Rockingham Poultry Cooperative (*New Dominion Series*, No. 21) has grown rapidly in three years. It started with $50 of borrowed money in the treasury and only three employees. When the story was reported in 1942, the cooperative was shipping 13,000,000 pounds of poultry a year. During the first two years of its existence it had spent considerable time building up markets. Since then, it has been hard put to it to supply the demand created. When reported in "Programs Revisited" in September, 1944, it was just opening a branch plant in Moorefield, West Virginia, sixty miles from Timberville. Now the manager reports the opening of a second branch at Winchester, Virginia, fifty miles in another direction. These branches save long-distance hauling and make possible further expansion of poultry raising in the area immediately surrounding them.

The Maternity Center, Clayton, Georgia, (*New Dominion Series*, No. 36) is rapidly developing into a complete health center with public health offices and hospital facilities. The Health and Welfare Council, the county officials, and the local doctors are all cooperating in the new developments as they did in its beginnings.

The Lynchburg Civic Committee for Children's Service (*New Dominion Series,* No. 25, December, 1942) has several offspring. One of them, the Child Care Center, has reached maturity and is now incorporated as a separate entity. It owns its own home and serves hundreds of children. The Youth Center, another offspring of the civic committee, provides evening recreation for young people. The civic committee itself made a survey of recreation needs in 1944 and followed it up by getting together a citizens' recreation committee to interpret needs to the city recreation department. Along with its study and action program, the civic committee carries on an educational program of lectures and discussions to "gradually enlighten more and more citizens." The Lenten study class that started it all back in 1941 could not possibly have foreseen all this when it decided that study of problems "should lead to doing something about them."

The museum at Big Stone Gap, Virginia, continues to grow (*New Dominion Series,* No. 27, January, 1943). Since the story was told, its founder, the Hon. C. Bascom Slemp, has died. The museum has been taken over by the state and will be operated by the State Conservation Commission. The collection will continue to be housed at Big Stone Gap. Traveling exhibits are being planned in order to extend its usefulness. The project will continue to "rescue from oblivion the history, arts, and crafts of the pioneers of Southwestern Virginia" and to demonstrate what a community can do to preserve its heritage.

Big Lick, Tennessee, reports that loss of the young men who were the best leaders in the program of study for action among the farmers there (*New Dominion Series,* No. 29, March, 1943) retarded the development of some plans. These young men are now returning, however, and are looking forward to accomplishing many of the things previously discussed. In the meantime, the community has not lost ground. It was accepted as an Area Demonstration by the Soil Conservation Commission, and much has been accomplished in spite of the shortage of farm labor. Last year the people participated in the *Rural Community Improvement Contest* sponsored by Knoxville civic clubs. They won third place, with more than eighty other communities participating in the contest.

Patrick County, Virginia, began harvesting and canning its wild berries in 1944 (*New Dominion Series,* No. 61). That first year its people harvested 41,000 gallons of blackberries and 32,000 pounds of blueberries. The commercial cannery flourished in spite of the fact that local skeptics had predicted its speedy demise. In fact, it flourished to the extent of being able this year to erect a new cinderblock building and to install new and more modern equipment. The county agent reports greatly increased interest in and respect for the undertaking on the part of local business men.

Fresh Adversities to Be Overcome

The report from Ravenscroft, Tennessee, (*New Dominion Series,* No. 26, December, 1942) is one of the most interesting. The bulletin told the story of a group of stranded miners who through their own determination and the help of the Farm Security Administration had made themselves into farmers and had reclaimed almost worthless land abandoned by the coal company in 1936. For two years they were merely squatters on the land. Then, in 1938, a cooperative was formed to arrange leases and eventually to arrange for purchase of the land which the tenants were improving yearly. When the bulletin was written in December, 1942, yearly leases were being granted by the company. Plans for purchase were merely awaiting the arrangement of a loan from FSA. The story ended with the following paragraph:

> Ravenscroft is not a ghost town because its people have discovered the land. They have learned a new way of life. They have learned to participate in community affairs and to work things out as a group. Most families are better fed than when the men were earning good wages in the mines. As individuals they are much better prepared than they were in 1936 to cope with problems of living in Ravenscroft or elsewhere.

That they need to be "prepared to cope with problems" became clear soon after, when they faced an unexpected situation. We quote from a letter from one of the persons interested in the community from the beginning:

We thought we had everything lined up to go ahead with a great program at Ravenscroft. The FSA was all ready to purchase the tract of land, with money that was lying in Tennessee banks doing nothing. And then came the great outbreak against FSA in Congress, fostered by the Farm Bureau Federation and allied agencies. I enjoyed going up and testifying before the Senate sub-committee on behalf of FSA. But the agency was afraid to move in the Ravenscroft situation.

And then without anyone's letting us know, the company that owned the land just turned around and sold it to a real estate operator. He got the benefit of all the labor we had put in securing a good price from the company, having the tract surveyed, etc. He started in immediately demanding large amounts from the people for their old company houses that they had taken care of themselves for years. And he wanted about $20 an acre for the land they had improved.

Of course, all our plans were knocked out. We could not continue the community house; it was sold to one of the families. We did get to keep the company store (we had bought the building but, of course, not the land before that) and he was reasonable and sold the co-op the land—at a high price. The co-op had made a very real success and promised to continue as an effective agency. Fortunately our ablest families knew enough not to plunge for the real estate man's original demands and I believe that some of them got their places at not too bad a price later. . . . . Still I know that some permanent results were achieved. It is likely that a permanent community will continue and that the cooperative movement will grow.

We look forward to another visit to Ravenscroft and opportunity to report the progress it has obviously made even in the face of fresh adversity at a time when the people had barely achieved some degree of mastery over their fate.

Spiritual Growth and Intangible Values

The Jordan Area, Greenville County, South Carolina, has been revisited this year, four years after the first report. Our comments in "Programs Revisited," September, 1944, can be repeated with one more year of steady growth added. There is no better summary with which to end these reports selected as typical of the fifty-eight continuing programs:

Probably the most exciting of the revisits was to the Jordan Area of Greenville County, S. C., (No. 11—"A Planned Rural Community"). In the first place almost three years had passed since our first visit—time enough for the program to prove itself or to die a slow death. In the second place, there had been two changes in school superintendents during that time, and this should afford a chance to judge whether the program truly had its roots in the community or depended for its vitality on the leadership of the superintendent who had started it. In the third place, we were accompanied on the visit by ten community leaders who last summer, in a workshop at the University of Virginia, had had the Jordan Area held up as a kind of model. Now they wanted to see for themselves.

What they saw was in no sense disappointing. The entire area shows remarkable progress in diversified farming. Cotton has been largely replaced by peaches, small grain, sweet potatoes and pastures for the herds which are steadily increasing. Well cared-for orchards and contoured fields with strip crops offer a sight pleasing to the eye. Buildings, both private and public, reflect the increased prosperity and fine morale of the community. The orchards are now producing so well that large sheds are being erected with belt conveyors and other mechanized devices for sorting and packing the increasingly large yield of peaches. Because of the size of the individual orchards, members of the community say that cooperative sheds are impractical. At the same time, the spirit of cooperation which has grown so strong in the area results in a generous sharing of this new equipment.

The cooperative potato-curing house on the school grounds has encouraged the production of sweet potatoes and improved the quality. They now are important not only as food but also as a small cash crop. Truckers come to the curing house and buy whatever producers do not need for their own families. The house is long since paid for. Its earnings and those of other cooperative projects now go to get additional services for the people. A new seed-treater is among the most recent acquisitions. Additional land for the nursery has been bought. The night following our visit a meeting had been called to make plans for a freezer-locker plant.

The cooperative store continues to serve the community. Last year's business amounted to more than $50,000 as compared with about $1,700 a month in 1941. There are now 122 paid-up members and 50 more whose shares will be paid for as their patronage dividends amount to enough. All earnings, of course, go back to members.

"We sell whatever the people want," says the manager, "and we buy from the farmers anything which it is possible to sell in the community."

The credit union which has been operating for five years has never lost a cent. It started with a $50 loan limit but later was able to raise that to $300. The boy who wants to buy a calf or start a poultry flock may become a member along with the adults. To get cans for the cannery, to increase the stock in the store, or to acquire some new service, the community has been able to borrow from itself and pay interest to itself. At present, there is little need for loans to individuals. The credit union has been buying war bonds. It has also sold war bonds to the extent of $22,000.

Careful planning for future needs carries over from individuals and the cooperative to other groups in the community. The church which was reported in the previous bulletin to have built a new parsonage now has collected a building fund during these days of prosperity. The money is invested in bonds and will be available when the war ends.

Some things have not lasted. The health center, for example, for which there was considerable outside help is no longer functioning save in a very limited way. Members of the cooperative, however, have availed themselves of a group insurance plan for hospitalization at a low cost. The area council set up under the Greenville County Council is no longer active. This does not mean the community no longer plans together. Meetings of the cooperative and of agricultural groups provide the opportunity. The community has perhaps found for itself a more natural planning setup.

Changes in school superintendents have been commented on. It should be noted that there has been no change in the teacher of vocational agriculture. To him must go much of the credit for vision, inspiration, and sound development. At the same time it is safe to say that the members of the community are guiding their own course. Several farmers, when asked what would happen if they lost their agriculture teacher, agreed that progress might be slowed up but they would keep moving in the same direction.

"We won't ever go back," said one man.

"We have lost our suspicion of new things," said another. "We are in an experimental state of mind."

Another said that they no longer felt that failure of one undertaking would mean that other things would stop. "If one thing doesn't work, we've learned that something else may."

There was everywhere expression of growth in the spirit of brotherly love and neighborliness. A minister who has recently come to the community remarked that he is continuously reminded of the text, "Behold how pleasant and good it is to dwell in unity."

As we revisit community programs or hear from persons actively engaged in them, we rejoice in the tangible evidence of actual accomplishments. Yet we feel that the intangible values, so readily apparent, are important in the enrichment of life. They cannot be reduced to statistics. They elude even expression in words. We agree heartily with a colleague who shares our faith but who, after a struggle to express it, invariably ends with the statement, "Well, anyway, there's *something* there!"

Even of the six programs that are reported as discontinued we do not despair. There is a residue of these intangibles. And, in most of them, there are still sparks that may serve to kindle fresh fuel as attention returns more fully to the constructive living made possible under peacetime conditions.

Wartime Planning—Peacetime Program

It was gratifying to be able to begin the fifth year of publication (which actually does not belong in this report because the *New Dominion Series* is now a regular rather than an experimental publication of the Extension Division) with

the story of the Washington County Development Association
(*New Dominion Series,* No. 73). This association began planning for peace in the midst of war. This was specially appropriate for the first story after V-J Day. The introductory
paragraphs follow:

"Now is the time to plan and act. . . . . It is not enough to dream
and to hope."

These were the words of citizens to citizens in Washington County,
Virginia, more than a year ago. The world was still in the throes of
war. Washington County was bending its energies toward ending the
struggle as earnestly as any other place. Of its 36,000 inhabitants, 3,000
young men and women were in the armed services. Others were busy
on the home front augmenting the world's food supply and serving
their country through the Red Cross, in salvage drives, in bond campaigns, by blood donations, and in whatever other activities presented themselves to civilians. Yet there was an urgent feeling on
the part of a few citizens that "while the flames of war blaze around
the world, we should lift our vision to a better era."

"We are winning the war," they said, "as a result of careful
plans, aggressive action, and a determination to win. With this same
approach—planning, action, and determination—we can be ready for
the peace."

Thus the Washington County Development Association, Inc., with
offices at Abingdon, came into being. This association is now vigorously attacking the job of building a better world in the community in
which it exists. But it did not wait until the war ended to make its
start. It is more than a year ago that a few citizens said, "Now is
the time." The intervening months have been busy ones with many
persons doubling in leadership in order to wage the war and, at the
same time, prepare for the peace. Now more than 500 citizens are
actively engaged in planning and doing.

And Washington County was by no means unique. Evidence could be found in many communities that wartime organization and planning were carrying over into better peacetime programs.

CHAPTER 5

Observed But Not Reported

"Tell us about some of the programs you have visited but have not thought models for other communities to follow."

This request, in one form or another, has come to us often enough to make us feel that some report should be made. The *New Dominion Series* set out to stress the positive on the assumption that we learn from our successes. That is one reason programs about which we are skeptical or of which we are frankly critical have not been included. The other reason is that, although most communities like to be held up as worthy of emulation, few communities — or individuals — are willing to serve as bad examples. It has seemed better, therefore, to point out their weaknesses in private to those most intimately concerned. In this chapter we are summarizing a dozen stories typical of those not reported in the *Series*. We have made some changes in non-essential details to preserve their anonymity.

Insufficient Evidence

One program that came to our attenion when we were collecting file materials in 1941 had an excellent blueprint for development of a rural community. It covered a period of years. The goal for each year was indicated in terms of number of acres of pasture to be built, number of acres to be reforested, number of houses to be painted, amount of food to be raised, number and kind of community services to be added. There was a community organization with committees responsible for each aspect of the program. The cooperation of all agencies such as schools, agricultural extension service, churches, and farmers' organizations was part of the plan.

The idea had received considerable publicity. Correspondence at that time with the young man responsible for it indicated that the goals were being attained and that, as each was reached, the community was more ready to start on the next lap. It had the promise of a good grass-roots development.

It was two years before a visit to the community became possible. The man who had started the program had gone to a good position in a federal agency as a result, we were told, of the publicity his program had received. The school principal had moved to another community. The superintendent had gone into the army. The office of the county agent had a new incumbent.

None of the new professional workers knew anything about the program. On the part of some of them, we thought we detected willful rather than accidental ignorance. There had been a political upheaval in the county, and the *ins* of two years before were now the *outs*. This seemed to have some relation to lapses in memory on the part of those who should have known.

A day of rambling about and chatting with farmers in the area revealed that there "had been something"—but, we were told by one man, it was *"only a citizens' organization;* the authorities were never behind it."

Another admitted to having been a part of it. "It all seems to have died down now. But you might see Mr. Blank."

Mr. Blank agreed that it had "died down" but felt there might still be sparks in the ashes. A man at the college, he said, was "nuts about community stuff." One of his students got this started. It was good. But it went too fast. When he left, his ideas were away ahead of the people in the community.

We were not entirely satisfied that there might not be a spark left strong enough to start the fire again. On the other hand, we could find no heat nor even a bit of smoke. Letters to the former professional workers of the area, including the enthusiastic maker of the blueprint, brought no response. Their attention was apparently on new ventures.

Our conclusion about this program, as about a number of others started by graduate students full of idealism and social theory and eager for material for theses, was that its value to the student was undoubtedly great; its value to the community was questionable.

"I don't guess it did any harm," is the way a man in a similar situation summed it up.

Possibly the good that accrues to other communities from the experience gained by the student in the community "not harmed" may more than justify the procedure. We have not enough evidence to say with finality. Perhaps here is subject for research and even a thesis.

Premature and Over-enthusiastic Publicity

A program in another community was reported to us as an excellent example of a principal's enlisting the interest of the patrons in school-community problems and then stepping back while they proceeded to find and apply solutions. It sounded like the answer to a principal's prayer. We hurried to the spot.

The principal was on the homemade athletic field coaching games. He put on his coat and greeted his visitors from the University cordially. After chatting with him about his school for a few minutes and finding deep understanding and responsiveness on his part, we mentioned the person who had directed us to him. He immediately became reticent.

The gist of his report, borne out by facts we were able to gather later, was that his patrons had been persuaded to take a normal interest in school affairs. They had used their influence to get for the school much needed equipment and improvements to the physical plant. They had acquired a broader comprehension of education and had insisted on such "frills" as art and music for their children. What they had learned to do for the school through cooperative thinking and effort might have carried over to community affairs but it had not.

An enthusiastic observer had given the program premature publicity. His fine vision of what such activity might lead to in terms of community life made him tell what could be as if it were already accomplished. The people in the community had, as yet, no idea of doing the "radical" things he imputed to them—though in the process of normal growth they might have done them all. They became self-conscious and suspicious. The leaders found that they were too busy at other things to continue their activities in relation to the school program.

The principal was sure that at some time they could start again but equally sure that they must make haste slowly. Too bright a vision of things as they might be had made them turn aside from the road they were following, but he thought they would return if left to themselves. Certainly it was not the time to turn the light of more publicity in their direction.

Insufficient Understanding

A program for "older young people" in one community caught our attention. Its purpose, according to its instigator, was to make life in that rural community more attractive to those older young people who had to stay there. Their brothers and sisters had escaped to the supposedly greener fields of urban life but they were caught by force of circumstance over which they felt they had no control.

The economic factor, he decided, was at the basis of their dissatisfaction. Cooperatives he saw as the answer. So a cooperative store was started. It prospered. Earnings made possible expansion as well as the payment of patronage dividends. A gas station was the next venture. It, too, was successful from the economic point of view. The leader's plans included cooperative ownership of farm machinery; cooperative marketing; a building which would house all activities and serve as a social center; and a homestead plan which would make possible the purchase of land by young couples wishing to have their own farms.

On our first visit, we saw the store and gas station. We found enthusiasm on the part of the leader who was a professional worker in the area. We could find little either of enthusiasm or of understanding among the few members he took us to see though they were the ones he considered the most active. The books, which he kept, showed financial gain. The meetings he described seemed to afford little else than opportunity for him to report the earnings and divulge future plans.

A year after the first visit, we were again in that community. The store windows were boarded up. The gas pumps were empty and padlocked. The "leader" had gone to another community. No leadership had developed within the group.

Two thriving activities had stopped, and plans were apparently forgotten. One observer offered as explanation of the failure "the inadequacy of the theoretical knowledge that underlay the practical expression." That coincided with our impression when, on our first visit, we found inability on the part of those participating to explain their program. *The degree to which participating laymen can interpret any program is a significant indication of whether it is rooted in their lives —always allowing, of course, for inarticulateness and lack of technical vocabulary.*

Right Deed for Wrong Reason

In several instances "the right deed for the wrong reason" has made us unwilling to label a program *good.* One of the finest community canneries in the South fell into this category. It was modern, well equipped, scientifically managed, and at the service of hundreds of citizens not usually within reach of canneries. But every piece of publicity about it (and there were many) featured the officeholder who "gave it to the people." It served as an excellent means of advancing his political ambitions. To be sure, it was tax money that paid for the publicity he received. But the community service, as he pointed out, was "free." It had been given to the people. It could be withdrawn at the whim of the giver. The people had no voice in either planning or control.

A medical care program in one county was reported to us by a social worker as taking care of the situation more adequately than any other she had known. Investigation revealed that public money was certainly provided for medical care and that anyone recommended by the welfare department or the board of supervisors received the care needed. Moreover, the plan had been inaugurated at the suggestion of the local doctors. These same doctors took care of cases referred. They kept an informal record in their heads of services rendered and they met once a year to divide the appropriation among them, always making what they all considered an equitable distribution. Undoubtedly they received less money for service thus rendered than if they had collected regular fees from each person. But they did not complain. It was their job to take care of sick people.

Their explanation of the plan concluded with their reason for starting it: They had been determined to defeat the health insurance program of the Farm Security Administration which they considered "socialized medicine." They had succeeded. *The fact that giving people a chance to pay might develop better citizens for democracy than giving them charity seemed incomprehensible to them. Yet they complained of the "triflin' shiftless people" who were willing to take and take!*

"Doing Good"

Another program was called to our attention as worthy of a place in the *Series,* by the persons responsible for it. In a small industrial town, the wives of mill executives and owners had established a library for the workers. Funds were collected from citizens, including workers, for purchase of books. The books were then rented for ten cents a week to the ladies sponsoring the project. When the ladies had finished reading them, those *which met with the approval of the wife of the owner* were put in the "library" for general circulation.

The library was a small dark room with shelves for the books and a tiny desk for the woman who, in return for a pittance, guarded the collection allowing "reliable people" to borrow some of the less valuable books. There was no place for a reader to sit even while he browsed long enough to make a selection. Certain shelves contained books that were not allowed to circulate because "they cost five or ten dollars apiece." Since there was no place to use them in the library and they could not be taken away, they were never read. Most of these expensive books had been gifts of persons "outside" who had heard of the worthy enterprise.

A casual drive through the part of the town where the workers lived convinced one that there was little space, privacy, or light for reading at home. The claim of the ladies that books were returned in distressingly soiled condition seemed plausible. To have kept a book away from the food, the flies, the babies, and the clutter in those overcrowded, unscreened shabby little shacks would have required superhuman effort.

The "librarian," who had first been put on as a WPA worker and was later retained on money collected by the ladies, deplored the irrresponsibility of the people as loudly as the ladies themselves in the beginning of the interview. Later, after carefully looking over both shoulders, she opined, "If the ladies had to live in them houses, they'd get the books dirty too." In fact they sometimes did anyway. And she displayed a book she was then cleaning up and mending for general circulation after its rental existence. Several pages were badly torn. "The baby got hold of it," the renter had explained.

Discussion with the sponsors brought out many complaints about irresponsibility of "people like them" and about lack of appreciation of efforts in their behalf. There had been no attempt to analyze needs and try to meet them. The library had not resulted from a conviction that it would meet a real need. The ladies had wanted to do something for the workers in the mill. Someone thought of a library which, with its rental plan, could serve the dual purpose of providing the ladies with current books at low cost and of gradually building up a collection for general circulation. Making books available satisfied their urge to do good. Beyond that they were not concerned.

Supplementing Farm Income

Stories of small industries brought into rural areas to supplement farm income have been investigated. They have been difficult to report as approaches to democratic living. The most promising one gave evidence of local initiative and local financing. In fifteen years its $75,000 annual payroll had added considerably to the prosperity of the county.

Yet no analysis of local resources had been made. Raw material for the factory was all brought in on trains while other trains hauled local products away to be processed elsewhere.

The only resource considered in the planning was unskilled labor. Skilled workers were imported for the higher-salaried jobs and they had continued to hold them. No provision was made for training young people in the skills required. Like other local products, the ambitious youngsters

continued to go elsewhere to make their contribution—using
their skills in some instances, we hazard a guess, in processing the very products exported by their county.

Though this community had done a good job, others can
do a much better one with the help of state services now available. They can analyze their total resources and plan their
industries much more scientifically.

Good Foundations Disregarded by Community

Failure of communities to build on excellent foundations
laid by WPA programs are numerous. Good hot-lunch programs in rural schools in the late Thirties were making a real
contribution to the welfare of future citizens. In 1941-42, we
were urged to include several of these in the *Series*. They
had been in operation long enough to prove their value. The
test would come, we felt, however, when WPA workers and
surplus commodities were no longer available. When that
time came, few school boards were ready with the funds necessary to continue what the WPA had begun. *Much evidence
was available that communities do not learn to help themselves by having something done for them. Citizens must
understand a program and demonstrate their determination
to have it before officials who are elected to protect public
funds will accept innovations.*

In one mountain county more than sixty weavers had
been supplied with looms and supervisors by WPA. A craft,
not yet quite forgotten in the area, was revived. Local wool
was used in the program and a fine demonstration given of
the possibility of production for the handicraft market which
is never able to meet the demand. Under the setup which did
not permit the sale of goods produced by WPA workers, markets could not be established. But other groups such as the
Southern Highland Handicraft Guild had demonstrated the
practicality of such production. When we visited the county
in 1943, every loom had been taken away. Sixty trained
weavers were seeking what unskilled work was available. The
supervisor was reluctantly closing the little workshop she and
her husband had struggled to keep going with three looms
he had made. And county officials and business men were try-

ing to lure small industries into the area to supplement income from the mountain farms. Local resources, traditions, and skills had no place in their planning.

In many rural areas WPA libraries were giving limited but much needed service as late as 1941. Old trucks converted into bookmobiles and even pack-saddles played a part in getting books to folks in isolated areas. Facts and figures proved that these people wanted and read books when they were available. In one county there were upward of 100 one-room schools with no books. In 1934 a WPA library began carrying books to both schools and individuals. By 1939, some 12,000 volumes were available, some from the state library, some locally owned, but all distributed through efficiently working machinery established under WPA. There were several enthusiastic, full-time, trained workers. Following the demise of WPA, one untrained, poorly paid worker was assigned by the county to keep the program going. It was a superhuman task. Some interested residents predict that now, with the war ended, the citizens will demand library service such as they once enjoyed. Time will tell. But if too much time elapses, the story will be the usual one of no carry-over, for the memory of man is short unless his own thought and labor have made an idea a part of his bone and sinew.

Community Programs Disregarded by Planning Boards

Reports of a log cabin community center, the building and use of which had regenerated an entire community in an isolated and completely rural area—so rural that it had no name —kept coming to our attention as we searched for good community programs. Its exact location was rather vague except for the information that it was within a 25-mile radius of a certain state university. Mimeographed reports were undated and gave no names of interested persons. From these reports we gathered evidence that it had flourished during the Thirties. When visiting the university referred to in June, 1942, we inquired about the community center. One professor knew of its rather thrilling beginnings and knew that members of the extension division had helped with programs. The extension division staff reported that they, too, knew vaguely of its existence but that the only man who had worked directly with it had gone to the army. Delving into records turned up names of enough landmarks to indicate its general location. Our curiosity as to the present vagueness about something that had seemed so fine made us continue the search. Landmarks were located—but no log cabin where it should have been. Inquiries at a humble cabin brought the information that the "government tore it down." The old lady who reported this was somewhat incoherent but insistent upon the wanton destructiveness of "the government." But, she insisted, she had not let them tear her cabin down. She had lived there all her life. Her husband had died there. She intended to die there, and those two box bushes growing in the yard were to be placed at the head and the foot of her grave. She and her husband had brought them with two more as tiny slips from the old box at the homeplace of her family. The other two already marked her husband's grave. And no government could make her move from her cabin and her boxwood.

Finally she told us the name of the schoolteacher who years before had persuaded the people to build the community center. The teacher now lived in the city. The "city" was a small town some twenty miles away. Inquiries in town uncovered no one of the name given by the old lady. As we were leaving town, we mentioned the matter to a man from whom we bought gas—and, at last, we struck gold. The teacher had married his cousin and lived right here in town. She could tell us the whole story. His directions took us directly to her home and a delicious luncheon.

She had come to teach in the little one-room school that served the community, in 1928. She knew the people well because she had been a sickly child and her mother had bought a farm there to let her run wild in the healthy out-of-doors. She loved the simple folk who had been their neighbors but knew the community was a difficult one.

All the people were very poor. Although there was a school, many children could not attend for lack of decent clothing to wear. The people quarreled continuously. It was unsafe to be out after dark. The quarrels were carried into both church and school. In what started as fist fights, knives were frequently drawn. Rumor had it that the older boys brought whiskey to school with their lunches.

Aside from the church and the school there was no meeting place of any kind and no provision for sociability. The young teacher, just out of college and filled with fine social theories, sensed the need of a place where people of all ages could get together to have some wholesome fun. The farm which her mother owned had plenty of logs and stones. The idea of building a rustic cabin there for a recreation center did not seem to her an impractical one.

One Sunday in church she told the people of her idea and asked whether they would like to help. Jeers and derisive laughter greeted her suggestion. Nevertheless she persisted. When the noise had died down, she announced a meeting date when anyone interested might come to make plans for a building where they could have ballad singing, fiddlers' conventions, storytelling, dances, and plays. On the appointed night three boys and the county superintendent of schools appeared. The small response did not discourage the teacher. The superintendent, at first suspicious of so radical a departure from the three R's, withdrew his objections. The teacher and the three boys spent almost a year organizing a group of neighbors who liked to play musical instruments and to sing. This group of "Rustic Revelers" then undertook to enlist the cooperation of other people in the community in helping to build the recreation center.

The teacher's farm furnished the land, the logs, and the rocks. The men and boys of the community furnished the labor. One of the most scornful when the first announcement was made in church built the fireplace and chimney. His interest became so great that he spent countless hours carving an Indian's head for the center of the chimney and finding just the right stones of graduated sizes to make a headdress for his Indian. His artistry was matter of pride for the entire community. Before the end of 1929, the cabin was completed. It had one large room, 50 by 25 feet, with a tremendous fireplace occupying the entire end.

While the building was in process, the teacher had organized the older children into Boy Scouts and Campfire Girls. She had found leadership in a nearby city and at the college. These groups were ready for the center when it was completed as were the "Rustic Revelers." Basketball leagues and general recreation nights were organized. The entire community, young and old, came together to play games including the old dances which Mammy Jones was able to teach younger people who had forgotten them. Petty feuds and neighborhood fusses were forgotten. Drinking and fighting ceased to be the only diversion. Informal classes, not called by that name, helped young married women to learn something about nutrition, health, and homemaking. There was no lack of activity in the community center.

When the little school was closed and the children taken by bus to the consolidated school, the community was glad. The children had better opportunities, and the cabin remained to serve the community. The former teacher, though no longer living on her farm, continued to help, but the people had become accustomed to planning their own programs and needed less and less help as time went on.

In 1937, the Department of Interior began to buy land in the area for a demonstration recreation center. Purchases included the farm on which the cabin stood, but the people were assured that nothing useful would be destroyed. It seemed to them particularly fitting that their cabin should be a part of such a center.

The teacher married about that time and went to Florida for a month. On her return, she was informed by people from the community that their cabin had been torn down. She investigated and found that only the chimney remained standing. She found the man in charge of the project. His explanation was simple. The specifications called for such cabins but did not call for one in this particular spot. She suggested that he leave the chimney for an outdoor fireplace since it was situated on a hill overlooking one of the prettiest views in the entire area. He thanked her for the suggestion and agreed to carry it out. Three days later she returned to get some ladyslipper plants which she and her Campfire Girls had planted near the cabin. Not only had the chimney been torn down, but the stones were already in the stone crusher making material for a new road. Even the Indian's head, which had become a kind of symbol of community achievement, had been destroyed.

Former residents who sold their land for the park and moved to nearby communities are as sad about the loss of their cabin as those who stayed on as had the old lady we had talked with. Cabins for Boy Scouts and other camping groups from nearby towns and cities have been erected in the park area but these are not used by the people who had been so well served for several years by their own cabin.

The teacher admits that many of the people sold to the park and are now a part of communities that have better educational and recreational facilities. They think they would have continued to use the cabin but their interest may be more sentimental than real. It would have been matter of great satisfaction to them if their little recreation project could have been a part of the demonstration center. But specifications took no note of what was, in planning what should be. Perhaps, the former teacher thinks, the cabin had actually served its purpose in its rehabilitation of the community. The sense of achievement and the pleasant memories of those who were a part of the program may be of as much value to them as the cabin itself. Yet with so little readjustment in "specifications" the program could have been given continuity in extending the purpose of the community center to serve a wider area.

Practice Belies Purpose

A rural school, whose leaders boast that its purpose is to make life in that rural community so attractive that young people will not want to leave, lays great stress on democracy. The stress is so great, in fact, that the principal says, "There *shall be democracy!*" He has set up a rigid framework within the confines of which children, teachers, and patrons are forced to go through the motions of democratic processes to arrive at decisions he has made in advance. He sees no contradiction in his theory and his practice. One bit of evidence

he produces to prove that democracy is at work is that the
students select their own models from among successful
alumni.   Nor does he see any evidence of failure to achieve
the school's stated purpose in the fact that those voted "most
successful" are always those who have made money in business or reputations in professions in parts of the country far
removed from their own rural community.   In fact he himself points with pride to those products of his school who
"have made good on the outside."

Cooperatives for Whom?

"Cooperative" ventures present as varied a picture as
any other type when viewed as "experimental approaches to
democratic living."   All too frequently they are "cooperative"
only in that a group of underprivileged persons cooperate
with someone who uses them to advance his own ends.

Handicraft programs of this kind are not uncommon.   In
these the people who do the work in their isolated mountain
cabins receive almost no remuneration.   Yet the high prices
received by the promoter of the project are paid at least in
part because of a sentimental interest in the poor mountain
folk on the part of the purchasers in the northern city or the
southern resort. Occasionally, even money is collected from
such people for the "educational" program which trains the
weavers to produce. Not infrequently the individual or agency
sponsoring the program is convinced that the useful employment of people who would otherwise "waste their time" is
ample justification.   The financial gains of the one who makes
the work possible are his just reward.

In one instance the "cooperative" was run by a Negro for
members of his own race.   In return for giving whole families
a questionable "education by doing," he had built up a substantial private fortune from sale of their products. He, too,
was among those who played upon the sentiment of well-
wishers of his race.

Cooperatives by Whom?

Another "cooperative" showed no evidence of personal
gain for its promoter.   In fact, he and his family had lived a

Spartan existence for a quarter of a century in a sparsely furnished, uncomfortable rural parsonage which served also as business office for the cooperative. It all started with a group of his parishioners whom he brought together to buy fertilizer cooperatively. There had developed from this beginning a large consumers' cooperative and a marketing cooperative. Material gains among the farmers in the community were unquestionably great. There were no evidences of growth in any other areas of living.

The minister, even after twenty-five years, kept all the records, did all the business, and was "the leader," at great cost to his health and personal life. When asked what would happen if he were to withdraw, he insisted that the cooperatives "had become the accepted way of life and therefore would continue." His failure to give the people concerned a part in the planning or an understanding of the process seemed to him to have no implications for the future.

In another large farmers' cooperative, a similar situation existed. Here, however, in addition to financial gains throughout the area, there had been great improvement in agricultural techniques. These could not fail to result in some permanent progress.

Yet here, too, there was one-man domination of the program that made it anything but "an experimental approach to democratic living." Likewise large amounts of money were collected from wealthy persons in distant cities and poured into the "cooperative." For this the backwardness and quaintness of the people were thoroughly exploited.

A local person who knew something of the cooperative movement elsewhere maintained that this leader had consistently refused to let "his people" know about it. "They think," our informant said, "that all this development is the unique brainchild of their friend. They stand in great awe of his unparalleled ingenuity." He was unsympathetic with small self-help cooperatives that were starting in the area. In fact, he opened one of his cooperative stores beside one which had enjoyed several years of successful history without outside help.

There is no evidence of spiritual or cultural growth of his people, in spite of great economic gains. Likewise there is no evidence of developing leadership. There is always an annual meeting at which the "leader" is elected president and his slate of board members is unquestioningly approved. Earnings are announced at these meetings with loud huzzas and handclapping led always by the president. Items of business are slipped in between song and dance numbers so that they are hardly noticed. Nobody is bored; everybody has a feeling of fellowship and well-being. Old-time revival methods are used to work up enthusiasm. And one wonders how in the world, when their leader is gone, these people are ever going to carry on the tremendous and complex business which they ostensibly own and manage. Again, time will tell.

Who Gets the Credit?

In at least two cases programs were not reported because organizations initiating them had been so tenacious of credit that the growth and usefulness of the projects were restricted. One was a library, the beginnings of which made an exciting story of initiative and determination on the part of a few women. So zealous were their efforts that the library soon outgrew what they could administer. They had demonstrated the need for a county library when no one believed it possible, but when state and local funds might have been procured to carry the program through the next stages of its development, they would not let go. The activity had become an end in itself.

In another community a recreation program for young people was an obvious need. Interested friends from a nearby community which had a good program offered to train local leaders. About a dozen persons attended the training program, a large part of which consisted of actually planning and carrying through community nights. At the end of the training course the young people were ready to carry responsibility for the programs. Adult sponsorship was needed. A church organization volunteered. Soon its name replaced the word *community* in the name Community Recreation Program. In all publicity the sponsoring group was named. At first this seemed important in order to give the program status in the community. Later, parents belonging to other denominations began to wonder whether their children should participate. The children wanted to, for there was no other recreation available. One leader suggested that with the amount of interest that had been aroused a community committee might now be asked to take over the sponsorship. The church group protested. Petty bickering began. Old interdenominational feuds were revived. Three sincere attempt were made by interested individuals from all denominations to remove the denominational label. The entrenched sponsoring organization held on.

The last straw that broke the back of this community program was dropped gently by one of the ladies of the sponsoring organization. An out-of-town guest at one of the most successful community night parties had remarked at the unusually large number of young people.

"We have a large church," she said, "but we haven't one-fifth as many young people."

"Oh," the lady of the sponsoring group replied (or was said to have replied), "these are not all in our church—but they will be if we continue to have programs like this."

It was the last "program like this" to be held in that community.

Planning FOR Rather Than Planning BY

Reports of a community center which the Negroes of one community had built for themselves sounded promising enough to warrant investigation. A tangled situation which developed as the project progressed cast some doubt upon it as a model of democratic achievement.

There had been no meeting place for Negroes in the area. Schools were too small and otherwise not suitable for adult meetings. The types of activities that could take place in churches were limited. Negro organizations appointed a committee to find a building or even a suitable room centrally located. None was available. The group decided to build. They collected funds. They found a good site that could be bought at a reasonable price. They asked a white friend to represent them in the business transaction. He was at first doubtful of the wisdom of their undertaking but was finally convinced that they had figured carefully and knew exactly what they were getting into and where their money was coming from.

The purchase was completed and plans for a modest building were drawn up. Then came the possibility of getting NYA and WPA help. A sponsor was necessary. This had to be a public agency to meet WPA requirements. Finally the town council agreed to sponsor the building. It was necessary for the group to deed the land to the town before the town could build on it. This was done. A board of trustees, three white and two colored, was appointed by the town council.

By this time white friends had become enthusiastic about the undertaking. A much more pretentious building was planned with services of a fine architect. Money was contributed by well-wishers. Costs went far beyond the few hundred dollars the Negroes had planned to raise. From that point on, the project so carefully begun by those whose lives were affected was taken out of their hands. When the .fine building was completed, it was dedicated at an impressive ceremony planned entirely by white friends who did not even consult with the Negro organizations which had bought the land and raised the few hundred dollars they planned to use for building.

The building consists of a large auditorium with movable seats so that it can be used for parties as well as for activities requiring seating space. There is a well equipped kitchen and good library. The kitchen was equipped entirely by the Negro women's clubs with money they raised at baked food sales and other similar activities. This took time but gave great satisfaction. They had planned as their next project to furnish and equip the little library. One day they came and found it to be entirely furnished and supplied with books. They were appreciative of the interest of their friends but were somewhat disappointed not to have the kind of library they wanted. Their experience with plans for a cultural program was similar. They wished to have a musical program or a lecture about once a month. They knew what artists and lecturers they wanted to invite. They planned to charge admission to cover cost. Plans were going forward when, unexpectedly, they were presented with a program with speakers and dates fixed and the entire cost underwritten. It was a good program and was well attended. But it was not exactly what they had been looking forward to in their own planning.

The Negro clubs have a place to hold their meetings. It is large enough for conferences or large gatherings they may wish to sponsor jointly or separately. On the other hand, it is not really theirs. Plans are being made for them by others when they wish to make their own. The pretentiousness of the center has attracted the attention and stirred the envy of white organizations which have no similar community center. Whether their friends have helped or hindered remains something of a problem. And appreciation is tempered by some questioning of the not unmixed purpose of those who so readily took the affair out of their hands.

The Good Program Is Part of a Process

All the programs investigated but not reported in the *Series* cannot be designated "failures." Some were omitted because publicity at the time might have hindered their best development, or because more testing time was needed before one could be sure a good plan was going to work. In a few cases we needed more evidence to substantiate the claims made for a program. All these may move along into the "success story" class. Other reasons for not reporting programs will be found in stories referred to above. They include domination by one individual or agency to the exclusion of others who should have a part; exploitation of a community for personal gain, individual prestige, or institutional aggrandizement under the guise of doing good; unwillingness on the part of one group to let another group they consider inferior have a part in planning their own programs; graciously tossing a crust by those entrenched so that those less fortunate will not be hungry enough to demand the full loaf of bread their needs require; failure of local leaders to erect structures on substantial foundations laid by programs not politically acceptable to the powers-that-be (e.g., WPA and FSA); failure of state or federal programs to take into account local patterns and achievements.

The most discouraging reaction to the stories in *New Dominion Series* has not been from persons who disagree. It has been from those who do not comprehend that our concern is with process rather than product.

"I never miss a single story. They are the best things of the kind I have ever come across," says an enthusiast. "But I can't understand why you have never told the story of . . . . ." Then there will follow reference to a hospital planned and financed by a foundation not stinting any part for lack of funds; or a library built and equipped by a public-spirited citizen for people who have no reading habit or concern with books; or a community center so well planned by some benefactor of mankind as to be a model but so carefully protected by the city fathers as to defeat entirely the purpose it should serve; or a model housing program provided by an employer who, by meeting even the unconscious needs of his employees, has made them perhaps more comfortable temporarily but less able to cope with the problems of living when they leave his beneficent care. We have not told such stories because we agree with the rustic philosopher who assured his friends: "Taint no use telling what you done when you aint done it any more than it is telling whar you been when you aint been thar."

There may be real evidence of community betterment in stories not reported. But we reiterate that it was our purpose to report in the *Series,* first of all, only those experimental approaches to democratic living that might well be tried in other communities. Hence some programs, perhaps good in themselves, have been excluded as not generally practicable. Others that can point to achievements that are indeed impressive have attained their goal through the gift of some good angel. Although the people may share to greater or lesser degrees in the benefits, they are no better able to help themselves in other areas of living. *A project that educates people to help themselves is never an isolated achievement. It is one in a chain of related events. The people concerned not only strengthen their techniques for self-development but also broaden their vision of the good community as the program progresses.*

CHAPTER 6

Trends As Indicated By Programs In Action

In connection with looking at programs, both for our own education and for stories to pass on to others, we have observed closely more than one hundred communities in the Southeast at work on some aspect of self-improvement. Up to September, 1945, we had reported sixty-four of these as success stories in *New Dominion Series*.

From programs observed but not reported, as well as from those reported, certain general trends emerge. In these trends are encouraging indications that communities are shaking off their lethargy. Viewed as a whole, the trend is toward working problems out on the local level through democratic processes. There are, at the same time, evidences of conflicts, so strong in specific situations as to make for a temporary *impasse*.

Conflicts Exist

Communities everywhere are accepting their *responsibilities with reluctance*. They are, with equal tenaciousness, clinging to their *right* to control their own destinies through efforts of their own citizens.

A community, for example, may have no public health service. Leaders may have recognized the need for many years without having done anything to overcome the inertia of we-have-always-managed-pretty-well-without-it. Then there may come a rumor that the state or the federal government is making a plan that will affect the local situation.

The citizens' reluctant acceptance of responsibilities collides head on with their equally tenacious clinging to the right to do things their own way. The latter is likely to triumph. State and federal funds are acceptable, they decide, but the control must rest with the local community. This insistence on control necessitates a variety in patterns to fit the diversified *mores* of communities.

In the insistence on "doing it our own way" are the seeds

of another conflict. This time it is between the local group and outside forces. Many state and federal agencies, as well as private agencies on the state or national level, have not accepted the idea that each community can do its own planning and may need its own pattern. In their handbooks or manuals, they have printed procedures that they consider the most efficient. Usually these involve appointing a committee. But the community may already have a committee.

Take one county as an example. It had an excellent organization of home demonstration clubs organized into a county council. They were centering their year's work in nutrition education. The high school home economics teachers, likewise, worked throughout the county with adults as well as with school-age children. There was a citizens' council that had a nutrition committee which coordinated the work of these other agencies, supplementing their programs where there was need. Why, citizens asked, should the State Nutrition Committee appoint a County Nutrition Committee in addition, in view of the fact that the same persons would be involved? Would it not be possible for the existing coordinating group to act as the local committee?

Such a plan might serve the purpose but would mar the pattern. Hence another committee was appointed. The result was complete inactivity of the new committee, not because the community was indifferent to nutritional problems but because it had already mapped out its campaign. It was perfectly willing to have this tied into the state program, but could not see the need for uniformity in organizational procedures.

State and national groups undoubtedly find it difficult to work through existing local groups. It does mean flexibility with reference to plans outlined in handbooks. It may mean consideration of individual community cases for which little staff time is allowed. The result, when reports are printed, may even look like *lack of planning* because of the differences in pattern. Certainly the process is neither so neat nor so simple as a plan which admits of no exceptions. But democracy is not neat and simple.

The conflicts both within communities and between communities and "outside" groups frequently are closely related
to divergent basic philosophies. These can be broadly grouped
as the doing-for and the doing-with philosophies. In the former is a survival of the powerful tradition of *noblesse oblige*;
in the latter are the seeds of democracy. The doing-for philosophy has been strengthened by the tendency of citizens to
think of the government as something apart from them and
to ask, "What are *they* going to do about it?" Where the doing-with philosophy is dominant, there exist no longer the
conflicts of the split personality of we-the-people and they-
the-public-officials (or agencies).

Confusion as to Purpose, Leadership, and Organization

Out of the conflicts there arise certain confusions in almost every community that attempts to organize for action—
and that means most communities nowadays. First, the purpose is not clear. Is the community organization merely an
avenue for channeling programs that originate on the state or
national level? Is it only a clearinghouse that may make for
greater economy and for elimination of duplication of effort on
the part of existing agencies within and without the community? Or has it a *raison d'être* in the nature of democracy
itself—an obligation to analyze local needs, to understand
available resources, and to initiate programs important to the
welfare of the community? Too many community organizations can be found which have never taken thought to clarify
their purpose.

Second, there is confusion as to leadership. Should leadership come from the public official? Should it come from the
professional—that is, the person employed by the agency to
render a certain type of community service? Or should it
come from the citizens of the community whose public servants the officials and the professional workers are? Lack of
clarity in this matter frequently leads to the let-George-do-it
attitude.

Third, there is confusion as to the type of organization
best suited to the promotion of community welfare. This, of
course, bears a direct relation to the other two. The term

"council" is the one most commonly used to denote any organization that exists. How the council should be organized and who should belong is by no means clear. Should it be made up of professional workers who feel the need of a clearinghouse? Or should it go a step further and include, along with the professional workers, heads of organizations such as local service clubs, parent-teacher organizations, and women's clubs? Or should it be a citizens' council, which may take responsibility for planning; for mobilizing the resources of the various agencies—local, state, and national; and for helping to carry out plans—including, perhaps, professionals and officials either as citizens or as representatives of agencies?

May the "council" be a self-constituted group taking its authority from the people composing it? Or must it be set up by a public agency? Or should it be an official group appointed by the local governing body authorized by state law to make such appointment, and acting in accordance with a pattern established by a state planning commission?

The confusion as to type of organization is apparent not only in different communities but often within the same community. There may be, for example, a professional workers' council, a citizens' council, and a planning committee all within the same community, having no relationship to each other save that a few individuals, who are "into everything," are members of two or, perhaps, all three of them. Frequently such individuals succeed in keeping the plans of each group so carefully compartmentalized that they do not see obvious relationships or overlappings.

Certain Trends Emerge

In spite of these and other conflicts and confusions, certain trends are persistent. Some of these have been noted in the six issues of the *Series* "telling of devices used by communities to make their programs more effective."[1] A brief summary is included below.

Study Leads to Action

A glance over the field of community development shows

---

[1]See *New Dominion Series*, Nos. 56, 58, 60, 62, 70, 72.

that a surprisingly large number of programs begin with study groups of one kind or another. These vary in purpose; in size; in sponsorship; in subject matter considered; in educational level, age, and sex of participants; in geographical area represented. In fact, they are as varied as communities themselves. The one thing they seem to have in common is a more or less serious consideration of some subject by two or more persons meeting together over a period of time. Viewed as a whole they present rather convincing evidence that study of even abstract ideas or "cultural" subjects may lead to programs of action that are far-reaching in their effect. In one community, for example, the seventeen persons enrolled in a class checked *culture* as their reason for being there. A community cannery and a recreation program were among the tangible outcomes.

At some point in every program careful analysis or study of the total situation becomes necessary. It may start because a group is disturbed by a bad situation and wants to consider possible solutions; or it may begin as a more generalized consideration of the community and serve as the means of defining problems and planning methods of attack.

In either case three things are clear: (1) no one pattern of procedure fits all situations or communities; (2) where effective, the study program is *closely related in time as well as purpose* to a program of action growing out of the analysis of resources and needs; and (3) the process, where it has proved most effective, is a cumulative one with new possibilities continuously emerging as the program gets under way.

Logical Progression as Program Develops

A community is much more likely to start with an obvious need than with a carefully worked out plan. In the process of meeting that need, very often those concerned become aware of other needs, and a sequence of activities gets under way. A good community program in one field is seldom an isolated instance. It is one expression of something at work in that community which will by the same process lead to other developments. The fine hospital or recreation program or cannery which is the only sign of progress in an otherwise backward community is probably an accident or an inheritance. It is not necessarily evidence of growth.

Organization to Facilitate Action

Also at some point in its development, every community is likely to "organize." In some instances the organization precedes the program it sponsors; in others, it grows out of the program as the need for better coordination of all resources and groups becomes apparent. Sometimes it outlives its usefulness and drops by the wayside while the program sponsored by it continues to flourish.

The multiplicity in form and purpose of such organization and the resulting confusion in the picture have been noted above. "Council" is the term by which it is most generally designated.

In our exploration of programs for *New Dominion Series,* wide variety in councils has been found. In one respect there seems to be consistency. The councils that have played and continue to play a vital part in the communities they serve not only are adapted to the social patterns of those communities, but also are flexible enough to adapt themselves to changing patterns as a program develops. This flexibility may account, to some extent, for the ephemeral nature of many councils. Their demise is not always evidence of failure.

From Study to Action

Councils, like study groups, have been effective in various stages of the development of many community programs. On the other hand, they do not constitute a panacea. Their mortality rate is high. Many, after brilliant beginnings, slip quietly out of existence. Others linger on without realizing or being willing to admit that they have no vital place in their communities. Divers reasons can be found for the untimely end of promising councils. The most common cause is inability to move from the study to the action phase of a program. The council which has the strength and leadership necessary to make that critical transition is likely to continue to serve the community long and well. And never have communities been in greater need of such service!

People Must Know

In the summer of 1944, a community development work-shop group from the University of Virginia visited Rabun County, Georgia. They wanted to know some of the things that made community projects so successful there. The editor of the paper was among the ten local people who met with the visitors. He listened quietly throughout most of the discussion. As the group was breaking up, however, he offered his answer to their question. To get cooperation, he said, *all the people must be kept informed all the time.* If people have the facts, they can be depended on to do the right thing.

Almost every community that is dealing successfully with its problems has discovered this. Each has tried to find a way of telling the people about needs and programs in such a way as to make them care.

Much of what they need to know is already in print. But only the very unusual person will take the trouble to find a pamphlet or a book and, when he has found it, know how to use it to meet the little problems of everyday living. It is these little problems that must be met if levels of living are to be raised to the degree that is made possible by our scientific knowledge. Letting the people know is the job of adult education. The translating of available materials into terms of the community group is one step in that direction. It is a step that many local groups are taking. People *will know in such a way as to take necessary action* only if they understand the language of the printed page and recognize the relation of the facts to their own lives. Distribution of carefully prepared local newsletters and bulletins, as well as wise use of local papers, is proving effective.

"Let's have a meeting," is the most frequently suggested way of getting a new idea before people or of trying to get community action on a problem.

"But there are so many meetings, and they never get any-where," is the most general reaction to the suggestion.

There is a contradiction here that indicates a real problem. Getting together to talk things over and make a plan seems to be a natural method of procedure for a group or a community. Yet there have been so many unsatisfying experiences that there is general skepticism about the wisdom of meetings.

In looking at community programs, we have been especially interested in the place of meetings in their development. Our conclusion is that there is no magic in *meeting* any more than there is in sending out a bulletin, or forming a study group, or organizing a council. On the other hand, a *meeting* occurs at some point in almost every community story we find. Whether or not the meeting has played a vital role in the growth of the program depends on its relation to what has gone before and what is to come after. Its relation to the sequence of events depends on whether it is so planned as to make an audience think and to give it a chance to continue to the point of *thinking things through.*

Who Starts and Who Gets the Credit?

Initiation of a program may come from many and varied groups. It may center around an individual, school, church, extension services, health department, or some other agency. It may be the outgrowth of a study group or of a planning committee. But whatever the initiation or the sponsorship, there is a growing conviction on the part of citizens that agencies, institutions, and individuals must no longer exploit community programs for their own prestige.

There are a gratifying number of instances of wholehearted acceptance of this principle by the groups involved. One young minister who has been the inspiration of a very fine, church-centered program expresses this trend when he says that the emphasis throughout his program has been "upon human needs and their satisfaction through cooperative community effort and planning rather than upon the aggrandizement of the church as an institution."

To be sure, petty jealousies between agencies still exist in most communities, but, more and more, their subversive influence is being recognized. In the long run the group that starts a program must be willing to lose its identity in order to find a more abundant life in the finer community made possible through cooperative efforts. The trend in this direction is more apparent on the local level than in the organizational setup which is farther removed from the people. Too frequently pressures for numbers or for showing results come to local workers from the state or federal level. Then the question of credit may take precedence over the best interests of the community. The agency worker in the community is more likely to see his relationship to other local programs than are his superiors in state, regional, or national headquarters.

Leadership Comes from the People

"Are the people who do these things ordinary people like me or are they of a genus not to be found elsewhere?" So writes one of the regular readers of *New Dominion Series*.

The answer to that question is one we have been seeking as we have visited some hundred communities in search of "techniques whereby communities can help themselves." To discover the answer, we have asked directly and indirectly: Who started it? What, in his—or her—background or training, made him start it? Did he do all the planning himself or did he seek the help of others whose lives would be affected by what happened? Did he do all the work himself or did he delegate jobs? If the latter, how did he select the people to whom he delegated? Did he do anything that could be labeled *leadership training*? Did the growth of the program provide for the growth of leadership to the degree that the instigator of it all could eventually withdraw with some degree of certainty that the program would continue?

In the answers to these questions we have felt that we might get at some of those intangibles that go into the development of leadership. We have hoped to be able to point to ways of overcoming the too common complaint: "But we can't do things in this community; we lack leadership." Looking back over the programs investigated, we feel there are a few basic principles exemplified in those which have had continuous growth.

"Helping communities to help themselves" implies a different philosophy from "helping communities." It implies a different understanding of the role of leader. It implies a different procedure. In both philosophy and procedure a *faith*

in people is basic—the same faith in people which is fundamental to a belief that democracy is the best way of life. The
procedure depends on *leadership*—more or less widespread—
rather than on *a leader*.

"Do you not possibly underestimate the role of the leader
in these programs?" is another question from a reader. The
question is not unrelated to the one above. *We do not underestimate the role of the leader, but we may differ from the
questioner in interpreting that role.* To one person, perhaps,
must go the credit for having the necessary vision—for inspiring, for motivating. But his success can be measured by the
degree to which he has developed leadership and thus worked
himself out of a job. The *leadership* (and very frequently the
leader) is found among "ordinary people like me."

In most good programs it is easy to point to the person,
agency, or institution from which the original inspiration has
come. The more closely a program approaches the democratic ideal, however, the more difficult it becomes to put one's
finger on *the leader.* Each person concerned assumes increasing responsibility. The readiness with which the original
leader relinquishes his place in the picture is one important
test of his mastery of the process of developing real leadership.
The readiness with which others accept their full share of
leadership is the test of whether the program really is rooted
in the community.

The stimulation does not, by any means, always come
from a professional or from a person with special training for
community work. *Many of the best programs we have found
have had their initiation or their leadership in "mere laymen"
in the community.*

The tendency on the part of people to look to the "natural
leaders" is one of the best indicators to the outsider or the professional who wants to discover or to develop leadership. Frequently these people are accepted as leaders but not so designated by those whom they lead. For this reason we have seldom found who were the leaders in answer to a direct question. Labeling them leaders frequently results in the same
kind of puzzlement implicit in the old joke: "Why she's not a

lady; she's my wife!" Yet this is the leadership that must be found and given a chance to continue to lead. It can only develop from the conviction that *everyone in the community has a contribution to make.*

To answer directly the question at the beginning of this section, the leaders in the programs described *are ordinary people like you*—like you, that is, if you have a faith in people and in democratic processes; if you wish to make communities not only better but *better able to help themselves;* if you believe that leadership should be widespread; if you, as a leader, *truly believe* in relinquishing the reins as others learn to hold them; if you are willing to lose your identity as a leader (or as an organization in a position of leadership) to find a richer life in the democratic processes you, the people, have helped to create for us, the people. There is no special genus discoverable! We are forced to report the finding of not a single superman on whom we can unhesitatingly lay our responsibilities as citizens in a democracy.

What Is "Community"?

The tendency has been to consider the "community" as identical with the political subdivision. Where this is the case a so-called county council not infrequently finds itself planning less for the county as a whole than for its industrialized area which has problems quite different from those of the surrounding open-country neighborhoods. Or the agricultural groups which began the planning job when their interests alone were involved have failed to make a place for the encroachments of other interests. Or the small independent city may proudly plan a fine health and welfare program for "the corporate limits" disregarding the fact that germs and delinquency are no respecters of imaginary lines determined by a board of supervisors or aldermen.

There is a trend toward redefining the community. It is based on a recognition of the fact that social planning may need to include a greater or lesser area than that designated as a unit for purposes of local government.

There is evidence that citizens' committees and elected officials are getting together on planning. In most cases, the

citizens' committee still has to play the gadfly role, acting primarily as a pressure group. While there are relatively few
situations where the public official has taken the initiative—
as in Clayton, Georgia—in establishing an advisory group and
has voluntarily submitted himself to its planning, there are
increasing instances in which studies and recommendations
of citizens' groups are welcomed by officials as a basis for action.

There is, as has been intimated before, a definite trend toward the acceptance of responsibility on the part of citizens.
There is a desire to understand what is being done and to consider what should be done. There is rather exciting evidence
of ways in which community planning groups—by whatever
name they are called—are attempting to get information and
understanding to all the people. Even where there is no coordinating group, women's clubs, service clubs, Chambers of
Commerce, and similar organizations, are seeing the need for
a more scientific approach to community problems. They are
asking state universities to conduct workshops for their officers and members in order to give them a more comprehensive
understanding of the implications of their programs. They
are seeking help in developing "adult education techniques" in
order to become more effective in reaching the rest of the
people.

There is a trend—or, perhaps, evidence in all these trends
—toward a reversal of delegation. Citizens are beginning to
plan and officials and agencies to carry out citizens' plans.
Truculent determination "not to be told by Washington or
Richmond" is gradually giving place to a more positive approach. Communities are analyzing needs, considering local,
state, and federal resources, and asking for what help is available in meeting their needs. Communities are trying to shake
off their lethargy for a positive attack on their responsibilities.

Problems Exist

Readers of *New Dominion Series* occasionally have asked
that more attention be given the "problems and difficulties
encountered" in programs described. An honest attempt has
been made to present them in each story, but the emphasis

has purposely been upon what was being done rather than upon what had to be overcome. This emphasis was not determined entirely by the writers. The participants in a good program when telling us the story generally "accentuated the positive." Observation and careful questioning of many persons have convinced us that opposition frequently does not develop or, at least, does not assume great importance *where faith in a program is strong.* Those who have put their hand to the plow firmly and purposefully have not kept looking over their shoulders. Opposition has been dealt with as it occurred but has not been anticipated nor feared. There have been problems—expected and unforeseen—but they assume a proper proportion when the purpose is positive and constructive.

It would, however, be unfair to leave anyone with the impression that any community group finds the way to more abundant life a broad smooth highway. There are always problems—even in that community which can point with pride to enviable achievements made entirely through the efforts of its own citizens.

There are the problems of traditional ways of doing things. "It was good enough for my grandfather and it is good enough for me," either spoken or implied, must be met on every newly opened front.

There are the problems of hereditary office and hereditary leadership. A certain citizen has always been chairman of every committee and must, therefore, always be offered the chairmanship of every committee. Usually he accepts — not because he wants to do anything about what the committee is set up to do, but because he has the habit of being chairman, or because it is the sort of thing his family stands for in that community. Here this problem tends to merge with those of *noblesse oblige* and the aristocratic tradition. The motives of the hereditary leaders are usually most altruistic, but theirs is the philosophy of doing things for people rather than of helping people to become increasingly able to do things for themselves.

The problem of who constitutes "the people" is one that every community attempting to control its own destiny must

decide. Do "the people" concerned include only those obviously prepared by education and social status to direct the
destinies of all? Or does the term apply to "even the least
of these" who at first glance may seem so insignificant as to be
worthless in any far-reaching scheme for the common welfare? What about that one-half, one-third, or two-thirds
that may be "underprivileged" because of race or economic
and social status? Have they the right and the responsibility
to participate in planning programs that affect their lives? Or
are they merely to share to some degree in the benefits of
plans made by others? Are they to be ignored, considered,
consulted, or included?

These and other problems exist. That they do exist is
not cause for discouragement. In fact, where they are recognized as problems and squarely faced, even though the "solution" is not immediate, there is reason for hope of their ultimate solution through democratic processes. Progress is
slow and uneven. Communities are full of contradictions. But
there is progress. And when contradictions and variations
cease to exist we shall need to re-examine our democracy to see
whether it, too, has vanished in the face of some efficient authoritarian pattern of social organization.

Part Three

TRYING THINGS OURSELVES

CHAPTER 7

Three Experimental Counties

To choose three counties in which to experiment with techniques for stimulating community development programs was not easy. Virginia's one hundred counties offered wide variation but almost every one of them had something to recommend its selection. Some were immediately eliminated by their distance from the University which is located in almost the exact center of the state except for the long stretch of the southwestern corner. If a small staff were to give personal attention to several areas at one time, all must be within reasonable driving distance of the University.

A second important consideration was the desire to choose counties typical of other areas in the Southeast. There was discussion by the staff of the Extension Division and consultation with many persons throughout the state as well as with some in regional or federal supervisory positions in agencies working in the state. Before the Special Projects staff had been selected, the choice had been narowed to about a dozen counties.

These represented three types—the southern Appalachian with problems typical of the whole range from Virginia on through North Carolina and Tennessee; the central Virginian piedmont area in which timber and general agriculture are the chief sources of income; and the Southside counties which have conditions similar to those resulting in the one-crop and tenancy problems of the deeper South.

Information on sixteen counties of these three types was gathered by the Extension Division staff from such sources as the State Departments of Public Health, Welfare, Agriculture, and Education; the Division of Population Studies of the State Planning Board; records and officials of the counties concerned.

After facts and figures had been put together, members of the Extension Division staff made many exploratory trips. They gathered impressions from looking at the farms, the dwellings, the schools, the churches, and public buildings.

They went off the main-traveled roads to discover the hinter-lands. They stopped to chat with farmers mending fences or, planting their crops. They consulted school superinten-dents, county agents, welfare workers, and other persons who might be expected to have given some thought to needs of their county.

The preliminary investigations were in no sense scientific or comprehensive. A casual survey was sufficient to indicate that any of the counties considered had conditions that could be improved through the efforts of their own citizens. Some were more backward or more progressive than others; some showed evidence of better leadership, developed or potential; some had officials who seemed more, or less, eager to cooperate with the proposed experiment; all presented challenges of one kind or another.

Even after the three counties had been selected, nothing approaching a sociological study was undertaken. An under-standing of the background was, of course, necessary if citi-zens were to be helped to become more proficient in analyzing and meeting their own needs. The staff of the Special Projects, therefore, made every effort to get as quickly and as thor-oughly as possible a good working knowledge of each county, including general physical characteristics; historical back-ground; economic conditions and potentialities; institutions, agencies, and services; folkways, local idioms and manner of speech of the people; attitudes and interests of officials, ordi-nary citizens, and professional workers.

In two of the counties data were gathered by two mem-bers of the Special Projects staff from documentary and hu-man sources. The latter, though perhaps less carefully ac-curate as to statistical detail, gave a local slant and flavor lacking in the former. In the third county, the chief source of information was a study made by the high school principal before the beginning of the experimental program with which he later worked. He was assisted by students and teachers in his school in gathering information and by members of the lo-cal Ruritan Club in interpreting it. Brief descriptions of each of the three counties follow. *These are of conditions when the project began in 1941. There are brief comments on wartime changes at the end of the chapter.*

THE MOUNTAIN COUNTY

The mountain county was the first to be definitely decided upon. Its choice was announced by Mr. Zehmer to the advisory committee in March, 1941. The fact that Farm Security Administration and several other agencies were especially interested in seeing something tried there had tipped the scales in favor of Greene. Also it had the advantage of being accessible. Its county seat was within twenty-five miles of the University. It was small enough both in area and in population to be possible of coverage in spite of mountain roads and isolated hollows.

Physical Characteristics[1]

The county comprises 153 square miles lying on the east side of the Blue Ridge Mountains with the Skyline Drive and a section of the Shenandoah National Park extending along its western border. About one-third of the total area is mountainous. There are two rivers—the Middle (or Conway) and the South which further along their courses join to become the Rapidan. The soil is red and grey loam. Mountain areas are extremely rocky; the lowlands are fertile.

Its mountains, streams, woodlands, and colorful soil afford a wealth of natural beauty. Off the main highways, it is unusually picturesque as are similar areas of the southern Appalachians. Many of the cabins are tucked away in secluded nooks beyond the streams and far from the rough mountain roads their inhabitants must follow to reach their fellow men.

There is no railroad in the county. Two trunk highways traverse it. Route 33, stretching from Richmond to the West Virginia line, runs the length of the county crossing the Skyline Drive at the west line. Route 29, connecting Washington with Florida, crosses its eastern end. The only other paved road is that part of Route 230 which lies between Stanards-

---

[1]The information that follows is taken from *Comments and Suggestions on Work in Greene County* submitted to G. B. Zehmer by Jess S. Ogden, October, 1941.

ville and the Madison County line. A few of the dirt roads are "improved." In the mountain areas, however, many roads are still almost impossible for automobile travel. Cross-country bus service on 33 and 29 connects the county with Charlottesville, Elkton, Orange, and Madison.

History and People

Greene County was formed in 1838 from the western part of Orange County and "named in memory of General Nathaniel Greene who served his country in the Revolutionary War." The local story of the division of Greene from Orange is that it was forced by the mountain people in the western end of the county under the leadership of a shrewd politician. He found it a simple matter to persuade them that Orange Courthouse was inconveniently far away and that they had a right to a more easily accessible county seat. The new court house was built at what is now Stanardsville. Whether or not this report of the origin of Greene as a separate county is true, it is in keeping with the character and temperament of its residents. They are characterized by a sturdy individualism with a trace of truculence when their rights are threatened.

The present total population is 5,218 (1940 census). There has been a steady decrease in population during the past twenty years, reaching a peak in the 1930-1940 decade. In nationality background the county is 74.2 British with the remainder almost entirely German. Many of the latter are said to be descendants of the Hessians who were allowed to escape from the Revolutionary War prison camp near Charlottesville. Most of the families in the county have been there since colonial or Revolutionary days, but one does not find among them that pride in their past which is so prevalent in piedmont and tidewater counties.

Like most mountain counties, Greene has a very small Negro population. There are 785 Negroes or 1 to every 7 of total population as compared with 1 to 3 in the farm population of the state as a whole. These Negroes are relatively prosperous.

Community Patterns

To a large extent "natural neighborhoods" rather than political districts determine communities in Greene County. In the mountain areas, hollows keep people together or ridges separate them from those of other hollows. The feeling of separation from the outside is likely to be stronger than any feeling of *community* within the area. In a few cases, however, loyalty to "the Hollow" is very strong on the part of those who live there. This finds expression in a solid front against outsiders rather than in cooperative undertakings among themselves.

Country stores and post offices have served perhaps more than other institutions as community centers. Since roads have been improved and mail delivery increased, post offices have decreased in number. The machine age has also encroached on the little country store. The farmer who in the past invariably traded his eggs at the local store and lingered for sociability now frequently pays a neighbor with an automobile to take him and his eggs to Stanardsville or Madison or even Charlottesville. He may use his entire return for the eggs to pay for the ride—but he has found other compensations in the trip. Churches and schools also determine communities or serve as centers of sociability. In general, however, the people have no strong group feeling. There is practically no constructive rivalry between communities.

Stanardsville, the county seat and the only incorporated village in the county, has a population of 212. It is on Route 33 and geographically is about the center of the county. It is also, of course, the center so far as governmental activities and services are concerned. Whether it could be considered a cultural or recreational center is a question. By way of recreation Stanardsville offers, in addition to slot machines in drug store and gas stations, a motion picture two evenings a week in a tiny frame building which seats about 150. It is almost never filled. People come to town on Saturdays and court days and appear to find their chief interest in sociability with others from the farms and mountains. The mountain people resent what they consider a feeling of unwarranted superiority on the part of residents of the county seat and the lower end of the county.

Ruckersville, the only other "town" in the county, is in the eastern and more prosperous end. It is smaller than Stanards-

ville but a good bit of rivalry exists between them. The needs
of the Ruckersville area are much less pressing than are those
of the central and western parts of the county. Ruckersville
has a number of public-spirited citizens but their "public
spirit" does not seem to extend into the county. Their interests turn rather to the neighboring counties of Orange and Albemarle. This cleavage makes it difficult to unite the people
of Stanardsville and Ruckersville with each other or with the
mountain folks in projects for the general welfare.

Economic Conditions and Potentialities

In merely driving through Greene County, one is impressed with its poorness. As one becomes better acquainted the impression deepens. Available figures bear this out. According
to 1935 figures found in various reports, 66 per cent of the
families in Greene had marginal incomes as compared with 47
per cent for all agricultural counties in Virginia. "Marginal"
is defined in the Department of Agriculture reports from which
these figures were taken as "annual income, including value of
products consumed, of $600 or less." A somewhat loose com-
mon use of the term includes those families not poor enough
to constitute a relief problem but unable to live according to
decent minimum standards. In this sense, Greene had an even
larger proportion of marginal families. Taking the most conservative definition of "marginal," 771 families fell under the
classification in 1940.

In spite of the poorness of the county, it has no larger
public welfare load in proportion to population than other counties. Likewise, in spite of greater concentration of poverty in
the mountains and hollows, welfare clients, as shown on the
map in the superintendent's office, are scattered throughout
the county. The largest portion of cases are old age assistance;
second comes aid for dependent children; and, lowest of all,
families on public relief. In addition to actual financial assistance, the public welfare department gives services of various kinds to a large number of "marginal families." But people tend to live on what they have. Though this may be ad-
mirable, it inevitably results in a low standard of living.

The following bits of information furnish rough indices

of the standard of living in the county. In 1935, nine persons
out of approximately 6,000 filed income tax returns; of these
only two reported incomes of over $3,000. The per capita re-
tail sales that same year were $39 as compared with $195
average for the total rural population of the state. Radios in
Greene totaled 29.3 for every hundred families as compared
with 46.9 for farm families in the state and 60.2 for farm families in the United States. Telephones numbered 7 per hundred families as compared with 25 for the state rural average.
Of 828 farm families in 1940, 250 had automobiles, 65 had farm
trucks, and 26 had tractors.

Almost the only source of income is the farm. According
to available figures the average value of farm land does not
compare unfavorably with values in many counties though it
is well below state average. The lower end of the county, however, brings the average up considerably, for in this section
the farms are superior to those in the western and higher parts
and farmers are much more prosperous. Hence averages are
misleading.

Many of the farms are small as a result of generations of
subdividing. More than one-third the total number have less
than 50 acres; almost two-thirds have less than 100 acres; and
only 9 farms have above 500 acres. In 1936 reports of the Department of Agriculture, more than 50 per cent of the farms
(456 out of 908) were classified as "self-sufficing." This means
that the farm consumed the major portion of products and no
appreciable amount was turned into cash. There is nothing
to indicate how many of these so-called "self-sufficing" farms
approached an adequate living.

For those that have products to sell, there is no market
readily available. As has been said above, there is no railroad, and farm trucks are scarce. In 1941, there was one man
with two trucks in the county who bought livestock, poultry,
and eggs from farmers to haul to market for re-sale. They
complained mildly about his prices but apparently never had
made any attempt at a different plan of marketing. A large
proportion of poultry, poultry products, and hams are bartered
at local stores.

The chestnut crop was once important to the mountain folk for cash to buy shoes and winter clothing. Since the blight, they have tried to substitute the sale of walnuts. One family in 1941 gathered and cracked enough to make eighty pounds of kernels. These they sold to local stores for 20 cents a pound when, at the same time, kernels were selling in cities for 90 cents a pound. Cash is scarce enough to make even such small amounts important. Yet the people show little initiative in utilizing or developing their resources.

There is no industry or establishment employing workers except for the small retail stores. Census figures for 1940 classifying employed workers by occupational groups showed 73.4 per cent employed as farmers or farm laborers. Others were distributed among professional workers, clerical workers, craftsmen (2.8 per cent), and domestic service (4.2 per cent). A sawmill from another state was beginning operations in the county in the summer of 1941. It has since provided some employment for local men.

For several years the tourist cabins and "rooms for tourists" brought a considerable amount of cash into the county particularly along Route 33. One woman, who was merely supplementing an already ample family income by taking "overnight guests," says she earned $700 in one year. In 1940, though her lighted sign still swung before her attractive home, not a single tourist had sought a bed. With the coming of the Skyline Drive expectations of increased tourist trade were high but these were not realized. Particularly after the opening of the lower end of the drive, trade dwindled rapidly until, in 1941, rooms were seldom rented and even the best of the cabins stood empty too often to bring a fair return on capital invested. No special effort had been made by Greene County people to induce tourists to turn in their direction. This acceptance of what happens as inevitable is a characteristic attitude.

A feeble attempt to encourage handcrafts was made by the Episcopal missions located in the area. Their role was primarily to provide an outlet through the shop called the Weaving Cabin on Route 33 for rugs, quilts, and homespuns the women might produce. Little effort was made to stimulate production, and the purpose behind the enterprise was primarily cultural or leisure-time rather than economic. For a few individuals the supplementary income from their handcrafts was really important, but production was so limited that, in order to have material to sell, the Cabin drew its stock largely from the shops at Blue Ridge School where products were made by the school children rather than the community; from the FSA shop at Ida Resettlement in Page County; and from the various handcraft centers in North Carolina, Kentucky, and Tennessee. The Cabin, however, was available until the war for sale of local wares if their production could be stimulated.

Institutions, Agencies, and Services

Among the institutions and agencies serving the county, churches are the most numerous. There are 29 white churches, and 2 Negro. The latter are both Baptist. The former are of the following denominations: Episcopal, 10; Methodist, 7; Brethren, 6; Baptist, 4; Christian, 1; Mennonite, 1. Services are held at irregular intervals because each of the four ministers serves several churches. Congregations are small even though churches are easily accessible. The number of churches each minister serves seriously limits his activities. The fact that the minister seldom resides in the community in which the church is located tends to decrease the social effectiveness of the church in that community. Of the four ministers in the county in 1941, three had residence in Stanardsville, and one in Ruckersville. There was little cooperation among the denominations.

The Archdeaconry of the Blue Ridge, with four mission centers in Greene County in addition to the Blue Ridge Industrial School, has been at work in this area for more than thirty years. One of the early jobs of the missions was to open schools. These were later taken over by the county. Only one mission schoolhouse was still in use in 1941 and here the teacher was being paid by the county. The missions also had helped to make it possible for the county to have a home demonstration agent and had concerned themselves from the beginning with public health and sanitation, though little actual evidence could be found of progress in this direction. Their greatest weakness, perhaps, had been in their eagerness to get things for the people, thus making them increasingly dependent. There was no evidence of their having developed leadership or of their having inspired the people to find better ways of living for themselves.

Though schools are reported to have improved considerably during the past twenty-five years, they still leave much to be desired. One high school located in Stanardsville serves the entire county. The same building houses the elementary school for that district. It is unattractive and inadequate though built as recently as 1925. Enrollment in the high school is below 150. Adults seldom use the building for any purpose.

There are eleven other elementary schools for white children and three for Negroes. Nine of the white schools have only one teacher. Most of the buildings are poorly equipped and in poor repair. Two schools are housed in good buildings and have four teachers each.

Accurate figures on school attendance in relation to school population are not available. Report and observation indicate that many families had been casual about sending their children to school. Improvement during recent years in this respect is said to have taken place. Accessibility of schools does not seem to be the determining factor. Just off the main highway in 1941 was a family of four girls, the youngest sixteen years of age, none of whom could either read or tell time. They had never availed themselves of the services of the school bus which passed within five minutes of their door. In the same community was another girl who had just completed high school at the head of her class and with a record of perfect attendance from the first grade on.

Illiteracy among adults is high. Census figures in 1940 reported 17.9 of every 100 persons over seventeen years of age as illiterate. So far as ability to use printed materials is concerned, the proportion is much higher. Yet there seem to be few families in which there is not someone who can read. There is no indication that men regard reading as "sissy" as they are said to do in some mountain areas. "I'd like if you would read it for me; I forgot my specs," usually means reluctance to admit inability to read. The proportion of illiteracy is, of course, much higher in the mountains than in the lowlands.

For those who read, there was in 1941 no reading matter available. There was no library service. Schools had only those textbooks considered essential. In the mountain areas, few families had a newspaper. Magazines could not be bought anywhere in the county. In reply to a comment on this fact, we were told that "most people subscribe." The total subscriptions, however, were so few as to be reported at zero in a census of circulation of the ten magazines most popular nationally. Yet we found a general interest even in the isolated mountain neighborhoods in what was going on in the world. In the lower end of the county, people were as well read and informed as the average in rural areas.

There was nothing that might be regarded as adult education in the schools. There was no work in home economics or vocational agriculture in the county schools for either children or adults. Greene and Madison Counties share a school superintendent who resides in Madison. He said he preferred not to take any initiative in an adult education program in Greene County but was not opposed to use of schools provided the request came from the patrons. We found that schools throughout the county were used for meetings of home demonstration clubs and 4-H clubs, for furniture clinics or FSA meetings, for money-making affairs for various organizations, for meetings of the Southern States Cooperative in the two communities where it existed, and for meetings of the Young Democrats Club. Arrangements for meetings were usually made by organizations directly with the principal or teacher. The latter were generally eager to have the adult community use the schools.

There were two or three abandoned school buildings available for adult work. Their use, however, was negligible since teachers had been depended upon to furnish leadership. Seventeen of the twenty-eight teachers in the county in 1941 were local people, and it was among them the most interested leadership could be found. What they could be expected to do was limited by the fact that most of them carried heavy home responsibilities in addition to heavy teaching loads under not-too-ideal conditions.

The Blue Ridge Industrial School originally was set up by the Episcopal Church as a kind of folk school to serve the entire community. In the course of the years it had become a boarding school for children from other areas, many of them behavior problems or from broken homes. It had ceased by 1941 to be an important social force in the area.

The home demonstration work in Greene County dated back fourteen years. Reports are that the first agent did some remarkable pioneer work, and there were still evidences of it in the existence of homemakers clubs among people of the lowest economic stratum who are frequently not reached by this program. The total membership of homemakers clubs in 1941 was about 200 in a county in which there were 1,375 adult women, most of them homemakers. With no home-making instruction in the schools, this left a large proportion of the families untouched. The work of the county agent, which was more recently established, reached even fewer families than that of the home demonstration agent. The 4-H club program was almost exclusively for girls.

There were two Farm Security workers in the county—a supervisor of rural rehabilitation and a home management supervisor. Because of the poorness of Greene County, an experiment had been tried there of "lending" money to farmers who had very little prospect of being able to repay. The supervisor had been urged to get 100 clients in the county and see what could be done with them. Because he chose people not considered "worthy" by other members of the community, there was rather bitter feeling about the program.[2] The supervisor had discovered the need for doing more than giving money to people and through his meetings with clients was at-

---

[2]The unusually high proportion of the borrowers who have paid back their loans and have improved their farms shows that local opinion was based on prejudice rather than fact.

tempting to conduct an educational program. He frankly admitted that he needed help since he was not an "educator." The home management supervisor, in addition to doing work with individual families to whom loans had been made, conducted meetings on nutrition, clothing, and simliar subjects. She was working with some families who were not FSA clients, having in all, she said, about 165 families on her list. They were for the most part not in home demonstration clubs. Yet because of the similarity of subject matter for meetings and because in Greene County the work of the home demonstration agent went further down in the economic scale than in many counties, there were some overlappings and considerable friction between the two agencies. The program was terminated in the county in 1943, before it had a fair chance to show results.

There was a rather sad attempt at a Farm Security resettlement project in the county under the administration of the Shenandoah Homesteads. Families who had been moved out of the Shenandoah National Park had been established in a kind of French village with farms at some distance from their homes. The utter disregard of their folkways in planning the project resulted in its limping along for a few years until the families gradually disappeared.

Medical and dental care are totally inadequate to the needs of an area suffering from malnutritional ills in addition to those that ordinary flesh is heir to. There is only one physician in the county. There is no public health service. At one time Greene was served by the Valley Health District composed of seven counties. The service was discontinued in 1939 because of failure of the county to appropriate adequate funds. This failure was due only in part to the scarcity of public funds for any purpose. A fair share of the blame must be credited to the fact that the county was dissatisfied with the service. The State Department of Public Health admits that the "seven-county district was entirely too large to be served satisfactorily by the available health personnel." This unsatisfactory experience plus the lack of interest in public health on the part of the local medical profession will undoubtedly retard progress in this field for years to come. Attempts of the Farm Security Administration to improve medical care for its clients were met with antagonism.

Habits and Attitudes

The few financially secure farmers in the county, the 1941 report points out, are in many instances the elected officials as well as the generally accepted leaders. They are shrewd, industrious, elderly men who are sure that lack of ambition is at the root of all poverty. They tend to condemn as shiftless and triflin' all who do not "get ahead." Especially they blame the younger generation because of their inability to "manage" or to be satisfied under circumstances their fathers had accepted without question. If they do not blame, they are at least puzzled and unable to comprehend "what has come over people."

"I can't understand it," one of these men said of a neighboring family. "Their father brought up fourteen of them in that cabin and he managed. He was too proud to ask for help. If they didn't have enough to eat they got along somehow. But the sons all want WPA jobs or something easy."

The fact that "fourteen of them" had grown up in that little two-room cabin without enough to eat and without the clothes necessary for school attendance, and the fact that six grown sons now tried to make a living on the farm their father had found inadequate for one family seemed to have no relation to their all "wanting WPA jobs or something easy." Little attempt has been made to get at causes of "not being able to manage."

There is general acceptance on the part of these leading citizens that the best young people will go to the cities. Their desire to "get out" is considered laudable. No attempt is made to find opportunities for the ambitious youth within the county. At the same time, when a local boy does make good at home they point to him with great pride.

The well-to-do are few in number. With them must be grouped, so far as attitudes are concerned, members of old families who own fairly good farms, hold a public office which brings in a little steady income, have an established place in

the community, and thus feel financially and emotionally secure. They are almost all genuine, sincere, well-meaning, and
kindly people with a desire to have everyone as comfortable as
possible. In a few cases there is strong resistance to new ideas.
With these people the favorite remark is, "It's been tried; it
won't work." Most of them, however, are by no means closed-
minded.

The county is divided in the minds of these "better people," as most communities are, into "we" and "they." *They*
include the less prosperous farmers, tenants, and mountain
or hollow folk. *They* are almost all characterized by a powerful inertia. Getting at a motivation important enough in their
minds to overcome the inertia is the key to solving their problems. The inertia has a temperamental and possibly a physical
basis. They seem to have accepted the standard of living they
have been able to attain without too great effort, and they
have not looked beyond. The fact that most of their neighbors have no better standard makes the desire to "keep up
with the Joneses" an almost non-existent stimulus. Complete
acceptance has left almost no spark of "divine discontent."

There is an unbelievable backwardness and a supreme indifference in matters of health, sanitation, and decent **standard**
of living. At the same time there is a high degree of native
intelligence. There is lack of information and motivation
rather than of ability to comprehend.

There is to be found little ambition among the young people of this group, nor for them on the part of their parents.
"What are you going to do when you grow up?" is a question
seldom asked. When young people go out to get jobs, there is
frequently resentment on the part of their families. One
mountain girl who graduated from high school at seventeen
with the highest record ever made in Stanardsville was persuaded by a mission worker that nursing would be a good profession for her. Plans were made for her training.

"I reckon I kin use her at home," said the aunt with whom
she lived; and the matter was closed.

In the case of another very promising girl permission to
go on to high school was withheld by the family—this time,

too, an aunt—lest she become interested in people "outside" and unwilling to marry the man selected for her.

In spite of this lack of ambition for their children, there is no lack of love for them. Family loyalties are strong and the devotion of the older children to the younger in large families is exceptionally marked.

There is, as in many rural communities, a lack of any tradition for cooperative undertakings. With changing conditions, the rural and mountain people are being more and more exposed to "luxuries." They are seeing and hearing of better standards of living; they are beginning to want a change, but the stirrings are feeble.

Supplementary income is important for people in this group. But learning to translate financial gains into social and cultural gains is even more important. Lack of money is less of a handicap than lack of knowing what to do with money. There is need for careful "education" as well as economic planning.

The third group in the county whose habits of thinking and social attitudes are of great importance is made up of the professional workers. They include mission workers and clergy as well as school people and those employed in various government agencies and county departments. Obviously this is not an entirely homogeneous group. They do, however, have common aims and have in general achieved a high degree of cooperation among themselves. They are almost all conscientious and devoted workers, but they are baffled by the serious social and economic problems with which they are continuously confronted.

The professionals do not share with the well-to-do citizens the opinion that the less privileged people are "triflin' and no-account." One superintendent of public welfare said he came to his job feeling that the people with whom he would be working were hopeless. During two years of close contact with them he said his respect and admiration had grown steadily—"They do much more with the chance they have than I ever could—or than any of my friends who call them triflin'."

This expresses the feeling of most of the workers, but at the same time they are filled with a kind of hopelessness and frustration because the people do well with the chance they have—but can they have a better chance? The eagerness of the professional workers for new methods, for new ideas, for finding ways to help the people of Greene County to a better way of living offers a real foundation on which to build.

The 1941 report made by two members of the staff after four months' residence in the county ended as follows:

> Greene County is a problem and knows it is a problem—in fact it has been told so often that one experiment or another is to be tried on it that, like a problem child, it enjoys the attention it gets and is rather truculently proud that it is a problem county. That this pride can become a constructive force to make the county want to solve its own problems we feel certain, but only as others stop trying to do for it, and it takes hold itself with the determination of which we know it is capable, will any real change come.
>
> People from the "outside" can help Greene County people to understand themselves better, to acquire necessary skills and tools, to know how other communities have pulled themselves out of the Slough of Despond; even, perhaps, help them to discover that they want to help themselves. Beyond that, the job is theirs. And it seems to us a not impossible one.

THE SOUTHSIDE COUNTY

The determining factor in the choice of a Southside county was the interest of a high school principal in promoting a school-centered community program. His was a consolidated high school serving the Holy Neck District of Nansemond County.

Preceding the beginning of the Extension Division's experimental program, he had made a survey of the community in cooperation with his students and teachers and the local Ruritan Club. The study stage had ended and next steps were under consideration when the Extension Division was selecting areas for experimental work. Since the county met specifications as to location, and the Holy Neck District was "ready to go," it offered an unusually promising opportunity. Though diversified agriculture had largely replaced cotton in the area, it presented another aspect important of the South—the encroachment of industry and the resulting problems. The area was chosen with the understanding that here the program

would be concerned with one district rather than with the
county as a whole, and that the staff of the Extension Division
would serve in a merely advisory capacity.

The information which follows concerning Nansemond
County and the Holy Neck District is adapted from the survey referred to above, the results of which were summarized
by Mr. William Savage, principal of the Holland High School.[3]

General Characteristics

Nansemond County, in the extreme southern tier of Virginia, is a typical tidewater area. Norfolk and Princess Anne
Counties separate it from the ocean but it extends to Hampton
Roads. The Nansemond River is a direct waterway from the
Roads to Suffolk, its largest city. The terrain is flat. The soil
in the eastern section is excellent for truck crops and in the
western area for general farm crops. The mysterious and ro-
mantic Dismal Swamp lies partly within its borders. Here
there are rich timber resources—long leaf pine, cypress, jun-
iper, and gum. Its rivers and coastline abound in fish and
waterfowl. Its climate is mild with a sixty degree mean annual temperature.

The entire county covers 421 square miles. The Holy Neck
District comprises 186 square miles or almost one-half the entire area. It is located in the southwestern corner of the county
touching North Carolina to the south and Southampton County
to the west.

Markets are accessible. More than 500 miles of improved
highways traverse the county—186 of these being within the
Holy Neck District. The highways and railroad converge at
Suffolk which has direct egress to the ocean.

Today Nansemond is one of the most fertile and productive counties in the state. Cotton is rapidly disappearing as a
leading crop in the district, as well as in the county. In 1934
the number of bales reported from the county was 3,870. By
1938, the number had dropped to 1,660. This decline is not
due to a lessened productivity, for the acreage in cotton shows

---

[3]William Richard Savage, "A Village Consolidated School in Relation to Its Community." Durham, N. C. Duke University Press.
1941. Typed. 117 pp.

a proportionate decline. Peanuts and hogs furnish the main money crops of the county. The county ranks second in the state in the total number of peanuts raised and also in the number of bags per acre. A large proportion of these are produced in Holy Neck District. The city of Suffolk is the largest market for peanuts in the country. Corn is grown in considerable quantity but, instead of marketing it, the farmers use most of it to feed the hogs, thereby converting it into meat and marketing it for a greater profit. Nansemond County ranks second in the state in the number of hogs sold for slaughter at the auction markets. There were 28,200 hogs sold in 1938. Data secured from the office of the county agent indicate that 7,467 hogs were slaughtered for market in Holy Neck District alone.

History and People

The county, one of the oldest in the state, received its name in 1642 from a local Indian tribe long-since extinct. Since its settlement in 1638, it has had an eventful history. By 1700 Nansemond County had furnished a colonial governor, and two speakers to the House of Burgesses. By the end of the eighteenth century one of the earliest mail routes in Virginia had been established there and a few small public schools were already in operation. By the middle of the nineteenth century a railroad had been built in the county and newspapers were being published. During the early part of the twentieth century Nansemond County continued to grow and develop consistently, with special progress in road construction, telephone lines, and electric power.

During the past twenty years, when purely rural counties have had a steadily declining population, Nansemond has shown a steady increase. The population for the county was 22,530 in 1930, an increase of 2,331 since 1920. Holy Neck District, with 6,710, was larger than any of the four remaining magisterial districts in the county. It had 29.8 per cent of the total population. Of this number 62.9 per cent was Negro.

The population for persons less than twenty years of age has declined for both whites and Negroes between 1930 and 1940, though there was an increase in total population. The white young people declined from 911 to 825, and the Negroes dropped from 2,514 to 2,206 during that period. The decline was sharpest for persons under five years of age.

Community Patterns

Suffolk, a city of 11,000 inhabitants, is located in the center of the county. Though it has been an independent city since 1910, it continues to serve as the county seat, and its market and industries play an important part in the economic life of the area. It is the center of trade and commercialized recreation for the county.

Holland is the next largest town with about 400 population. Here is located the consolidated high school which serves the Holy Neck District. The cotton market centers in Holland and likewise an experiment station for cotton and peanuts.

There are a number of rather well defined, though small, communities throughout the county. Those lying within the Holy Neck District are Bethlehem, Box Elder, Holy Neck, and Buckhorn. Box Elder is generally progressive and its people socially minded. Buckhorn, poorest of the communities, constitutes something of a social and economic problem.

Institutions and Agencies

When the survey was made, the school was the only agency which served the entire Holy Neck District and that alone. The county as a whole had the usual agencies and services which could be called upon by the district.

There had been for many years a two-county health unit shared with Isle of Wight County. There were the usual workers in the Department of Public Welfare. There were Extension Service workers for both white and colored farmers and a Farm Security Administration program. Service clubs and women's clubs existed in Holland as well as in Suffolk.

Churches played an important role in the social as well as in the religious life of the community. There were seven white churches in the Holy Neck District including Baptist, Methodist, Congregationalist, and Friends. Many of the white people, according to the survey, participated in no recreational, social, or cultural pursuits other than those fostered by the churches.

The Holland School

The consolidated elementary and high school in Holland served the white pupils of the entire Holy Neck District with the exception of one elementary school with thirty pupils enrolled. Consolidation was begun in 1920 when there were seven schools in the district. It was completed in 1935.

The school plant was good. In addition to the elementary and high school buildings, there were a gymnasium, a school bus garage, an agriculture building, a cafeteria. Play space was provided on the three-and-one-half-acre campus behind the buildings. The space in front was attractively shrubbed and well kept. There was a library of about 3,000 volumes with a trained librarian in charge. The auditorium seated 500. An attractive three-room apartment in the high school building housed the home economics department. Seventeen teachers comprised the school staff. These included persons specially trained in agriculture, home economics, music, dramatics, and physical education as well as the usual academic subjects.

Ten busses brought approximately 450 children to the school. Most of them came from farm homes, some of them as far as fifteen miles distant. Only the children living in the village were within walking distance. Although located in Holland, the school served a community much more scattered and diversified than the town itself. It was to get acquainted with this larger community that the school principal, teachers, and children had undertaken a survey in 1929. The idea was based on the principal's assumption that "intelligent planning and administration of school problems necessitates that prevailing situations and trends in the community served by the school be taken into account."

Situation as Summarized

To complete the picture of the community used as a basis for planning the program, we quote from Mr. Savage's summary and conclusions:[4]

---

[4] *Ibid.*

"The survey shows that in 1940 nearly three-fourths of all white male adults were engaged in farming. With absentee ownership of farms seeming to be a trend in the district, the fact that farm tenancy is likely to increase presents a significant problem. In 1935 more than 40 per cent of all white farm operators were tenants. Many of these people of necessity have a low standard of living because they have a marginal income. Should this high percentage of tenancy continue, with the accompanying low marginal incomes, the effect on community life and institutions can be nearly disastrous. The fact that there is a much higher percentage of Negro farm operators who are tenants and wage earners with marginal incomes does not lessen the problem for all.

"Aside from the town of Holland, where the homes have more modern conveniences and the people generally have a higher standard of living, about one-third of the white residences in the district have electric lights, while less than one residence in six has running water. One residence in ten has a telephone.

". . . . Tuberculosis is the cause of a high percentage of the deaths in the district. While the larger proportion of deaths caused by this disease is among the Negro population, the prevalence of the disease in the community can have a dire effect on the health of the entire population. One Negro death in four was due to tuberculosis for the years 1933-34 and 1938-39.

"Of the white children attending school in the district, less than one-half of those with physical defects have had corrections made. A large proportion of pupils needing immunization treatment have had such treatment, largely because the health department clinics held in the school furnish a very convenient and economical situation for the child, especially since the school pays the slight fee for most children who are regarded as indigent. There appears to be a large number of children with defective vision, teeth and throats, who leave such defects uncorrected. Possibly this is due chiefly to the fact that the cost of corrective treatment makes it prohibitive.

"A sad commentary on the pride or ability of white adults

to provide healthful surroundings for their famliies is the fact that nearly one adult in five lives in a residence that has no toilet facilities, or has toilets that lack doors, ventilators, or other proper health precautions. There must be many more children who live under such circumstances.

"Even though Holy Neck District is a rural community with farming as the main occupation, approximately one-half of all white adults have less than one pint of milk per day, or no milk at all. When it is remembered that possibly a majority of the children come from homes where no milk is served as a food, it becomes somewhat evident why a large number of the children in school have defective teeth and are underweight.

"Approximately one-third of all white adults in the district have less than an elementary education, while about one-fourth of them finished high school. Very few attended college, except in the case of Holland where one-third of all adults attended college.

"Nearly 80 per cent of all white children of school age are enrolled in school, and slightly more than 90 per cent of the enrollment are in average daily attendance. As the Negro pupils lack transportation facilities, and as other unfavorable conditions prevail, only 54 per cent of the Negroes of school age are enrolled, and not quite 80 per cent of the Negro pupils enrolled are in attendance. For both the Negroes and whites there has been a decrease in school enrollment since 1930. However, the per cent of pupils enrolled and in attendance has increased for both races since then.

"Since 1930 Holy Neck District has spent approximately three times as much per capita for instruction of white pupils enrolled in school as for Negro pupils enrolled. There appears, however, to be a tendency to increase the per capita expenditure for Negro instruction.

"More than half of the white residences in the district have a radio and daily newspaper. The reading of current periodicals by white adults seems to consist chiefly of farmers' magazines, such as *The Progressive Farmer* and *The Southern Planter*. Nearly half of the residences have these magazines, while very few residences have such magazine as *Time, Life,* or *Reader's Digest.*

"While sports like hunting and fishing seem to be the chief forms of outdoor recreational activity for the men, more than half of the male adults participate in no sports or games whatever. A very small percentage of them plays tennis, baseball, basketball, or swims with any frequency, while games like pingpong, badminton, and such games as can be conveniently played at home, were not listed at all. For the women, bridge is played by one in ten. Very few women participate in other games or sports frequently, while half of of them indicated they take part in no games or sports at any time. While movies are attended by 20 per cent of the men and women, few attend programs like concerts, plays, musicals, and lectures. More than half of the whites attend no forms of entertainment programs.

"Of the out-of-school youth in the community, one-third of the boys are working on farms, and more than one-third of both boys and girls have no occupation. More than one-third of the boys in this group have less than an elementary education, while less than one-third finished high school. Of the girls in this group, nearly one-half finished high school. With the small amount of education that a great many of these boys and girls have received in school, the opportunities for successful employment appear slight.

"It appears that approximately one-half of the men and women graduated from the Holland school since 1930 still live in Holy Neck District. Of the others, many live in nearby communities in Nansemond County. Only 7.6 per cent live outside the state of Virginia. Of these graduates, about one person in five has attended college, and slightly less than half of that number remained to graduate from college. Nearly 70 per cent of all graduates since 1930 have received no further training after high school. This percentage has increased since 1936. While more of the men graduates are engaged in farming than in other occupations, about 60 per cent of all the men graduates are distributed over several occupations."

Mr. Savage's report ended with specific recommendations

as to ways in which the school might effectively serve the entire community. He suggested a comprehensive adult education program including everything from vocational and cultural courses to "classes in social living." For out-of-school youth, he proposed that "the Holland Consolidated School make provision for the continued training and guidance of those people who are no longer in regular attendance in the public scool, and who have not yet become adjusted as adults in their social order and engaged in gainful employment." Suggestions included both classes and recreational activities. There were likewise suggestions for planning that might eliminate, or at least alleviate, some of the social and economic ills disclosed by the survey.

The plan, he concluded, would make "the public school the center of community life in fact as well as in theory. The people would be encouraged to use its facilities for their meetings, their discussions, and their development of those talents and traits that will somehow enable them to live healthier, happier, and more useful lives for themselves, their children, and their community."

THE PIEDMONT COUNTY

Selection of the piedmont county was not definitely made until the end of the summer of 1941. There were under consideration several that offered excellent possibilities. The staff continued to explore them during the summer, as work got under way in other areas. Finally all but Louisa were eliminated for such reasons as difficult political situations, extremes of wealth and poverty not typical of the state, frictions or uncertainties among agencies that made it seem unlikely that anything could be accomplished within the time provided by the experimental program.

In reporting to the advisory committee on the final selection of Louisa, Mr. Zehmer stated: "Our conclusion is that Louisa is a very conservative county but one in which the need for cooperative effort is apparent to many of the citizens and officials. There is skepticism on the part of the people of the county concerning our Special Projects, but no definite opposition and some real willingness to cooperate. Progress will necessarily be slow."

Historical Background

Explanation of the prediction of slow progress is to be found, at least partially, in the county's history. Louisa was first settled in the early eighteenth century. It became a separate county in 1742. During the intervening years, the county had been "transformed from a wilderness into a community of citizens *who wished to handle their own affairs.*"[5] This desire, two hundred years later, remained as one of their outstanding characteristics.

In many respects, getting acquainted with Louisa County was like stepping into a history book. Five signers of the Declaration of Independence and three presidents of the United States had attended school there. The school was conducted by the Rev. James Maury, grandfather of Commodore Matthew F. Maury, the great geographer. It was from Louisa County that Patrick Henry went to make his famous Stamp Act speech in the House of Burgesses. Jack Jouett rode from Cuckoo to Monticello to warn Jefferson of Tarleton's approach. The Marquis de Lafayette re-opened an old, forgotten road through the county to get between Cornwallis and the supplies at Charlottesville. The road is still known as the "Marquises Road." Markers and monuments indicate that the county was the scene of bloodshed and pillaging in the War between the States. Over its roads Jackson and Lee traveled to reach Richmond.

The county has always been on the direct routes from Richmond to the West. The Old Mountain Road, developed along an Indian trail, was the first road connecting the mountains with the tidewater. It played an important part in the early development of the west-central part of the state. Later it was replaced by the Louisa Road (now the Jefferson Highway) leading from Richmond to Charlottesville and on west-

[5]Malcolm H. Harris, A History of Louisa County, Virginia. Richmond, Va. Dietz Press. 1936.

ward, and the Three Notched (or Three Chopt) Road so named
from the three chops made in honor of George III by surveyors
who first marked the course. These roads not only made Louisa
County accessible but also made of it a main thoroughfare over
which makers of American history continuously passed.

During the nineteenth century, the coming of railroads
changed the character of the county somewhat. Fredericks-
burg, which could be reached by water, was replaced by Richmond as the marketing and trade center. The Louisa Railroad is said to be one of the first in the country. It was completed in 1837, and on December 20 of that year the first trip
was made from Doswell to Frederick Hall with an engine and
three cars traveling at the unprecedented rate of fifteen miles
an hour.

Frederick Hall, now a sleepy little community centered
about a store and a post office, with a lumberyard as its chief
scene of activity, was once an important railroad terminal.
Here passengers took the stage westward to the springs to
seek health from the mineral waters supposed to have unusual
therapeutic values. The once flourishing spa at Green Springs
was destroyed by fire many years ago. But the springs with
their greenish waters are still to be seen. And the glamor persists in retrospect.

Soon the railroad cut through the county to Gordonsville
and on to Clifton Forge, finally becoming a part of the present
Chesapeake and Ohio. The way to the West was opened up,
and Louisa furnished its full quota of pioneers.

Yet, for those who stayed behind, past and present seemed
to merge in Louisa County. Its history has a continuity not
so readily sensed in communities in which shifting populations
have been the rule. Names found in the original land grants
are still those of the county's leading families. County offices
have been handed down in some cases from father to son for
several generations. There has been a similar line of descent
in the professions. The following example from the medical
profession indicates the pattern:[6]

---

[6]*Ibid.*

No Louisa family has furnished as many of its sons to the medical profession as the Pendletons. . . Joseph W. Pendleton practiced at Cuckoo for many years. His brother, Dr. William J. Pendleton, father of the late Dr. Lewis Pendleton. . . . lived at Frederickshall. Dr. Madison Pendleton, of Hermitage, and Dr. Philip Pendleton, of Cuckoo, nephews of the first two doctors both served the people of the county for many years. Dr. Edmund Pendleton, son of Dr. Madison, later practiced in Louisa . . . Dr. Eugene, son of Dr. Phil, succeeded to his father's practice and in later years occupied the house at Cuckoo. After his death his son, Dr. E. Barbour Pendleton, has continued the practice, which has passed through four generations of his family . . . Red mud, slush, and rain did not hinder them in following their line of duty.

In 1942, the high school presented a pageant marking the completion of two centuries of history. The audience reaction indicated that those living in the present felt a close relationship with their past. Events commemorated in the pageant were matters of common knowledge. Yet there was also evidence of a desire to face forward which intimated that the ideas expressed in the prologue of the pageant were more than mere wishful thinking:[7]

. . . . . Louisa has not been doomed by the will of the pessimist who wishes things to stand still, though her boundaries remain unchanged and her people of the same stock as at the time of the Revolution. There has been such a marked improvement in her soil in late years that we have a new day dawning agriculturally. Men of distinction have come from the county, and from the same background more will come. It is in a spirit of hope for a bright future that we the seniors of Louisa County High School present the pageant "Louisa's 200 Years."

One cannot but question the temerity of outsiders who would attempt to help such a community find ways of helping itself through the efforts of its own citizens!

Physical Characteristics

Louisa today has 516 square miles of timber and farm land located just east of central Virginia and about midway of the north and south borders of the state. It is gentle, undulating country extending from tidewater to the foot of the mountains. Its average elevation is about 500 feet. The central plateau serves as a watershed for the two main streams—the North and South Anna Rivers. There are numerous small

---

[7]Louisa's 200 years. Louisa County High School. 1942.

streams and creeks with picturesque names — Roundabout, Duckinghole, Contrary, Goldmine, Little Rockey.

The soil is of average fertility and yields good crops when given good care. Many years of tobacco with no attention to rebuilding the used-up soil has left some parts of the county much less productive than need be. In some parts the colorful but profligate broomsedge, so discouraging to any other vegetation, has taken over acre after acre of neglected lands. Contrasting with these wasted acres, there are lush pastures and bluegrass for fine dairy herds where careful and scientific farming has restored the original fertility to the soil. Ellen Glasgow is said to have based her story, *Barren Ground*, on her impressions of Louisa County. Evidences of both the discouragement she expresses and the hopefulness she suggests in the spread of scientific farming are to be found there.

It is traversed by Route 33, a direct route from Harrisonburg to Richmond which is about forty-five miles from Louisa Courthouse. There are other paved roads, but there remain also many miles of red dirt roads leading to the more remote neighborhoods. Both highways and railroads make markets readily accessible to all parts of the county.

Population Trends and Characteristics

In 1920, Louisa County had 17,089 people. It has since that time shown a steady decrease. In 1940, the census reported a population of 13,665. Of this number 59 per cent were white and 41 per cent were Negro. As the size of the population declined, its average age increased. The youth left the county in large numbers. The average age of Louisa County farmer in 1943 was stated by a school principal to be fifty-eight years— and 81.4 per cent of the total population was on the farms.

Economic Conditions

The chief source of income is the farm. There were, in 1940, in the county 2,256 farms with an average size of 95.6 acres. Most of these were owner occupied. The percentage of tenancy was listed as 14.7 as compared with a state figure of 26.9. Percentage of farms mortgaged was 21.3 as compared to 24.3 in the state as a whole. Of the total products of the farm, 42.4 per cent were used by farm households. This figure has gone steadily up as diversified farming has increased.

Changes in the agricultural pattern are perhaps significant. In 1880, Louisa County had 1,813 farms with a total of 273,159 acres. Of these acres 106,642 were improved land. By 1935 the number of farms had increased by one-third. Their average size had decreased from 151 acres to 88. The amount of improved land had decreased by 21,560 acres. Reasons given for the decrease were wastage due to erosion and fertility depletion.

Between 1930 and 1935, according to the Federal Farm Census figures, farmers reduced their tobacco acreage 33 per cent. This drop was accompanied by a 17 per cent increase in hay. Small grain also showed a definite increase. Among the outstanding changes during this period was the great increase in dairy cows. These trends have continued together with concerted efforts at rebuilding the soil.

About 29 per cent of the total acreage in 1935 was in timber. The cutting rate was reported at 155 per cent of the average reproduction rate. This trend has continued with little attention to replanting or even to careful cutting which would assure the greatest return from the woodlands. Local lumber men, unlike those in some areas, have tended to encourage this profligacy.

In addition to farming, opportunity for employment was offered to about four hundred wage earners in twenty-eight sawmills, a small furniture factory, and a small garment factory. Total wages paid by these manufacturing concerns in 1940 was $152,958. The war did nothing to change this situation except to hasten the rate of migration to areas offering more and better job opportunities.

The following figures indicate something of living standards: Per capita retail sales in the county in 1940 were $108.59 (state figures for farm population, $195). On 97 per cent of the farms, wood was used for cooking; on only 1.3 per cent was there central heating. These figures contrast with national percentages of 69.5 per cent of the farm population cooking with wood and 10.1 per cent having central heating. Radios in the county numbered 44 per hundred families (national farm family, 60.2); telephones 4 per hundred; passenger cars 51 per hundred families.

In general, the county is poor. There are not great extremes of wealth or, save for the abandoned mine area, of poverty. The income tax reports for 1930 recorded six individual incomes of above $5,000.

The escape of youth from the county is accepted with the explanation, "You can't make a decent living here;" or "There are more people in the county than the farms can support." At the same time, facts can be offered contradictory to both these explanations: Shortage of farm labor is given as the reason for the encroachment of broomsedge on many potentially fine acres; and a few farms, not different from others except in application of scientific methods, yield excellent incomes.

Communities and Neighborhoods

Louisa, the county seat, and Mineral, about five miles distant, are the two largest towns. One falls just below four hundred in population and the other just above. The courthouse town is attractive and compact. Transacting the county's business is its chief activity. Mineral, only slightly larger in population, is more spread out in area. In the Nineties, it is said, its streets were laid out in the hope that it would become a flourishing city serving the nearby iron pyrite mines. These hopes vanished when surface mining in Louisiana made working the shaft mines of Louisa too expensive to compete. What remains of the abandoned mine community north of Mineral constitutes one of the social problems of the county—though many residents of other parts of the county are unaware of the existence of this ghost community.

The rivalry between Louisa Courthouse and Mineral has continued from the days preceding the establishing of the county seat at the former. The die was cast in that instance, according to local tradition, because an early judge refused to move out of his own tavern to hold court. He later gave his land and buildings to the county for court house and gaol. Those early officials, the same faction reports, were brought in from Charlottesville or Spotsylvania or Hanover; they were "not even old county families"—and to some they are still not old county families in spite of the fact that their residence in the county predates the Revolutionary War.

Although there are only two small towns, there are many clearly defined communities — Trevillians, Cuckoo, Apple Grove, Frederick Hall (or Frederick's Hall or Frederickhall), Bells X-Roads, Poindexter, Waldrop, Shelfar, Bumpass, Buckner, and others. Each of these has its own peculiar quality, and the loyalty of residents is likely to be to the community rather than to the county as a whole.

Institutions, Agencies, and Services

Inevitably in such an area, pooling of interests for more efficient administration of public affairs has not come without effort. In 1939, the opening of a fine new consolidated high school serving the entire county marked a real milestone in education. The scars of consolidation, however, were not quickly healed in spite of the fact that the new school was centrally located in the open country with allegiance to no particular community.

Early private schools in the county, as has been pointed out, had many students who later won distinction in the state and nation. Yet little impetus was given by this fact to the development of general education. The existence of these private schools and the custom of several well-to-do farmers pooling their resources to have a teacher for their children retarded the growth of public education. During recent years real progress has been made in this direction for both the white and Negro population. In addition to the excellent modern consolidated high school for white children, there are six elementary schools, five of which have four rooms or over. Attendance is good, but school population is shrinking at an even more rapid rate than the total population.

For Negroes, there is a high school at Louisa Courthouse with bus service. The plant is admittedly inadequate, but there are plans for improvement. Elementary schools for Negroes number twenty-four. Only two of these have as many as four rooms.

Of the population above twenty-five, the average school grade completed is 5.8 for males and 7.3 for females. Two factors must be considered in interpreting these figures—the annual migration from the county of large numbers of high school graduates, and, until recent years, the lack of educational facilities for Negroes.

Illiteracy in the county is not higher than for similar rural areas. Books, however, are not easy to come by. During WPA days the county had bookmobile service from the State Library. The board of supervisors did not appropriate money to continue such service when relief funds were withdrawn. Schools meet the needs of adults in their areas to a limited extent. Books from the high school library circulate *via* the school busses. Sporadic attempts by neighborhoods to establish some kind of library service indicate a feeling of need. Magazines circulate rather widely in the county. A report of twelve most popular national magazines in 1940 showed twenty-six per hundred families. In addition, agricultural magazines and six women's magazines were circulated in about the same proportion.

Churches are numerous and, as in most rural counties, are an important part of the social as well as the spiritual life. Some of the church buildings are colonial in origin and are pointed out with pride. Of 39 white churches listed in the *Central Virginian,* the county's weekly paper, in 1941 there were 12 Baptist, 11 Christian, 9 Methodist, 3 Presbyterian, 2 Episcopalian, 1 Brethren, and 1 Holiness. Of the 18 ministers serving these churches, at least 15 had residence in various neighborhoods of the county.

Negro churches are about as numerous as white. Baptist is the predominant denomination. The buildings are well kept and share with the schools the responsibility for furnishing meeting places for various organizations including the community clubs organized by the home demonstration agent. The churchyard not infrequently serves as a picnic ground where the community gathers for sociability usually related to church activities.

The county, at first glimpse, seems highly organized. Most school communities have active parent-teacher organiza-

tions. A few churches have young people's societies. There
are many homemakers and 4-H clubs throughout the county.
There are three Granges. Both Ruritan and Rotary have active groups concerned about county affairs. To find a meeting
night that will not conflict with some activity is difficult. Yet
the majority of people belong to no organizations; a few belong to everything; and even fewer carry the active responsibility.

Public services, in general, have not increased greatly in
the county's two hundred years. There is a department of public
welfare as required by state law. There is no public health
service. Agricultural and homemaking needs are excellently
served by the white county farm and home demonstration
agents and a Negro home demonstration agent. In addition,
the high school has teachers of home economics and vocational agriculture who work with adults as well as with school
girls and boys. The county is also a part of the Thomas Jefferson Soil Conservation District and has the full-time services
of a technician.

General Attitudes

The county is a good one with fine old families. They
have contributed generously of their sons and daughters to
the building of the state and nation. Going without some nice-
ties of living on the home front has been accepted as a necessary concomitant of this contribution.

To be poor is in no sense to be unrespected. In fact, wealth
is considered a bit ostentatious. Simplicity in private living
and in public services is the pattern. Unless positively uncomfortable, most people in the county prefer not to disturb
their way of living.

"I reckon Louisa has a bit of whatever any other county
has," one citizen remarked. It has. And it has no burning desire for more than "a bit" of whatever it may be.

Yet the following statements are likewise typical:

"If as citizens we cannot, or will not, locate the pressing
problems facing us and take steps to solve them, we are in a
pretty bad fix."

"The basic problem is that of making all the people fully
aware of problems which need thought and action."

"When you're through changing, you're through!"

And Louisa County, proud as it is of its past, is by no means ready to think of itself as "being through."

The fine heritage is, generally speaking, a real asset. Some aspects of it, however, tend toward the liability side of the ledger. The county has made history and can therefore rest on its past. The fact that certain families always have carried heavy public responsibility has led to an acceptance on the part of all that these same families should continue to carry it. The burden has become too great. Yet those who are most weighed down by it are among the last to see the potentially fine leadership but waiting for an opportunity to serve. *Noblesse oblige* here, as in many other old Virginia communities, has hindered as it has tried to help.

APPROACHING THE PROBLEM

The selection of communities that differed widely as a result of topography and location was purposefully made. As a basis of approach was sought in each, even greater divergencies than had been anticipated emerged. These consisted more in customs and attitudes than in economic status, educational levels, or standards of living. Census figures, for example, might show that two counties had almost identical percentages so far as number of telephones or kinds of toilet facilities were concerned. Yet their people might differ widely in actual degree of isolation, in personal habits of health and sanitation, and in attitudes toward change. First-hand impressions and locally gathered information served a much more useful purpose than the statistical material. Even the inaccuracies and biases of the human sources were significant and helped to build up a working understanding that was in no sense a comprehensive or scientific study, but which suggested possible motivations and methods of procedure.

The differences are implicit in the analyses of the three counties given above. In part those differences determined the emphases in the analyses. Physical characteristics and temperament of the people in Greene, for example, had more bearing on the job to be done than had local history. In

Louisa, the history was an inescapable part of the present and a foundation on which to build for the future.

The other factor determining emphases was the method of approach decided upon. In Nansemond, for example, the school stands out as a focal point because the study there was school centered rather than because the school was a more influential factor in community life than in the other areas. The analysis of this county, unlike the other two, is not the result of firsthand observation. Our report is based on that of the principal. His report was based upon answers to questionnaires carefully checked and tabulated rather than upon personal observation.

Living in the Community

In the mountain county, the first problem seemed to be one of socialization. Aside from the county seat and the few progressive communities in the lower end of the county, the people had little habit of getting together for any purpose. It was necessary first to get acquainted with those living in each isolated hollow or along the ridges, to find ways of bringing them together in their communities, and then to set up intercommunity relationships, striving to break down mutual prejudices of the mountain folk and those in other areas of the county. This necessitated much talking with individuals, joining the natural discussion groups that gathered on the porches of country stores, whittling, strumming a guitar, exchanging songs, attending church and church activities, having "gatherin's" in little schoolhouses, and in every way becoming as much a part of life in the several communities as was possible.

To facilitate this process of knowing the people and becoming known to them, actual residence in the county was thought desirable. Two members of the staff lived there for four months the first summer (1941) and for a somewhat longer period the next summer. An explanation of their presence was given whenever interest offered opportunity. There was less curiosity about it among the people than might have been desired. Officials and professional workers were sought out and an explanation offered. They listened politely

to the story of the purpose of the Special Projects with varying degrees of interest. Only in a few individual cases was
there positive expression of a desire to cooperate with an experimental program which, through the work in their county,
might find ways of helping other communities. At the same
time, there was no antagonism. The county as a whole was
most hospitable.

A detailed analysis of what was done and an evaluation
of this approach to community development are given in the
next chapter, "Living in the Community."

Consultants in Community Affairs

In the piedmont county, social organization had progressed much further than in the mountain county. Many unrelated activities were under way and were consuming a major portion of the time and interest of the recognized leaders.
No centralized planning was being done. Here the role of the
project was more clearly that of a coordinating agency that
might help toward a better local understanding of existing
problems and of resources available for their solution. The
eventual goal might be to work toward a unified county planning program.

Procedure involved making the acquaintance of county
leaders and professional workers in the various agencies, explaining the purpose of the project to them, asking their advice as to next steps, and finally inviting them to meet as a
group and talk things over with representatives of the Extension Division.

The interest of the Extension Division, it was carefully explained, was not only in helping this particular county, but
also in discovering through what was done here whether university extension could serve similar counties interested in
"raising themselves by their own bootstraps." Those who attended the first discussion agreed to cooperate in such an undertaking. Unquestionably they were willing to do it largely
out of politeness to the agency which asked that their county
serve as a guinea pig rather than out of any conviction that
their county would benefit greatly.

Once cooperation was agreed upon, a local committee was

appointed to work with the staff on future plans. Out of this
eventually came a citizens' council with subcommittees working on various aspects of community life.

The step-by-step progress and the possibilities in this
method of approach are given in detail in chapter 9, "Consultants in Community Affairs."

Guiding by Remote Control

The southside-tidewater approach was a kind of absentee
treatment with the high school principal giving actual guidance to the program. It was a conscious experiment in extending the service of the rural consolidated high school to
the entire community. The principal was paid from the funds
of the Special Projects for the summer months in order that
he might devote his time entirely to developing a community
program. Members of the Extension Division staff served as
consultants to the principal, advising when he sought advice
but in no sense attempting to direct or shape the program.
They visited the community only when invited.

The principal's interest was primarily in finding the difficult
road from survey to action. His exploratory journeys included
cooperating with existing organizations, such as Ruritan and
the women's club; setting up a council; and initiating activities both at the consolidated school center and in the neighborhoods which were so remote from the school that they had
never come to feel a part of it.

Although no secret was made of the fact that the principal was working with the Extension Division, no special
effort was made to interpret the whole experimental program
to the people of the community and enlist their interest in the
implications of the local effort for other areas.

Details of the program developed and an evaluation of
this approach are given in chapter 10, "Guiding by Remote
Control."

Came the War

The actual work in two counties began in the early summer of 1941. In the third it was fall before the selection was
definitely made. In December of that same year, we were
plunged into a war that seriously affected life in even the most

remote hollow. In Greene and Louisa Counties there were great migrations to defense industries as well as heavy losses of youth to the armed forces. The population of Greene decreased by about 1,000 or slightly under 20 per cent. In Louisa the drop was well over 20 per cent.

In the former county, in addition to the migration, hundreds of workers were taken out daily in trucks to the steel mills of Orange, or the silk mills of Charlottesville. From one hollow, eighty workers of both sexes left their homes each day. This involved almost every home in the neighborhood. In some families every able-bodied adult was employed. Older children were kept home from school to take care of younger. School attendance dropped until, for the first time, the school board put on a truant officer primarily in an attempt not to lose state funds. There was more cash money coming into the county than ever before—except possibly in prohibition days when moonshine is said to have brought fabulous sums to a few people. Much of the money was squandered. But some families built up substantial bank accounts to buy land or build homes in the county after the war.

In Louisa, the loss of young men seriously crippled agriculture in which there had begun to be real progress. Increased returns from the farms had not yet changed the financial status of youth enough to make those who could stay on the farms want to. High wages for less arduous labor lured them from the county with apparently little intention of returning. Timber resources were used up at an even greater rate than before the war as a result of high prices and appeals to patriotism.

In Nansemond County, on the other hand, newcomers to the area almost balanced losses to the armed services. Civilian population increased in the period between 1940 and 1943. The Holy Neck District had no defense industries within its area but sent many residents daily to the shipyards in Suffolk and Norfolk and housed many newcomers who worked there. Farm labor became inadequate to the demand. This community felt the pressures and knew the problems of all impacted war areas.

The consolidated school suffered from loss of teachers. Some went to more remunerative jobs. Others married and left to be near their husbands in camps or industries. The older boys and girls found employment, and student leadership was weakened. More and more, the entire time and energy of principal and faculty had to be given to making ends meet so far as regular school assignments were concerned. Little attention could be given the broader community program.

Objectives in Review

Toward the end of the first year, what could be hoped for by the end of a two-year experimental program had been stated as follows:[8]

Although those working on the project hope that each county will have made a significant beginning toward solving its problems by the end of the two years set for intensive experimentation, they know the task will not be completed. Plans, therefore, growing out of this fact as well as out of the primary purpose of the experiment—helping people to help themselves—include increasing the awareness of available services and agencies, placing responsibility on local people, discovering the natural leadership, helping potential leaders become better leaders, and building up in each county a group that will carry on. The future relationship of the Extension Division to the local work will be determined as the program develops.

Progress toward these ends has been steady and sure. Loss of young people inevitably meant more concentration of leadership in older groups than had been anticipated. Yet, even here much new leadership was discovered and "helping potential leaders become better leaders" was rewarding in its results.

Curtailments of some activities as a result of the war made a longer period of experimentation possible financially. This was particularly fortunate in view of shifts in emphasis after Pearl Harbor, and resulting loss of time that cut seriously into the original two-year period.

The effect of the war on the experimental program is difficult to judge. In some ways, war conditions were as much

---

[8]Jean and Jess Ogden, "Opportunity for Choice," Adult Education Journal. American Association for Adult Education. New York. April, 1942.

an asset as a liability to Special Projects. Normal inertia was disturbed, life was unsettled, and immediate problems pressed for attention. There was a motivation both in cooperating with the war effort and in planning for the postwar life of the community that could be utilized to advantage in helping people gain control of techniques of cooperative effort and planning. The projects had been set up with flexibility a basic principle. This principle was put to an unexpected test and, we believe, met the challenge. The staff might even be accused of stretching flexibility to the point of opportunism. At any rate, they made use of the emergency to help people and communities become more adept at foreseeing and meeting needs and problems. If this meant shifting some immediate goals, it did not change the ultimate purpose of the program.

The progress of planning and development in the postwar period in each area will be the real test of whether a foundation laid on emergency needs is a solid one on which to build. It is too soon to know what problems the peace has brought and whether the tools developed in each area are adequate to meeting them.

Whether the extended time was better than more intensive work during a shorter period, we shall never know. Our opinion is that the absence of high-pressure, or time-pressure, methods was a real asset.

In spite of the fact that what had been thought of as a two-year program in communities had four years of experimental activity, the principle of placing more and more of the responsibility on local people was adhered to from the beginning. The tapering-off process is evident in the decreasing number of trips and amount of time spent by the staff in each area toward the end of the period. It seems certain that, had the program ended in 1943, its termination would have been too abrupt to assure the desired carry-over. At that time the staff was still stimulating communities as well as meeting needs of which they were already aware. It was during the next two years that the staff was able to confine activities to helping when asked to, with reasonable certainty that the local group would ask. During those years acceptance of the principle of local initiation and responsibility was clinched. The Extension Division became to the experimental counties one of several state agencies to which they could turn for help.

As to the question of the best approach, we can say that all three are good. As is indicated more specifically in the following chapters, probably no others would have worked so well in the mountain and piedmont counties, for the methods selected grew out of and proved to be peculiarly adapted to the mores of the area. In the southside-tidewater area this was not the case. Some other approach might have served even better. There was no predisposition on the part of the people toward the school as a center of community life and there was no enthusiasm on the part of the superintendent in having it become such a center. The principal upon whom the responsibility rested left at the end of the second year. His successor for many reasons found it difficult to carry on what had been barely started. Yet even in the face of these adversities, the approach to community development by way of a school-centered program was good. In fact, it was so good, that out of it developed the extended experiment described in chapter 11.

To get light from our experience as to the best approach in his own community, the reader must consider procedures in relation to the customs, habits, attitudes, interests, and aspirations of the community concerned; in the light of his own experience, temperament and abilities; and in relation to the scope and potentialities of sponsoring agencies.

Our conviction in the importance of an experimental approach and of flexibility as the program develops has been strengthened a hundredfold. Our faith that the "community can do it" has received even greater reenforcement.

CHAPTER 8

Living in the Community (Greene)

No one ever made a formal decision that the work of the Special Projects in Greene County should start with a period of residence there. Yet the conviction that such an approach should be tried certainly influenced the decision. The fact that the two staff members directly concerned had come to Virginia from a Settlement House experience made them especially eager to try the effectiveness of living in the community as an approach to working with rural people on their problems. Moreover, the mountain county chosen for experimentation differed more sharply from their previous experience than did other areas in Virginia. It would require some kind of intensive program for getting acquainted.

Our first trip to Greene County had for its purpose merely to see the farms and the houses and to observe the general character of this part of Virginia. It was more or less by chance that on this trip we found a house in which we felt we could spend a very comfortable summer just on the edge of the mountain area. In the beginning, establishing residence in the county was as much a personal as a professional matter. Almost immediately, however, we found that it was to play an important part in our method of working there. We also found later in the summer when a water shortage became acute in the house where we were living that our decision to move out could not be made on the basis of purely personal considerations.

The situation was a complicated one involving two factions, one of which had believed that the source of supply was adequate when the water system had been put in with WPA help, and the other of which had been sure from the beginning that it would never do. The former were now sure that the fault lay not in the supply but in the mechanics of the system; the latter were, without investigation, saying, "I told you so." Since our house was higher above the water main and the reservoir than others it was affected first and for the longest period of time, and since it was new it had none of the old facilities, such as wells and outside toilets, which the others had retained. We, therefore, became a focal point in the controversy.

"I wouldn't take it," an adherent of one point of view would advise. "If Miss Dora lost a renter, I bet she'd tell that council a thing or two about their water system."

"All we need is a new valve to control the pressure," a member of the council on the other side would assure us. "You'll have water tomorrow if we can find the plumber this afternoon."

"Tomorrow" prolonged itself into twenty-eight waterless days, but our being able to "take it" rather than running back to the city raised our stock in the minds of our country neighbors. At the same time we felt we could do the project and our effectiveness as workers a good deal of harm by allowing "Miss Dora's losing a renter" to become the whip to be used on the council. By the time the water shortage ended we had an established place in the community bestowed upon us after a kind of prolonged initiation. So residence had become inextricably involved with working in Greene County. Four months later when the opening of school necessitated our moving into Charlottesville with our family, we were assured on all sides: "You'll be back in the spring. Once Greene County gets you, you can't get away from it." Our own feelings coincided with this sentiment. And the next spring found us returning for another five months of living in the county—this time because we wanted to and because we had a definite job to do there.

It was, however, those first four months of residence that established the firm foundation of mutual understanding on which future building depended. Those months were among the busiest we have known. Our Greene County home was twenty-five miles from the University. Several times a week we drove in for consultation with other members of the staff or for meetings with the advisory committee. We explored Buckingham, Fluvanna, Orange, and Louisa Counties in order to help in the selection of a piedmont county in which the experimental program might be tried. We began the investigations of good community projects throughout the state, made plans for *New Dominion Series,* and wrote the first two stories during those four months.

But our life was lived in Greene County. There was no separation of hours for working and hours for personal living. Every mile of driving, every mountain path explored, every casual exchange of greetings, every social contact, every friendship made, every purchase at a local store or gas station, even just sitting at home and listening to the comments of those who passed by on their way to or from Stanardsville on Court Day, strengthened our understanding.

We did not *do* anything by way of a program during those first months. We did not even say very much. In the words of one of our mountain friends, we "were sitting with our chins on our hands to keep our mouths from running while we studied on what to do."

This took self-control for, at first, what should be done seemed obvious—much more obvious, we hasten to add, than it seemed after longer acquaintance. We were well aware when we went into the county of the dangers of the new broom which sweeps so clean that everyone runs away from it. We were not aware—but learned that summer—that our delay in beginning to sweep was in itself an effective technique. By the time we were ready to start "doing something," the natural resistance to a new broom had been replaced by an eagerness to see it in action. We were able to cooperate with established agencies at their invitation as a part of the whole rather than as something new which had been reluctantly or apprehensively added.

Natural Relationships Established

The friendliness of our immediate neighbors and the feeling of responsibility of older residents for our comfort and happiness in their county made us feel at home immediately. Soon our "social life" was difficult to separate from our professional. Our invitation to go with the Stanardsville banker and his wife to the festival of sacred music at Massanetta Springs on Sunday evening came because he and Mr. Ogden had enjoyed singing at the evening service of the Methodist Church a few Sundays before. The banker's family had lived in Greene County for generations, and the background of understanding we got on that ride was greater than we could have acquired in several months of "objective study." Similar experiences with other persons with whom we shared interests resulted not only in increasing our store of understanding but in building up a mutual liking and respect.

Mrs. Ogden accepted an invitation to join the Stanardsville Homemakers Club and at meetings and social gatherings became well acquainted with the women of the county seat. She soon found herself promising to direct a play for them *as a member of the club rather than as a professional worker in the county.*

The Episcopal rector and his wife called, and this was the beginning of a friendship which we think would have been difficult to build up had we not been living in their parish. Later in the summer, they gave a tea at their new rectory at which we were "guests of honor." They asked us to tell the people there about the project on which we were working. Again, sociability and job became intermingled. Out of the chatter at the tea evolved a plan for opening the Parish House for a recreation program for the community. Later a leadership training program grew out of this plan. But we must not get ahead of our story.

Off the Main Highways

These first contacts were primarily with our immediate neighbors on the main highway and with the people in Stanardsville. They were natural and pleasant for us personally and important to carrying out future plans for the county. But equally important to initiating a program that would be far-reaching in its effects was acquaintance with the more remote farm families and the mountain folks. We had been warned that they would be suspicious of "outsiders" and we were apprehensive. We need not have been.

They, too, were extremely hospitable to us as guests in their county. Everyone seemed to know about us. "You live in Miss Dora's new bunga-low," was a greeting and a statement of fact rather than a question. The next remark was almost invariably, "How do you like Greene County?" The fact that we chose to live there was evidence that we did like it. Thus the first barrier was down. Our liking for the county and our genuine interest in its background and welfare brought us a wealth of information, local traditions, and attitudes which we would have gathered much more slowly as casual callers from the University. In fact, our connection with the University seemed to puzzle the mountain folk. We, in turn, were puzzled by their not infrequent remarks, such as, "I went there once," or "I went to see my mother when she was there." Gradually we realized that to most of them the University meant the hospital or clinic—and nothing more.

Off the main roads our out-of-state license plates frequently broke down barriers. This was a surprise to us. We had planned to put Virginia plates on the car as soon as they could be obtained. Before this was done, however, we decided that we must not discard too quickly the excellent opening to conversation found in our Illinois plates: "What's hit like whar you come from?"

The mountain people were deeply interested as we tried to describe the prairie land of Illinois, and often remarked, "I can't think what it would be like not to have hills." One woman, at whose little country store we occasionally stopped for gas, always examined the yellow plates, saying, "I can't rightly remember whar that place is that don't have no hills."

Our exploration of back roads and the hollows was continuous. We asked directions whenever we saw people with whom we might talk. On one occasion we had asked some little girls where the road led. They did not seem to understand. We explained, "We don't know where we are going and thought perhaps you could tell us."

The oldest child said, "I don't know whar *you're goin'* but we're goin' three mile and hit's all up."

We invited them to get in and thus made our first trip to Pocosan. It *is* "all up." But we found there one of the most needy and promising communities in which to work.

Occasionally response was brief and conclusive; more often we found both men and women ready to stop what they were doing for a bit of talk.

"I kin work anytime," one woman said when we apologized for keeping her from her canning. "But I don't often get a chance to talk."

One farmer left his work in midmorning urging us into the house: "I hear you-all are musicians. We got a piano but we can't none of us play."

He could not play but he could sing and strum his guitar. So before he went back to his fields, we had an hour's concert in one of the two rooms of the house which was full to overflowing with a large double bed in one end and, in the other, the old square piano which had belonged to "Great-Aunt Ellie." The wife, the three smallest children, and Mrs. Ogden sat on the bed; the two older girls stood by the piano using eyes as well as ears to enjoy the music.

The porches of the crossroads stores became favorite resting places as the summer went on. We drank Coca-Cola, whittled, talked, played the guitar, or just sat, as is the custom of the country. To stop briefly and exchange a few words gave us very little by way of understanding; to stay, as the others did, till we "got our settin' done" usually brought rich results. To learn to do this was difficult, for we are accustomed to leave when our business is finished and we felt awkward just sitting idly by. At first we consumed second and third bottles of Coca-Cola to give us an excuse for staying. Mrs. Ogden, whose capacity was greater, succeeded in gaining a reputation for having a passion for Coca-Cola, and one storekeeper and his wife stopped at our house late one night with a large bottle of the stuff.

"We saw your light and thought you was still up," the wife explained. "And I says to Him, Mrs. Ogden *loves* Coca-Cola." (*Him* and *Her* we find are the regular appellations of husband and wife for each other.)

The conversation during their call was again one of the best we had all summer so far as gaining insight is concerned.

In addition to informal chats with people at stores or on the roadside by their farms, we sought out key people in various neighborhoods, told them of the project and asked for an opportunity to discuss the county with them. In most cases several talks were necessary before we got through the barrier of their wondering just what we were going to ask for. They were sure there must "be a catch in it somewhere." This feeling was gradually dispelled, and we were invited to spend an evening or to come to dinner. They were interested but somewhat skeptical of all programs to help the county. So many had tried and failed. They sincerely wished to help "their people," but found the idea of helping people so they would be better able to help themselves incomprehensible.

Intensive Exploration of One Community

We were eager to get well acquainted with one mountain community for two reasons: (1) to verify our impressions as to actual needs; and (2) to prove to ourselves that we could gain the confidence of the people and perhaps hope to do an effective piece of work with them.

We chose a community in which we had made the acquaintance of the teacher. She belonged to an important family in the neighborhood. For many years she had taught in the one-room school built and owned by her family but later rented from them by the county. Her father had come from "outside" to teach there. Her mother's family had lived in that community for generations and owned several hundred acres of land. The teacher also ran the little store which served the entire community and furnished a meeting place on "Sat'd'y ev'nin' "—which, we discovered, meant from about one till seven on Saturday when everyone came to buy supplies and exchange news or just sit. There were few cash transactions at these times. A live hen or duck or a basket of eggs or a few pounds of walnut meats were handed over the counter in exchange for the inevitable can of kerosene and whatever other store supplies were essential to a meager existence. The one indulgence seemed to be soda pop—usually lukewarm and of poisonous color. Sometimes each child had a bottle; sometimes they shared one among many. The baby was given some from the bottles of his older brothers and sisters—orange on top of cherry on top of sarsaparilla. And, if later the baby cried, a bottle of another color was borrowed from another child and "jist a mite more" was forced down his throat.

But back to reasons for choosing this community. The teacher-storekeeper encouraged it when we talked with her; the professional workers in the county agreed that it was a difficult community and that the people were "shiftless and triflin';" the Farm Security Administrator had a number of clients in that neighborhood and had discovered that there was need for something more than money if loans were to be used intelligently; then, last but most important, we thought there was potential leadership among the people we had come to know, if a way could be found to develop it. So we chose this community for a bit of intensive cultivation.

"But they won't come to meetings," the teacher warned us.

So we sat through a hot afternoon on boxes in the stifling little store swarming with flies talking with her about what might bring them together. Each suggestion brought the same response: "That's been tried and it won't work." It was not until we mentioned music that she brightened. We said we were much interested in the music we had heard about here in the southern mountains and would like to hear some of it. "Ruby Lillian and the Jarrell boys would be proud to play for you," she said when convinced of the genuineness of our interest. "And I'll invite the others to come to listen. If it's in the paper they will like it."

So she inserted in the county paper a notice of a "musicale" to be held at the school. And they came—five "musicians," about twenty-five adults and uncountable children. The women and children crowded into the tiny schoolroom but most of the men gathered round the door and steps outside. As the young people played and sang, the men scattered about the building, one or two sticking their heads in each of the windows. Toward the end of the afternoon some of them began to edge their way into the school and nearer to us.

Mr. Ogden had brought his guitar but found their rhythms difficult for his fingers. He handed his guitar over to one of the boys standing eagerly by who said he could play but had no guitar. They "were proud" to entertain us but as the afternoon went on we were forgotten in their own enjoyment of the music.

When, after about three hours, the music was over, we said that we would like to meet some of the people. Thus far the teacher had introduced only the musicians. She looked at us appraisingly and remarked, "If I introduce you, you'll have to shake hands and then you'll always have to know the names of those you've met." We assured her we were good at names, and she proceeded with the introductions. Names presented a simple problem since three surnames accounted for most of the community. Fortunately, getting interrelationships straightened out and knowing to whom the children belonged was not required of us at first.

At the "musicale" several persons had remarked that it was a shame to let this good music go to waste, intimating that music was primarily for dancing. Later we talked with the teacher about combining some square dances with the music at the next get-together. She was hesitant at first saying that they had stopped having dances years ago because of the drinking that had come to be a part of them. Several of the people suggested that dancing in the afternoon instead of at night might be a way to separate it from the drinking. The teacher agreed. She suggested that we invite Richard Chase and some members of the Albemarle Country Dance Society to come out.

This time the little school was not nearly big enough for the crowd even when the stove had been taken from the center of the floor. Members of the Albemarle group were in favor of dancing on the grass outside. This was entirely out of the pattern and met with no response at first. Finally, however, after several sets inside, the dancers were warmed up enough to be willing to come out where more could participate. Many did not dance; some did not even talk; but everyone was reluctant to leave, and the party, which had started at one, went on till about seven when we left exhausted.

Richard Chase tried throughout the afternoon to discover whether any of the old ballads survived in this neighborhood. He found it difficult to make his meaning understood, but late in the afternoon one woman confided to Mrs. Ogden, "I know what that man was talking about. My husband and his uncle sing those songs."

That determined the pattern for the next party. Due to everybody's uncertainty about the singers, no attempt was made to get a crowd. Nevertheless, about thirty adults gathered at the store. On each preceding occasion we had assembled at the store and had then gone on to the little schoolhouse. This time we decided to try the experiment of sitting right there on the porch to sing and talk. A much more informal atmosphere was established immediately.

Only one singer arrived. He was shy but not at all self-conscious about his singing. While he rested between songs, Mr. Ogden sang. The other singer sat during these songs with his eyes closed and his lips moving. After the third, someone volunteered, "He'll be singin' them songs tomorrow."

"Will you?" asked Mr. Ogden. "Did you get them?"

"I didn't get quite all that Joshua one," was the apologetic reply. "I'd like if you'd do it again."

We heard later that he had learned the new songs that day. He cannot read but has a remarkable memory. This is not unusual among these mountain folk.

Our faith in these people and in our ability to help them to help themselves was strengthened greatly by this closer acquaintance with them, in spite of our gradual introduction, as the summer progressed, to neighborhood quarrels and points of friction. Hearing these "family secrets" helped to convince us that we had been accepted and were no longer looked on as "outsiders" for whom company manners were put on.

In other communities we did not attempt any meetings or program of our own, but went to lawn socials, graduation exercises of daily vacation Bible schools, and any meetings to which the public was invited. At first we had to depend almost entirely on the *Greene County Record* for notices of events. Soon, however, we established connection with the "grapevine" over which news of coming events spreads through the county. This achievement we accepted as further evidence of "belonging."

One day we met a county acquaintance who said, "We had a lawn social at the South River Church last Sat'd'y, and I kep' saying, 'I wish I'd told the Ogdens; they certainly would like this.' You always have such a good time." And we always did. Though our primary purpose in going to any affair was to get acquainted, we invariably had a good time. This fact, we are sure, facilitated the getting acquainted process.

The Professional Workers

While getting acquainted with the people of various communities and on various social and economic levels, we were not neglecting the professional workers and officials in the county. We made repeated calls on them to get information or to ask advice in relation to some matter in which we were interested. Our specific question usually led to discussion. We began to accumulate a store of information and points of view. With professional workers as with "leading citizens" we had more suspicion to break down than with the people themselves. We soon succeeded in convincing them that we had not come to take their jobs, nor yet to tell them what to do. They accepted the fact that we wanted to learn about the county and that we felt they were the people from whom we could learn.

We were always ready to cooperate but always careful not to move in any direction until sure of our welcome. When asked about the use that might be made of the idle Parish House, we were ready to make and to help implement suggestions. When asked by the home demonstration agent whether there were free movies available so that the homemakers club at the Celt School could have a "picture show" to make money for equipping a school lunchroom, we took lists and helped her to select. In the end we "put on the show" with the advice of Mr. Rorer and the help of Mr. Cheney. At that meeting we were able to draw sound conclusions as to the possible effectiveness of pictures as an educational device in Greene County. The audience responded with an eagerness and interest such as we had never seen in more sophisticated communities. So while helping the home demonstration agent, we were actually gaining valuable experience in adult education techniques for ourselves and making the acquaintance of a neighborhood we had not previously known. The amusement of the people at the appearance of big Mr. Ogden as he played the little portable organ for their "cakewalk" was an excellent ice-breaker. And by the time Mrs. Ogden had stood in the center of a circle of solemn couples "walking" for cakes through six separate "walks" and had dropped the broom over her shoulder six times to determine the winners, she and they felt like old friends.

Soon invitations began to come from the professional workers for us to attend meetings of homemakers clubs, FSA clients, the buyers cooperatives in the Dyke and Ruckersville areas, and finally even to meetings of professional workers themselves. By the end of the summer we felt the professional workers were no longer being politely hospitable to strangers in their midst but were including us in their deliberations because they thought we had a genuine interest in the county and a real contribution to make. Skeletons carefully kept in the county closet in the early summer began to be exposed to our friendly view. As with the people, we interpreted the laying aside of company manners and reticences as evidence that we belonged. Though relations with professional workers in other counties have been close and pleasant, nowhere have we become a part of the family as in Greene. Residence in the county undoubtedly brought this about.

Going on from There

Moving into Charlottesville at the end of four months did not mean withdrawal from activities. We continued to be included in meetings of homemakers clubs, Farm Security clients and advisory board, professional workers council, county nutrition committee, and whatever meetings were planned by the various agencies. We were still learners. But, more and more, we were invited to advise and to help in programs.

In May, when we had moved into the county, we had thought that a county committee or council should probably be set up when the time came "to launch a program." Four months of close association with the people had convinced us that this should be a step well along the way rather than the starting point. In the first place, there were already many committees and boards. The same few people served on all of them. Professional workers continued to go through the motions of appointing committees, but had long since ceased expecting them to do more than hold an occasional perfunctory meeting called and presided over by the professional worker. Observing meetings of local committees we were invited to attend had convinced us that many undesirable procedures had become accepted as the way a committee should function. We felt that to start under a committee banner might invalidate the purpose of the program at the outset.

In the second place, a large portion of the county was not yet ready to participate in a countywide planning group. The same few people who were already on every committee would, of necessity, be the group upon which we might call. A very elementary job of socialization had to be done within small natural neighborhood groupings for the hollows and hinterlands. Many prejudices between groups— mountains and lowlands, county and county seat, Methodists and Episcopalians, "we" and "they"—had to be broken down and groups united on a common interest. Until there had been time for socialization and breaking down prejudices, nothing like a representative council could have been organized.

In the third place, it developed that there was to be no "launching of a program." Activities had begun quietly and naturally during our period of residence and getting acquainted. In the extension of these activities was the promise of a foundation program on which sound building might be done. But there was need for much spadework before any imposing structure could, or should, appear.

Activities that Led on

In the report written in October, 1941, appears this statement:

A modest program for adults is already under way in the plays and chorus we are directing in Stanardsville. If the groups participating wish to continue after their "show," our desire is to train local leadership as quickly as possible. Those who are now participating are getting the beginning of such training.

They did want to continue. The chorus, particularly, had met a real need. Someone suggested keeping together to sing Christmas carols. But Christmas programs, said someone else, were something the individual churches planned. But, another pointed out, this group had people from every denomination. Someone else observed that no church had enough singers for a really good chorus. Finally the revolutionary suggestion came from the group that an interdenominational choir might offer a Christmas program for those who wanted it. It did. Its program in five churches of three denominations during Christmas week took people into enemy territory, and they returned unscathed. Breaking down one barrier of prejudice was begun. Another step was taken the next summer when, as a result of the choir experience, an interdenominational daily vacation Bible school was held. Here we assisted in training leaders. But again we get ahead of our story in our eagerness to show how one thing led naturally to another!

Throughout our first summer in the county, two needs had been so obvious as to be inescapable. In almost every discussion, we were told that there was a lack of anything in the county of interest to young people; that as many young people as could were leaving to find a more interesting as well as a more profitable life elsewhere; that among those who could not leave there were many with a great deal of leisure and nothing to do. At the same time, everyone bewailed the lack of leaders for all kinds of activities. Ministers complained that they could not have Sunday school unless they themselves did the teaching. The home demonstration agent said that only two of her seven clubs had the kind of leadership that made a meeting possible if she were not there to conduct it. Whenever consolidation of schools removed a teacher from a community, 4-H clubs and other activities stopped because the sole leadership had come from the teacher.

As we discussed this situation with the ministers, school people, and professional workers in the county, it seemed as if the need of young people for something to do and the need for leadership might be combined to mutual advantage. The young people, who had time on their hands, might be trained to assume responsibility for certain activities throughout the county including the proposed use of the Parish House in Stanardsville for community programs.

In the plays and chorus there had been five young people who showed promise as leaders. One of these left the county to take a defense job. With the other four as a nucleus, we invited a larger group suggested by the home demonstration agent, the trial justice, and two ministers, to meet with us to talk about a program of leadership training for recreational and cultural activities within the county.

In February this group began weekly meetings to learn how to plan recreational and cultural programs and how to lead games and singing. A part of each meeting was spent in discussion of leadership qualities and how to develop them, but most of the time was spent in learning and practicing skills. Twice members of the group were taken to visit programs in other counties. In April they planned their first community party for the Parish House. Thirty selected guests were invited with the understanding that they were "guinea pigs." This affair was so successful that the next party was announced for the entire community. From then on weekly community nights were held with seventy-five to one hundred in attendance. It is on our June calendar that a penciled note appears saying, "Stanardsville Community Night—*Do Not Go.*" That was to remind us that this group no longer needed our help. Our attendance had become purely recreational—and our help was needed elsewhere.

Neighborhood Meetings

The above activities served primarily Stanardsville and the area immediately surrounding it. People from five different communities had sung with the chorus, and young people from four were in the training group at first. But that winter we entered the war; gas rationing began; and neighborhoods had to become self-sufficient.

Moreover, as has been indicated, the communities most needing help in learning to help themselves had to start on a very elementary level. Our experience with music in one

community the first summer and with the "picture show" in
another had indicated a way of beginning. From Christmas
until March, however, the outlying communities hibernated.
Roads were bad, the weather was unpleasant, clothing was
inadequate. Hence the season when farmers were not busy
proved to be, contrary to our expectations, the season when
least could be done. With the first signs of spring came a general awakening. The summary report of activities in Greene
County, October, 1941, to April, 1942, includes those described
above and ends with the two following:

> In cooperation with the teacher of agriculture at the Blue Ridge
> Industrial School, we have shown a series of motion pictures at the
> Dyke School on March 12, 19, 26, and April 9. The Dyke Community
> League has sponsored this program but farmers and their families
> from the surrounding area were invited whether or not they were
> members of the league. Attendance has ranged from 100 to 150. The
> movies have dealt primarily with such subjects as soil erosion, modern
> farming methods, food production and preservation. There has been
> some discussion (participated in by only a few) and group singing (in
> which everyone took part) at most of the meetings.
>
> On March 30, the presidents of all the Greene County homemakers
> clubs and the home demonstration agent were invited to come to the
> University to preview a number of films on nutrition and discuss a
> program of movies for the county. All seven clubs were represented.
> . . . . . These women decided that they would like to suggest to their
> clubs: that each sponsor a program for its own neighborhood, at
> which nutrition pictures would be shown; and that each club attempt
> to get as many as possible of the women who were not members to
> attend these meetings.
>
> Ten meetings are planned for the first three weeks in May. These
> meetings are to be held in the least accessible parts of the county, as
> well as in the larger communities, so that everyone will have an oppor-
> tunity to get to a meeting.

These two items herald the beginning of the intensive
movie program reported in chapter 13. They also lead directly to the beginning of the second summer of residence in
Greene County. This differed markedly from the first in that
it was filled to overflowing with activities for which we carried primary responsibility. We had become not only members of the community but *working members* who found it
difficult to give attention to activities elsewhere.

JULY-AUGUST, 1942
During Period of Residence in Greene County

MONDAY	TUESDAY	WEDNESDAY	THURSDAY	FRIDAY	SATURDAY
13 9 a. m. Daily Vacation Bible School (Greene) 7 p. m. Nutrition Films—Mineral (Louisa Co.)	14 9 a. m. Daily Vacation Bible School (Greene) 8 p. m. Movies—Rising Sun Church—(Louisa)	15 9 a. m. Bible School (Greene) 8 p. m. Movies—Mt. Gilliam Church (Louisa)	16 9 a. m. Bible School (Greene) 2 p. m. Meeting of Vocational Ag. Teachers (Massanetta Springs) 8 p. m. Movies—Kinderhook (Greene)	17 9 a. m. Bible School (Greene) 8 p. m. Movies—Wyatts Mt. (Greene)	18
20 9 a. m. Bible School (Greene) 2 p. m. Office	21 9 a. m. Bible School (Greene) 7 p. m. Movies for Greene Co. Nutrition Committee	22 9 a. m. Bible School (Greene)	23 9 a. m. Bible School (Greene) 8 p. m. Community Sing—Mineral (Louisa Co.)	24 9 a. m. Bible School (Greene)	25
27 Office all day	28 8 p. m. Movies—Middle River—(Greene)	29 9 a. m. Take movies of community garden for school lunch 10 a. m. to Bealeton to get N.D.S. story of farm machinery repair	30 3 p. m. Recreation meeting—Louisa 8 p. m. Community sing—Mineral (Louisa Co.)	31 Office all day	1
3 Office all day		5	6	7	8

NANSEMOND COUNTY TO VISIT PROGRAM THERE TUESDAY THROUGH FRIDAY

10	11	12	13	14	15
Office all day 8 p. m. Greene Co. Leadership Training		3 p. m. Movies Stanardsville (Greene Co.)	*Jess:* 4 p. m. Louisa Recreation Group 8 p. m. Mineral Community Sing *Jean:* 8 p. m. Lawn Party and Movies, Dyke (Greene Co.)	8 p. m. Movies at Wyatt's Mt. (Greene Co.)	

17	18	19	20	21	22
Office all day p. m. 4-H Club Stanardsville to plan movie 8 p. m.—Leadership Group—Stanardsville	3 p. m. Movies— Louisa (cancelled because of blackout)		*Jean:* 6 p. m. Lawn Party and Movies—Stanardsville (Greene Co.) *Jess:* 8 p. m. Community Sing Mineral (Louisa Co.)		

24	25	26	27	28	29
Office all day 7 p. m. 4-H Club Stanardsville to Plan Movie 8 p. m. Leadership Group Stanardsville	Visit Page County Clinic for NDS story 8 p. m. Community Sing—Louisa	Visit Timberville Poultry Co-Op for NDS story 8:30 p. m. 4-H Club Meeting Stanardsville to plan Movie	*Jean:* 8 p. m. Community Night, Stanardsville *Jess:* Community Sing Mineral (Louisa Co.)		

Louisa County is about the same distance from Stanardsville as from Charlottesville. Hence residence in Greene
County did not necessitate absence from Louisa where our job
was largely that of consultants. The summer of 1942 was one
of unusual activity in that county also. During the summer
months we had twenty-three meetings—nutrition, movies,
singing, recreation, and council committees — in Louisa and
spent four days in Nansemond where we were still working
by remote control. The sample page from our calendar for July
—August, 1942, will answer the oft repeated question, "But
what did you do when you lived in the county?" No mere
calendar can convey our feeling that we certainly had "talked
up a storm" so far as activity was concerned.

During our second summer in Greene County we held
fifty meetings in eighteen centers. Audiences included more
than 50 per cent of the total population. The wartime emphasis on food production and preservation and defense determined to a large extent the subject matter of the meetings.
Cooperating agencies were the home demonstration clubs, the
Farm Security Administration, the civilian defense committees, and the teachers in the communities concerned. There
has been some attempt to evaluate the program from the point
of view of participants in chapter 13. So far as we were concerned, the greatest value was in our intimate association with
people in every part of the county. We began to feel that we
had a working knowledge of the county and had learned
really to communicate with the people.

The Second Winter

In October, we again moved back to Charlottesville with
even greater reluctance than the preceding year. Activities
of the winter can best be indicated by excerpts from a progress
summary dated April 6, 1943:

1. Cooperation with Professional Workers

    Close cooperation with all the professional workers in the county
continues. We attend meetings of the professional workers council no
longer as visitors but as regular members "with voice and vote." The
fact that there has been a 50 per cent change in personnel in this group
in the less than two years we have worked in the county means slower
progress toward coordination than we had hoped.

2. Leadership Training in a Specific Technique

Having, through our use of motion pictures, convinced the county (professional workers, church groups, schools, and community organizations) of the educational value of movies, particularly in the more remote sections of the county, we are having more requests for film showings for adult groups than it is possible for us to fill. Partly because of our lack of time but more because we wish the local groups to become increasingly independent of us, we are more and more supplying films for meetings which we do not attend.

The high school already owns a projector which it allows other groups to use. The professional workers council is discussing the advisability of getting one for all agencies to use or, possibly, of getting a film strip projector and a lantern for showing slides, thus supplementing the visual aids available to the county.

The high school principal is the only local person who can operate the projector. Others wish to learn. Mr. Rorer has consented to teach a group and will have his first meeting with them Monday afternoon, April 12. At least two subsequent meetings will be planned at that time.

This visual education leadership group will include the home demonstration agent; the Farm Security supervisor and home management agent; an adult leader from each of the two Stanardsville church groups—Episcopal and Methodist; lay leaders from Stanardsville, Dyke, and Ruckersville home demonstration clubs; two young people who were in last spring's leadership training group; and the superintendent of public welfare.

In addition to teaching members of the group to operate the machines (movie projectors—sound and silent—film strip projector, and lantern), Mr. Rorer will discuss with them the effective use of visual materials. Most of them have already had a practical demonstration of this from our rather intensive program during the past year, but this training class offers opportunity to point out what procedures have been followed.

3. Recreation Program

Through January the leadership group with which we worked last spring continued to conduct weekly recreation nights in the Parish House. By that time there were almost no young people of the out-of-school group left. The army or jobs had taken them all. The older people preferred singing to the more general recreation program. The Odd Fellows decided to sponsor community sings every Tuesday night with Mr. Ogden in charge. We welcomed the change to the Odd Fellows Hall because of the continuous struggle to keep Parish House meetings non-denominational. The sings were well attended and included a number of young high school people as well as the adults. Toward the end of February, interest in an Easter sunrise service began to show itself. The four ministers (Episcopal, Brethren, Methodist, and Baptist) with a member of each church were asked to serve as a committee on arrangements. Mr. Ogden was asked to find music. He had done this and had also asked an alto and a soprano from Charlottesville to help. They went out twice and the "choir" found that it could actually do four-part singing with the help of a strong lead in each part. Enthusiasm ran high at the last rehearsal. Mr. Ogden went to the hospital the next day—and the choir has given up its ambitious Easter music program. Plans are still going forward, however, for the interdenominational Easter service, and the choir is eager to continue when Mr. Ogden can meet with it again.

There are only four members of the young people's leadership training group still in the county. Two of these have full-time jobs with rationing and draft boards. The other two have more leisure and are now learning to operate the movie projector in order to help with community meetings.

4. Community and Neighborhood Programs

　　　(Note: This part of the progress report describes seven com-
　-　munity programs of which we select one to present here as
　　　typical.)

Bacon Hollow: The Bacon Hollow people attending the Dyke meetings began to ask in July, 1942, whether they might have meetings in their own abandoned school because of the difficulty of transportation. We were reluctant to plan a neighborhood meeting if the broader community approach could be continued, for since the Bacon Hollow children are now brought out to the Dyke School, it seemed wise to have the adults feel that they, too, are a part of that school community.

The October floods, followed by impassable roads, and the continued need for curtailing use of tires and gas changed the situation so that planning a neighborhood program for the Hollow seemed desirable. It was not until January that the road was open to within walking distance of the Victory Hill School about half way up the Hollow. Then in cooperation with the Farm Security supervisor we planned a meeting for the evening of January 15. Mr. Olcott and Mr. Ogden had to carry the projector, battery, and screen the last half mile over rocks and debris left by the flood but the eager audience of fifty-three adults made the effort seem worthwhile.

Following the pictures (two current news reels and two short comedies) there was discussion of some of the problems of Bacon Hollow. Getting their road rebuilt was the major concern of the group. Those who lived beyond the old Victory Hill School to which their children formerly went were not willing to have their children come that far now to meet the school bus which since the first of January had been able to get up there. They were sure that if they made that concession, the county would never bother to complete the work on the road. The other problem bothering them was how they were to get their land cleared of rocks for spring planting. It was agreed to continue having neighborhood meetings and discussions.

A short time before the January meeting, Mr. Poling, a young Brethren minister who came to Greene County in the fall of 1941, moved to a house on the edge of Bacon Hollow. His church at Victory Hill is the only one in the Hollow, and Miss Niely Wampler, a missionary of the same faith, has taught Sunday school and had a women's club there for many years. We found that Mr. Poling, having become a resident of the Hollow and having planned to devote most of his time to its problems, was concerned at what he felt to be "too many approaches from too many points of view." In analyzing the situation with him we found that the only conflict in "approaches" in his mind was concerned with attitudes toward the war. It seemed to us that we might help work out a better coordinated program for the Hollow by calling a meeting of all the professional workers in the county who touched the lives of the people there.

It was the first time we had officially taken responsibility for calling such a meeting. We invited nine persons to meet with us on the evening of February 23. All nine came! (This is a remarkable response in Greene County.) They included: Mr. Poling and Miss Niely of the Brethren Church; Mr. Knight, principal, and Miss Winona Morris, teacher, of the Dyke School to which the Hollow children go; Mrs. Whorley, the home demonstration agent; Miss Bolton, superintendent of public welfare; Mr. Olcott and Miss Bristow, FSA supervisors; and Mr. John M. Morris, trial justice, who grew up in Bacon Hollow and continues to be much interested in the people there. Mr. Knight was also a Bacon Hollow boy and Miss Winona Morris has always lived just on the edge of the Hollow and knows the people and their problems very well.

We met promptly at eight and found it difficult to bring the discussion to a close at eleven.

In addition to a clarification of aims and the loss of any feeling that some of us might be working at cross purposes, there were some definite outcomes of the discussion, as follows:

a. Learning to work together, it was agreed, was the greatest need of the Hollow folk and we might help toward this end by deciding on a single simple objective and all working toward it with a committee from the community. (Food production seemed to be the most urgent. It could honestly be stressed as a live-at-home rather than a food-for-freedom program.)

b. The three agencies working with women (home demonstration, FSA, and church women's club) decided to hold joint meetings and to agree on a single program.

c. A committee was appointed from among those present to plan a community meeting in the Hollow in which the rest of us would cooperate. At that meeting, it was hoped, there might be appointed a community committee to cooperate in planning future programs.

A Bacon Hollow neighborhood meeting in the Victory Hill School was planned by this committee for the evening of March 12 to discuss food production. We were asked to show the pictures of gardens and canning we had taken in the county last summer and to suggest the possibility of taking similar pictures of especially good gardens and well planned storage space in Bacon Hollow this year.

This time we were able to drive to within a short distance of the school. Climbing a rail fence with the battery, projector, and screen, and getting them up a steep slippery hillside in the rain were the only hazards. The schoolroom was filled to capacity. More than seventy-five had come out in the rain for the meeting. A "hill-billy band" which Mr. Poling has organized among the boys opened the meeting. There followed talks (too long and too many) by Mr. Olcott,

Miss Niely, Mr. Poling, and Mrs. Ogden. Everyone was very patient though whispered questions indicated throughout the evening an eagnerness for "the picture." Interest was great in seeing on the screen people and places they knew, and we feel sure that a chance "to be in the movies" themselves will be a real incentive in garden making and storage planning this year.

At Mr. Poling's suggestion the group agreed that a Bacon Hollow live-at-home committee would be a good idea—or at least, as one man expressed it, "a committee couldn't do no harm." Mr. Poling suggested that they name five members to such a committee. After much hesitation, the naming began, and a committee of *six* was necessary in order to satisfy all factions. Three men and three women were named. The committee got together briefly after the program had ended to plan a time and place for their first meeting.

They met the following Wednesday with Mr. Poling and Mr. Olcott. Only three committee members came, one excusing himself because "the day didn't suit" and the other two saying frankly they thought the Hollow folks would resent having a committee tell them what to do and they were afraid to be a part of it. Those present, however, decided to proceed with plans for gardens. They listed thirty-three vegetables that they knew would grow well in the Hollow and decided to advise every family to plant at least fifteen this year because of rationing. They also decided to ask us to have their list printed for distribution to every family in the Hollow. This was done.

A second meeting of the committee was called for the next Tuesday evening (March 23). All members but one attended this time since the others had suffered no dire results. The one absent was really ill and sent word that she would do whatever she could thereafter. Each member took copies of the printed list to distribute to those neighbors nearest him, all the families being divided among committee members. Another neighborhood meeting was thought to be desirable "with more pictures." The date set for this is April 29.

The school in which these meetings are held is a very good two-room building which is still owned by the county though no longer used. The Hollow people have a strong feeling of loyalty to it. It is centrally located and would make an excellent community house. The seats and desks have been removed to other schools. Making furniture for the building might make an excellent beginning for a wood-working program there when the busy farm season is over.

What Happened Then

The April, 1943, report ends there. Again one is tempted to get ahead of the story of the total program to tell what happened next. There had been four or five community meetings in the two-room abandoned school when, in June, the school board suddenly announced that it was to be sold. A few of the Hollow folks had a meeting. They invited the FSA supervisor, the trial justice, and the Ogdens to come to help them decide what they wanted to do. Several persons who had earned money in war industries in an adjoining county wanted to buy the building which was better than most houses in the area. Others felt it should remain for the community to use. Their opinion became unanimous when the trial justice told them how much money was being offered for it. The sum was greater than anyone in the Hollow could or would **pay.** The question then became one of how to get all the people in the community behind a request to the school board not to sell the building. Each of the professionals present was asked in turn to present an appeal to the board. Each objected on the basis that any appeal to carry weight must come from the people themselves—and from a larger proportion of them than the half dozen present at that meeting. There were only three days in which to act; Mr. Morris suggested a petition. The people, however, felt that they needed a mass meeting and set the next night as the time. The professional workers present said they would not come, for to them it seemed better that the people carry on by themselves. They proved that they were ready to do it. Not only was a petition presented to the board, but about thirty men walked the five dusty miles to Stanardsville to see that it was presented. The board decided to let them keep their school as long as possible.

In the fall it was the scene of an impressive Achievement-Day display of food produced and preserved. To the live-at-home committee and the now united women's organizations must go the credit. It was the first such program in that community. The home demonstration agent had said at the February meeting of professional workers referred to above that there was supposedly a home demonstration club there but she had never been able to find any evidence of it since coming to the county. Our experience in the summer of 1941 had been the same when twice we had gone to furniture clinics announced for the community. At the first, no one had appeared. At the second, as the agent and we were about to leave, a small child slid up quietly and reported, "Ma says they's a old chair on the porch you-all can fix if you want." And this was the community that was revitalizing itself.

Progress continued—though it was slowed up by the termination in the county of the Farm Security Administration which was doing more than any other agency in that community to help individuals; by a change in ministers at the little church and another change in home demonstration leadership; and by really crippling losses of community leaders to armed services and defense industries. Many of them will never return. Yet there comes the news that the people have raised money and are about to build their own community house to replace the school which now after two years' delay the board must sell; and that they are organizing to get REA lines extended to furnish electricity for their farms and homes.

This is only one of a score of communities that make up the county. It is one of the poorest, the least socialized, and the most difficult. It was described to us by a sympathetic resident of the county who knew it intimately as being "spiritually, as well as financially, bankrupt." The newcomer would still consider it pretty hopeless. But those who have known it long feel that these folks have become definitely more capable of helping themselves and have turned in the direction of finding a better living.

Evaluation of Two-Year Program

The program of the Special Projects had first been thought of in terms of two years. The April, 1943, report from which we have quoted above was made at just about the end of the two-year period. The paragraphs that follow it telling of subsequent progress in one community up to the fall of 1945 might be cited as evidence that there would have been a carry-over had the entire program terminated then. The staff of the Special Projects have attended only one meeting in that community since the Achievement Day in September, 1943. The FSA supervisor had been withdrawn before that time. The minister left soon after. The home demonstration agent left the next summer. Yet the people continue to help themselves and to turn to the new professional workers for help rather than to depend entirely on them for leadership.

This same is true to a greater extent in the more progressive communities of the county. They no longer ask us to "bring a show" as they did in 1942. They now ask for specific help in relation to something they wish to do—leadership training for a recreation program in one community, planning for revival of handicrafts in another, discussion of possible harvesting and marketing of the wild berries that grow on the mountainsides, extension of rural electrification lines, health programs, and library service.

At the end of two years, had Special Projects terminated then, we should probably have tried to organize a county council to carry on. It was not the time. The few people who served on countywide programs were, in 1943, approaching a state of complete exhaustion as a result of emergency demands of the war program. The best potential leadership from the areas we had hoped to have ready to unite in a countywide program had gone from the county for war service or work. Since the Special Projects could continue for a longer period, it seemed wiser to wait until the county was ready to organize itself without our taking the initiative.

The spadework had been done. Into it went nine months of residence in the county during the summers of 1941 and 1942; and, during the winters following, a total of sixty trips from Charlottesville to call on or confer with individuals, fourteen to attend committee meetings of various agencies kind enough to include us, fifty for study groups and leadership training meetings (including choir and daily vacation Bible school), and seventy-two community meetings for which we carried program responsibility but most of which we planned in cooperation with county agencies. Thus, in two years we spent nine months of residence in the county and made 196 trips to it.

In 1943, the tapering off process began. That year we made 113 trips, each for the purpose of attending a meeting or answering a specific request. In 1944 and 1945, the number of trips (exclusive of those for personal sociability) totaled less than fifty for each year.

When we left the county in the fall of 1942, we had hoped for another period of residence there. The next spring we rented a house. The workshop program and experiment with principals (see chapter 11) which began that summer kept us in Charlottesville. Later, follow-up work with members of this group and activities in other counties still kept us from living in Greene County. After eight months of paying rent and never spending a single night in the little house, we gave it up. We still feel that another period of living in the county would clinch the program there. But possibly it would be only self-indulgence, for there are many signs that it is unnecessary.

The People Take Hold

In 1945, three people from Greene County attended the summer workshop at the University—a school teacher, a school principal, and the welfare superintendent. All are permanent residents as well as workers in the county. It is one of them who reports:

Ruckersville and Stanardsville are now seeing their recreation programs in county terms. We are helping the home demonstration agent carry out a recreation program not only in our own communities (Stanardsville and Ruckersville) but also in other communities in the county.

Our little library has grown from 100 to 1,000 books which belong to the county, and 600 loaned by the state. They are scattered about in thirteen different communities—in schools, homes, and country stores— and serve the whole county. There is talk of uniting with Madison County to get bookmobile service for both.

We want a countywide study and planning group—not only the three of us who attended the workshop, but people from all communities. Many people have suggested it. They are asking how they can make it sound important enough to get the Ogdens back here to help and are saying, "It's too bad we weren't ready for it when they lived right here."

For a long time I have wanted to change things, but it seemed like there was so much to be done, the load was too heavy for one person to pull. Now I have learned to *get behind and push,* and I don't have to wear myself out because I am just one of many pushers!

We are convinced in Greene County that people can change a county if they once see the way. Right now it looks like we are seeing the way and are ready to start really working at it.

Some Things We Learned

We made mistakes—undoubtedly many more than we recognize. But, so far as techniques are concerned, we learned as much from our mistakes as from our successes. We believe that same is true of those with whom we worked (professional and laymen) because we were willing to admit our mistakes. *We were sincerely trying to learn.* Such an attitude on the part of a leader, we are convinced, makes for a better learning situation for all concerned—provided, of course, the leader is the kind of person for whom people have enough liking and respect to permit him a mistake or two and a chance try again.

In our desire not to establish a new agency and to cooperate fully with those that were already working in the area, we bent over backward to let them take the lead. In some cases, they were not ready. This idea is developed in the chapter on "Meetings with Movies." Likewise we relied at first too much on the professional workers to give continuity to the program. Many of them moved on: In five years, there has been a complete turnover in personnel among ministers; the FSA workers, who were most eager for our program, have gone; the present home demonstration agent and welfare superintendent are the third persons in those positions since first we went into the county. From the point of view of extension of the program into other counties of Virginia, this has had some good results. From the point of view of Greene County, it has meant starting over again with each newcomer.

Even lay leaders in rural areas, we learned, must be chosen with care if they are to continue to serve the community in which they are trained. Migration of youth from these areas has to be reckoned with. The fact that there are only two of the fourteen young people we trained in 1942 still in the county is only partly due to war conditions. Yet one does not wish to leave leadership entirely in the hands of those too old or too tired or too unassertive to move on. Over the years, we have learned to identify more accurately those with potential leadership ability and roots in the community deep enough to suggest permanence. The worker in a rural area needs a divining rod for this purpose!

We learned that basic to any program of helping individuals or communities to help themselves is the individual's sense of his own importance in the scheme of things. Once he *believes in himself,* he accepts responsibility for the community and is ready to contribute to the common welfare.

Familiarity with methods of procedure is perhaps second in importance. Nobody wants to "make a fool of himself" by trying to do something he does not know how to do. "It doesn't suit," was an answer often given when someone refused to accept a job that needed to be done.

Such an answer, our experience proved, seldom meant indifference to one's job in a democracy. It could usually be interpreted to mean: "My goodness! I don't know how to do what you are asking me to do and I'd be scared to death to try!" *Teach people how* (to conduct a meeting, to organize a committee, to lead discussion, to direct a recreation program) *and they are willing to work.*

Before Christmas in 1945, we are told, someone in Stanardsville wished "the Ogdens would get the chorus together to sing carols." Someone else echoed the wish but then had a second thought: "Why, they're busy with a hundred things, why should we sit here and wait for them to come to get us together? We can get together if we want to." They did get together and had lusty community sings all by themselves.

There has been a definite increase in self-reliance in Greene County. There has also been a strengthening of the belief that people must do things for themselves and of willingness to try things rather than to brush off each new idea with the remark, "It won't work." This willingness to try things is not yet strong enough to be termed an "experimental state of mind" as in the Jordan Area. But it is a start in that direction.

CHAPTER 9

Consultants in Community Affairs (Louisa County)

The approach of Special Projects in Louisa County was deliberately planned by the director and the staff. It was not predetermined in relation to an already existing program as in Nansemond, nor was it allowed to evolve in the course of events as in Greene. It was clearly indicated in the conversations with officials, professional workers, and citizens of the county before the decision was made to choose Louisa as one of the three experimental areas.

The county was an old one justly proud of its fine heritage. The sense of *noblesse oblige* on the part of leading citizens was something which could be appealed to in relation both to helping their own county and to sharing their experience with others. In all early conversations, the experimental nature of the Special Projects was explained together with the desire to discover techniques that might be broadly applied. The most general reaction was, "If we can help the University in this undertaking, we shall be happy to oblige."

At the same time, it was apparent from the earliest conversations that there were some leading citizens who were willing to face the fact that their county could be improved in some respects by carefully planned change, even though it had been a good one since the days when Jefferson, Madison, and Monroe attended school there. A few of these same citizens seemed willing to face problems and to accept their responsibilities for finding solutions.

The setting up of a citizens' council was in the minds of the staff from the beginning. Yet the council did not become a reality until February, 1943. This was twenty months after the informal visits of staff members to the county had begun and thirteen months after the first formal meeting of citizens and staff to consider the county's needs and plan ways to meet them.

Preliminary Calls and Conversations

During the summer and fall of 1941, the director of the Extension Division and members of the staff made numerous

calls in the county. Twenty-seven of these are recorded. At
first the question discussed was whether Louisa should be
selected as one of the three experimental counties. Reactions
of those consulted were, in general, polite rather than enthusiastic. The following memorandum on a visit is typical:

> Mr. Zehmer and Mr. Finley spent Tuesday, July 1, in Louisa
> County. Conferences concerning the proposed experiment were held
> with Mr. D. B. Webb, superintendent of schools; Mr. J. J. James and
> Mrs. Ellis, Farm Security Administration representatives; Mr. L. A.
> Keller, clerk of the court; and Mr. W. Earle Crank, commonwealth's
> attorney for Louisa.
> All of those seen approved the experiment and expressed the hope
> that we would select Louisa as a county in which to work. They said
> they would cooperate.

Such an expression of willingness to cooperate, however,
did not always settle the matter. One of the persons mentioned
in this memorandum had interpreted "study of county problems" to mean a survey. When a staff member called on him
a little later he said he had been thinking about it and he did
not want to have anything to do with another survey. There
had already been too many of them. They got people all stirred
up and then nothing happened. The interest of the Special
Projects in a study-for-action program rather than a survey
was again explained. But his apprehension persisted for several
months after the group meetings had been started.

Difficulties that would be met in the county came out in
these early conversations. One prominent citizen assured Mr.
Finley that "Louisa is a tough county to deal with. Citizens
are pretty independent. Professional workers do not have as
much influence as they do in other counties."

Comments of professional workers bore this out. Their
feelings ranged from frustration to bitterness, with a few
saying they received "fair cooperation." In general, it was observed that those representing "outside agencies"—especially
those sponsored by the federal government—found most cause
for complaint about lack of cooperation in the county.

Even those citizens and officials most willing to cooperate
did not suggest that the job would be an easy one. The same
man who intimated that it would be "tough" was asked whether
we "would get the best results from work in Louisa or Flu-

vanna." His opinion was that the "ultimate results would probably be about the same, but that in Louisa it would take about twice as long and be twice as hard."

Planning Procedure

After the question of *whether* we should work in Louisa had been thoroughly discussed in preliminary visits, the subject of each call became *how* and *what*. Problems that should be attacked were enumerated. Criticisms of previous or present methods of attack by various agencies were frequent and sometimes assumed the proportions of a tirade. Yet constructive suggestions as to *how* were few. Members of the staff began early in the fall to suggest a meeting of citizens to consider a plan of attack. There was no opposition but little enthusiasm. No one had any inclination to take the initiative. It was not until December that a plan was made, and even then, it will be noted, there was some insistence from the Extension Division:

> *Memo on Trip to Louisa, December 2, 1941*
>
> Mr. and Mrs. Ogden and Mr. Zehmer went to Louisa to confer with Superintendent Webb, Mr. Keller, Dr. Daniel, and Mr. Fisher with reference to next steps. Messrs. Keller and Fisher and Dr. Daniel agreed with us that an informal conference of a small group to consider some of the major problems and methods of attack might be the next step in the program. For various reasons, it was felt that it would be better to hold this conference after the Christmas holidays than before. There was fairly general agreement that the following persons should be invited. . . . . It was assumed that those with whom we conferred today would attend.
>
> The question of who should call this first meeting was raised but no definite decision was reached. It was suggested that Dr. Daniel call the meeting, but he demurred saying he would prefer that the Extension Division call it.

And the Extension Division finally did call the meeting for January 14, 1942, thus, perhaps, admitting that it had "lost the first round." The staff had done six months of spadework conferring with citizens who agreed to the importance of the program. Yet they had inspired no one to the point of being willing to take the initiative in inviting a group of fellow citizens to meet to consider their county. There was comfort in the historical fact that it has sometimes been necessary to lose battles in order to win wars. Subsequent events have indicated that this first defeat in Louisa County might be so classified.

The First Citizens' Meeting

Eighteen local persons and four members of the Extension staff attended the meeting. The director of the Extension Division presided and stated briefly his purpose in calling the meeting. His statement is summed up in the minutes as follows:

At a time when everyone is interested in defense, it is appropriate to ask what we want to defend, and we find the answer in one word: democracy. Although the project of which this meeting is a part goes back two or three years, it is primarily concerned with the defense of democracy, particularly in smaller and larger rural neighborhoods, in towns and counties as units. The interests of the Extension Division in this problem though practical are broad. They are concerned with certain questions to which trustworthy and intelligent answers can be found only by rural people who experience and live with rural problems.

Some questions facing us as citizens in a democracy are these:

1. Has authority and responsibility concerning the really important things in life been taken too largely out of the hands of rural people?

2. If so, what can and should be done about it?

    (a) What can rural people do themselves, on their own, to take a more active and effective part in solving their their problems?

    (b) How can we bring about more wholehearted and effective cooperation between local, county, state, and federal officers and agencies?

3. What, in the opinion of rural people, are the really important problems (economic, health, educational, recreational, social, religious) facing people living in rural and small-town communities?

4. Can we find through discussion and cooperative effort, perhaps through some trial and error methods, a more satisfactory solution to these problems?

The Extension Division staff has no formula for finding the answers to these questions. After conferring with citizens in a number of counties and other interested persons in various agencies, we decided to ask citizens of three counties to work with us in trying to find answers to the questions we are considering with reference to rural life. The three counties are Greene, Nansemond, and Louisa.

The one suggestion we make is that immediate procedure might be to continue to get together informally, as we are doing tonight, for discussion of some of the problems confronting Louisa County. Though it cannot give the answers, the Extension Division does offer its time and cooperation, the services of its staff, and help in securing cooperation of experts in various fields. We hope that you will help us tackle this job of finding answers to these questions as they relate to Louisa County. We can then seek ways of sharing the results of our cooperative efforts with other communities. They may have far-reaching implications.

Following these remarks, Mr. Zehmer invited comments from the group. Discussion was free and pointed. It was later summarized and distributed to those who had attended the meeting and to others invited but not present. The summary follows:

Discussion by the group brought out the opinions that counties had, perhaps, made as great progress as urban areas in finding solutions to problems; that Louisa had made definite progress in some areas, such as schools and agriculture, but had not been as aggressive as it might in attacking other problems, and that, as a result, outside agencies had taken on responsibilities that could possibly be better handled locally; that the soil conservation service was in some cases giving very practical help in demonstration plantings, in marking wood lots for proper cutting, and in running fire lanes, but that no way had been found of arousing the public to the importance of such a program or of disseminating the information to the people most in need of it.

Some specific problems suggested as needing more thoughtful attention included: rapid depletion of Louisa County's timber resources with special attention to arousing a feeling of concern on the part of the public, and to making more adequate use of opportunities afforded by such agencies as the Soil Conservation Service; increasing responsibility assumed by the state and federal governments in local affairs such as welfare, roads, and schools; indifference of the public concerning such matters, and the relation of this indifference to the greater centralization that now exists; need for planning medical care and hospitalization for rural people.

It was agreed that there could be value in informal meetings to analyze the county's problems, to seek practical solutions, and to work out better ways of making full use of available resources. Real value would, however, result only if discussions were definitely related to doing something to improve conditions. Experts can advise, it was pointed out, but progress takes place only when people are enough interested to make practical application of the information to their own local situations.

As a result of this agreement, the group accepted Mr. Zehmer's suggestion that these meetings be continued and set February 4 for the next one. A committee was named to plan questions to be attacked first, and to suggest additional persons who should be invited to the meetings.

The Committee Takes Hold—or Does It?

The committee named to make plans for the next meeting took hold with a will. It called a meeting for January 28. It invited members of the Extension staff to attend. The chairman of the committee presided and guided discussion. Members of the committee had many suggestions to offer. Staff members

were merely consultants. It was an enthusiastic meeting characterized in the minutes as "highly succesful, with no difficulty
at all in getting the committee down to work." Excellent plans
were made. The staff felt that initiative was now in local
hands where it belonged. They were doomed to disappointment.

Again the responsibility for calling the meeting of the
citizens' committee was placed on the Extension Division. This
time it was at least possible to include in the notice the names
of the local planning group. Two notices were sent out by the
director of the Extension Division as follows:

1. *To those who had attended the January 14 meeting*

The special committee consisting of Messrs. Keller, Crank, Quisenberry, and Dr. Daniel met Wednesday afternoon, January 28, and
took the following action concerning which they asked me to inform
you:

(1) Decided that the next meeting of the general committee will
be held in the Louisa County court house next Wednesday evening,
February 4, commencing at 7:30.

(2) Approved the minutes of the meeting held on January 14 and
requested me to send copies of these minutes to each person in attendance at the former meeting. A copy of these minutes is enclosed
with this report.

(3) Agreed unanimously that each person attending the first
meeting of the group be given the privilege of inviting one or more
citizens of Louisa County to accompany him to the meeting on February 4.

(4) Suggested the names of some fifteen others to be especially
invited to attend the next general meeting.

(5) Tentatively agreed on some of the more pressing problems
in Louisa County which might be considered at greater length at the
meeting on February 4.

I join with the committee in expressing the hope that you can be
with us next Wednesday.

2. *To those whose names had been suggested by the planning committee*

There was held in Louisa Wednesday evening, January 11, an
informal meeting between representatives of the University of Virginia and citizens of Louisa County to consider very tentatively some
problems affecting Louisa County. At the end of the meeting it was
generally agreed that it would be desirable to continue the discussions,
and a committee consisting of Messrs. L. A. Keller, Jr., W. Earle Crank,
J. H. Quisenberry, and Dr. H. S. Daniel was appointed to make plans
for the next meeting. This committee met at Louisa Wednesday afternoon, January 28, and among other things decided to call the next
general meeting in the Louisa court house Wednesday evening, February 4, commencing at 7:30.

This committee requested me, as acting chairman, to extend to you an invitation to attend this next meeting, and in the meantime to send you a copy of the minutes of the meeting held on January 14. A copy of these minutes is enclosed herewith.

I join with the planning committee in expressing the hope that you will meet with us next Wednesday evening, February 4, at 7:30.

In response to some thirty-five letters, eighteen persons came to this second meeting. Of these, ten had attended the first meeting. Excerpts from the minutes indicate the direction of thinking:

. . . . . it had been suggested in the meeting of the planning committee that this group might be asked to list those problems of the county in which they were most interested and then select those which need immediate attention. The planning committee urged that those be selected which are non-controversial and in which reasonable progress can be expected. Otherwise this group might become divided or discouraged before having had time to become a working unit.

Following this general discussion, five subjects were selected to be investigated by special committees and to be reported back by these committees to the group as a whole. These were forestry, soil improvement, nutrition, health, and recreation. The planning committee was asked to appoint special committees in these areas of interest. To help it in this task each person attending the meeting was asked to check and return a postal card, given out at that time, indicating his special interests.

Time and subject of the next meeting were left to the planning committee.

Committees Are Organized

At a meeting of the planning committee the next week, the chairman announced that only eight persons had returned cards indicating interest in subjects selected for investigation. He was, nevertheless, sure that interest was more general and proceeded to appoint committee chairmen for forestry, soil improvement, and nutrition. In the appointment of a recreation committee chairman, according to the minutes, "procedure was less clear" as a result of unfortunate experience in the past. Further investigation was thought advisable by the committee. The steps taken and their results are discussed later.

Other committee chairmen were to be notified of their appointments and asked to meet with the planning committee to select members for their committees and plan procedure. It was at this time that the question of the relation of professional workers in the county to the citizens' committee was raised.

The results of the discussion set the policy which has been adhered to ever since both in committees and, after its organization, in the council itself. It is recorded in the minutes as follows: "The consensus of opinion seemed to be that there should be no rigid ruling, and that they might serve in varied capacities (as chairmen, committee members, or consultants) according to their interests and abilities." Of the committee chairmen appointed at that meeting, three were laymen and one a professional worker.

At the second meeting of the citizens' group, it had been suggested that the committees to be appointed by the planning committee "investigate and report back" to the larger group. The minutes of the February 10 meeting of the planning committee conclude with the statement:

Of the committees that could be ready to report within a month, nutrition and forestry seemed the most likely. Since it was thought that interest in forestry would be more general, this was decided on as the subject for the next meeting of the larger group which will probably be called for the date already tentatively set, March 4. The planning committee will proceed with plans and notify the Extension Division of the date of the next meeting.

That last sentence is typical of the slight intimations of progress toward local autonomy with which the staff had to be content during the early months of the program.

How One Committee Went to Work

On February 26, the forestry committee met with five members present. They became so interested in the matter under discussion that they listed sixteen questions on the answers to which they would base their report to the larger group. The questions follow:

What per cent of the income of Louisa County comes from timber or timber products and industries?

What is the comparative cost of cutting and milling timber when the stumpage is between six inches and eight inches, in comparison with the cost of cutting and milling timber of larger stumpage?

Has the county the authority to pass legislation placing a minimum on the size of timber that can be cut for commercial purposes?

Do pulp and paper mills tend to encourage the cutting of very small timber?

In view of the fact that there are no pulp or paper mills in Louisa, is the practical problem one of regulating the practices of sawmills?

Will it be possible and practical to get the sawmills operating in Louisa County to agree not to cut timber below a certain stumpage?

In reporting the sales from forest products on selected tracts, will it be possible to estimate the increase in sales that might have come as a result of better marketing practices?

How much faster is timber being marketed in Louisa than it is growing?

What is the rate of production (growth) per acre in Louisa County? Can this rate of growth be stated in terms of cords or feet of lumber per acre?

What is the best method for determining the ratio of growth to that of timber cut in Louisa?

Will it be possible to select a few farms or tracts of land in Louisa on which records have been kept, and to show how often and in what amount sales of timber have been made?

Is it true that the less valuable types of pine are being produced much more rapidly than the more valuable types?

Can practical steps be taken to produce more generally the better types of pine in Louisa?

Will not the officers associated with the lumberyards in Louisa be the most effective people in bringing about better forestry and marketing practices?

What group will the committee have especially in mind in its general educational program: landowners, mill operators, or future farmers?

At this same meeting the committee agreed that its long range program could be summarized in the following questions:

1. What facts do we need to know?

2. What specific things can we do to improve forestry practices and the marketing of forest products in Louisa?

3. What steps should be taken to realize our objectives?

As the committee went to work finding answers to their sixteen questions, it became obvious that they had set themselves so big a job they would be unable to complete it by the date set for the meeting. At their request this meeting was postponed while the planning committee turned its attention to a mass meeting on recreation discussed later. This need for postponement was in no sense an admission of failure to meet a deadline. It was rather evidence that serious research on a local problem was going forward and that genuine interest had been stirred.

The forestry committee was ready with an excellent report six weeks later covering the questions listed. At the committee's request, the Extension Division had invited someone from the state forester's office to be present to help with the discussion. Attendance of thirty-six, the largest up to that time, indicated general interest in the subject. There was enthusiastic discussion with almost everyone present participating. The discussion reflected genuine concern for more careful planning in relation to Louisa's timber resources. Before the meeting adjourned, three subjects were selected by the group and referred back to the committee for further investigation. This time the committee was asked to bring in specific recommendations on: (1) steps leading to control of fires in Louisa, (2) practical methods of reforestation, and (3) most advantageous cutting practices from point of view of husbanding Louisa's timber resources.

The committee went back to work with renewed enthusiasm. Its meeting on May 4 resulted in several practical plans that were put into action. The minutes reflect the purposefulness of the group not only in the practical nature of the plans but also in the specific assignments of jobs to people:

Forestry Committee Meeting, May 4, 1942

1. *Distribution of Literature on Forest Fires*

   Dr. Daniel reported that he had been in communication with Mr. Dean of the state forester's office in Charlottesville and had obtained a large supply of bulletins, pamphlets, and posters on forestry for distribution in Louisa. The committee's first problem was to consider a plan for the best distribution of these materials. It was decided that certain of the materials should go into each home in Louisa; others should be placed in each school in the county; while certain posters and placards should be posted in each store in the county and in other buildings and centers. Dr. Daniel reported that he had arranged for Miss Motley, the home demonstration agent, to distribute the literature that was to go to each home while she was gathering some data for other bureaus. Mr. Loving agreed to distribute posters and other materials in the white schools of the county and to arrange, if possible, for the materials in the Negro schools to be distributed by the Negro school supervisor. Mr. Pendleton was to distribute the posters for the stores in the Cuckoo, Jackson, and Mineral districts. Dr. Daniel would distribute these materials in the Green Springs district, while Mr. Crank would attend to the Louisa district. Mr. Purcell was to distribute certain leaflets to mill operators, especially the leaflets on "Forest Fire Control" and "Keep Fires Out."

2. *School Poster Contest*

   The question of a school poster contest was next considered, and the committee voted unanimously to sponsor such a contest provided it met with the approval of the superintendent of schools and the school board. Mr. Loving was asked to present the matter at the next meeting of the board.

It was agreed that, if approved, there would be four contests: one for the consolidated white grade schools, one for the consolidated Negro grade schools, one for the white high school, and a fourth for the Negro high school. A first and second prize would be offered in each such school, and there would be a first and second county prize for high school students and elementary school students.

Mr. Crank was asked to raise the money, and it was suggested that the prizes consist of cash money or Defense Savings Stamps.

Mr. Zehmer was asked to select a committee of judges consisting of one representative from the state forester's office, one from the University School of Fine Arts, and one layman from the University or Charlottesville.

3. *Centers for Local Meetings.*

The committee was of the opinion that meetings in other centers in the county should be held—at least at Buckner and at Apple Grove. Mr. Pendleton was asked to assume responsibility for discussing the proposed meetings with citizens in these communities. Mr. Zehmer was asked to see Mr. Dean and find out if and when he would be available for talks in Apple Grove and Buckner, and to report to Mr. Pendleton.

The use of motion pictures in connection with further meetings was considered, and it was recommended that the pictures be used as an experiment. The idea of taking and showing pictures of devastated areas in Louisa was heartily approved. The committee recommended that, if possible, pictures be taken of devastated young forests and of older forests, and, if possible, of some fires in progress.

4. *Report on Cause and Damage of Each Fire*

Consideration was given to a suggestion that a committee be appointed to discover the cause and to estimate the damage of each fire, and then to report both to the Louisa people and to the committee on forestry. Rather than to appoint such a special committee, it was agreed that the suggestion would be referred to Mr. Powell and Mr. Dean, with the request that they report such facts following each forest fire in Louisa to the editor of the *Central Virginian.*

5. *Instruction on Fire-Fighting Methods*

Dr. Daniel and Mr. Crank stated that while they did not mean to be critical, they observed during the recent fire-fighting in Louisa the lack of thorough knowledge of how to fight fires and of coordination and cooperation among fire-fighters, both officials and volunteers. Mr. Zehmer was asked to discuss this question with Mr. Dean and to suggest that a short course on fire-fighting methods be offered in Louisa.

At the next general meeting, the forestry committee again reported. Because fires had been the worst in many years, it was natural that steps for their control should receive special attention. Recommendations were made, discussed enthusiastically, approved, and later carried out in excellent fashion.

Someone suggested, however, that the problems of reforestation and selective cutting had also been referred to the committee for recommendations. At this point an influential lumberman categorically stated that, barring fires, trees would reseed themselves; that, even when there had been a fire, loosening the earth with a harrow was all that was necessary if a seed pine were within a mile; and that God did not need man's help in such matters. This was in direct contradiction to facts reported by the committee and the representative of the state forester's office. It was so stated, however, as to effectively end discussion. The matter has never been reopened for general consideration, though the forestry committee has continued to be active. Of course one cannot be positive in relating cause and effect. Usually reasons for a change in course are not simple, and they probably are not in this case. It is, by no means, the only instance of abrupt termination after enthusiastic exploration of a problem in the history of this council and similar groups elsewhere.

The recommendations with reference to fire-fighting and control were carried out, including neighborhood meetings, a course in fire-fighting methods by the state forester, the contest in the schools with winning essays printed in the *Central Virginian,* and a publicity campaign which reached the entire county and resulted in the development of the tailor-made bulletins described in chapter 14. With reference to other objectives of this committee, interest persists on the part of individuals. Some work has been done in collecting information from local and state sources. The wartime emergency needs for wood may have influenced the delay in pursuing these objectives. The work of the committee, however, undoubtedly has influenced the state forester's office in offering special services to Louisa County.

Progress Slow but Not Steady

This detailed account of how one committee went to work may serve as an example of what has proved to be the strongest unit of the Louisa County program—the special interest group. Space does not permit a complete reporting of deliberations and activities of the various committees working with the Extension staff preceding the formal organization of the council. Yet the apparent zeal of the one described should not give a false impression of rapid and easy progress. One must remember the time and patience required in doing the spadework of calling on individuals preceding the group meeting in January, 1942, and in laying the foundations in special interest groups between January, 1942, and February, 1943, when the council was formed.

Throughout the remainder of the winter and the spring of 1942, the Extension Division continued to call monthly meetings of the citizens' group with the advice and consent of the planning committee. Though size of meetings increased steadily, the makeup of the group changed with each meeting. Eight or ten persons attended regularly—some to give enthusiastic cooperation; others apparently to see that nothing untoward was done. More than forty participated, but for the majority, attendance was a most irregular affair.

Between these monthly meetings there were always at least one meeting of the planning committee and one or more meetings of committees in special interest fields such as forestry. From three to five members of the Extension Division staff attended all these as well as the meetings of the larger group. Also, the Extension Division continued to send out notices of meetings, to keep minutes, and to remind the chairman of the planning committee or special interest group that a meeting should be held.

Yet when the subcommittees or the larger group met, there seemed to be developing progressively more interest and desire for doing something concrete about problems. This fact made the staff feel that though they had underestimated the time it would take for the groups to become self-starting and self-directing, there was little real basis for discouragement.

The Staff Demonstrates Possibilities

Activities of the busy summer of 1942 (see calendar, page 158) preceded the formation of the council. Although they grew out of discussions of the planning committee, they were carried out by the staff and were, in a sense, a demonstration of the type of programs they felt might be helpful in the county.

These activities were in two areas—nutrition education and recreation. Both programs were reported when the citizens' group resumed meetings in October. Reports and results are summarized below.

Nutrition Education Experiment[1]

Miss Motley invited us to meet with a group planning county Red Cross nutrition classes, on Saturday morning, May 9, 1942. Most of the discussion at this meeting was concerned with setting up regular Red Cross classes to be taught by home economics graduates within the county.

There was, however, some discussion of parts of the county that needed a more elementary kind of nutrition program. These included Dabney, Holly Grove, the sulphur mines area near Mineral, and Bells Crossroads. It seemed as if the Extension Division might be able to make a contribution in developing techniques for reaching these groups and presenting materials to them simply and pictorially. We offered to work with Miss Motley on such a program after her Red Cross classes were under way.

At this meeting we had described an intensive program of nutrition movies we were planning for Greene County. Miss Crawford, a home economics teacher who was present, asked whether we could show some of these pictures at the high school on Monday, May 18. (On that date Mr. Ogden and Mr. Cheney showed "Food Makes a Difference." The entire high school attended.)

Miss Blanche Harrison, the colored home demonstration agent, was also present at Miss Motley's meeting. She said she had already organized some very elementary classes in nutrition with her groups and asked whether we could show pictures at the regular meeting of her Bells Crossroads club on June 12. This meeting led to the scheduling of nutrition and live-at-home pictures for colored groups throughout the county as follows:

Group	Date	Attendance
Bells Crossroads	6/12/42	95
Red Cross Class	6/15/42	23
Rising Sun	7/14/42	125
Mt. Gilliam (Community Club)	7/15/42	150
Mt. Gilliam Church	7/23/42	95
Louisa Courthouse (Baptist Church)	7/25/42	167
Louisa Courthouse (Colored School)	7/29/42	300
Ferncliff (Galilee Church)	7/29/42	67
Buckner (Watch Tower Church)	7/30/42	51

Number of meetings............ 9

Total attendance ....1,073 (one-fifth total Negro population)

[1]Reports of Meetings and Minutes of the Louisa County Citizens' Council.

We offer for consideration of the planning committee the following comments on this experiment:

The use of motion pictures seems to be an easy and effective way of reaching large numbers of the colored people.

In every group there was great interest in the "lessons" of the nutrition pictures and excellent follow-up work by the home demonstration agent in helping her people apply the lessons to their own living.

In two communities we showed the pictures Mr. Cheney had taken of last spring's fires in Louisa. Interest in this subject was as keen as in nutrition. It seems as if a good job of educating Louisa's colored population for care in preventing and controlling fires could be done through movies of which there are several good ones available.

A similarly eager response to "The Negro Farmer," a picture prepared by the United States Department of Agriculture, suggests the possibility of doing much more in this field also.

In the minutes of the meeting at which this report was given, discussion is summarized as follows:

Dr. Daniel expressed appreciation for the activities of the Extension Division in presenting motion pictures on nutrition, stating that "the colored groups had shown more thirst for knowledge than the white people." Mr. Zehmer pointed out that members of the staff had taken no initiative in promoting this program but that all meetings with colored groups had been at their request and that other groups were asking for further programs. He raised the question: "How can we reach the white people, arousing their desire to see these pictures?" Mrs. Ogden reported that some of these colored groups are in isolated communities where other attractions are not found and that there are probably equally isolated white communities where people would come to see educational pictures simply for the recreational value. The results of the use of pictures during the past summer indicates that people will come to see movies in spite of their educational value. Mr. Zehmer presented a brief report of the film resources available from the Extension Division.

There was no follow-up on the part of the planning or nutrition committee so far as this program was concerned. The staff continued to cooperate with the Negro home demonstration agent, whenever she requested their help, until she left the county the next year.

Report on Recreation Program—October, 1942[2]

Background

At a meeting of a planning committee in the court house, February 10, 1942, committee chairmen were appointed for forestry, soil, nutrition, and tuberculosis—four of the subjects selected at a previous meeting for further study and planning. The fifth subject—recreation—

[2]Ibid.

presented some difficulties, and procedure here seemed less clear than in the other fields of interest.

Problems that had arisen in the past out of disagreements about use of the community hall and some unfortunate experiences with WPA leadership were cited by the committee. The desirability of giving youth a voice in the matter was recognized. It was suggested that there be a meeting to which young people should be urged to come and at which they would be given opportunity to express their opinions. The Boy Scouts, Girl Scouts, 4-H clubs, and Girls Friendly Society were mentioned as organizations whose leaders should be consulted. The planning committee agreed to confer with these leaders and make plans for calling a meeting of young people leaving the program plans entirely in the hands of the Extension staff. The date for the meeting was tentatively set for early April.

The April Meeting

After the Extension Division had been informed that April 8 was a good date for a meeting of young people and that the auditorium of the grade school was available, arrangements were completed with the Lane High School choir of Charlottesville to give a concert. Twenty-seven young people and their choir director were taken to Louisa in cars provided by the Extension Division and staff members.

The concert was attended by approximately eighty-five persons, about equally divided between youth and interested adults. Following the musical program, Mr. Zehmer led a discussion on recreation in Louisa. Everyone agreed that a countywide program would be difficult if not impossible, and that local community centers offered the best approach.

In response to the chairman's suggestion, a motion was carried that *the meeting go on record as being vitally interested in the problems of recreation in Louisa County and that they recommend to the informal "steering committee" already set up in the county the appointment of a special committee on recreation to discuss problems and possible approaches to solutions.*

Summer Program

Since interest had been expressed at the April 8 meeting in holding "community sings," and since the services of the director of the Lane choir could be secured during the summer vacation, Mr. Zehmer discussed this possibility with several members of the steering committee referred to above. It was decided to experiment with programs in two communities—Mineral and Louisa Courthouse.

1. *The Mineral Program*—After several weeks of discussion with Mineral citizens, the first meeting was held on the evening of July 23 at the school with an attendance of eighteen. At this meeting three persons volunteered to work on publicity through the churches and the local paper. As a result of their good work, subsequent meetings about doubled in attendance.

Seven meetings were held on consecutive Thursday nights. The group continued to be enthusiastic and was eager to go on with the program. The opening of school made it impossible for the director to continue her work in the county, and it has not yet been possible to replace her. Plans are now under way for combining the Mineral program with some music in the high school.

2. *Louisa Courthouse*—Several persons had said there was great need for a recreation program for young people in Louisa. There was, however, no specific request as there had been in Mineral. Since a trip was to be made to Mineral each Thursday, it was decided to try a late afternoon meeting in Louisa on the same day.

Mr. Webb agreed to let the auditorium of the grade school be used for the meetings. Staff members procured a list of about sixty young people who, in the opinion of adults consulted, would be interested in getting together. Cards were sent inviting them to come for singing and for discussion of a broader recreation program.

At the same time, letters were sent out to ten adults who had expressed interest in working on the recreation problem.

Twelve young people attended the first meeting and one adult not among those who had previously expressed interest. The group was less ready for singing than the Mineral group, but in the discussion all but one said they would like to meet for singing once a week and would also like other recreational activities but were vague as to what these should be. Several who were there said they would bring their friends next time.

This group continued to meet as long as the one at Mineral. It started one week later and had six meetings in all. It grew to twenty-seven, all but seven of whom were girls. With few exceptions the group was made up of high school students and there seemed little reason for continuing it after the opening of school.

Several conclusions could be drawn from the experiment in singing in Louisa Courthouse: (1) the meeting place was unsuitable because of size, formality of seating arrangement, and noise and dust from repairs that were being made; (2) afternoon was, in the opinion of those who came, a less desirable time for meeting than later in the evening; (3) singing, though mildly enjoyed by the majority who attended, was not a primary recreational interest; (4) the fact that twenty-seven persisted in spite of these difficulties is evidence of a need on the part of young people for something to do or some place to go; (5) a broader program in more congenial surroundings would meet a very real need which the present world situation has made even more vital to the welfare of a community if it is to fill the gap left by decreased transportation to places of amusement and at the same time meet its responsbility in the physical fitness and civilian morale programs.

Discussion of this report on the recreation program, as summarized in the October 27 minutes, follows:

It was pointed out by the chairman that there is as yet no recreation committee and that what has been done in this field thus far has been done by members of the staff of the Extension Division. In reply to a question from the chairman, Mr. Gill said that perhaps the recreation problem is not so acute in winter when schools are in session offering an opportunity for sociability to young people from all parts of the county. Dr. Daniel stated that he felt it might be very difficult to carry on a good recreation program during the school year when young people are not only busy with studies during the day but also have the opportunity of attending movies six nights a week. It was observed that movies are available only in Louisa Courthouse. There was also some discussion of the quality of motion pictures shown commercially and the desirability of these as the sole form of recreation for young people. Mr. Webb pointed out the fact that there are also church groups, Boy Scouts, Girl Scouts, and other organizations, but admitted that these were largely restricted to the area immediately surrounding Louisa Courthouse.

Mr. Ogden urged that the consideration of recreation should not be confined to children or young people still in school. He pointed out that the Mineral group which is anxious to resume the weekly sings contains a larger proportion of out-of-school persons than of school age. He further urged that the older group is the one that needs special consideration. The Louisa group, he said, which had met six times during the summer for singing was largely a school group and that may be one reason that there has been less interest in resuming activities here. Mr. Porter Wright stated that the fact that this group had met in the afternoon had made it impossible for a number of older persons who are deeply interested, to attend meetings. There is, he said, considerable interest on the part of this group in starting something again.

Mr. Gill reported that the high school is eager to cooperate with the Mineral group in establishing a music program. He hoped that until a full-time teacher could be engaged, Mr. Ogden would be willing to help them out. The plan they have in mind, he said, is to provide singing for school groups during one afternoon each week and for the adult group in Mineral on the same evening.

The chairman suggested that a recreation committee be appointed by the new committee chairman to be elected and that the recreation committee explore needs throughout the county and bring in recommendations.

In connection with this report, as with the preceding, there was no further committee action. Requests to the staff continued to come *from communities* for help in planning recreation activities. Singing at the high school for both young people and adults continued throughout the winter. The school board made an attempt (unsuccessful at the time and not repeated later) to find a music teacher for the high school. One community set up a good recreation program with local leadership following a workshop conducted, at their request, by the staff. Later the new home demonstration agent attacked the problem for Louisa Courthouse. *The council has, to date, not considered the matter again nor has it appointed a recreation committee.*

Organization and Program of Citizens' Council

At the October meeting at which the above reports were given, the director of the Extension Division suggested the "need for a simple statement of purpose and scope of this general committee." Committees were appointed to draw up a constitution and to nominate officers for the organization.

The constitution committee had several long meetings at which thoughtful attention was given to the organization in relation to its role in the county. A staff member attended only one of these meetings at the invitation of the group after its deliberations were well along toward crystallization. The resulting constitution was an authentic local product.

In February, 1943, with the adoption of this constitution and the election of officers, the Louisa County Citizens' Council began its official existence. It differed little from the informal citizens' group which had been meeting for the thirteen months preceding.

The organization is a simple one. Membership is open to all white citizens. The members elect officers annually. These officers with two members at large, also elected, constitute the executive committee. Standing and special committees are appointed by the president with the advice of the executive committee.

The purpose of the council as stated in the constitution is to aid and promote community development in Louisa County by:

1. Informing the people of Louisa County of community needs and assets as shown by studies made from time to time under the supervision of this council.
2. Planning with the people of Louisa County ways and means of meeting community needs and taking full advantage of the assets available in every community of Louisa County.
3. Coordinating all the agencies and organizations working in Louisa County so that their efforts will be of maximum benefit to the county as a whole.

The constitution provides for quarterly meetings of the council. Between council meetings, research and activities are carried on in various fields of interest. Three of these committees and their programs predate the constitution and were made official after its adoption. They are forestry, nutrition, and soil conservation. Later a committee on publications was appointed to prepare and finance the bulletins described in chapter 14. Still later, one was appointed on economics and post-war planning. This has, as might be expected, become one of the most important. Since timber and soil are the two basic resources of the county, committees dealing with those subjects have naturally assumed great importance. Their programs, like that of the council as a whole, have evolved slowly—with forestry following the direction already indicated.

The soil conservation committee has cooperated with the county agent and the Thomas Jefferson Soil Conservation District of which Louisa County is a part. Its "educational program" has been largely informal, consisting of talk about good soil practices wherever two or three were gathered together.

In June, 1944, this committee prepared and distributed a *Bulletin* on soil which attracted widespread attention locally and throughout the country. Out of this grew the program in cooperation with the Thomas Jefferson Soil Conservation District described in chapter 12.

It was also this committee that first brought to the council the idea of getting behind a plan for a locker refrigeration plant for the county. The subject had come up for discussion by chance at one of the committee's meetings. There had been considerable enthusiasm. The committee chairman suggested to the council that one issue of the *Bulletin* carry a supplement asking about interest in such a plant. Discussion revealed that people needed to know much more about locker plants before they could express an opinion for or against. A special committee was appointed to prepare an entire *Bulletin* on the subject.

In December, 1943, the publication carried to every family in the county such elementary information as what a frozen food locker plant is for, what it is like, what it costs the locker holder. Thirteen months later a second *Bulletin* on the subject announced the opening of the plant which had been built with the cooperation of the Southern States Cooperative. *The council does not claim credit for the locker plant. It played an important part, however, both in initiating the idea and in informing the people.*

The same is true of the health center which is now being considered. The need for public health and medical care programs in the county was stressed at the very first meeting. It has continued to come up in one form or another at almost every meeting. A health committee, however, was never appointed. It was when the committee on postwar planning began to put together the ideas of a living war memorial and a health center that things really began to happen. The idea had the backing of every organization, of the home demonstration clubs, of the local doctors, and of all citizens who knew about it. The chairman of the postwar planning committee was asked to head up a fact-finding committee on health centers. A council meeting in March, 1945, was devoted to the subject. The *Bulletin* carried the facts about local health needs to every family in the county. A campaign to raise funds is now in progress under the direction of a county committee especially appointed for the purpose. Again the council is helping with the job of "telling the people."

Has the Council Taken Over?

Had the program terminated at the end of two years in accordance with the original plan, the council would have been in existence about three months. It is altogether likely it would not have survived the withdrawal of the staff from the county. Even yet, it is doubtful whether it can be regarded as ready to assume initiative in directing its own destiny.

In attempting to analyze recently the role of the council in the county, several members agreed that (1) it had met a real need in a noteworthy way in getting information to all families in the county by means of the Louisa County Citizens' Council *Bulletin;* (2) it had served the county well in initiating several programs and stimulating the interest of other groups in their execution; (3) it had served less well as a coordinating agency. With respect to this last purpose, these members thought that, whereas the council felt that it should perform the function of a coordinator, it had not yet been accepted in this role by the various organizations and agencies in the county. The explanation, they pointed out, probably was to be found in the fact that no effort had been made by the council to interpret this need to other groups or to get official representation from each on the council. Next steps, they suggested, should be planning ways of making the idea of coordination of county activities a two-way process. Yet there was strong feeling expressed that the jobs of initiating programs and stimulating organizations and individuals to action were perhaps even more important.

Members of the staff concur in this opinion. Real progress has been made by the council in initiating projects and facilitating their execution. Its role as a coordinating agency, however, is practically nil except as individual members of various groups who attend council meetings may see the needs of a total program more clearly and help their organizations do a better planning job. Evidence that agencies and organizations do not think of the council as a clearinghouse is to be found in the fact that they continue to turn to the staff of the Special Projects rather than to the council for help and advice in planning their programs in relation to county needs. The same is true of neighborhoods and communities within the county. They have developed a feeling of *rapport* with the staff and the Extension Division rather than with the local citizens' council.

The explanation of progress in the first two areas probably lies in the fact that the interest groups or committees have really gone to work. When they have become excited about plans, members have naturally turned to the agencies or organizations through which they have been accustomed to work, and action has resulted. Even the method of letting all the people know about what is being considered by way of soil improvement, or locker plant, or nutrition, or medical center grew out of the work of the forestry committee. Their interest in circularizing the county with just the right material on forest fires resulted in the *Bulletin*. The interest of the Special Projects in exploring the effectiveness of this method, and the fact that not only staff time but also project money were available during its early days undoubtedly account for its development. When financing the *Bulletin* became a local responsibility, the Council strengthened the committees and probably weakened its position as a coordinating agency by deciding that each committee wishing to prepare and distribute an issue of the

Bulletin should find an organization or agency to sponsor and finance it.

It was only after repeated insistence by the staff that a publications committee was appointed to carry responsibility. It, like other committees, has really worked. The staff was likewise insistent that the name of the council and local sponsoring group appear on each copy of the *Bulletin* rather than the name of the University of Virginia Extension Division. This policy was adhered to even when it was discovered that it meant the refusal of second-class mailing privileges and an increased cost of $16 for mailing each issue. Seeing the name of the Louisa County Citizens' Council prominently displayed on the masthead of each *Bulletin* has impressed on organizations and individuals the *fact of a council.* Having a working committee to turn to has made procedure clear and easy. The last two issues of the *Bulletin* were prepared at joint meetings of the publications committee and committees of the interested organizations *at the request of the organization in each instance.* Members of the staff were invited to help in preparation and editing *by the publications committee of the council* rather than by the groups immediately concerned with publicizing the particular projects. This may be interpreted as evidence that organizations are beginning to turn to the council and hence coordination is beginning to be a two-way process. Clarification of procedures by the council in other matters where coordination is desirable might be the most helpful next step.

What Went into the Program

At the meeting at which the constitution was adopted and officers elected, Dr. Daniel, the chairman, expressed his conviction that there was a real job to be done by such a council. He ended his remarks with the statement: *"But what comes out of it depends on what we put into it."* This was repeating from the point of view of the citizen the conviction on which the Special Projects had been established: only by learning to help themselves could communities really be helped. Some attempt has been made to indicate what has come out of the program to date so far as the county is concerned. What went into it might well be analyzed from the point of view of both the county and Special Projects.

In the first place the citizens consulted gave their cooperation to the University in exploring effective methods of improving communities. They gave generously of their time and
experience both in conversations and later in group meetings
even at the stage when they were convinced that they were
"helping the University" rather than accepting a service that
might have great value for them and their community.

For four years, nine of the eighteen persons who attended
the first group meeting have continued to attend all meetings
and to work with committees. Many of them have served as
officers and committee chairmen. One of them, Dr. H. S. Daniel,
accepted the chairmanship of the first planning or steering committee in 1942 and has continued as leader of the council in
spite of the heavy demands made on his time and energy by
his professional duties and his many activities in relation to
wartime needs. Other citizens have come to meetings at the
invitation of the original group and some have accepted responsibility for committee work. Now more than eighty names
are included on the council list. These few citizens have been
willing to consider problems and try to do something about
them. They have accepted their responsibilities as well as their
privileges. They have been willing to shake off their own
lethargy and to take steps to disturb the inertia of those who
seem only too willing to let well enough alone.

Though deeply interested in Louisa County development,
the Special Projects had as its primary purpose learning about
techniques that might prove effective in similar areas throughout the Southeast. Hence, because of the intention to apply
widely what was learned locally, considerable effort and time
of staff members went into developing a program in Louisa
County.

Preceding the first group meeting, the director and members of the staff had made at least 50 trips into the county to
consult with leading citizens, officials, and professional workers.
During the next 13 months, preceding the formal setting up of
the council, they had made an additional 87 trips, each involving 3 to 5 members of the staff for attendance at committee
meetings, showing movies at neighborhood meetings, and conducting the recreation program reported above. An additional

staff member had been engaged for the summer to help with the community sings. She made 8 trips to the county for 14 group meetings. She was accompanied each time by at least 1 member of the regular staff.

Any accurate estimate of man hours or miles of travel would be impossible. There is no doubt that it would be more of both than any agency not engaged in an experimental program could hope to devote to the development of any one community. Up to February, 1943, there had been a total of at least 137 trips. Minimum mileage on any one trip was 60, if the destination were Louisa Courthouse, more if it were Mineral or some other community. Minimum hours consumed were 4. Not infrequently, especially during the summer of 1942, as many as 3 staff members were in the county (or on the way to and from it) from noon till midnight. Records were established, according to the date book of that summer, on 3 days when the starting time was 8:30 a. m. and returning time was frequently as late as 1:30 a. m. This was during the movie program when the show could not begin until about 9:30 or 10 o'clock. *Hence at a minimum estimate more than 1,500 man hours and more than 10,000 miles of travel had been expended by members of the staff prior to the meeting of February, 1943, when the council became a fact.*

In 1943, '44 and '45, there was a total of about 40 trips each year into the county. Most of these were made for the purpose of meeting with specific groups *at the request of the groups.* Few of the trips during these years involved more than 2 staff members. So the total amount of time devoted to Louisa County decreased even more than is indicated in the decrease in number of trips. Yet interest and activities continued. During the first two years, the staff had offered their services rather insistently. During the next two, they cooperated when invited. But it had taken a full two years to become what they had meant to be at the outset—merely consultants in community affairs.

Some Things We Have Learned

What the Special Projects learned in the experimental areas about specific techniques is recorded in the next section. A few general observations growing out of the approach in Louisa might be given here.

Working first with the recognized leaders and trying to build a program from the top down or from the center out presents some real problems. Recognized leaders are inevitably busy with many things. Though they may—and frequently do—have the social vision and attitudes necessary for good community building, they are likely not to have the time for attention to detail required for sound planning. Moreover the continued acceptance of responsibility by these recognized leaders may effectively block the discovery and development of potential leadership among those who have more time at their disposal.

Studying local needs in relation to local resources and planning a program of action based on such study affords an excellent opportunity for discovering and developing hitherto unsuspected natural leaders. Committee work in Louisa brought this out. The method was adapted and process expedited later in local workshops.

Having a program center in the county seat inevitably results in reluctance to cooperate on the part of outlying and rival communities. Sooner or later a community education job must be done. Even after four years, most communities in the county do not identify themselves with the council. They are coming in as study of community needs and resources brings a realization that they are identified with those of the wider community which is the county. *If a county council does not develop from community programs, it must find a way later of identifying itself with them.*

Staff members perhaps erred on the side of caution in giving guidance to the program. They did not wish to determine its direction in line with their special interests. At the first meeting, citizens were assured the Extension Division had no preconceived answers, that it had not even a *special formula for finding promptly and accurately the answers to community problems.* The staff felt this sincerely. Yet, in retrospect, it seems that the group they were responsible for bringing together was, at times, permitted to flounder unnecessarily. Certainly there should have been no attempt on the part of the staff of Special Projects to impose ideas or to determine policy. They might, however, have facilitated matters *by of-*

*fering the results of their experience and tested techniques
more insistently at times.*

The progress made by the publications committee is an example of this having been done effectively. On the other hand,
the failure of the very good beginnings in the movie program
for Negroes and the recreation activities to carry over may
prove that insistence is not an effective method. These were
staff demonstrations. They were successful in themselves. They
did not become a part of the local pattern. Perhaps programs
must be allowed to evolve, muddling through the difficult spots
in order to acquire strength.

But the evolving process is time consuming. It had not gone
far in the two-year period set for this experiment. At the end
of that period, the council was only three months old and was
by no means a self-assured or self-reliant infant. The *Bulletin,*
which has been one of the most effective jobs locally and one
of the most far-reaching for other programs, did not start until
the very end of that period. Like the council, it was not yet
ready to walk alone. The time required for establishing a program by this method had been greatly underestimated.

Yet those who worked in Louisa County learned from the
experience there how to proceed more rapidly in other communities. Study of local resources in relation to local needs, and
planning a program of action as a result of this study were basic
in the Louisa County approach. Offering the services of the
Extension Division to citizens in working out such a program
was the method of implementing this approach. The same approach and method were later applied in other communities
through the extension of local workshops. Here a plan of intensive study over a period of weeks provided a foundation which
in Louisa County had to develop from trial and error procedures.

Undoubtedly the staff learned much from its experimental
approach. Likewise the county has obviously made some strides
forward. It can honestly be said that the Extension Division
of the University of Virginia and the Louisa County Citizens'
Council feel the experiment to be mutually beneficial. They
look forward to a long period of cooperative endeavor.

CHAPTER 10

Guiding By Remote Control (Nansemond)

Procedures in Nansemond County differed markedly from those of the other experimental counties—Greene and Louisa. First, the program was planned for only the Holy Neck District rather than for the county as a whole. Second, the community had surveyed itself and was searching for next steps when the Special Projects came into the picture. Third, one agency—the consolidated high school—was the focal point in the program. Fourth, direct leadership came from a professional worker within the community; the director of the Extension Division and the staff of the Special Projects served as consultants to him giving advice and going into the county only when invited.

What Had Been Done

What had happened before the Special Projects came into the picture can be summarized briefly. In 1939, the Holland Ruritan Club faced the fact that it had no significant objective. Although its general interest was in improving community life, it had no plans other than to cooperate in whatever worthy cause chance brought to its attention. To be sure, it had a creditable record of achievement; but, since Holland was the birthplace of Ruritan, the local club felt that it had a special responsibility to continue its work as a pioneer.

About the same time that the club began taking stock of things it might do, the Holland Consolidated High School was considering a plan for getting to know its community better in order to serve it in the most constructive way. Through its superintendent, principal, and teachers, the school had recognized the desirability of a community survey. The means of conducting such a survey presented a problem, but there was agreement as to the fact that participation of many persons other than the school group was essential.

The principal of the high school was also a member of the Ruritan Club. The desire of the club for a specific objective and the need of the school for getting a definite job done afforded a happy coincidence. The idea of a survey was presented to the club by the principal. Club members felt that they would gain much from discovering the most significant community problems and attempting to determine effective ways of dealing with them. They agreed, therefore, to cooperate fully with the school group in planning and conducting the survey and in analyzing the data secured. A committee was appointed and the cooperative venture was begun.

Before the necessary questionnaire was devised, the committee discussed and selected the matters of community interest about which more facts should be gathered. These included health, education, housing, occupations, recreation, out-of-school youth, and other factors affecting community life. The questionnaire, in tentative form, was discussed by all participating adults and by the pupils in high school social studies classes. In its final form it was designed to give information not otherwise available which would round out the community picture.

There followed a house-to-house canvass conducted by the pupils as a social studies project with each pupil working in his home locality. The thoroughness with which they did this part of the job shows in statistical results: Of the 603 white residences in the community, 565, or 93 per cent, were visited, and a total of 1,219 questionnaires was completed in an area having 1,934 as its total white population over seventeen years of age.

Specific tasks were assigned also to adults. They collected data already compiled by such local agencies as the commissioner of revenue, county treasurer, agricultural agent, county school board, health department, department of public welfare, and juvenile court. Their data covered valuation of real and personal property, merchants' capital, tax collections and expenditures, names of farm owners and tenants, number of farm laborers, value and acreage of crops, and similar subjects which might be considered as indices of the social and economic status of the community.

Once collected, all data was tabulated and organized in such a manner as to have meaning for the ordinary person to whom statistics are but so many figures. In this, too, the services of both high school pupils and adults were used. Pupils worked under careful supervision and with continuous guidance from principal and teachers. The final summary was primarily the work of the high school principal. The findings (see chapter 7) indicated need for programs of adult education and recreation, for planning for public health and sanitation, for devising ways of making the community generally more attractive to its citizens.

After all Ruritan Club members had had opportunity to discuss the findings, a committee was appointed to consider in detail their significance in terms of community service and planning. Other organizations became interested. The Holland Women's Club and the Home Demonstration Club each devoted a meeting to a discussion of the survey. The interest thus aroused in such groups and their desire to "do something about it" pointed to the need for wider understanding and collective action.

A brief summary of the "highlights" was mimeographed and distributed to the presidents of all organizations, to the pastors of churches in the community, and to other interested persons. Some organizations, including churches, used the study in formulating new objectives or strengthening old ones. Several pastors used materials from the survey in their sermons to draw attention to social needs and citizen responsibilities. In the 1940-41 program of classes for adults at the high school, one in community problems, led by the principal, studied the findings of the survey. An effort had been made to have this class include representation from every agency and organization in the community, but it was felt at the end of the session that many more persons should be included if a plan of action involving community participation were to be made. The twenty-five persons who had attended thought the class should continue the following year.

The Special Projects Enter

It was at this point in the history of the program that the high school principal and the Extension Division joined forces. Someone in the State Ruritan who had been consulted about the Special Projects had suggested that clubs in other communities could well follow the example of Holland if they had some guidance. Mr. Savage, the principal of the Holland High School and the member of the local Ruritan Club who had initiated the survey in his community, could give such guidance. The Special Projects might employ him during the summer vacation for this purpose. It was with this idea in mind that the director of Extension first discussed the matter with Mr. Savage. In the course of their discussions, it became apparent that there was much still to be done in the Holy Neck District to move the program along from survey to action. After considerable discussion of the matter with members of the advisory committee of the Special Projects and with President Newcomb, Mr. Zehmer decided to make the Holy Neck District of Nansemond County one of the three experimental areas and to ask the principal to give direction to the program there.

Mr. Savage was employed during the summer months in 1941 and 1942 by the Special Projects. He was asked to do two things: (1) to work with Ruritan leaders in other communities that might be interested in programs similar to the one initiated in Holland; and (2) to work with those groups in his own community that might plan procedures for taking action on some of the problems uncovered by the survey. Before the end of the first summer, it was evident that more could be accomplished by concentrating on the second of these objectives. In fact, from the beginning emphasis had been given to meeting the needs of the Holy Neck District first. In a letter of June 26, 1941, confirming his official appointment, Mr. Zehmer wrote Mr. Savage: "President Newcomb's chief interest is in your work in the Holland community. You will naturally be thinking about next steps to take there. We will be interested in knowing what you think these should be."

The need for a continued experimental approach and for keeping sensitive to techniques that might have wider application were stressed in that same letter:[1]

"While we don't wish to let any grass grow under our feet, neither do we wish to rush pell mell into any of this work. Pro-

---

[1]Letter from George Zehmer to William R. Savage, June 25, 1941.

cedure at first must be slow and cautious. We are not expecting you to deliver to us at the end of the summer any communities all organized and functioning. The purpose is rather to lay a firm background on broad educational lines for more thorough-going community study, cooperation, and planning later. Remember that we are experimenting, trying to discover more effective ways for helping individuals and communities to help themselves. Hence the necessity for caution and open-mindedness, and the willingness to try new approaches if the original ones fail.

"Don't feel that you have to write long letters or submit reports of great length. On the other hand, do not hesitate to call or write when you think we may be of assistance or when you want our advice or approval of a course of action. From time to time, we shall be asking you to come to the University for conferences."

Remote Control Indicated

That last paragraph indicated the "remote control" pattern set up and adhered to in relation to this phase of the experimental program. Four times that summer Mr. Savage came to Charlottesville to confer with the director and members of the staff. They exchanged ideas and, as work got under way in other counties, experiences. Mr. Cheney, the librarian, supplied materials on community organization from the pamphlet files he was assembling. Staff members did not visit the community during that first summer. Weekly letters were exchanged. Progress and procedure can best be indicated by excerpts from those letters. (References to conferences with Ruritan officials in other communities which were frequent in the early letters are omitted since we are concerned here with the program in the Holy Neck District.)

Mr. Savage to Mr. Zehmer, June 27, 1941:

Thank you for your letter of June 25 and the helpful suggestions contained therein. . . . . It is my sincere hope that my time will be spent effectively in these summer months. There is much to do here.

This week, I have been taking time to get oriented in other areas and have done little that is tangible in Holland. We are planning, however, a group conference one evening next week for the purpose of evaluating what we have done and planning where to go now. I shall report later.

Mr. Savage to Mr. Zehmer, July 4, 1941:

During the past week I have spent considerable time here in the Holland community. I have met with two small groups, one from our Ruritan Club and one from other organizations. I have also had very satisfactory conversations with many representatives of various groups and organizations in the community. We have agreed, tentatively, to have a conference on the evening of July 17 with those people now being selected, who, we hope, will constitute our community council.

I shall plan, according to your suggestion, to come to Charlottesville July 8, to confer with you and the staff. I can then tell you in more detail of some of the ideas and suggestions that have come from our conferences and discussions thus far.

Mr. Savage to Mr. Zehmer, July 14, 1941:

The past week has provided experiences that have been, in some respects, the most satisfying yet. I have talked with individuals not previously contacted who live in various parts of the Holy Neck District, and I feel more than ever that we have a fine nucleus for work in community planning. There seems to be a high degree of interest in the possibilities of cooperative planning, as well as an expressed willingness to participate. This, perhaps, sounds like mere repetition of former comments, but I feel more and more that a firm understanding is being built up by means of these individual conversations and that the foundation is being laid for more consistent development later.

I plan to talk with a small group from our Ruritan Club this evening relative to the proposed meeting on July 17 of people from the various organizations and others not identified with organizations. Out of that meeting, as I have indicated before, we hope may come the formation of a community council. When this happens, I think we shall have the framework for group attention to community needs.

Mr. Savage to Mr. Zehmer, July 24, 1941:

We have selected a committee of three (two men and one woman) to consider further and to determine the most suit-

able manner to form our community council. I plan to meet
with this group again soon. We believe that our council may be
a reality before very long. Mr. White [superintendent of
schools] has been immensely helpful with suggestions, and I
feel that he is going to be of great help later. His position and
interest in the community make his assistance very important
to the future development of the program.

I shall plan to attend the staff conference, about which you
have written, with Mr. Pomeroy, Director of the State Planning
Board on July 30. I shall arrive in Charlottesville the preceding
day since I need to see Mr. Cheney relative to some material
that might be helpful at our present stage of planning here.

Mr. Savage to Mr. Zehmer, August 9, 1941:

Last evening we had a small committee meeting to discuss
further the matter of policy in forming our community council.
It goes slowly!

I am enclosing a brief synopsis of our experiences here
preceding this summer. Members of the staff have asked me for
this background to give them a better grasp of the whole picture. I shall be glad to discuss these notes with them when I
come to Charlottesville next week.

Mr. Savage to Mr. Zehmer, August 27, 1941:

(*Note:* This letter is a summary and final report of the
first two months' work in cooperation with Special Projects. It
is, therefore, quoted in full.)

I believe that it can be said that our major emphasis in
the Holland Community for the summer months has been to set
the stage for the formation of the community council. As has
been stated before, a community survey had been made; some
attempt had been made to make the findings easily understood
through reports of the study to organizations, by discussions
of the findings in adult education classes, by summarizing the
data for ministers and others; some progress had been made in
the dissemination of the facts as revealed from the study before the summer months.

During these past weeks several meetings or conferences
have been held with small groups, never larger than twenty-
five, sometimes only four or five persons, for the purpose of

discussing what our next steps might be in the Holland community and what some of the benefits might be if a council were formed. I have had numerous conversations or conferences with many persons representing a cross section of the community. In many cases I have talked with these people two, three, or four times, relative to possibilities for the future, with the idea in mind that it is most desirable that as many of the people as possible have a clear concept of what some of our desirable goals might be. The results of these meetings and conferences seem to indicate very definitely that there is now a real desire to form a community council. They seem to believe that such a group is necessary now to give direction to future activities. A committee of three persons was selected from one of our recent meetings to work with the Ruritan committee on social needs to make plans for the organization of the council and to consider some of the related problems. As the matter now stands, a council is being formed formally sponsored by the Ruritan group. We hope to have it well enough organized by the latter part of September to hold our first meeting and then to set up our plans for the future in the light of developments thus far.

On Wednesday night, August 20, I had an interesting conference with Mr. W. W. Eure, field agent for the Extension Division at V. P. I. We talked at length as to how our program and such activities as are sponsored by V. P. I. through its agencies and county agriculture committee can be integrated or correlated without duplication or working at cross purposes. It was his belief that such a council as we contemplate is the very thing that is needed to enable people in the community to consider problems that affect *any* and *all* phases of living. Mr. Eure suggested that it might be a fine idea to have a conference early in September with you, Mr. Pomeroy, Mr. Hummel, Mr. Eure, and others in attendance who might consider together what further cooperation or supplementation of effort is possible. I would like to have your opinion on this matter.

At Wakefield [a neighboring town] some progress has been made in formulating a plan for their study. They have spent some profitable time in thinking about the kind and extent of information they need. They are now working, through committees who are *definitely interested,* on the questionnaires or study forms they will use. The Wakefield Ruritan members who are undertaking this work are calling on other people for assistance and suggestions in planning their course and will enlist their aid in the actual study.

While statistical data here are somewhat meaningless, it should be stated, perhaps, that I have made four trips to Boykins this summer and have talked to individuals and groups; there have been seven trips to Wakefield for conferences, and there will be more conferences with that group as they request assistance in the fall or winter; there was one trip to Blacksburg to talk on the general theme of community planning to the conference of vocational agriculture teachers in the state; one trip was made to Louisa County to talk to a group assembled for a countywide farmers' picnic with their families.

While it would be presumptuous to attempt to comment relative to the effectiveness of my work, I can state quite sincerely that my experiences have been highly interesting and very pleasant. Surely I have been helped immensely, if no one else has! I have seen a very definite but gradual modification and growth take place in my own thinking as I have read, thought, and talked with people this summer regarding the possibilities of agencies, institutions, and groups "teaming up together" to create better conditions for all that affects living.

It is my hope that our community council will have organized and set up a plan of action or objectives before the fall or early winter. I shall, of course, give whatever time and thought I can to that end.

Mr. Zehmer to Mr. Savage, August 30, 1941:

I am pleased with what you have accomplished this summer. Several movements which, I think, may be of far-reaching significance are now under way.

I observe with particular interest the suggestions [in your letter] of a conference in the Holland community during September with representatives of other agencies. I approve of the suggestion. Since I am planning to get away for a short vacation, I should prefer that the meeting be held in late September or early October. Let me hear more about this at your convenience.

It has been a pleasure to work with you this summer, and I look forward to continuing associations in this community work in which we are mutually interested and concerned.

Mr. Zehmer to Mr. Savage, October 23, 1941:

I remember my promise not to bother you too much during the regular session about the community work in Holland. I hope that you will not think that I am presuming too much then to ask if you are going ahead with the organization of a community council. If you are, I should be interested in hearing about the plans and in knowing if those of us in Charlottesville can be of any assistance.

Mr. and Mrs. Ogden have been pretty active in Greene and Louisa Counties. There are some very favorable developments in Greene. Progress in Louisa is slow and has not yet gone far enough to enable us to draw any conclusions.

Mr. Savage to Mr. Zehmer, October 25, 1941:

"Time marches on!" Sometimes I wish it didn't "march" quite so rapidly. Then, perhaps, I could find time I need for a variety of activities—all of which seem to require so much attention.

This is by way of saying that I have been planning to write long before this and comment on developments here— *or lack of them.* There have, of course, been so many requirements on my time and thinking—conferences on the course of study, the problems of new teachers, the extracurricular program, the adult education committee, the Ruritan committee, the guidance program, the community council committees—I have procrastinated with respect to some of these things, I fear. Nevertheless, through this maze of activities, functions, obligations, and responsibilities, I can see emerging more and more clearly a unified plan of attack on these problems of ours by *all* groups. Others, too, insist they are aware of order in viewpoint and action slowly developing. Now, that's progress, I think.

Our community council, on its own, has done little yet, but, indirectly, it has furnished the impetus in thinking for significant developments. The planning committee of the council has held two meetings since September. Plans are being completed

now to call the entire council together for its first meeting as
an officially organized body within a week or ten days.

Following are some recent developments in our community
life that seem to indicate progress:

1. A board of health for the entire community is being
formed. Membership on this board will include the health
committees of the Ruritan Club, the PTA, the Women's Club,
the home demonstration clubs; representatives from one church
where such a committee exists; and representatives from the
county health department. The organizations have already
voted to merge these committees on welfare and health into
one planning board. Our community health and welfare work
can be much more effective under that kind of broad, cooperative planning.

2. The Women's Club, the Ruritan Club, and the Holland
school officials are in process of forming a committee with
representatives from each of these groups to formulate plans
for cooperative action in financing adequately their activities.
It is felt that where each organization sets up its budget independently of the other and plans its money-raising activities,
there is frequently conflict in planning and purposes that works
a hardship on all groups. You would have been thrilled to wit-
ness the growth in understanding at a conference a few days
ago where the school's extracurricular budget was discussed,
the Ruritan plans were presented, and the Women's Club financial needs were recognized. Several commented to the effect
that never before had they understood so well the total problem.

The two developments mentioned above resulted from discussion and suggestions from the members of our planning committee of the council. There are other objectives that I will
discuss with you when they have emerged a little further from
the nebulous stage. Something has been said about a joint
project in play production—perhaps a commnuity pageant with
children and adults participating. Would it be possible for us to
borrow Mr. and Mrs. Ogden if that plan should materialize?

I regret that I simply have not had time to plan for the
conference with Mr. Pomeroy, Mr. Hummel, you, and some

others, that I spoke to you about. It may be that I will be able to work out the details for such a conference soon. I hope so.

Conversations are so much more satisfactory than letter writing. I want very much, therefore, to come to Charlottesville sometime soon and talk with all of you if it should be convenient.

Mr. Zehmer to Mr. Savage, October 29, 1941:

Your report is certainly an interesting, stimulating, and encouraging one. Some of us here will plan to drive down to Holland sometime soon when we can see you. In the meantime, I don't wish our proposed trip to interfere with your trip here. We should be very glad to see you at any time that suits your convenience. In this connection, you will be interested to know that Dr. R. B. House, dean of administration at the University of North Carolina, is coming here for a staff conference on Monday evening, November 10. Dr. House is in the field of sociology and is particularly interested in rural life. He is going to talk with us informally about these problems as he sees them and understands them. While Monday might be a bad day for you, I believe you will enjoy Dr. House and profit by the discussion if you can attend.

Members of our staff will be here most of the day on the tenth, and we could confer with you on that day. I have to leave late that night for New York and so could not see you the next morning. If the tenth is not convenient, we could see you almost any other time that you suggest.

I am particularly interested in committees that you now have at work. Apparently they are very wisely proceeding slowly. It is our opinion here that such movements cannot be hurried along. In fact, I think you are going about as fast as you can and should in laying the groundwork for a council that will know how to function.

Mr. Zehmer to Mr. Savage, February 24, 1942:

I am enclosing copies of the minutes of some meetings that we have held in Louisa County. These may be of interest to you. As further copies are available, I shall send them on to you.

I wonder if I may ask how the community planning project is coming at Holland. In a recent staff conference here, we raised the question as to whether a visit from some of us might be helpful. If you have a 16mm motion picture projector, we might bring along and show some pictures dealing with community organization, cooperation, and planning.

Mr. Savage to Mr. Zehmer, March 12, 1942:

The information relative to meetings at Louisa was very much appreciated. I hope you will send me subsequent reports on the work there.

The work in community planning in Holland is going forward. However, *progress is slow.* One difficulty particularly evident now is the question of *how* to get at some of the things that we agree are in need of attention. Many of us have been pleased at the thinking and cooperation evidenced in setting up objectives and goals in our community, but it seems difficult to frame the most practical course of action.

The group of twenty-five or thirty who consider themselves members of our council have had only two meetings since October. I am enclosing a brief summary of the most recent, held last week. I believe that I can safely say that our people feel the need of planning for the solution of our local problems now more than ever before, even though the war has made unusual demands on people in this vicinity.

I believe I told you last fall that we have formed a community health and welfare board that can be thought of as an appendage of the community council. This group, made up of representatives of all organizations and agencies, has been going forward with plans. I am enclosing a copy of its objectives.

I sincerely regret that I have procrastinated in the matter of making definite arrangements for you and other members of the staff to visit us here and attend some of our community meetings. I know that you all could make a contribution to our work. We need particular help on how to plan wisely for recreation for youth and adults during the present period when transportation is becoming more of a problem. Please let me know whether you and other members of the staff can visit us early in April. We could arrange for you to meet with our community planning board, with the Ruritan Club, or with both.

I appreciated your comment regarding plans for next summer. I am very much interested in carrying on the work in a more effective manner. Time permits so much less planning and activity during the regular school session when there are so many demands.

Mr. Zehmer to Superintendent White, March 17, 1942:[2]

You will recall that I have discussed with you briefly on one or two occasions our experimental work in community organization and planning. You are familiar also with our cooperative work with Mr. Savage in this connection. As you also know, we have a new state superintendent of public instruction, and, although I have discussed our program with him briefly, I felt that it would be highly desirable to give him an opportunity to ask questions and to learn more about our objectives and our methods. Accordingly, I invited Mr. Lancaster some time ago to come and spend an evening with us at his first opportunity when our staff could sit around a table and discuss the project informally. He has set the date of Wednesday evening, March 25.

Our chief purpose is to give Mr. Lancaster an opportunity to question us on aims and procedures. We will be prepared to give a brief report on progress that we have made in the experimental centers of Greene and Louisa Counties. My hope is that you and Mr. Savage may join with us at this meeting and discuss any questions that are directed to the community work that has been done in Holland. This letter is to extend to you a hearty invitation to meet with us next Wednesday evening.

Mr. Zehmer to Mr. Savage, March 30, 1942:

Mr. and Mrs. Ogden and I have just finished discussing the proposed trip to Holland. The week of April 12 would be the best one for us to make the trip. We are tentatively reserving Thursday, the sixteenth. However, if some other day of that week would suit better, we can make a change.

We inferred from the minutes of your recent council meetings and from our informal talks with you that perhaps the

---

[2]The meeting referred to in this letter marks the beginning of the idea of the experiment with twelve-month employment of high school principals described in chapter 11.

problem of procedure is the one that is now giving you more difficulty than any other. It occurs to us, therefore, that we might be of most assistance to you and your council by discussing with you informally questions of procedure. However, if you have some other subject which you would prefer to discuss, please let us know and we will adjust our plans to your wishes.

We enjoyed so much having you with us last week. We are only sorry that Mr. White could not join you.

Mr. Savage to Mr. Zehmer, April 1, 1942:

Thursday, April 16, will be a very satisfactory date for your visit to Holland. I shall make plans to have our people get together at that time for a conference. You will hear from me again within a few days concerning the hour of the meeting. I hope that you and the Ogdens will arrive early enough in the day to enable you to see a little of our community. (*Note:* The program had been under way almost a year before this first visit of the staff to the Holland community.)

Memo from the Ogdens to Mr. Zehmer on First Visit of the Staff to Nansemond County Project:

The Ogdens and Mr. Cheney met with the Holland Community Council on Thursday afternoon, April 16, 1942, at the high school. Mr. Savage presided at the meeting. Other members present included Mrs. Butler and Mrs. Davidson, representing the Women's Club and the home demonstration clubs; Mr. Edwin Felton, chairman of the county agriculture committee; Dr. O'Neil, pastor of the Christian Congregational Church; Mr. Ragsdale, teacher of vocational agriculture; and Mr. Clark, social science teacher in the Holland High School.

At the suggestion of the chairman, the council proceeded with discussion of its regular business and we were asked to participate in the discussion at any point we wished. Two specific projects were under consideration: (1) the development of picnic grounds with fireplace and other necessary equipment on the school campus; and (2) the use of two acres of land belonging to the school for a community garden, the produce of which would be used for school lunches for children unable to provide their own. It was decided to proceed with both programs.

The picnic grounds are particularly important this year since it will be impossible to transport large groups to the lake at which picnics have usually been held. In connection with the discussion of this project, there was also some discussion of whether there was still need for a centralized program of community recreation or whether this program should give place to decentralized neighborhood activities. Leadership for both centralized and neighborhood programs presents a problem about which, apparently, there had been little thinking. The feeling of the group was that even with the difficulties of transportation there was need for a centralized program. Because it seemed so important to have people from the various communities in touch with each other, there was a reluctance on the part of those present to give up the idea of occasional central meetings until experience had proved that it was impracticable. It was felt, however, that the development of neighborhood programs might go on at the same time and that, possibly, leadership for neighborhoods might be developed through a centralized program.

Though no definite decision was arrived at concerning regular recreation activities, it was decided that this group might well attempt to have a community picnic sometime during the summer and that this picnic might be the starting point for a recreation program which should include a softball league, well supervised dances for young people at the high school, and community sings. The group asked that the Ogdens come to help them get such a program started.

Following the meeting, we had opportunity to talk with the persons who had attended. Afterward Mr. Savage drove with us through the area, helping us to get acquainted with the neighborhoods that are a part of the Holy Neck District. We spent some little time seeing Box Elder, where there is an abandoned elementary school in excellent condition that could very easily be made into a community center; Holy Neck, which already has a building for a community center which belongs to one of the churches but is used by the entire community for social programs; Buckhorn, which is the poorest community and presents the most difficult social problems of the entire area.

We were favorably impressed both by the Holland community and by those members of the council whom we met. The community certainly presents problems. None of them seems insurmountable. The council is well aware of the problems but needs a clear-cut idea as to *what should be done and how to do it. Members have dealt with generalizations and analysis until they have reached the point of diminishing returns. They now need a very definite program of action. They need help in planning and are ready for it.*

We found an intense interest in knowing what other communities are doing. Members of the council would benefit from trips to visit successful programs or from seminar or workshop programs which would get right down to doing something.

There is a strongly felt need for leadership for recreation and related activities. We should like to be able to cooperate with them in their community rally and in getting the recreation program under way but feel that they need more permanent help than we should be able to give with the time at our disposal.

Mr. Savage to Mr. Zehmer, April 17, 1942:

We certainly enjoyed having the Ogdens and Mr. Cheney at our small conference yesterday. They made suggestions that will be helpful, and I believe they are now in a position to make further suggestions in the future since they have a general picture of our situation. The group here yesterday *insists* that they return!

We all regretted very much that you were unable to come. I hope that it will be possible for you to get down here sometime soon.

(*Note*: Following the above memo and letter in the files there is voluminous correspondence representing an unsuccessful attempt on the part of Special Projects to find someone who could work with Mr. Savage in developing the recreation program during the coming summer. The war had taken everyone. So it was decided to try the experiment of developing local leadership. Results are described later.)

Mr. Zehmer to Mr. Savage, May 6, 1942:

I thought that you and members of the Holland community working on community problems might be interested in the recent minutes of a meeting of the committee on forestry in Louisa County. I think that the direct way in which the committee tackled the problem before them at this meeting is pretty suggestive of the way in which such committees may and can act.

We are showing a number of films on such subjects as forestry and nutrition in Greene and Louisa and they are attracting noteworthy attention. You might consider such pictures as a means of arousing interest and suggesting methods of procedure.

Mr. Zehmer to Mr. Savage, June 1, 1942:

With further reference to work this summer, I should like to see you at your earliest convenience following the closing of your school. Since I should like you to meet with members of the staff, also, I believe it would be better if you could come here for the conference. We could see you any day during the next two weeks except Monday, June 8.

Mr. Zehmer to Superintendent White, June 16, 1942:

You will recall that last year we engaged Mr. Savage for the summer months to help us in some experimental work in community planning. Mr. Savage was engaged with the understanding that he would give much of his time to the Holy Neck District, but that he would be available also to work in other communities, especially communities where Ruritan National had local chapters that were particularly interested in community projects. From our point of view, we were very pleased with the work done in the Holy Neck District. We were somewhat disappointed with the apparent results accomplished with Ruritan clubs.

For this summer we would like to engage Mr. Savage again, with the idea that he would devote practically all his time to work in his community. The arrangement would make it possible for him to follow through in some detail on certain undertakings which grow out of the notion that the school has certain community responsibilities beyond those of teaching children during the regular school year. Although, in a sense,

the experimental work in which we are engaged is separate
from and independent of the work of the school, there is another sense in which it is so closely related that I have some
hesitancy in continuing the relation suggested with Mr. Savage
without keeping you fully informed and getting your approval
of the plan adopted. I think Mr. Savage has similar feelings in
the matter. I would appreciate it, therefore, if you would let
me know if you approve this plan for employing Mr. Savage
this summer to give his time to the community work in Holy
Neck District.

Mr. Savage to Mr. Zehmer, July 3, 1942:

It is my opinion that we have made satisfactory progress
in getting our preliminary planning under way for our program of recreation in the Holland community. I am working
with the committees now that have been set up to guide and
assist the program for each age group. They are very cooperative and will, I believe, prove to be helpful in the development of the program we have in mind.

The Holland Women's Club has assisted with the selection
of these committees, and that organization is making plans to
help with the publicity and explanation of the purposes of our
program.

While we have already done some work with the young
people's group, our organized work will actually get under
way next week. So far I have spent considerable time with
people serving on these committees; in selecting time suitable
for each group; in planning activities that might be carried on;
and in analyzing the kind of assistance and material needed.
Mr. White, [superintendent of schools] has assured me that he
feels the school board members will be pleased to have us
make use of the campus and some of the equipment here at
school in developing our plans.

I have done some work with the neighborhood committees, set up by the AAA program in our district, in obtaining
definite data on our health and welfare problems. Since this
was one of the objectives set up by our community council in
the spring, it is felt that such information will be very helpful
in the work of the community health and welfare committee
in their action during the fall and winter. I hope to continue

this work during the mornings whenever time is available.

Observations on Developments

It was at this point that the program in the Holy Neck District reached the stage of "getting out of hand," which is both the hope and the despair of everyone who gives direction to a community program. The painstaking and the time-consuming conversations with individuals reported in the letters of the first summer were bearing fruit. The problem had ceased to be one of "getting something started;" it had become one of finding enough hours in the day to give guidance to the many activities "rarin' to go." Working with lay leaders rather than with a trained recreation person further complicated Mr. Savage's problem though he was convinced that in the long run it was sound procedure.

"I am so hopeful," he wrote (July 10, 1942), "that our activities here this summer will be something of a demonstration of how people *in any community* can work out a sound, wholesome recreation program for all ages and develop local leadership at the same time."

The letters of this second summer take on a new tone of enthusiastic busyness. By the same token, they become fewer and more hurried, with time available only for referring to activities rather than for giving play-by-play descriptions as had been possible the year before. Requests for materials are specific and those for help from other members of the staff are urgent.

It was during this same summer that activities in Greene and Louisa Counties likewise had reached a point of intensity that left little time for the staff to give to Nansemond.[3] In retrospect this seems unfortunate, for the program was in a crucial stage of its development. Two members of the staff spent four days in August visiting in the community, thus equipping themselves to do a better job as consultants but unable to render any tangible assistance. Their observations on progress of the community program may serve as a briefer and, at the same time, more complete summary than excerpts from letters.

---

[3]See calendar on page 158.

Memo by the Ogdens Following Visit to Holland,
August 3-7, 1942:

The community council in Holland has found the same
difficulty that other communities have faced in moving along
to the second phase—a program of action. Now the transfer
seems to have been made. The war may have given the necessary final push.

The problem of recreation noted in the survey as one of
the most serious became even more acute as a result of difficulties of transportation. Thrown completely upon its own
resources, the community saw and developed the possibilities
at its disposal. The school campus became a playground and
the school building itself was opened for dancing and other
indoor programs. The Women's Club has actively sponsored
the program. Equipment and refreshments for parties have
been made possible by appropriations from this organization,
the PTA, the Ruritan, some church groups, and interested individuals. Three days a week there have been planned activities supervised by the high school principal.

On Wednesdays about 150 adults have come together for
softball, tennis, croquet, badminton, and a community sing.
Tournaments in the various activities have added interest
and have stimulated use of the tennis courts and other facilities during the week as individuals or small groups have
come for practice. On Thursdays the younger children
have come for games, stories, and educational movies. The
last have been made possible by the gift of a projector by last
June's high school graduating class. All groups are enjoying
it for both recreational and educational purposes. Each Friday the teen-age youngsters have their special program. They
have enjoyed games and singing, but the Friday night dance
has proved their most popular activity. At first an adult committee took care of refreshments, but the young people volunteered to do the work themselves and have done a creditable
job.

On one Sunday evening each month the churches have
joined forces to hold a community vespers service in the
schoolyard. A master choir made up of the combined talent

of the various churches has made possible unusually fine music. Community singing has also been enjoyed on these occasions as at the Thursday night programs.

Holland has been particularly fortunate in finding that it had within its own community leadership for the various activities. The leaders and the people who have participated in this summer's program are looking forward to a community night at the school this winter and to a perhaps expanded program next summer. They are also discussing tentative plans for helping to build up neighborhood programs in some of the outlying communities from which people cannot come to a central place such as the consolidated school.

The other area in which the Holland Community Council is getting some real work done is health and welfare. The committee, again pushed by the Women's Club, is setting up a master file and offering to serve as a clearinghouse for all organizations and agencies interested in health and welfare work. This necessitates the continuous gathering of new data.

The council says modestly that there are many problems revealed by the survey that are as yet untouched. Nevertheless, a visit to Holland and the Holy Neck District surrounding it convinces one that the community has definitely entered the action phase of its program.

Mr. Savage to Mr. Zehmer, August 26, 1942:

It has been a busy summer but a pleasant one. People have continually pleased me with their interest and enthusiasm. We are convinced that any community can work out a very sound and practical recreation program with the lay leadership which almost certainly exists there.

Statistics mean very little in evaluating a community program, yet the simple table below does indicate something as to *quantity*.

	Number of Meetings	Aggregate Attendance	Average Attendance
Children's group	8	249	31
Young people's group	9	192	21
Adult group	7	995	142

Community vespers held on the school campus are not included in these figures. Nor are the numbers of small groups of two or four persons who were using the facilities continuously for tennis, croquet, and badminton. While the number of people who attended was not as high as had been hoped for, particularly for the young people's groups, it may be significant that those who came to early meetings were regular in attendance and that numbers in each group increased as the weeks passed.

Perhaps it is too early to appraise the quality of the program that has just come to a close. As time passes it will become more evident how effective such a program is in developing local leadership, building morale on the part of those who participate, and creating an interest in a variety of sports and games that will carry over.

It appeared significant, however, that there were several people in the community who were *eager to help* in carrying out a recreation program for all people. There were many more who were enthusiastic about possibilities and wanted to see the plan succeed. There is still definite need for further development of responsibility on the part of lay people for initiating and carrying through a program rather than merely helping with one for which someone else carries responsibility.

To meet the needs for social intercourse and recreation for more people, it will be necessary in the future to take into account inability of people [during the war period] to travel considerable distance for such meetings. The Holland school serves a ten-mile radius. Perhaps we should plan many meetings and activities on a neighborhood basis where people are within walking distance.

Plans have been discussed for taking some of the leaders developed this summer, and possibly some of the teachers from the high school, to outlying districts for community sings and movies. The movie projector has already played an important part in the community program. The county home demonstration agent has asked whether the school will cooperate with her clubs this fall in a program of educational films. This offers the school another opportunity to work with families in the district outside of Holland.

It is too early yet to state definitely what can or should be done during the winter and next summer in the field of recreation. The following things appear desirable and will be further considered by the council in making definite plans:

(1) One evening a week at school for adult recreation, including singing, dramatics, games, and movies.

(2) Similar programs for young people—possibly a "family night" plan could be arranged.

(3) Having local leaders work in neighborhood churches, halls, and schools to develop participation in singing, folk dancing, games, and movies.

It is my intention to write you from time to time during the fall and winter relative to our progress in the general area of planning and putting into effect such procedures as seem sound. We shall continue to need help and advice from you and the staff who have made many friends here who want to see them again.

Should you have suggestions, send them along. The staff is now better acquainted with the general situation since their visit this summer. We had time to move over the community and chat with many people. They were impressed with the well informed and sincere interest of you people in the whole problem of community betterment. We all look forward to working closely with you in the future.

Mr. Zehmer to Mr. Savage, August 28, 1942:

I am pleased with what you have accomplished. What you are doing may have far-reaching implications. I am not certain but that it points the way to a new policy of engaging principals of our high schools for twelve months with the understanding that the summer months, excepting a vacation period, shall be devoted largely to the problem of school-community relationships. I think that such a step might lead the way to a much richer life in Virginia.[4]

Shadows of Future Obstacles

A letter from Mr. Savage to a staff member about the same time contains foreshadowing of things to come that were

---

[4]This marks a second step toward the experiment with principals described in chapter 11.

to affect the future of the program seriously: "I am very much aware that school begins next week and that many woes begin with it. We have learned only yesterday of the resignation of two more teachers. You can realize what that involves with the present scarcity of teachers. With nine new teachers, I shall probably spend most of my time in teacher training!" He had not even guessed the worst, as is indicated in his next letter.

Mr. Savage to the Staff, November 19, 1942:

You are aware, I know, of the definite modifications we are making in public school education in terms of war needs. These matters have required much administrative attention. Added to that, the facts that I have no clerical assistance and have had to take on increased teaching duties, due to our inability to fill the place of one teacher who resigned, keep me exceedingly busy.

Sounds pitiful, doesn't it? It isn't though! I'm really thrilled to see a program in operation that seems to have a real purpose.

The plans for the fall and winter months which we discussed last summer for the community seem to be going forward in promising fashion. Our council is holding together through an executive committee. Our real work now, however, is through several neighborhood committees or councils. We have held planning sessions in two neighborhoods other than Holland. In each of these smaller communities (Box Elder and Bethlehem) we have planned to have family get-together nights. At these sessions there will be group meetings for men (mostly farmers), separate meetings for women, and a group for children. After these separate meetings there will be a general discussion on timely problems, followed by singing, games, and a movie. We hope to make these evening affairs about two hours long with about equal emphasis on adult education and recreation. We have tentatively planned for these sessions to be held one evening a month in each of these places. We may decide to meet more often after Christmas.

In the Bethlehem neighborhood the three-room school is just right for our needs. We held our first session there last week after our preliminary planning conferences, and it was great! About sixty people were present and you should have heard them help plan for subsequent meetings! We are in the planning stage now with the Box Elder people. They will use the Friends' meeting house. (You remember our visit with the Hares.) At the Holy Neck churchgrounds there is a hall that will be suitable for meetings if the people there care to plan with us. We haven't done much work there yet, but I believe they, too, will want some of these things.

Since transportation becomes more and more of a problem, we are beginning to see clearly that in the local neighborhoods we have an excellent opportunity to help people understand contemporary problems and learn how to work together for their solution. The recreational aspect of this approach is another point in its favor, I believe. We had two of our primary teachers helping some of the mothers and youngsters with games for the children at the Bethlehem meeting, and it was fun for all concerned.

Do you have any good films for such groups that are not available in the state film library? Let me know if you have such material.

Mrs. Savage and others are quite busy now getting ready to put on a radio program that will deal with the summer's activities in which the Women's Club was particularly active. (You will recall your avid discussion of such a program when you were in our home last summer.) It is built around various committees working on plans for recreation in a small community with a couple of brief skits taken from some of our recreation meetings. It is to be presented next Sunday afternoon over WLPM.

We still want to come to Charlottesville to talk with you and to visit the programs in Greene and Louisa. There just does not seem to be time enough to do all the things that should be done. Maybe we'll get to that later. In the meantime, we want you to come down here again.

Later when we have more definite ideas as to how effective our approach for meeting neighborhood needs is, I shall write you more about it.

Mr. Savage to Mr. Zehmer, February 24, 1943:

We have had twelve family night meetings so far at Bethlehem and Box Elder. Other meetings are being planned for Holy Neck and South Quay. These are all neighborhood centers (as the Ogdens will remember) that help make up the larger magisterial district served by the Holland school. At Bethlehem we use the elementary school for our meetings; at Box Elder we have used the Friends' church though many of the people attending are not members of that denomination. Our average attendance for both places has been slightly more than fifty thus far, with about equal representation among men, women, and children.

Procedures at all meetings have been planned around the general session for discussion, films, singing, and announcements, followed by smaller group conferences. The general meeting usually runs from forty-five minutes to an hour in length, and group sessions are about the same length. The films we have used have been mostly OWI and others sponsored by the State Board of Education through the A.V.P. plan. We have exercised care in choosing these films, and we have been immensely pleased with their effectiveness. For the group sessions we have had the aid of our agriculture and home economics teachers, county agent, home demonstration agent, farm leaders, and others.

The young people have furnished leaders to help with games, stunts, discussion and the like. Some of our teachers went at first to help, but we soon found that there was leadership already in the community. The teachers, however, have continued to go, for, they insist, it is an excellent way to understand the community better. Also it's downright fun, they say! We felt that we simply would not have time to hold these meetings in all the local neighborhoods this year since we have our regular meetings here at Holland still, but the people in Holy Neck and South Quay have asked for meetings of their own. We hope now to go to each of these places, for two meetings at least.

It was interesting to be in on the planning for these meetings. At each of the places a local council discussed the type of get-together that would be most practical and effective for that area. We have assured them that we want them to have the use of our equipment and personnel for as many meetings as they desire. These meetings will probably be temporarily discontinued during the spring planting season.

On two or three occasions the people who live in these neighborhoods removed from Holland have voiced the hope that they could have recreational meetings for all ages during the summer somewhat like those we had in Holland last summer. I am vey hopeful that we can work out plans that will meet these needs.

Mr. Zehmer to Mr. Savage, March 1, 1943:

I was very glad to have your letter of the twenty-fourth and the report on the community work now under way. I think the report is a very good and encouraging one. In this the Ogdens concur.

While I am not yet ready to make final commitments, I am hoping that you will be available this summer under the general plan of last summer. I am making plans to that end. It may be possible for us to try a somewhat similar program in several other high schools, working through the principals. We will know about that soon.

If we undertake such a program, we shall start off with a two- or three-week workshop. We will want you here for that undertaking so as to give the new principals an opportunity to profit by your experience.

Mr. Zehmer to Mr. Savage, March 5, 1943:

I know that you will be interested in learning that our requests for funds to conduct in several other high school communities the kind of experiment that you have been carrying on in the Holy Neck District have been granted. We will, therefore, now be able to make plans for this extended program.

As I indicated to you in my recent letter, we will want you to continue in Holland during the summer of 1943 anyway. We are all the more anxious for you to continue since we can extend the experiment to other communities.

Mr. Savage to Mr. Zehmer, March 11, 1943:

Indeed I am delighted to learn that funds have been made available for extending the kind of program that we are so interested in to other communities. It has been a dream of mine that educational leaders would sometimes see the wisdom of having their personnel use available resources throughout the year for community betterment. It certainly begins to look like the splendid pioneering of the Extension Division of the University is becoming significant.

A Program Expands Abroad—Declines at Home

As soon as principals were selected for the extended experiment with school-community programs, they were invited to a preliminary planning conference at the University. This was April, 1943. Mr. Savage attended and shared generously with others his experiences in the Holy Neck District. On this foundation, building was begun for school-community programs in other areas and for the first three-week summer workshop at the University.

Then the inevitable happened. As has been observed in connection with other experimental areas, disaster awaits the program which leans too heavily on a single professional worker. This is especially true when his job of earning a living is only indirectly related to the total community program. Also there is the strange paradox that the more capable the professional worker is, the more questionable becomes the procedure of placing chief responsibility on his shoulders. There are bound to be better jobs offered him, and he is bound to consider professional advancement in his specialized field. This may necessitate his withdrawal from the community program before it has become strong enough to continue through the mazes of problems and pressures without his guidance. He may carry the gospel to another community that may need it just as urgently. But there is, at best, a period of floundering and readjustment in the community he leaves and, at worst, complete collapse of the program there.

In the Holy Neck District, the worst did not happen when Mr. Savage left. The period of wavering and adjustment, however, was aggravated by the wartime emergency demands on lay leaders and on the principal who followed him.

This new principal was interested in continuing with the experimental program. He attended the three-week workshop at the University along with the other principals who were about to begin community programs. In pre-planning his community activities he was aware that his was an even more difficult job than theirs, for he must take up where someone else had left off, whereas they were starting "from scratch."

Following the workshop, he faced the problem of finding housing in a war-impacted area. It was almost time for school to open before this problem was solved. In the meantime, he had driven into the community as frequently as his gasoline ration permitted. The summer was spent, he reported, in getting acquainted with people and "studying the files in an attempt to familiarize myself with the community and school programs."

The community council did not rush to his assistance. He talked with individual members but no meeting of the council was suggested. On August 19, he wrote, "I think it will be some time before such a meeting is held unless something unforeseen happens. I am trying to decide whether it would be wise for me to ask for a meeting of the council."

But it had not seemed wise before the opening of school. Then there was no time. The "foreshadowing" apparent in the letters of the fall of 1942 was realized completely in the fall of 1943 when school personnel was even more drastically curtailed by losses of men to service and defense plants and women to join their husbands wherever service had taken them.

Some neighborhoods continued the meetings begun the year before. No one person kept in touch with them and there are no records to indicate just how much carry-over there was. Opinion locally is that the neighborhood leadership, though not organized as formally as during the preceding year, continued to function pretty effectively. Teachers in the high school were unable to give as much time to the program because of the increasing pressure of their regular duties.

At the end of his second year, the principal reported with reference to community activities, *"Getting the job done is still difficult."* Nevertheless, he cited as tangible evidence of good

community spirit, the general interest in civic clubs, in the
Parent-Teacher Association, and in the community recreation
program which had continued, though never on so extensive
a scale as in the summer of 1942. Evidence of improvement
in the past two years, he felt, was less in "concrete achievements than in an intangible feeling that we are making
progress and are all working together toward common ends."

Some Things We Learned

Here, as in other counties, we learned from failures as well
as from successes, and in the extended program with high
school principals have already had opportunity to profit by
mistakes made in this first cooperative venture.

Moving from survey to action has proved difficult in many
communities. The Holy Neck District had, in addition to the
usual handicaps, a wartime situation to meet which necessitated a shift in emphasis just when the point of transfer had
been reached.

In retrospect, it seems as if there may have been a weakness in the survey itself. It resulted in a pretty thorough
analysis of conditions and problems but did not do a similar
job for resources upon which the community might draw in
improving conditions or solving problems. It was assumed
that the school and the Ruritan Club were the agencies
through which the program should find expression. A careful
study of the many agencies upon which these groups could
draw might have brought about a coordination of effort which
would have strengthened the program. In subsequent planning with local groups, the staff of Special Projects stressed
the importance of *knowing resources and agencies and seeing
them as well as problems in relation to the total picture.*

After the Special Projects had extended the right hand of
fellowship to the local program and had accepted the Holy
Neck District of Nansemond County as its third experimental
area, the staff may have adhered too rigidly to the policy of
guiding by remote control. They had waited for special invitations to help or even to visit the community. The principal had waited to find something specific to ask for or important to exhibit before extending an invitation. Everyone
was feeling his way. Probably opportunities for mutual help-

fulness were missed. In later experiments with principals and local workshop groups the staff took the initiative in familiarizing themselves with the situation, and, as a result, were more sensitive to needs and less hesitant about making concrete suggestions.

During the first summer, Mr. Savage had come to the University for conferences with the director and staff four times and had sent weekly reports that were acknowledged with occasional suggestions. Similar, but less frequent, contacts were continued throughout the winter. It was not till April, 1942, ten months after embarking on the cooperative venture, that members of the staff visited the community and began to "get the feel" of it. The following summer, when their help was urgently needed, they were able to spend only four days there. Mr. Savage's program that summer precluded the possibility of his getting to the University for conferences. Long letters were exchanged, but letters became increasingly unsatisfactory as a means of exchanging ideas as complexities in the program emerged.

Again in retrospect, it becomes apparent that the basis of communication between Special Projects and the Holy Neck program should have been broader. Contacts with the two agencies most active locally were made entirely through one person in the beginning. The high school principal had been president of Ruritan when the idea of the survey was conceived. He had carried chief responsibility for it in both school and club. He had later been employed in a dual capacity by Special Projects to promote similar programs in other Ruritan clubs and to develop a school-community program in his own district.

It was toward the end of the first of his two summers of employment that it became clear that he could work most effectively as the school principal serving the community throughout the summer months. Up to this time there had been no attempt on the part of Special Projects to ascertain whether or not the superintendent of schools was in sympathy with the program. When he was consulted, the plan was already made, the principal engaged, and activities under way. Although the superintendent then expressed his confidence in the principal and in the Extension Division and his willingness to cooperate, it is perhaps not surprising that he never took any initiative in later planning nor seemed to feel any direct responsibility for the program's continuance.

In selecting the principals in 1943 for the demonstration of the effectiveness of twelve-month employment, interest of the superintendents, as well as of the principals concerned, was one of the prerequisites. The director of the Extension Division and a member of the State Board of Education conferred red with them in their own communities before decisions were made. Superintendents were then invited to come with their principals to the planning conference in April and to visit the three-week workshop as often as they could. *The principle of participation in planning is as important among professional workers and officials as in citizens' groups.*

As It Is Now

The results of the experimental program in the Holy Neck District of Nansemond County are far-reaching so far as the state is concerned. What the community has gained is not so readily apparent.

A visit by the staff to the community in the fall of 1945 convinced them that there are signs of a return to life on the part of individuals and organized groups. Whether the school will be the center of the revitalized program is doubtful. Certainly the part it has played in the past cannot be discounted, and its continued activity as one interested agency is assured. There is not the "total collapse" that can result from loss of a leader. The period of wavering brought about by the change in leadership here was aggravated and prolonged by wartime conditions. As a result, the experimental period of Special Projects has ended and this report is being written at a time when one cannot yet see "the shape of things to come" in the Holy Neck District. The "remote control" through employment of the high school principal terminated following the summer of 1944 after two years of promising growth followed by two years of steadily declining activity. Services of the Extension Division continue to be available to this community as to any other in Virginia, but at present there is no official relationship between any local group and the staff.

CHAPTER 11

The Extended Program

In the summer of 1941, news began to get about that the Extension Division of the University of Virginia had embarked on an experimental program. There was little clear understanding of its nature or purpose but two phrases seemed to have caught attention. These were "projects in adult education" and "helping communities."

Requests for advice or help began to come in. The first came from a newly organized adult education council in Harrisonburg. Its purpose was closely related to that of Special Projects. The Shenandoah Valley was different from the three experimental areas. In their eagerness to have all types of Virginia communities represented, the staff at first thought they might extend the program to include the Valley. Several visits were made for the purpose of conferring with officers and meeting with the council.

By that time requests from other sections of the state had come in, each having as valid reasons for attention as the first. Work in the mountain and piedmont counties had become intensive and time-consuming. It was obvious that, if the field staff were to do a thorough job anywhere, careful restrictions had to be adhered to. Therefore the policy of limiting their personal attention to the already selected experimental areas was adopted, with the understanding that requests for printed materials would be met and that consultation and advice would be furnished when this did not necessitate extra trips but could be done in regular line of duty. Visits to programs to get stories for *New Dominion Series,* it later developed, offered excellent opportunity and almost always resulted in such service. This the staff labeled "incidental sowing of seed." Much of the seed thus sown bore excellent fruit.

When requests could not be met, an explanation of the experimental nature of the intensive program was always given and hope expressed that ways would develop from it of extending the service to the entire state. This chapter deals with some of those ways.

THE GRUNDY PROGRAM

In the spring of 1942, a request came from Buchanan, one of the extreme southwestern counties. The interested group was made up primarily of teachers in the small city of Grundy. Their concern was with community problems. What they asked for was a regular extension class in which their study of the community might be directed and for which they would receive credit toward certificate renewal.

The southwestern counties are so far from Charlottesville that they are likely to receive less attention than is their due when general extension programs are being planned. Moreover the Southwest is very different from central and eastern Virginia in topography, attitudes, and social and economic problems. In these respects, it is similar to some other areas of the South, especially some in Tennessee, West Virginia and Kentucky. What might be learned there about methods of procedure, therefore, could have rather broad application.

It seemed wise to try to work out a special arrangement for that area. Virginia Polytechnic Institute at Blacksburg is in the southwestern part of the state. In accordance with his usual policy, Mr. Zehmer, director of the University of Virginia Extension Division, turned to the institution located in the area to find someone to work on the program there.[1]

The General Plan

Dr. Leland Tate, professor of rural sociology at V.P.I., was asked to come to Charlottesville to discuss the program with the staff. A cooperative undertaking was planned with the division of extension teaching, the Special Projects, and Dr. Tate participating. Students were to pay the usual extension class fee. (In the three experimental counties, no fees were being charged for services of the staff.) These fees would take care of the professor's honorarium. His travel and field expenses were to be paid by Special Projects. The class would meet once a week for twelve weeks. At the end of that time

---

[1]In Virginia, the University of Virginia carries administrative responsibility for general extension. Agricultural extension services are headed up at V. P. I.

Dr. Tate was to make recommendations about follow-up work he considered necessary or desirable.

Summarizing the discussion of the preliminary conference, Mr. Zehmer wrote Dr. Tate as follows:

Our principal interest in this particular class is in having you experiment in using the class method in developing interest among a responsible group of citizens in community welfare, looking particularly to a matter-of-fact study of the community and especially to community planning and the coordination of community efforts in meeting the vital problems of the community. In other words, we are trying to find out more about methods for helping people, especially those living in rural communities and small towns, to help themselves. We are trying several different approaches, and the idea of a course of study as a basis for community planning and cooperative effort seems worth undertaking.

As the work goes forward, we would want you to keep a brief record of your procedures so that at the end of the experiment you could submit a brief but accurate report on the methods that you followed and the results.

If, after trying this approach to community study and organization in Grundy, you might like to try a somewhat similar approach in other communities in the general vicinity of V. P. I., we will be glad to consider that. . . . . In our attempts to find out more about effective methods for working with people and especially for developing a technique by which people can more effectively solve their own problems, we would like to have your cooperation and that of V. P. I.

This approach, based as it was on regular extension teaching, was much more closely related to established patterns than were those being tried in other areas. It could be used only in communities that had a group already aware of needs and interested in study and planning. It should be less time-consuming than the type of work which was being undertaken in communities where no awareness existed. If it achieved results, the extension of Special Projects to serve more communities would be simplified.

The Class

The class had twenty regular members, mostly teachers. Visitors were encouraged to come. For the final meeting, a special invitation brought out more than twenty-five representative citizens to hear a report of the findings of the class. These included persons in positions of leadership, such as ministers; the school superintendent; officers of Rotary, Chamber of Commerce, and Women's Club; county officials; and "just good citizens."

In submitting to Mr. Zehmer his outline of work covered in the course Dr. Tate commented as follows:[2]

You will note that we first went into the background information pertaining to communities and community study, and followed this by a general study of Grundy and a special diagnosis of its solidarity and organizational effectiveness. We then returned to a study of the factors affecting community development, past, present and future.

The class showed unusual enthusiasm for the general study and diagnosis, and insisted that we try to make our findings functional. This was attempted by two means. First, we decided upon a directory of service agencies, and then upon a joint meeting with community leaders at which we would tell them of our findings and the future possibilities for coordination and development.

Committees from the class were chosen to handle these two projects. One compiled the directory, had it mimeographed and obtained funds from the town council for its publication. The other committee contacted local leaders, invited them to our last class meeting in the high school library, and had a fine representation of leaders present for this meeting.

It was hoped that these things would make the local leaders more conscious of their community needs and point the way to future activities. Mrs. Minnie Padbury, a member of the class, had already sensed the need for a calendar of community events, and hoped to complete this and thereby show the overlapping of meetings and the need for better coordination. Other ideas were also expressed, but just how many of them will be carried out I do not know. I do feel, however, that the method we used has definite possibilities.

Members of the class also were enthusiastic about what they were able to accomplish. Their directory of local service agencies, mimeographed and distributed at the expense of the town council, was useful to the entire community. How much carry-over there has been during the three years that have elapsed since is not known.

Relation to Total Experiment

Though the Grundy approach was obviously sound for that type of community, it had one great weakness so far as the experimental program was concerned. It remained an isolated case never tied in with the rest of the program. Distance was one important reason for this. Another was the fact that Dr. Tate with full-time teaching responsibilities in another institution could give little more than class time to the project.

In a program, the primary purpose of which is to "dis-

---

[2]Letter from Dr. Leland B. Tate to Mr. Zehmer, July 27, 1942.

cover techniques whereby communities can help themselves through the efforts of their own citizens," continuous analysis of what is being tried is necessary. During the first two years of Special Projects, there were numerous staff meetings for the purpose of analysis, stock-taking, and planning. Specialists from other areas and specific fields of interest met with the staff to help in this process of analysis. Continuous exchange of experience resulted in frequent re-shaping of details as the several programs developed. The Grundy program was never subjected to this type of planning, analysis, and re-planning that went on in relation to the other experimental areas. After one preliminary conference, Dr. Tate had almost no contact with the rest of the staff.

The members of the class naturally associated their class with V.P.I. from which their professor came. Other members of the Special Projects staff had never met with them. The group had no comprehension of the class as a part of a broader program. They did not turn to the Extension Division for the follow-up help they should have had. Both Dr. Tate and the Extension Division staff were busy with many things, and no one took responsibility for keeping in touch with Grundy.

All these things influenced procedures when, two years later, an adaptation of the Grundy approach was extended to many sections of the state. This later development was not an outgrowth of the Grundy program but of the experiment with high school principals the story of which follows. By the time it got under way channels had been found through which to assure continuity and exchange of experience.

EXPERIMENT WITH PRINCIPALS

As one experimental approach to helping communities help themselves, the Special Projects of the Extension Division had employed a high school principal during the summer months to work on a school-centered program in his community. (See chapter 10.) In 1942, the second summer of his employment, the program on which he was engaged attracted the attention of the State Board of Education. Superintendent Lancaster had for some time been interested in twelve-month employment of high school principals, and other members of the state department were also interested in school-community interaction. The experimental approach of Special Projects, as tried in the Holy Neck District, offered a way of combining the two interests. The Extension Division and the State Board of Education decided to join forces in extending the experiment to enough centers to afford a demonstration.

The General Plan

The plan was for them jointly to sponsor the employment of a few selected rural high school principals for twelve months instead of the usual nine. On the basis of its experience, the Extension Division would give them some guidance in planning the use of the additional time for community work. Both agencies felt sure that when the value to schools and communities had been demonstrated, state and local appropriations would make possible regular employment of high school principals for twelve months.

The State Board of Education and the Special Projects of the Extension Division each contributed one-third the funds necessary. A foundation grant provided the remainder. The request to the foundation stated the purpose as follows:[3]

. . . . to measure the advantages to a rural community in employing the high school principal on a year-round (twelve-month) basis rather than on the nine-month schedule now in effect. The proposed investigation is based upon the assumption that the modern rural high school has a general educational responsibility to the community that it serves, as well as the specific one of giving more or less formal instruction to those of legal school age. It is felt that the high school principal is the official upon whom the major responsibility rests for clearly understanding his school's obligation to the community and for taking whatever steps are necessary to enable it to meet this obligation. However for the principal the regular nine-month term is always crowded with duties connected with the established and more orthodox school program. The question is how much more effectively can the principal function as the educational leader of the community if he is employed for the summer months also when he will be largely free of regular session duties and can devote most of his time to studying community problems, establishing relations with the citizens of the community, and perfecting techniques that will make it possible for the school to better serve general community interests.

---

[3]Memo from G. B. Zehmer to the foundation submitted with request for funds, December 21, 1942.

Selecting the Principals

The beginning of the program was set for the summer of 1943. During the preceding winter careful attention was given to the selection of principals. The director of the Extension Division and officials of the State Board of Education spent many hours in discussion. Then they visited centers that were under consideration talking with the principals and their superintendents.

Interest on the part of the principal and willingness to cooperate on the part of his superintendent were, of course, among the primary considerations. Diversity in types of community and a geographical spread that would include all sections of the state also weighed heavily in the selection.

It was decided to continue the principal of the Holland High School of Nansemond County as a part of the extended experiment. This was considered especially important since Mr. Savage, who had been employed for the two preceding summers, was moving to a city school, and a new man with little experience in community work was taking over his duties in the Holy Neck District. The new principal expressed interest in the program and became one of the group.

By early spring, 1943, the entire group had been selected. The budget as set up had provided for five centers. In one of the five counties considered, the local board was beginning the next summer to pay the two high school principals for twelve months. The interest of their superintendent in having his principals learn more effective ways of using their summer months led him to bargain. The project, he pointed out, had contemplated paying one salary, expenses for a workshop at the University, and travel expenses throughout the summer for community work. Relieved of the salary, which was already provided for, why, he asked, shouldn't the project accept two from his county instead of one? No more money would be needed, and more individuals would be enabled to participate. His request was granted.

Later a seventh principal was included. He had not been among those originally selected but had turned to the Extension Division for help on a school-community problem after selections had been made. He obviously belonged in the

experimental program. The budget had provided for five.
Economies in several phases of the program, added to the saving of summer salaries of the two principals already being
paid for twelve months, made it possible to start the demonstration with seven high school principals from six different
counties. The counties were Fluvanna, Lunenburg, Bath,
Fauquier and Spotsylvania, in addition to Nansemond in
which some work had already been done.

The Group

It was a diversified group. No one had special achievements in community work to his credit. Only one had a special community program in mind. Two would be starting work
in new communities. One of these would be following the
principal engaged by the Extension Division during the two
preceding summers. A fourth was just starting as principal
though he had been in the schools of his community for several years. Four had been serving in the same positions for
periods of time ranging up to fourteen years.

Getting Together to Plan

The group met for the first time at the University on a
Saturday in April, 1943. Several of the principals were accompanied by their superintendents. There was discussion of
the general purpose of the program and of specific directions
it might take in the several communities. Mr. Savage who
had worked for two years in the Holland program participated in this conference. His concrete suggestions were helpful to those to whom the idea was new. Everyone felt the
need of considerable help in planning. It was decided to bring
the entire group together for a three-week workshop in community development at the University in the beginning of the
summer. Following that, help and advice of the staff were
promised to the extent permitted by its limited numbers and
the many miles they would have to travel to give personal
supervision.

Preliminary Workshop[4]

The workshop program provided background in the sociology of the community; presentation of "programs in action" by persons specially invited because of what they were doing in their communities; opportunity to get acquainted with the materials in the field—printed and visual; and time for individual planning in consultation with members of the staff of Special Projects.

The group lived in one of the fraternity houses and had meals together. Classes began at nine in the morning. Study, conferences, and discussions continued throughout the day. Officially the program ended at nine in the evening. The "post mortems" that followed, the staff were told, were a very important part of the educational process.

During the three weeks, members of the workshop were exposed to more than a dozen individuals enthusiastic about programs in which they had had a part. They brought inspiration. They were questioned about how to start, where to start, just how to proceed until, according to their own admissions, they had subjected their programs to more searching analysis than they had ever done before.

At the same time each participant put his own situation and community under the microscope. He analyzed needs and considered methods of attack. At the end of the three weeks, each principal emerged from the ordeal with a plan and with the conviction that plans might have to be scrapped when actual situations were faced. The need for careful planning and the equally strong need for complete flexibility were the inescapable lessons of every program discussed.

Back to the Community

On his return to his community, each principal approached the job of the remainder of the summer in a different way. All reported they were seeing things in a new perspective. Almost all felt the urge to get to know their people more intimately. One made 290 personal visits, calling on every family represented in his school and asking what, in their opinion,

---

[4]The summer residence workshop as a technique is discussed in detail in chapter 16.

the school might do to serve the community more adequately. He found some good suggestions. He also found a number of older boys and girls who had left school for no particular reason. Many of them were persuaded to return, and some modifications were made in the curriculum to meet their needs. Another called on all the elementary school principals to get their ideas about the role of the high school in the community. He also took occasion to speak on the subject before every organization of which he was a member. No one "organized" special activities that summer but everyone found himself very busy getting acquainted with the *total needs and resources of his community* rather than with only those phases that had direct bearing on the school. A recent questioning of the principals brought out the fact that only one had used the plan made in the workshop without major changes. Yet all agreed that the pre-planning process had been of inestimable value.

Some details of their accomplishments are given later, together with those of other professional workers who were a part of that first summer workshop and hence a part of the extended program. (See chapter 16.) Here, however, before ending the discussion of that part of the program concerned chiefly with principals, it should be said that the demonstration brought results.

The investigation of the value of employing high school principals for twelve months with emphasis on community leadership had begun in the fall of 1942. The selected group went to work the next spring and were paid salary, travel, and workshop expenses by Special Projects for two summers. Before the end of the first year, at least one school board had expressed itself as planning to continue the twelve-month salary. In the spring of 1945, funds were made available through the State Board of Education for the year-round employment of principals in 96 of the state's 110 high school divisions. The relation of the appropriation to the experiment seems to be more than coincidental!

EXTENSION VIA THE SUMMER WORKSHOP

Though the 1943 workshop was planned with the seven principals in mind, it was announced as a part of the regular summer school program. The State Department of Public Welfare sent three superintendents selected because of their interest in the total community. One rural elementary school teacher selected the course for himself. These four, added to the selected principals, brought the total of individual participants to eleven. Ten counties were represented—Franklin, Tazewell, Southhampton, and Floyd, in addition to those named above.

The three welfare superintendents each served an entire county. Of the principals, two had consolidated county high schools (Spotsylvania and Fluvanna); two (from Lunenburg) had schools each serving one-half the county; the others had consolidated schools serving a section of a county rather than the entire political subdivision. The elementary teacher had come from a one-room school but returned to a large consolidated elementary school serving about half the county and working under a supervisor who was responsible for the entire county.

With the workshop participants assuming responsibility for getting others interested, it was hoped (1) that countywide programs might be started in at least six counties and (2) that in the other four the idea might spread from the areas reached to the entire county. The first of these hopes seems to have been realized in five of the six counties; the second in at least two out of the four—possibly more, for relationships are less direct in these cases. But in the meantime, the summer workshop training was supplemented and given continuity by other types of experience.

Subsequent Conferences and Trips

Before the workshop had ended in July the participants made several recommendations. One of these was that the group meet again for a conference in October. The meeting was arranged at the University. Members of the State Board of Education and the State Department of Public Welfare attended along with the staff of the Extension Division and the workshop group. The day was much too short for the exchange of experience. At this time, it was urged that a second recommendation of the workshop group be carried out as soon as travel restrictions permitted. This one provided for visits to good programs that had been described. When made at the end of the summer, the recommendation had seemed a good one. After several months of trying "to do likewise" members of the group considered it imperative.

"We've got to see for ourselves," they said. "It doesn't work in our community—or maybe it does and we are not seeing the woods for the trees."

Programs they especially wished to visit were discussed. By the following spring, money and cars were available. A trip was planned—and all but two members of the first workshop went. Their experience is described in *We Went to See for Ourselves,* University of Virginia Extension Division, January, 1945.[5]

LOCAL WORKSHOPS DEVELOP

During the intervening winter, staff members had visited the centers—sometimes to participate in meetings, at others merely to talk things over. Two principals asked that the Extension Division conduct local workshops with content similar to that of the summer in order that more persons might begin to understand community relationships.

The staff hesitated. There were now only two field workers and a secretary giving full time to Special Projects. Their work had increased considerably in two years. The two field workers were investigating community programs throughout the Southeast and reporting eighteen of the best of these each year in *New Dominion Series*; they were meeting continuously increasing requests for help from the mountain and piedmont counties selected for the experiment; they were answering requests for printed materials which after having been almost non-existent for two years, had through the summer workshop acquired an audience;[6] and, although they had had assistance

---

[5] The itinerant workshop as a technique is described and evaluated in chapter 17.

[6] The librarian had left Special Projects the preceding January.

for the three weeks of the 1943 summer workshop, they must now carry chief responsibility for keeping in touch with the ten counties to which workshop participants had returned.

Yet the idea of local workshops was an excellent one. Already the program was taking the shape of ever-widening circles such as result from dropping a stone into a pool. These local groups centering around the principals suggested a logical next circle. The pattern must not be broken now because of the frailty of human flesh!

So, in cooperation with the division of extension teaching, local workshops were planned for Bath and Fluvanna Counties—one about 100 miles from the University and the other about 30 miles. Mr. Rorer, director of extension teaching, assisted the staff of Special Projects. Groups met for three or four hours one night a week for ten meetings. The four-hour group preceded the study and workshop with dinner.

In one county, the workshop was made up entirely of school people. These came not only from the area served by the principal who had attended the summer workshop, but also from "the other side of the mountain" which was served by another school. Alternate meetings were held on either side so that no one felt the program belonged to the other group. Bringing the two "sides of the mountain" together was an important step in the development of this county—and the workshop seemed to do it.

In the other county the group was more diversified. In addition to teachers, it included a minister, the county agent, a soil conservation worker, the leader of the Grange, and "just a housewife." Teachers from a local private school also joined the workshop. In this group clarification of aims seemed to be the chief outcome, and the group had opportunity to organize for action before the end of the year. The part that members played in getting an appropriation for a cannery from the board of supervisors after it had been refused was a fine culmination of their study.

A third request for a local workshop came after these two were well started. It came from a school community in the piedmont county which had been selected as one of the original three experimental areas. It was within twenty miles of the University. Work in Louisa County took the staff frequently in that direction. Yet again they hesitated, for weeks continued to have only seven days each. Their demurring was ended by the question, "Shouldn't our rights take precedence over those other counties? You said you were going to concentrate on the counties you picked."

This group met once a week for twelve weeks. It was sponsored by the community league. Meetings were held in the fine recently consolidated elementary school. Teachers and patrons participated in about equal numbers. The aim of the workshop was to plan ways to consolidate the communities served by the school. The group moved steadily toward that aim in addition to uncovering several other needs to be worked on.

Each of these local workshop groups had between 15 and 20 participants. In each, those desiring credit paid regular Extension Division fees. That number included the majority of the members of the first two groups, but was limited to two in the third where the interest was centered chiefly on a problem to be worked out.

Analysis and evaluation of the local workshop as a technique are given in some detail in chapter 18. Here it should be said that the value of the process was immediately apparent and requests increased at so rapid a rate that a way was sought to add someone to the staff to meet this need.

The Movement Spreads

Before plans were completed, however, for the spread of local workshops, a second summer workshop was held at the University. In accordance with recommendations of the 1943 group, a more diversified group was brought together in 1944. There was no new experiment with principals this summer to determine a nucleus. Members of the 1943 group had their itinerant workshop early in the summer of 1944 followed by a conference of several days at the University. Their experience and advice helped the staff in planning for the second group which was beginning that year. Several members of the first

year also came back to visit or to take part in the program of
the second workshop. They all urged the extension of the
local workshop idea. Hence this second group went back to
their communities determined to organize local workshops.

New Staff Member Extends Local Workshops

Early that fall, money was given by a foundation to pay
the salary of an additional staff member for two years to devote full time to conducting local workshops, Dr. Hayes, professor of sociology at Vanderbilt University, who had taught
in the two summer workshops was persuaded to take an eight-
month leave of absence to join the staff of Special Projects for
this purpose. His knowledge of the summer workshop groups
was an important asset in the extension of this part of the
program.

To get as much in planning as was possible from persons
living and working within the communities, a joint conference
of summer workshops of 1943 and 1944 was held in December
before Dr. Hayes joined the staff in January. Several groups
represented at the conference were ready to start immediately. It was agreed that the Extension Division would contribute the services of Dr. Hayes, but that each group would
pay enough to cover travel and field expenses. A flat sum of
$10 a meeting was agreed upon. This stipulation was in line
with the philosophy and purpose of the Special Projects to
help communities to help themselves.

From January till July, workshops met in Campbell,
Lunenburg, Rockingham, and Augusta Counties. Dr. Hayes
then assisted in the 1945 summer workshop which had an even
broader basis of community representation than the preceding
two. Two special programs developing out of interests in the
1944 and 1945 summer workshops centered in activities of organizations rather than geographical areas. These are described, together with a third growing out of the work in
Louisa County, in the next chapter.

At the end of the summer, it was necessary for Dr. Hayes
to return to Vanderbilt. He was replaced by Dr. William B.
Jones, professor of sociology at the University of Tennessee.
Four more local workshops started in October and were com-

pleted in December. These were in Charlotte, Hanover, Chesterfield, and Campbell Counties. The last was a second-year local workshop tried as an experimental way of assuring intensive planning.

In other areas where local workshops had been held, an attempt likewise was made to continue to give help to the developing programs. These, added to the experimental counties and the areas from which people had come to three summer workshops, again increased the work beyond the capacities of the limited staff. *Thirty-four counties were now involved instead of the original three. Scratching the surface was not the purpose of the program. Each community was gaining increasing control of analyzing local problems and meeting them. Yet the more they learned, the more articulate they became in asking for special services they must have if the result of the work was not to be primarily a feeling of frustration.*

Hence a plan was made to use the period beginning January, 1946, as a time for consolidating gains rather than for further extension. This will involve fresh experimentation as well as training of local persons in some of the special adult education techniques found effective in other communities.

CHAPTER 12

.... And Beyond

In Virginia it is the county that gives to people "a local habitation and a name." It is the important political subdivision. But it is much more than that. A person identifies himself as coming from Dinwiddie or Fauquier or Tazewell or Pittsylvania and feels a kinship for others from the same county. Though he may turn to the nearest city for his marketing, shopping, entertainment, and various services, his life is closely identified with the county in which he lives—and in which his family may have lived since the first land grants from the crown brought them there.

Hence it was natural that, in planning its experimental program, the Extension Division should consider the county as the unit. In selecting experimental areas, it chose three counties and later, through work with high school principals and superintendents of public' welfare, began rather intensive work in some dozen other counties. Local workshops, too, were first thought of as countywide in nature and were organized through county agencies.

It was out of the summer workshops at the University that later approaches through state and regional rather than county groups began to crystallize.

Public Welfare Suggests a Pattern

In the 1943 summer workshop, there were three superintendents of public welfare. Two of these came from southwestern Virginia counties. When, in December, 1944, a conference was held to plan local workshops, these two superintendents brought with them one of the field representatives of their area. They proposed a different type of local workshop. It was for the entire Southwest comprising twenty counties and three cities. It was an intensive residence conference extending over a period of several days and planned for one group of professional workers. Its purpose was to help these welfare workers see their program in relation to the total community. Against the background acquired in the workshop, each would analyze the situation in his own county and bend his own efforts toward stimulating new activities or helping to coordinate those already under way.

In preliminary conferences with the superintendents who had been in the summer workshop and their field representatives, details were worked out. The first week in June was set for the conference, and facilities in Hungry Mother State Park in southwestern Virginia were reserved for the group.

In order that members of the workshop might begin the process of community analysis before coming together, each person was asked to send to the staff a list of problems already recognized and to bring to the conference a rough map of the area that would indicate something of its topography and sociological nature.

Half a dozen had no problems to list—or so many that the task seemed hopeless. From the seventeen lists submitted a summary was made. Need for better health programs, for more adequate recreation facilities, and for coordination in planning appeared on almost every list. These were general enough to warrant the allocating of special discussion periods to their consideration. Others were left for individual conferences. Books and pamphlets dealing with the many problems listed were carried to the workshop.

Morning hours were devoted to lectures and discussions on the sociology of the community. Afternoons were given over to discussion of the general problems listed above. In the evening there was discussion of various techniques or ways of working. Individual conferences were sandwiched in between whenever there were moments to spare. The living arrangements plus the inclement weather which kept everyone close to the fireplace made it possible to use about fifteen hours of each day for discussion. Since everyone was talking about what concerned him most, nobody got tired of talking. There was no time for reading the materials that had been assembled but everyone had time to look them over and choose some to take home for more leisurely perusal.

As in the case of summer workshops, the staff promised to give whatever follow-up assistance time and distance permitted. During the succeeding five months personal visits were made to three of the counties to meet with local groups. In two cases representatives of the Bureau of Public Administration and the Bureau of Economic Research helped with this follow-up work. Several other participants have asked for advice by mail or have written for additional study material. Others have reported activities under way and have urged visits. One of these reports is from an isolated mountain county where an office assistant carries total responsibility for the welfare program. She was one who, preceding the conference, had considered her problems too many to list. Her report of November 10, 1945, reads in part as follows:

Immediately after my return from the Hungry Mother Park workshop in June, I began to talk the situation over with various citizens and officers of organizations in town. Most of the people approached appeared to be interested in a recreation plan, but no one knew just where to start. Definite action was not taken until August 6 when I was invited by the mayor to attend the meeting of the town council and put my plan before them. The town owned a good-sized lot in the heart of the village and, after a discussion, the council agreed to let a recreation organization that might be formed have the use of such lot for a playground for children. It also agreed to let swings and other equipment be placed there. A notice was then sent to the president of each organization—civic, religious, fraternal, etc. At our first meeting on August 11, we had about a dozen people. Plans for the new organization were discussed but, due to the small group present, we took no definite action. Further meetings were held on August 21, August 30, and September 20. The last meeting culminated in an organization called the Civic Betterment Club—and officers were elected.

Regular weekly meetings have been held since that time and our attendance is steadily growing. At our last meeting 41 were present. As the club has grown it has become apparent that the need of the county is far greater than for a recreational program alone. Other projects under consideration include town beautification, volunteer fire department, garbage disposal, and school improvement. But our beginning project is a teen-age recreation plan.

The report continues with the story of organizing sandlot football teams, a Girl Scout troop, a dramatics club. It tells of the uncovering of unexpected local talent and leadership, the search for a suitable clubroom for social activities, the plan for eventually having a town hall which will serve as a community center. From the stage of "no one knew just where to start," this community has moved along to the "beginning of a useful and valuable organization in our community." It is only one of the outcomes of the regional workshop at Hungry Mother Park but it alone would justify this method of attack on community problems.

A continuation committee is now planning a second-year workshop for the same group. One member writes that the first one was inspiring and that she went home and tried things she never thought would work. To her surprise, they did. Now she wants to get together with the group again to work on more plans, for "Now we know so much more than we did then."

The news has spread to other areas of the state and similar workshops are being planned. In each, however, the pattern will vary to meet the needs and interests of the local groups. *Participation in planning is as important a part of the process as actual participation in the workshop.*

Ruritan Extends the Program

The Ruritan Club in Virginia is important because it cuts across the division of the strictly rural from the strictly urban in sociability and in social planning. When the experimental program was under consideration, it was felt that Ruritan might play an important part in its development and might gain considerably from the experience. Mr. Zehmer mentioned this possibility in his memorandum of August 28, 1940, to Dr. Newcomb, as follows:

> Ruritan National is a new and principally Virginia organization, modeled rather closely after urban civic bodies. On paper, at least, this organization has formulated worthy objectives in rural and small-town leadership and community action. The organization has no paid officers or assistants at the present time who can keep in touch with local clubs and help direct their activities.
>
> The suggestion is that the project furnish the leadership to work with a few selected local Ruritan organizations. If the plan should be productive of good results, the state organization of Ruritans tentatively promises to provide a part or all the salary and expenses of an educational director, after the experimental period, thus setting up machinery for carrying on indefinitely a personnel for helping the local units realize some of their present very worthwhile objectives.

When the experimental program got under way almost a year later, this suggestion was not lost sight of. In the summer of 1941, Mr. William Savage, principal of the Holland High School of Nansemond County, was asked to give attention to carrying the plans forward during the time he served with the staff of the Special Projects. (See chapter 10.) Results, however, were somewhat disappointing. This was due in part to the fact that the Holland school-community program necessarily occupied a large portion of Mr. Savage's summer. It was due, perhaps, even more to the fact that the entire experimental program was just getting under way. Its purpose, as has been stated so many times, was to *discover techniques.* Probably it was too early in the search to attempt to give guidance to an organization that was likewise feeling its way.

At any rate, effective cooperation with Ruritan began almost four years later. Like the local workshops and the cooperation with the State Department of Public Welfare, it grew out of the summer workshops in community development held at the University.

In 1944, a leader in the state Ruritan organization attended the summer workshop. He thought he saw a technique which could well be extended throughout the state by way of Ruritan. That fall, preceding the state convention, he and the president had a conference with the staff. Since Dr. Hayes was about to join the staff to conduct local workshops, it was possible to promise leadership for any Ruritan Club that might like to organize one. It was suggested that workshops sponsored by Ruritan be open to the entire community. Mr. Zehmer was invited to present the matter at the state meeting. Those present were enthusiastic. It was voted that any local club sponsoring a workshop might have $25 toward expenses from the state organization.

Augusta County was the first to get under way. It was followed almost immediately by Rockingham. The next fall (1945) Chesterfield, Charlotte, and Hanover clubs organized workshops. Dr. Hayes had then returned to Vanderbilt, and these last three workshops were conducted by Dr. Jones. Ruritan-sponsored workshops are evaluated along with others in chapter 18.

Women's Clubs Seek Guidance

Another statewide organization through which further extension of the community development program is taking place is the Virginia Federation of Women's Clubs. Its pres-

ent president says she brought to the office "the aspiration
that the federation continue to contribute to the progress of
the state." She also brought the conviction that emphasis
must be "increased at the local level, for . . . . the state can be
no stronger than its local units." It was this conviction that
prompted her to turn to the Extension Division for help in
preparing materials for local clubs. The result was a study
guide of some sixty pages, with the title *Community Quiz:
Some $64 Questions.*

In her letter which serves as a foreword to this booklet.
Mrs. Northington tells its story as follows:[1]

. . . . Now that our duties connected with the war have been
largely completed, there are other matters which need the attention
of the fifteen thousand clubwomen in Virginia.

We are bound to the Commonwealth by a thousand ties. We are
steeped in its traditions. We have lived here for generations. We
have discovered, at least to a limited degree, the sources and the potentialities of good living. We have assumed that we knew much about
our community and state. However, we have been made conscious time
and again of our ignorance concerning our neighbors and their ambitions and needs, as well as our interdependence one upon another.
Who are our people? What are our racial and national backgrounds?
What are our traditions of culture, patterns of family life, habits of
industry, standards of behavior, hopes of success? How shall we as
alert citizens find ways to help ourselves?

The contribution which we as intelligent women shall make to
the state will be in direct proportion to our ability to answer these
questions. The solution to our problems will come through our own
efforts to understand them and in the degree to which we succeed in
arousing our neighbors.

Sometime in March, I talked with his Excellency, Colgate W.
Darden, Jr., Governor of Virginia, concerning the relationship of the
Federation to the welfare of the Commonwealth. I also discussed with
Mr. George B. Zehmer, Director of the Extension Division, University
of Virginia, the ways by which our organization might work with his
division most constructively. Out of these discussions it was finally
decided that several Federation women should attend a workshop on
community development which would be offered during the summer
session of the University. Three members of the Federation joined me
in attending the sessions of the workshop; they are Mesdames C. A.
Haden, Jr., James A. Izard, and Roy C. Kyle.

The workshop was conducted by Mr. Jess Ogden of the Extension
Division staff, and Dr. Wayland J. Hayes, a specialist in community
development; Dr. Hayes assisted us in making the general plan of study

---

[1]"A Letter From Your President." *Community Quiz.* Published by
the Virginia Federation of Women's Club in cooperation with the
Extension Division of the University of Virginia.

and guided the early work. From time to time we had the advice and help of the following people from the University of Virginia: Doctors George W. Spicer and Wilson Doyle in the field of government, Dr. Tipton R. Snavely on taxation, Doctors Lorin B. Thompson and Arthur M. Whitehill on population and economics, Dr. Francis Lankford on education, and Dr. Wilson Gee on rural conditions. Mr. Randolph Church, Assistant Librarian of the Virginia State Library, offered suggestions and prepared a bibliography for supplementary reading. Dr. I. C. Riggin, Commissioner of Health for Virginia, was helpful on the topic of public health. Dr. W. E. Garnett, Rural Sociologist of the Virginia Polytechnic Institute, supplied materials for the kits. Several welfare workers, members of the workshop, submitted pertinent questions on welfare and public health.

Out of our experience in the workshop we offer to our clubs this study guide as a help in evaluating their communities and in determining the share which they will contribute to a new understanding of local needs and problems. Through such an engaging search as we may make, we may find opportunities for expanding the services of existing community agencies and for curbing certain tendencies which, if allowed to develop, would limit the well-being of our localities. More important still, and the sole reason for this particular undertaking, is the opportunity which is ours of helping ourselves and others to discover channels for constructive thinking and action. It is my hope that divine discontent, without which no real mental development evolves, may be fostered now and may in years to come show the fruits of our present activities.

The study guide went out in December, 1945, to local clubs throughout the state. It is the hope of the federation that each of them will use it as a basis for studying one or more of the eleven phases of community living suggested in the guide. Kits of research materials have been assembled to accompany the guide. With the help of these kits and local sources suggested, answers to the $64 questions can be found by each community in terms of its own problems and needs.

Results must await the test of time. It is doubtful whether many club members will acquire from a study of the questions, the depth and breadth of insight and understanding that had to be gained by those who formulated them. Yet it is possible that some may go on from there to a vision of new fields to conquer.

The following reaction of the press to the quiz book is hopeful:[2]

. . . . while the questions seem to be refreshingly casual and spontaneously posed, they have the most carefully studied significance.

---

[2]Editorial, Richmond *Times-Dispatch,* December 14, 1945.

All were formulated at a summer workshop on community development at the University of Virginia. . . . .

The workshop students were unusual in that they went to school with proved interest and ability in their field of study. . . . . The workshop at the university furnishes the model for similar workshops which it is hoped will soon be conducted throughout Virginia, and for which Virginia club women can furnish the leadership. . . . .

The federation's quiz book contains the stuff which may ferment Virginia imaginations, if proper conditions for the magic process are cultivated. Its questions concern the state's past and present and how its people can use Virginia's resources to build a better future. The answers are not in the back of the book, for that would be too easy. One must go to the sources of patient students who have studied the problems over the years, and in going to them, catch the spirit of their research.

To the degree the members of local study groups catch this spirit ,they are furthering the aim of the Extension Division's Special Projects. They are proving the efficacy of yet another way of helping communities to help themselves through the efforts of their own citizens.

Soil Conservation Seeks Assistance

In the spring of 1945, a program of cooperation with the Thomas Jefferson Soil Conservation District offered opportunity for further experimentation and for application of some of the techniques of adult education which had already proved effective.

The Thomas Jefferson District is made up of five counties, one of which is Louisa. This was one of the project's three experimental counties. In their program there, the staff of Special Projects had worked with the various committees of the Louisa County Citizens' Council in getting out a series of bulletins spreading information throughout the county.[3] One of these committees was concerned especially with soil conservation. In June, 1944, this committee prepared and distributed its first bulletin. The material was prepared by the members of the soil conservation and publications committees of the council in joint session. The county agent and local soil conservationist were members of the committee together with a number of farmers. They had invited to the meeting

---

[3]The council is described in chapter 9 and the *Bulletin* in chapter 14.

also the soil technician for the Thomas Jefferson District and a
member of its board of supervisors from a neighboring county.

Out of the afternoon's discussion emerged a four-page bulletin. In addition to a quiz on soil, it gave specific facts about
the soil and soil practices of Louisa County. On a map were
located several Louisa farms where good soil practices were
being observed. Readers were invited to visit them.

Before the bulletin went to press the district technician,
Mr. John Smart, who had attended the meeting, was asked to
check it for facts. In writing the bulletin the staff had merely
carried out the suggestions of the committee. They made no
pretense of being specialists in the subject matter. Their skill
was only in expressing ideas simply and in such a way as to
catch attention. That is, they were attempting to apply a few
educational principles to educating adults in good soil practices.

The method appealed to Mr. Smart. After watching the
effectiveness of the bulletin in Louisa County, he discussed
with his board of supervisors the possibility of preparing and
distributing similar materials in the five counties comprising
the Thomas Jefferson District. They asked the help of the
Special Projects of the Extension Division in carrying out
such a plan.

Their request came at about the time a small grant had
been given to the Extension Division for preparation of materials for adults in natural resources of Virginia. This was a
part of a program growing out of two regional conferences
called by the Committee on Southern Regional Studies.[4] The
Thomas Jefferson Soil Conservation District offered a specially
promising audience for such experimentation.

In June, 1945, a conference was held at the University
with members of the district's board of supervisors, agricultural workers and farmers from the several counties, and members of the staff of the Extension Division. Needs of the district were discussed. The type of contribution which the Extension Division might make was explained. The point was

---

[4]See *Channeling Research into Education* by John E. Ivey, Jr.
American Council on Education Studies. 1944.

stressed that skills of the staff which would be put at the disposal of the district would be entirely interpretive or educational. Content and factual material must be supplied by the technicians in soil conservation and those applying their theories.

There was discussion of techniques other than the printed word. Mr. Rorer, director of the Extension Division's audiovisual library, showed two pictures and discussed the use of movies and slides. One of the pictures was a new one, and the soil conservation people were able to advise as to whether it was the type of material that would be useful enough to warrant its purchase by the Extension Division film library.

The entire conference was an exchange that indicated education could be a two-way process. It seemed wise to those present to try to pool the information and skills of the soil technicians with those of the adult education technicians in a campaign of "telling the people."

Several subsequent conferences were held. The *Soil Saver* evolved. By that time plans for trying other approaches had been worked out. These included plans for training lay leaders in various communities. With the beginning of the new year the campaign will really get under way.

From General Approaches to Specific Techniques

An attempt has been made in these chapters to show how one experiment in the total program has led to another. The stone dropped into the pool with its ever-widening circles seems to be the best figure to describe approaches to discovering techniques. The intensive work in a few areas, the geographical spread through workshops for community leaders, and the attempts to give assistance to programs of organizations or agencies working at the state or regional level—all these have afforded excellent opportunity for trying special techniques and evaluating their general effectiveness. Our experience with several specific techniques used in working with adults toward the end of better communities is described in the next section of the report.

Part Four

WAYS THAT HAVE WORKED—OR HAVE NOT

CHAPTER 13

Meetings with Movies[1]

"When you-all goin' to bring us another show? It'll be all right if you don't bring no more white rats next time!"

This question eagerly asked and this comment smilingly added became familiar to us toward the end of the summer of 1942 whenever we met our friends from the hollows and mountain tops at the county seat on "Sat'd'y ev'nin' " or "Co't-day." We had, throughout the summer, carried on an intensive experiment in nutrition education through use of films. We had held several meetings in every neighborhood in a small rural county. Our concern was less with nutrition than with discovering how effective films might be in getting information to people in such a way as to make them want to change their habits and attitudes. Nutrition was a timely subject and one in which this particular county needed help.

The question and comment above are indicative of the response to the pictures. The people were eager for "shows" and would come again and again regardless of the fact that not infrequently the pictures were entirely lacking in entertainment value. They came for entertainment. But they did not object in the least to having "educational" films, though sometimes the relation between their lives and the white rats and test tubes used to prove that "Food Makes a Difference" was too remote for people untutored in laboratory techniques.

Most of the films in nutrition then available were of more value to home economists than to laymen. *Yet people would come to see them.* Whole families would walk for miles, sometimes climbing down one mountain and up another. Occasionally a family, or the young people from two or three families, would share one horse, two or three riding at a time while the others walked alongside. A few of the old farm trucks still had tires and gasoline that first summer of our movie program and they carried as many as could crowd into them. But not

---

[1]Sections of this chapter have already been published in *Making Films Work for Your Community* and *Film Forum Review*.

infrequently our own car would be the only one parked outside the little schoolhouse where 60 to 160 people had gathered to "see the show."

More people would come to the second meeting than had come to the first and still more to the third. Often a community that had had its first "show" in the little one-room school had, by the second or third, entirely outgrown its restricted space so that the screen was set up against the building and the schoolyard became the theatre. On one mountain top, a snake-rail fence served as seats for those in the "back row."

Before the end of the summer we began to feel that we had a "b'ar by the tail" and that we must use care if our direction was not to be entirely changed. Attracting crowds "to see shows" was not our purpose. Our concern was rather in using films to stimulate individuals and communities to action. The line between putting on a show and using films effectively for educational purposes may be a narrow one. But therein lies the significance of the movie as an adult education technique. It is potentially powerful. *To realize its potentialities, however, one must use it as a step in the educational process rather than as an end in itself.*

This observation is based not on casual use of "movies" in connection with programs planned by others—but on several intensive experiments involving 101 meetings for which we ourselves carried chief responsibility. About half of them were in really remote areas, as in the county referred to above. The remainder were in various kinds of rural communities and for groups having varying degrees of education and sophistication. In addition, we cooperated in showing pictures at a number of meetings held by such groups as the PTA, the Women's Society for Christian Service, the FSA, lenten study groups, Red Cross home nursing classes, and community councils.

How We Went About It

We had spent almost a year studying the habits, interests, and needs of the people of Greene County (see chapters 7 and 8) before we decided to experiment with an intensive program of educational films there. The county is mountainous. There is no town except the county seat which has only 212 people. There is a commercial movie here once a week. Communities consist of scattered families who live in the same hollow or who come to the same little store for their groceries. One- or two-room schools are scattered throughout the area. Illiteracy is not more prevalent than in similar areas of the South. There is, however, no reading habit among the people, and there are no books or magazines available for those who might read. Changing life habits and attitudes of adults through use of the printed page is a slow process when one must start with persuading large numbers of them to read anything. In looking for a short cut, we decided to try movies.

In the first place, we felt that they would afford a method of getting information to people in a quick, easy-to-understand, pleasant manner. They might have a secondary value in an area where the population was scattered and opportunities for sociability were rare. Meeting to see and discuss movies might facilitate the process of socialization which must precede any attempt at cooperative endeavors leading to improved ways of living.

To test our theory, in the spring of 1942 we planned to experiment with two types of program at which educational movies would be the chief attraction: (1) a countywide program with at least one meeting in every neighborhood on a subject of general interest; (2) several series of neighborhood meetings over a period of several months on subjects of special interest. Later we added a third type for the least socialized areas: "putting on a show," with primary emphasis on entertainment until individuals became used to meeting together, and some semblance of a "group" had emerged.

That spring the "food-for-freedom program" was focusing the attention of the nation on nutrition. In Greene County, the number of rejections for Selective Service because of defects resulting from malnutrition gave the subject a special significance. The local home demonstration clubs had selected nutrition as their project for the year. There were seven of these clubs with a total membership of about 250. Since there was no home economics teacher in the county, the work of the home demonstration agent and of the FSA home management supervisor constituted the only available education in nutrition.

We discussed with them the possibility of a countywide program of meetings on nutrition for which we would provide films and at which they would be on hand to help with the discussion and plan what follow-up work seemed necessary. One agency was eager to cooperate; the other demurred, asking the question, "Who will get the credit for the meetings?" Finally a satisfactory agreement was reached. The home demonstration clubs would officially sponsor the program and serve as a kind of advisory group. Both professional workers would attend the meetings.

At our suggestion, the home demonstration agent asked the officers of her clubs to act as a previewing committee to help in selection of pictures to be used. They came to the University for this purpose because we felt it would give the job added importance in their minds. Moreover we wanted them to know the kinds of service for which they could turn to the Extension Division when we were no longer giving direct attention to their county.

This group of nine rural women took their job seriously. Their comments on the five pictures presented were a sound guide to selection. One they labeled excellent basic nutrition material presented in a simple way and suitable for use throughout the county. A second was considered too technical for any but groups "studying physiology." It was suggested that it might have value for the Red Cross classes which the home demonstration agent was about to start. A third which presented the possibility of disposing of surplus garden produce through a farm women's market was dismissed as not practical for a county which did not have a large town. A fourth which showed school children selecting balanced meals in a fine school cafeteria was considered suitable for the three largest communities in the county where school lunchrooms were being developed. It was thought, however, to present a situation too impossible of attainment for communities served by one-room schools with no kitchen or lunchroom space or equipment. The club members asked that we try to find one that would be of help to the one-room school teachers who were struggling with the problem of the school lunch. (We were never able to meet this request.) The fifth picture, in kodachrome, was by far the most pleasing to the eye. But though conceded to be attractive, it was rejected on the basis of being presented from the point of view of the city dweller. Also, the display of scantily clad bodies was thought to make it unsuitable for use in the county, "for farm folk are conventional."

Following the evaluation of the pictures there was discussion of the need for a nutrition program for the county. These facts were considered: According to the census, there are 1,375 women over twenty-one years of age. Of these practically all are heads of families. Not more than three hundred are receiving any kind of information on nutrition. Those who are in homemakers clubs are, to a large extent, the already privileged group who have less need for the information than many not in the clubs.

"What is our responsibility to our neighbors?" was the question presented for consideration. The women present decided that they would like to suggest to their clubs that each one sponsor a meeting on nutrition in its own community and that it "make every attempt to get women who do not belong to clubs to attend." These meetings would be planned in so far as possible to cover the entire county, and it was decided to experiment with a number of different kinds of publicity— notices sent home with school children, announcements in the county paper, printed posters in stores and post offices, and word-of-mouth.

From this point on, the planning was not done in quite the way we had hoped. It seemed to the home demonstration agent more simple to assign dates for meetings and to work directly with the school teachers in the various communities since most of the meetings must be held in schoolhouses. She handled newspaper publicity herself and asked the teachers to notify parents. Thus the fine enthusiasm and feeling of responsibility for their neighbors shown by the officers of the

home demonstration clubs was wasted. This fact did not re-
act unfavorably on attendance at the meetings but was unfortunate, we felt, from the point of view of encouraging citizens
to assume responsibility for making communities better places
in which to live. Also, more active participation by the clubs
might have resulted in more emphasis on education and less
on "a show" but this is only guess work.

The meetings were a success if judged by attendance. Interest was so great that it was not possible to limit the program to the summer. More and more responsibility for scheduling the meetings was shifted to us as requests came directly
from the people and the teachers. This was out of line with
our policy not to set up a new agency but to work through
those already in the field. Later the FSA workers in the
county assumed chief responsibility, even learning to operate
the projector and run the meetings themselves when we could
not find enough nights in the week to meet our engagements.

During that year in Greene County we held fifty meetings
in eighteen centers with audiences totaling 3,448 adults and
older children. The numerous small children and babies were
not included in the count though they made up a large part
of every audience. There were as many men as women in attendance and their interest was as great. The average size of
meeting was sixty-eight. The largest group (160) assembled
in one of the most remote areas of the county. The smallest
(15) was in the county seat where there are more opportunities for sociability and where there is a commercial movie
house open once or twice a week. The meetings held for colored people, who have no opportunity in that area to see
movies, had an attendance of 66 per cent of the entire colored
population of the county. The attendance of this group would
probably have totaled 100 per cent had it been possible to plan
a meeting in the third area of the county in which a number
of Negroes live.

How much the audiences actually learned about nutrition
can only be guessed at. The people of the hollows and mountains are reticent and "poker-faced." There was no way of
judging their reactions. Occasional comments from individuals indicated that the information in the pictures made a

lasting impression. A return to the communities after several months usually resulted in the reference to the "white rats" or a question as to whether we had pictures of rats this time. One young woman told us that she thought "all that about what milk does for teeth and bones" was good to know because she had a small baby and she wanted to "raise him right." Such comments, however, were the exception rather than the rule.

It is certain that there were better gardens with greater variety of vegetables planted the next spring. There was increased interest in the "fall and winter garden." There was an increase in home canning. Several families built storage pits. By the end of the second summer, two very backward communities produced enough in their gardens to hold their first "achievement days" for displaying their produce. Yet many forces were at work during this period to encourage production and preservation of food. The war and rationing had made everyone food conscious even in remote areas. The interested professional workers of the county had opportunity to talk with people at the meetings whom they might not have seen otherwise. The people had opportunity to exchange ideas about gardens, food preservation, and storage pits. How much they gained from these things and how much from the pictures themselves, there is no way of knowing. *But the pictures brought them together as nothing else had!*

What we gained in understanding strengths and pitfalls in use of movies for adult education is more definite. This is included in the general summary that follows the account of our other experiments with movies which were going forward at the same time.

Same Pictures with Different People

In order to test the same type of program with another group, we eagerly accepted an invitation that came from the Negro home demonstration agent in Louisa, the piedmont county in which we were working.

Just as the 1942 meetings were getting under way in Greene, the white home demonstration agent in Louisa invited us to meet with a county committee planning Red Cross nutrition classes. Most of the discussion at this meeting was concerned with setting up regular Red Cross classes which must cover specified subject matter and must be taught by licensed home economics teachers. There kept coming into the discussion, however, the need for a much more elementary kind of program for many of the poorer areas in the county. The movie program in Greene was referred to. The colored home demonstration agent had already organized some very elementary classes in nutrition and wanted help. She asked whether we would show for her groups the pictures we were showing in Greene County. We agreed to begin the next week. Subsequently we met with groups in nine communities and showed pictures to audiences totaling 1,073.

These meetings with Negro groups were very different from those with the mountain and hollow folk described above. Both were of limited educational background. Neither had access to printed materials or commercial movies. But the mountain audiences were made up of collections of separate individuals who were uncommunicative if not unresponsive. The Negro audiences, on the other hand, were more highly socialized. There was a feeling of "community" and a lack of self-consciousness. Individuals were ready to ask questions and make comments both during the pictures and afterward when the home demonstration agent led discussion. There was great interest in the "lessons" of the pictures. People in the audience got up and exhorted each other to "take the lesson home," explaining what they thought "the lesson" was. Thus it was possible to judge whether or not they understood the content of the pictures. Usually they did. In cases of misinterpretation, the home demonstration agent was very clever at correcting the impression without embarrassing those who were taking part in discussion.

Likewise she was very skillful at making the picture an important but not the all-important part of the meeting. There was no time before the first meeting for her to preview the picture, but, as we drove through the red dust to Bells Crossroads, we summarized the ideas of the picture for her. Her introductory material, even after having had only a verbal explanation of what was in the picture, was excellent.

So many came to that first meeting—presumably because pictures had been announced—that its locale had to be shifted from the tiny school to the yard. This was our first outdoor movie and their first outdoor meeting. Yet there was no confusion about getting under way. The regular business was transacted; announcements were made; and the nutrition lesson began. The picture supplemented and illustrated points made in a brief preliminary talk given by the agent. Then discussion followed the picture. It had, of course, been necessary to wait till it was "plumb dark" to show the picture out of doors. For the discussion period, two or three lanterns were lighted. The leader's face was lighted but voices from the audience spoke out of total or semi-darkness. Yet discussion flowed easily. At first the leader called on individuals on whom she could count for pertinent remarks. Then the discussion became general. No one seemed to find it embarrassing to ask questions which revealed lack of knowledge or lack of understanding of the picture. In the end we felt that the subject had been pretty thoroughly covered. If time had permitted a second showing of the picture, it would have had added meaning for the group. But this was never possible. Meetings started late (they were announced for nine) because these people must work in the fields until almost dark. Then they must "clean up," for, though the men might come in overalls, they were always fresh for the occasion. For some there was a walk of two or three miles before and after the meeting—and work in the fields began early the next morning. Hence the program could not run on indefinitely, and, though the home demonstration agent and we felt that a second showing of the picture would have been desirable, it was never feasible.

The home demonstration agent was clever in her use of publicity as well as in conducting meetings. Each month she sent to the county paper an announcement of meetings held, pictures shown, and numbers in attendance at each. A bit of healthy rivalry entered. One notice commented on the fact that sound pictures were shown in places wired for electricity whereas only silent ones could be used elsewhere. This resulted in getting the church wired in one community where materials had been on hand for some time but members had been too busy to get the work done. Mt. Gilliam was not to be outdone by Rising Sun or Watch Tower.

The nutrition work in these communities did not end with the meeting. The neighborhood leaders under the direction of the home demonstration agent did careful follow-up work with the families assigned to them. Better gardens, increased canning and drying of vegetables and fruits, and more carefully planned meals were reported.

Following the nutrition meetings, another series was begun. These were planned around the picture "The Negro Farmer." Later "Henry Browne, Farmer" and "Let My People Live" were used. These three, especially planned for the southern Negro, were among the most effective educational pictures we found. Although the groups had learned something from "Food Makes a Difference" and "For Health and Happiness," these others had dramatic values that stirred the emotions as well as the mind. One of the most touching tributes to the power of the pictures to give the illusion of reality came when we showed "Henry Browne, Farmer." In this picture a Negro farm family visiting a training camp proudly watch the oldest son take off in the plane he is learning to pilot. They watch and wave lovingly until he disappears in the sky. One old lady in the audience was so moved that she rose to her feet, shaded her eyes, and waved as did the family on the screen.

Never have we felt that a specific adult education technique had better demonstrated its usefulness than did movies in these Negro community meetings. This was partly because the pictures we could get were well adapted to the audiences. But the entire credit should not be given to the pictures. *The meetings were carefully planned and carefully followed up. The people came to learn. Their leader was an excellent teacher who knew how to use visual materials for her purpose.*

In these communities, the meetings had an educational emphasis. They never became "a show." The pictures were always a means to an end and never an end in themselves. We learned much about good use of films from this experience.

An Unsuccessful Attempt

We have not yet been able to demonstrate the effectiveness of movies with white audiences in this same county though we are not convinced that they cannot be effectively used. The Louisa County Citizens' Council had appointed a forestry committee which was ready to launch an educational campaign in the spring of 1942 about the same time we started the Greene County nutrition program. There were good movies available for this purpose and we suggested neighborhood meetings. In this case, too, we invited the local sponsoring group to come to the University to preview a number of pictures and make selections. Two members came. They eliminated two pictures which dealt with large-scale lumber industries on the west coast. Others they thought applicable to conditions in their county.

There was no great enthusiasm but a plan for neighborhood meetings was made. Only two of them materialized. Attendance was not good. There was little interest either in the pictures or the discussion in which members of the state forester's staff had been invited to participate. Sponsors admitted that there had been little publicity and this may have accounted for the poor attendance. The young man most interested in planning these meetings left for the navy. Unusually widespread forest fires that spring centered attention on fire prevention rather than reforestation and good cutting practices. Members of the committee were more interested in publication of a bulletin and sponsoring an essay contest on the subject of *Stop Forest Fires* (see chapter 9) than in promoting a program of neighborhood movies.

Organizations were told that movies were available. A few asked to have them shown at their meetings. Some of them considered sponsoring a countywide program, but none did so. In accordance with our policy of cooperating with local organizations and agencies rather than promoting a program independently, we let the matter drop.

Because we were curious as to whether there was some reason that educational films would not attract people in this county, we made a second attempt later. This time the soil conservation committee was really excited about spreading information. A citizens' council meeting was devoted to the discussion of soil needs of Louisa County. The meeting ended with the showing of "The River" under excellent conditions. The county soil conservation technician who happened to be present was moved by the picture to make a little speech on the relation between poor soil and poor people. Someone in the audience suggested that everyone in the county should have a chance to see that picture. Officers from two local Granges asked whether we would bring the picture and projector if they scheduled meetings. We were not only willing but eager. Exact procedures were worked out. Enthusiasm seemed genuine. But the matter stopped there.

Almost two years later, the county agent and the soil conservation technician from this county attended a meeting of the Thomas Jefferson Soil Conservation District at the University. At the request of the district technician, we showed an excellent new film called "The Living Rock." Again the conviction was expressed that "everyone in the county should see this." Thus far no one has—though neighboring counties began asking for it the following week.

This county is more highly socialized than some of the others in which educational films have been effective. Its more prosperous residents have easy access to Richmond and Charlottesville. Yet the general educational level is not higher than in other counties where pictures have been used, and there are a number of poor areas almost untouched by any agency. The problem seems to be one of interested leadership. The accepted leaders are busy in many organizations and activities. The very able but overworked professional workers have many demands made on them by the "enlightened" farmer. They find little time for experimentation which might reach those at the lower end of the social and economic scale. There is as yet no widespread conviction in the area that it is important to reach them. These factors rather than any indifference or aversion to educational films seem to us to account for the fact that films have never been really tried with adults there except in the Negro groups.

A Dual-Purpose Experiment

The two experiments with nutrition films were going on simultaneously. At the same time another, having for its purpose stimulating interest in better agricultural practices, was being tried in one community of Greene County. Initiative in this case came from the president of the community league of the Dyke school and the agriculture teacher of the Blue Ridge School in the late winter of 1942. The latter is a church school located near Dyke. It had the only agriculture teacher in the county. The majority of his students were not county boys, and he wished to be of service to the community as well as to the school. The cooperative program with the Dyke community league offered a way. The Dyke school is a consolidated elementary school serving the relatively prosperous agricultural area immediately surrounding it and two hollows runnning back into the Blue Ridge. Children from Shifletts Hollow had been brought by bus for several years to this fine new building and were fairly well assimilated. The Bacon Hollow children, on the other hand, had just started. The little school in the hollow, which had been closed this year, had served as something of a center of sociability for adults. Their interest had not yet been transferred to the new school. Hence the Dyke community league had a purpose somewhat different from the agriculture teacher's in planning these meetings. It wanted to consolidate the adult community and thus help the children in their adjustment to the new school.

The plan was to hold one meeting each week for four weeks beginning March 19, 1942, and thereafter one a month throughout the summer if interest continued. A previewing committee selected the best available films dealing with agricultural practices, farm machinery and equipment, and defense problems as they were related to the farm. It was decided to use school busses to bring people from both hollows for the four weekly meetings. This practice was continued until the close of school. It then had to be discontinued because scarcity of gas and rubber made it impossible to use school busses for any purpose other than to transport children to school.

Attendance at the meetings during the first four months

was well over 100. The largest audience, numbering 135, was
at the June meeting. In July when busses could no longer be
used, attendance fell to 71. This audience, however, still had
a number of people from Bacon Hollow who came on foot or
in an old truck.

By this time the agriculture teacher had gone from the
Blue Ridge School leaving the county without anyone to carry
on his instruction. The president of the community league
had gone into the army. The school principal was away working in a defense industry during the vacation. This meant that
there was little local leadership for the meetings during the
summer months. No meeting was held in September while
we were on our vacation. Early in October (1942) we met
with the committee of the community league and planned a
program of monthly meetings for the year at each of which
there was to be a speaker as well as a movie. The committee
planned to have the meeting of the Dyke community league
on the same night as the speaker and movie and hoped that,
as the year progressed, it might be possible to start one or
two study groups for the same evening.

Before the first meeting, the floods came; roads into Bacon and Shiflett's Hollows were entirely washed out. Until the
next spring it was not possible for the school bus to get into
Bacon Hollow to bring the children to school. Even walking
over what had once been a road was almost impossible because
of the huge rocks left by the flood. The people in the Dyke
community continued to be interested, but with the loss of the
agriculture teacher and the absence of the people from the
hollows the possibility of attaining either of the purposes of
the program became remote.

Monthly meetings, however, were continued until February with attendance of approximately fifty, a large proportion of whom were children. This latter fact made the committee's plan for picture and speaker unsuitable, for though
the children were well behaved they were too numerous to
be ignored, and a speaker on cooperatives or better rural
schools or the defense of democracy had a difficult assignment.

Yet the committee was persistent. In February, 1943, the
ban on pleasure driving presented another obstacle. The

committee wanted to try afternoon meetings for which all the
school children would remain and from which adults who
came might ride home in the school busses. One such meeting
was tried. It was not a success, for the preponderance of
children (75 in an audience of 100) changed its character entirely. Spring work on the farms made future adult attendance in the afternoon even less probable. Meetings were given
up until a better plan could be made.

This program is difficult to evaluate. The planning was
carefully done in relation to both purposes—agricultural education and breaking down mutual prejudices and misunder-
standings between the hollow folk and those of the Dyke community. With respect to the latter and really secondary purpose, the officers of the community league and the school
teachers and principal felt that considerable gains had been
made before the October floods. It is hard to say whether the
gains were then entirely counteracted by the ensuing con-
troversies over rebuilding the road; the refusal of parents to
send children to school until the busses could run; and the
discovery, during that winter, of the convenience of having
older children at home to care for younger so both parents
could go to the defense plants in an adjoining county. But
this problem has little relation to the use of motion pictures
to attain an educational purpose. In this case, content of the
pictures had little to do with the purpose. People came to
"see the show" who would never come to "just a meeting."
Hence the pictures facilitated the process of socialization, and
the "education" probably neither helped nor hindered.

So far as the primary purpose—agricultural education—
was concerned, the meetings began well. Pertinent discussion was planned by the president of the community league
and the agriculture teacher. The pictures we were able to
get served as little more than bait to get the people there and
very slender pegs on which to hang the discussion. "Plows,
Planes and Peace," "Frontiers of the Future," and similar pictures were pretty remote from the experience or customs of
the community. Thousands of acres of flat fields with tractors, combines, and other mechanized equipment had little re-

lation to the small mountain farms these people worked. "The River," though applicable, needed so much explanation that it is doubtful whether the real idea of the picture reached the minds of the audience. For the first time, we realized that this beautiful documentary film is for an audience of sophisticated movie-goers. Later experience in other groups with the same picture bore this out.

Better results were had with a few simple pictures on methods of cutting up and curing hogs after butchering, preservation of food, and making storage pits. Available pictures on cooperatives also seemed too remote from experience. "Fruits, Vegetables, and Cooperation" and "Marketing Livestock Cooperatively" dealt with such large-scale production and marketing as to be almost meaningless to these small farmers whose great need was obviously for cooperative undertakings. "The Lord Helps Those" showing the organization of the Nova Scotia fishermen was ably explained by one who had visited there. Yet it apparently made little impression.

It seemed to us that the agricultural education of the community was advanced very little by the program. After the first two meetings, discussions related to the pictures became perfunctory. The president of the community league and the agriculture teacher were getting ready to leave the community. Their attention had already been transferred to the next steps in their own lives. Plans for follow-up programs, such as the repair of farm machinery and possible ventures in joint ownership of farm machinery, were dropped. *The pictures themselves were not good enough to stimulate people who lacked enthusiastic and able professional leadership in agricultural matters.*

Incidental showing of newsreels, defense pictures, and pictures explaining why rubber must be conserved was eagerly welcomed in this group. Such pictures helped considerably in spreading understanding and building cooperative attitudes toward the war effort. Requests for more pictures of this kind increased faster than the supply. The failure to attain the primary purpose did not necessarily mean failure of the program. The people gave it up reluctantly—and so did we.

Several months after the end of the planned program, we went back twice for special meetings to show "Soldiers of the Soil" and "Prelude to War." The former, produced by a commercial concern, showed the importance of the farmer to the war effort in the dramatic story of one simple farm family. There were few dry eyes in the audience at its close. The sceond, produced by the War Department for the education of soldiers in the background causes of the war and loaned to us by one of the naval units at the University, held the audience at close attention for an hour and a half. At its end, there was spontaneous applause—the first we had ever heard in that community.

It happened that no male member of the staff was available for this last meeting at Dyke. Later an old gentleman who had been in the audience stopped Mr. Ogden at the court house to remark: "I just wanted to tell you those two women put on the best show I've ever seen in a theatre or out."

To the picture must go all the credit. It was an educational film made with a certain objective in mind. It aimed at making ordinary people understand complicated motives and abstract ideas. It neither talked down nor overshot the mark. It had the simplicity which is akin to greatness. Had we been able to find pictures as good for the purpose of educating mountain farmers in good agricultural pursuits and soil practices, life in this particular community might have been completely changed. *For people will come to see pictures and good pictures make an impression that can change lives.*

A Film-Forum Plus Books

In another community which was served by a one-room school we tried a simple film forum supplementing movies with some discussion and reading. Because the people in that community had been especially interested in current news pictures shown with the nutrition films, and because the teacher desired to have a better informed community, we planned a program the purpose of which was to present the past and present of American democracy and to give some understanding of other lands. The program had to depend on silent films since there was no electricity in this community and our battery projector could not show sound pictures. The Yale Historical Films furnished the background. For current material, we were able to get cuttings from current news releases. Good silent pictures were found on Mexico, South American countries, Alaska, and Canada.

The majority of the adults in this community are literate. They have no reading habit, however, because books are not available. We collected historical novels, biographies, travel books, and current events materials which were attractive and easy to read. Books written for older children seemed best suited to our purpose. We borrowed from our own and our friends' libraries, from the University, and from the state library. We bought ten-cent-store books with pictures of airplanes, rubber, army insignia, and similar subjects. We placed about one hundred carefully selected books in the school, in charge of the teacher.

Eight meetings were planned for this series. The same October floods which had interrupted the Dyke meetings made it necessary to postpone these. Roads remained impassable until March. Then afternoon meetings were held weekly in the one-room school. The children (25) all stayed and 25 to 40 adults attended. The men came in even greater numbers than the women until the spring work made it impossible for them to take the time. They then asked to have the meetings at night. Unfortunately our schedule and the bad roads made the shift impossible and many of the men missed the last meetings.

But they read the books. Before, during, and following each picture we attempted informal discussion. Real group participation was difficult to get, for it was not in the pattern of the community. But people listened attentively and liked to stay around to talk after meetings. We suggested specific books both in relation to the pictures and in conversation with individuals. The books were in continuous circulation and were read by both children and adults. They were left in the school for the rest of the year and came back showing signs of considerable use. The same community asked for more books the next year, and the teacher, who had moved to another community, asked for the same type of program. Unfortunately our schedules had become so crowded that we could not meet the request. But she was able to borrow books from the state library and soon she may have a projector of her own.

We considered the Yale films pretty dull. To the people in this community they did not seem so. Their interest in "old-timey" things and events was exceeded only by their eagerness for current material, for most of them had "kin" in the war, and they had little contact with "the outside."

Our best piece of evidence as to how much of our discussion "registered" came when one little boy attended an evening meeting in a neighboring community where we were showing some of the same pictures. He sat on the floor in front of the screen and explained accurately just what was coming next. Hearing the very words we had used in spots was rather startling and made us feel that our future remarks should be pretty carefully considered.

Movies for Socialization

In three communities movies were used purely for the purpose of bringing people out and getting them used to meeting together. Many of these programs were planned in cooperation with the FSA supervisor and subject matter was closely related to his interests. The socializing value of these meetings cannot be questioned. Over a period of several meetings one became aware of a change in the audience. At first it was a collection of separate individuals each keeping himself apart and unwilling to show too much interest in this new or unusual experience. Gradually this attitude gave place to one which was less self-protective. A desire to make comments to one's neighbors began to develop. Informal commenting by one of us or by the FSA supervisor frequently facilitated this process. After several meetings the audience had become a *group enjoying a common experience*. Then came the time for transfer from "a show" to a discussion or study group.

This was not as easy to achieve as we had expected. There were minor matters that were by no means insuperable but that did present difficulties. There were large numbers of children, many of them too young to be either included or ignored. In the outdoor meetings there was total darkness, and in the indoor only a lantern or two. Not to be able to see faces is a great hindrance to discussion in this kind of group. These difficulties could be obviated by planning but by the time we had discovered them ground had been lost.

The "entertainment" element gave a mind-set which was hard to shift. Often the home demonstration agent or school teacher planned to sell ice-cream sandwiches after the show. In communities that seldom saw either ice or ice cream, this gave the affair a really gala atmosphere. As soon as the picture ended, minds leapt to ice cream—and bodies followed almost immediately. All hope of discussion was gone.

Recognizing this as an obstacle to the transfer to "education," we tried to eliminate it by failing to bring the ice cream once when not specifically requested to. (Having it had never been our plan but bringing it out from Charlottesville was always our job.) On this occasion our audience was so subdued and we were so saddened by their uncomplaining acceptance of disappointment that no progress was made!

The real difficulty, however, lay in the fact that special skill was required for stimulating discussion among people who had no habit of getting together to talk things over. In the beginning it seemed to us that the person expert in subject matter (nutrition, agriculture, etc.) should lead the discussion. By the time we discovered that these persons usually made a little speech—or a long one—which was either technical or patronizing or preaching, there was no way we could say, "You are not doing well. Let us try." We might not have done any better at first but we were frankly *learning*. Among all the "experts" we worked with in this experiment we found only a few who could even admit the *need to learn*. With them we were able to start a discussion among ourselves about the picture just shown. Sometimes members of the audience joined in; sometimes they did not. The more informal our procedure, the better the response. We found often that it was better just to speak from where we happened to be in the audience with no one going up front as "leader." Then conversation might be started and perhaps guided toward a few simple conclusions.

In most cases, we undoubtedly delayed too long before attempting the transfer from a show to a meeting. The professional workers with whom we were cooperating were glad "just to get them there" and loath to risk "losing them." We ourselves found real satisfaction in giving pleasure to people whose opportunities for sociability were rare. So we continued to put on shows. Then, usually before the transfer could be effected, there had to be an interim period after which people were asked to come to a meeting rather than a show. Fewer would come but those who did had apparently gained something from the socialization process.

Making Movies as Motivation

By chance we happened on another way to use motion pictures to stimulate community development. It was necessary for us to miss the May Day program in a neighborhood where we had been showing pictures. The program had been planned in part for us. We knew that many of our friends would be disappointed when we did not come. We, therefore, asked the staff librarian to take movies of the program for us and to explain to the people that we would thus see it even though we could not be there. There was great interest in being "in the movies." Later when we showed the May Day picture in the county, audiences exceeded anything we had experienced before. The community where the picture had been made asked to have it run four times in one night, and people moved right up to the screen on the second, third, and fourth showings, to point out special features. Neighboring communities were interested to an almost equal extent.

This happened when we were showing nutrition pictures throughout the county. We announced at meetings where we showed the May Day picture that we would like to get pictures of good gardens as the summer went on and later of good canning programs, storage plans, and sorghum boiling.

We feel sure that this was an incentive to food production and preservation. Screening and sanitation pictures were added to our list because these are among the major needs of the county. We were too limited in skill with movie making and in money for film to carry the program through to anything conclusive. However, with the cooperation of Mr. James Brown, then state director of audio-visual instruction, we were able to take about 750 feet before the film he provided was used up and his camera had to be returned. The interest throughout Greene County in the local pictures even in their unedited condition convinced us that there is powerful motivation in a movie-making program.

In Louisa County that same spring forest fires destroyed thousands of dollars worth of timber. Mr. Cheney took pictures of burned-over areas, of the ruins of homes, and of one fire while it was still smoldering. When, early the next spring, we used films as part of a stop-forest-fires campaign there, we found that this picture caught and held the attention of local audiences much more effectively than the more dramatic ready-made films. This was true in spite of the fact that *there were no people in the entire picture*. Recognition of places and place names on roadside markers and railroad stations seemed to give as much satisfaction as recognition of people.

We had hoped to extend this experiment with movie-making as a motivation for learning and doing, recognizing the fact that the products would be less important than the process. Yet the slight experience we had, indicated that the product might have at least local value. Two pictures other than the Louisa forest fires gave proof of this. One was of a simply, but scientifically, constructed storage pit that inspired a number of others in the county. The second was the picture of a woman ironing comfortably with an *electric* iron on a *screened* porch. Interest both in extension of rural electrification lines and in screening was stirred among the women-folk who, we are convinced, wield more power in getting improved standards of living than their unassertive role in rural communities would lead one to expect. Wartime scarcity of materials left us with little tangible evidence of achievement, but we know that plans are now moving forward in both these areas. And the comfortable appearance of the woman ironing on a cool screened porch made a more lasting impression than all the talk about flies and disease.

Two groups were eager to act as guinea pigs in a movie-making experiment. One was a 4-H club and the second the Negro community clubs to which we had taken the nutrition pictures. But there was a war. Film was scarce. A skilled cameraman was lacking. Both home demonstration agents whose cooperation was assured left for better jobs. The program would have required more time and attention than we could give it with the other things that must be completed during our experimental period. It was therefore postponed. But we were convinced by limited experiment that movie making is a way that should be tried for stimulating communities to action and at the same time for getting a few simple local needs presented in familiar settings.

Training Others

The intensive movie program in Greene County and also among the Negroes in Louisa resulted in a demand from the people for more movies. Professional workers who cooperated with us in the programs became converts to visual education. This was especially true of the home demonstration agents and FSA workers. A demonstration on nutrition or first aid seldom reached more than a dozen women in a community. A movie on the same subject reached 50 to 150 men, women, and older children. Selling an idea to the whole family at one time had obvious advantages.

Church groups had also become interested. What they could learn about Latin American countries, for example, from one movie far exceeded what they could learn in a study group during the entire Lenten season. Pictures had also been found helpful in daily vacation Bible school.

School teachers had found a way of reaching the adult community as well as the children. The schools in one county alone could have filled our entire time. (In fact, one superintendent suggested our showing movies in schools instead of his hiring a truant officer!) Having asked the cooperation of teachers and professional workers in our experiment, we found it difficult to say, "We have learned what we wanted to know. Now we are busy elsewhere."

So we took the next step. A group of six professional workers in Greene County were taught to show movies and slides themselves. The Extension Division had a film library from which they could borrow. Mr. Rorer, director of audio-visual education, taught them to operate the projectors — sound, silent, and slides. We offered the use of our projectors as far as they would go. The high school owned one and was generous with it. The professional workers council decided to buy one but none was available at that time. This was unfortunate, for it would have been a practical demonstration in "joint ownership" which the FSA workers were then discussing with their clients in the county.

Several of these workers became more skillful with use of movies and slides than we had been. The need for visual materials in remote areas was so great that our small battery projector was in the county for months at a time and we borrowed it when we needed it. One of the most eager users was the new home demonstration agent. She had not been in the county during the intensive program, but she heard about it wherever she went. She asked for our report; she learned to run the projector; she became the best commentator we had worked with; then she, too, left.

In fact, after two years there was left in that county not one single person of the six who learned to show movies. And therein lies the problem of the professional worker in the small, rural county. He goes on to another and better job as soon as he has demonstrated his ability. The more he learns, the more quickly he moves. He takes his newly acquired skills with him and is better equipped for his next job. These Greene County workers continued to borrow our equipment to use in other communities. But we must begin at the beginning again in Greene—and this time with *lay leaders whose lives are identified with the community.*

A Movie for a Meeting

As soon as news spread that we had movies and a projector, requests to "bring a movie for a meeting" came much more rapidly than we could meet them. We found that we must be especially discriminating about these requests. Too often they came from a program chairman or professional worker who saw this as an easy way of filling time on a program that required a certain number of meetings each year. Usually in such cases it had little or no relation to anything else in the program. "Bring anything you like" was the kind of invitation we refused immediately.

On the other hand, we were eager to help leaders, both lay and professional, work out ways of using visual aids effectively. Even when the leader asked for a film to serve as a link in a chain, he (or she) was likely to expect the picture to do the entire job. It seldom will. We tried, therefore, to insist on previewing and preliminary planning. One professional worker who had become an enthusiastic user of films remarked that in the beginning she had thought they would save her work. Later she found that to use them effectively she had to work even harder than when she had no film. Yet she felt that the increased interest and the additional ground that could be covered in a short time repaid her amply for the work. Her discovery tallied with our general experience in many and varied groups: *The pictures are useful in the degree that the leader makes them useful.*

Our own mistakes led us to be more insistent on planning as time went on, for planning by us we discovered was not enough. We were delighted early in our experiment by one request for films on forestry for a county in which timber resources were important. The organization was devoting an entire meeting to the subject and the film was to be only a part of the program. In consultation with the state forester, we selected the film best suited to the community. A member of his staff agreed to go with us to introduce the picture and be ready with any technical information needed. He — and we—spent considerable time in selection and preparation. The meeting was a large one—and a long one. There were essays by school children and speeches by representatives of various agencies concerned with the subject under consideration. After almost two hours the chairman relaxed and announced, "Now, we will have our entertainment."

At first we did not recognize this as meaning our contribution to the program. It was confusing to the audience, too. We showed a film on good cutting practices and reforestation which should have been an integral part of the educational program. It was not "entertainment." People were already tired, they had been prepared for "entertainment," minds were turned off, and it was not surprising that no souls —or no trees—were saved by that movie.

Another experience came later—and we applied what we had learned from this one. An Armistice Day committee asked us to bring a suitable picture. We asked how it was to fit into the rest of the program.

"Oh, we'll have some singing, a speech, and the picture," was the reply.

"But why have a picture?" we asked.

"Because people will come to see the picture who would not come to hear a speech."

Convinced that pictures could and should serve as more than bait, we urged that the committee think through a unified program. Their purpose, they said, was to get people to think about the kind of peace that would prevent another war. We agreed to look for suitable films if the committee and the speaker would preview them and plan their use in relation to the rest of the program. The speaker was cooperative. He and the committee came to the University and spent an afternoon looking at the film selected and making plans. The meeting was a good one with everything directed toward the main purpose. The audience was definitely moved. The speaker later admitted that he had "really worked" on that speech to make it and the picture supplement each other. But he liked the results—and he saw a new use for films in his own community programs.

Frankly Entertainment

We have not personally experimented with movies solely for entertainment purposes. Three principals with whom we have worked as consultants or in workshops for planning community activities, however, have tried this type of community recreation program.

In two of the communities it was an "emergency" program to meet a wartime need when pleasure driving was not permitted. Both communities were twenty miles or more from commercial movies. They were able, therefore, to get somewhat more recent films than if they had been within a "competitive area." Each charged a low admission in order to cover cost of rental. The attendance was fair. Audiences in both cases were made up of people who, in normal times, saw movies occasionally or even regularly. They were generally dissatisfied with the type of pictures available and with the limitations of the small projector and school screen. The conclusion in each case was that community nights in which there was general participation in games furnished a more satisfying kind of entertainment. In one school a short comedy or feature became a part of the more diversified recreation program, but in neither case was the once-a-week movie continued after the trial period.

In the third school the approach was different and likewise the result. This is a large consolidated high school serving an entire rural county which has no motion picture theatre. The school is equipped with a 35mm projector and an excellent screen. The program predates the war. School busses were used to bring people to the movies. Everyone paid for both bus service and movie. The crowds were large enough to make good pictures financially possible. The program was successful both as a business venture and as entertainment. It had to be discontinued during the ban on pleasure driving but has now been resumed with satisfaction to both school and patrons.

Though the classroom visual education equipment may serve well the purpose of adult education in a school com-

munity, it is doubtful whether it can or should ever be adapted
to the needs of an extensive entertainment program.

Film Library for Adults

When the experiment with movies was begun, we borrowed pictures for the purpose from the film library of the
State Board of Education. Some of the films were useful;
many were so definitely supplements to classroom teaching
as to make their use in the informal adult audience difficult.
Most of our rural audiences were not yet at the "study group"
stage; many of them never would be. They needed a different kind of film.

"Food Makes a Difference," for example, was the best elementary nutrition film we could find. It contained basic principles simply presented by teachers of home economics. For
students of home economics it was excellent. But we discovered there were weaknesses for our audiences. Captions were
in technical language. There were two spots where it always
lost the attention of the audience. One was in a long sequence on experiments with white rats. The second was in
the details of intelligence testing. The results of both experiments were directly related to the purpose of the picture but
the techniques involved were meaningless and without interest to our audiences. It was possible to purchase a print
of this film and experiment with some judicious cutting and
some rewriting of captions on the basis of audience reaction.
Results were excellent. Unfortunately, borrowed films could
not be treated this way.

Moreover, there were some films available for adult audiences that did not belong in the classroom film collection.
These were borrowed or rented at first from their distributing
agencies. There were, however, obvious advantages in own-
ing prints and having them readily available. The local banks
were very much interested in the program and offered a small
sum for the establishment of an adult education film library
in the Extension Division. A collection of the best films is
being built up gradually.

Some Things We Have Learned

The "silver screen" is not an educational magic. But the good leader can use it to stimulate, to inspire, to inform, and to demonstrate, if he is willing to work as hard at it as he would in preparing any other kind of educational program. The picture itself will not do the job. It is—or can be made—a teaching aid. It does not and cannot take the place of the teacher or leader in an adult group any more than in the elementary school classroom. Adults who are accustomed to directing their own study can make use of movies just as they can of printed materials—but these are not the people who concern the adult educator in search of techniques. *No device we have found is more rewarding than the film when carefully used as one step in the educational process. None is more wasteful of time or stultifying of thought if casually treated.*

Defining the Purpose

The first step in planning use of films is careful definition of purpose. Movies as bait should not be confused with movies for teaching. They may serve a real purpose in either case but nothing is to be gained by fooling oneself as to what is really happening.

If the movies are being used frankly as bait—to "get the crowd" or to socialize a group of individuals unaccustomed to coming together—care must be taken not to continue past the point of achieving the purpose. Movies so used can have a narcotic and habit-forming effect on both leader and audience.

The publicity should be in line with the purpose. If the meeting and discussion are important, the affair should be announced as a *meeting with a picture,* not as a *show.* The entertainment element in the latter term places the leader at a definite disadvantage if the picture is merely incidental to speaking and discussion. In our cooperation with local groups that handled the publicity, we found this one of the most difficult problems to work out.

The desire of the local agency to take advantage of the meeting for money-making purposes likewise confused issues.

Though the movie can serve as well as many other forms of entertainment to raise money for the school lunchroom or other worthy cause, it should be announced frankly for this purpose when so used.

For the purpose of getting people out, the movie is undoubtedly more useful in unsophisticated communities and areas in which there are few opportunities for recreation or sociability. But this very fact of isolation and limited background presents a real problem in finding the right pictures. Thus we have the anomaly of the most spontaneous response from the people for whom there are few really good pictures available.

Problem of Selection

Selection of films is closely related to both purpose and audience. A film may be excellent from aesthetic and scientific points of view. But whether it is good for a specific purpose with a specific audience is another matter.

Only the person who knows *how* the film is to be used and *with whom* can make a wise selection. We have asked for help and we have tried to give it. We speak with feeling both as borrower and as lender of films.

Even when selecting from well known films for own own use in a particular situation, we have had to look at them again through the eyes of the new audience. Often a picture that we remembered as excellent when we looked at it with only general use of films in mind is not at all what we need for a specific purpose.

We once had a happy group-experience looking at a film on cooperatives at a meeting of the Southeastern Cooperative League. Later we used the same film with a rural Virginia audience who knew nothing of the "cooperative movement." The film left them just about where they started. Then we realized how much we, and other members of that enthusiastic conference audience, had read into the film from our own knowledge and experience.

Titles and catalogue descriptions are frequently misleading. We were asked to find a picture that would show the importance of milk in the diet. The title "Drink Milk for

Health" sounded right. Nothing in the description warned us that it was for city audiences only. Not till we looked at the film did we realize that it would not do. The tall shining bottles being filled and capped by beautiful machines and delivered at the door of the city home had little significance for a rural community in which the only milk came from the family cow. Here the problem was one of making people see the importance of having enough cows of good enough quality with enough feed to assure an adequate year-round supply of milk for a family of eight or ten children. We did not find such a film—though we found many groups where it would have served a real purpose.

Even the director of a film service or the custodian of a state or regional film library can only advise on the basis of the information you give him. "We need an elementary film on the care of the teeth for 4-H clubs and parents in a rural county" seemed like a simple order that we could pass on to the state film library. The film that came in response to that request stressed need for periodic checkup by a dentist and showed just what happened to a child in the dentist's chair. It was an excellent psychological preparation for a child likely to have such an experience. In the city where the film was made, dental hygienists visit the public schools, and every child has his teeth cleaned and checked periodically. But in an area where few children (or adults) own a toothbrush, where there is no dentist except an itinerant one who has more than he can do when he comes to pull decayed and aching teeth of suffering adults, the "periodic checkup" for children is not a suggestion that is possible of attainment.

Often we have looked at ten pictures that sounded right to find one that was possible. *There is no way to select but to see for yourself and to be sure you see through the eyes of the particular audience with which you plan to use the picture.*

The Previewing Committee

Local committees to preview films that are under consideration are of great value. The teacher or leader who meets many groups becomes so accustomed to the content of a picture that he needs the help of fresh eyes and minds. It had never occurred to us that, in one area not yet touched by rural electrification, the electric stove and refrigerator in a picture would mean nothing. When this was pointed out by a "previewer," we were prepared to make an explanation that would broaden the understanding and possibly make the picture serve as an incentive to rural electrification in that area. We have already pointed out the help to discussion from having members of a previewing committee in an audience.

In relation to purchase of films for building up a local or regional library, advice of such committees is more dependable than that of teachers, professional workers, salesmen, or so-called visual education specialists. It takes time to work with committees but it is time well spent.

Preparation—Mental and Physical

Even the best picture for a specific purpose, we reiterate, will not do the whole job. The leader must get ready to use it. He must look at it himself before showing it to his audience. Captions may use words that are too technical or otherwise unfamiliar. The leader may need to paraphrase them as they appear. For this he must be prepared in advance. In audiences in which there was some illiteracy, we found that paraphrasing was less likely to hurt the feelings of those who could read than direct reading of the words on the screen.

Ready-made guides are helpful but almost always need adapting to the audience. This, too, requires advance thinking on the part of the leader.

A part of the preparation must be done on the spot. Placing of screen and projector—and, especially of the loud speaker —for best results, focusing of lens, adjusting of speed and of sound so that everything is *right* are very important. The only way you can tell in a new place is by trying—and this should be done before the audience assembles.

"Our people won't come out to see movies," one school principal told us. Later we saw a film at one of his PTA meetings and we thought the people showed good judgment. The screen sat far back on the stage. The picture spilled over its edges. The speed of the film was such that we were quite

dizzy trying to watch it and were unable to complete the
reading of a single caption. The sound was turned to full
volume and echoed back from the cinder-block walls of the
auditorium so that no one could possibly understand a word.
The subject—transportation of freight by rail—had absolutely
no relation to anything else in the meeting. There was no
introduction of any kind. The lights went out, the noise began,
and the picture flashed along to its end. The lights came on,
everyone breathed a sigh of relief, and certainly there had
been nothing in that performance to make "our people come
out for movies."

So far as the film forum is concerned or discussion following a picture, preparation is also important. Experience taught
us that skill in discussion technique was more essential than
expertness in subject matter. Anyone having the former could
master the subject matter for a particular situation. The
expert in subject matter could also perhaps master the technique but, in our experience, he seldom recognized the need.
A few happy experiences with "experts" who would sit in
the audience ready to act as resources or consultants convinced us that this was an ideal kind of arrangement. But,
unfortunately, most experts felt that they could show their
willingness to cooperate only by assuming complete responsibility. And seldom were they able or willing to take the time
to prepare in advance whereas the person interested in perfecting the film forum technique would take time to master
subject matter.

*The leader who puts nothing into the "meeting with
movie" gets little by way of results.*

Further Development Needed

The potentialities of the movie in a program of adult
education which has for its purpose better living in better
communities are unlimited. The film can bring the necessary
inspiration, can furnish information and teach skills with
which to bring the inspiration closer to reality. It can influence
habits, attitudes, and ways of doing in more backward areas.
It can broaden horizons and increase understanding—doing in
a short time through visual means what years of travel and

wide reading might accomplish. But it can do all this only
if movies are as carefully planned for the purpose as the best
textbooks have been.

After a year's intensive movie program in rural Virginia,
we faced a real problem. We had made both the people and
their professional leaders movie-minded. The former were
clamoring for shows. The latter were clamoring for pictures
dealing with subjects they were trying to help the people
understand. The removal of several of these professional
workers to other areas spread the use of our films whenever
we could make them and, in some cases, the projectors available.

We had created a demand for pictures adapted to the rural
or small town adult audience. Subjects needed included good
farming practices for small farmers; home-making and nutrition education for homes not equipped with up-to-date facilities and with little cash to spend; cooperative undertakings
on a simple scale; public health and sanitation practices simple
and inexpensive enough to be applicable; home nursing, first
aid, and medical programs suited to the needs of an area where
hospitals are nonexistent, and doctors are scarce or cost too
much for most family budgets; construction of sweet-potato-
curing houses, storage pits, and other food preservation facilities.

A fine-tooth-combing of the lists of available films revealed
many that "would do" but few that actually answered the
need. Some good nutrition films, for example, were addressed
specifically to city audiences. Other assumed too high an
educational level or too broad an experience level for those
who would see them. Others were too blatant in their advertising. One good film in kodachrome was not usable because
it showed more of the human body than conventional rural
folk would tolerate. Pictures of cooperatives either showed
large midwestern developments that were bewildering rather
than inspiring, or told the story of a people whose livelihood
and folkways were foreign to the southern farmer. There
were films, many of them excellent, but few of them right
for our audiences in spite of the fact that the audiences are
typical of vast southern rural areas.

Our own experiments with movies sharpened our observation of the use of films by others. From both the experimentation and observation we were strengthened in our conviction that *the motion picture is outstanding among the techniques that have demonstrated their effectiveness and need for further development in relation to adult education.*

In its further development there are two aspects of the educational film that need consideration: (1) refinement of techniques for integration of the pictures with the entire educational process; and (2) preparation of pictures better adapted to the needs, interests, and background of specific types of adult audiences. The first of these can make some progress without relation to the latter. *Full realization of potentialities, however, depends on simultaneous development of both better techniques and better pictures.*

CHAPTER 14

The Printed Word:
Tailor-Made Versus Ready-Made

"Why don't we use the same bulletins over again?" asked a member of the council when a new bulletin on forest fires was under discussion.

"People like something new," was the answer of another member.

"But," persisted the first, "we read the Bible over and over. It tells us simple things we need to know. So do these bulletins. One reading is not enough."

This discussion came after a year of intensive experimentation with locally prepared printed materials on subjects of local importance expressed in simple language and distributed in small doses to all families in one rural Virginia county. The conclusion to the above discussion was that we had probably not yet acquired such great facility at saying the right thing in the right way as to warrant our simply repeating ourselves. Nevertheless the committee agreed to try to discover from talking with as many people as possible which ideas or approaches had made the greatest impression and to make further use of those that had proved most effective. The group as a whole wished to continue to experiment in refining this technique of analyzing local needs; selecting pertinent facts from materials of research workers and professional agencies in the field; putting them together into a small broadside aimed directly at the group they wished to reach; and becoming more and more adept at hitting the bullseye.

The Beginning of an Experiment

That they wished to continue to improve on what had been done delighted us when we remembered how this particular experiment had started. In the spring of 1942 there had been unusually devastating forest fires in the county. The citizens' council had decided to carry on an intensive campaign before the dangerous season of the next spring. It was as part of this campaign that one member of the forestry committee suggested that some of the printed material available from state and federal agencies be distributed throughout the county. These pamphlets had been very useful in essay contests and for committee study. That they be given wider distribution seemed a good suggestion.

Our files yielded scores of pamphlets. We checked with the state forester's office to be sure we had missed nothing. They were all turned over to the local committee for selection of one that would be right to send to every family in the county. Examination resulted in dissatisfaction. Every pamphlet said too much. The most attractive was printed in three colors, with excellent pictorial charts, and clearly expressed printed information. But it covered the entire field of forest husbandry with only incidental reference to fires—and it was addressed to a very general audience. It contained more material than any but the most determined seeker-after-information would read.

At the same time, committee members found specific facts the county needed in these pamphlets. It seemed to them to be a fairly simple matter to select those that pertained to the immediate local situation, rephrase them to suit the local vocabulary, use local names and incidents, and have the type of broadside that should go into every home in that county.

Since the important group to be reached was the less privileged educationally and economically, it could be assumed that they had no reading habit. Yet it was agreed that almost every family had someone who could read—and that what came through the mail was pretty sure to be read. Hence it was decided to stress one idea only on each leaflet, to present it arrestingly, to have it printed in large type that could be read at a glance, and to send it by mail personally addressed to the head of each family in the county.

Stop Forest Fires Series

After informal discussion with members of the council committee, the Extension Division staff worked out tentative copy for four leaflets on subjects the committee had suggested. These were *Burn Brush Early, Burn Brush Safely, Don't Burn Sedge,* and *In Case of Fire.* Copies were made before the next

meeting so that each ̲c̲o̲m̲m̲i̲t̲t̲e̲e̲   ̲ ̲u̲s̲e̲r̲ ̲c̲o̲u̲l̲d̲ ̲h̲a̲v̲e̲ ̲o̲n̲e̲   ̲
̲l̲o̲o̲k̲ ̲a̲t̲ as a starting point for discussion. The four subjects
were given thoughtful consideration. Three were accepted
unanimously as of primary and indisputable importance. The
one on burning sedge brought out strong differences of opinion.
Some people thought sedge burning absolutely unavoidable for
many local farmers who lacked the kind of equipment necessary to plow it under. A few even disagreed with the advice
of the forestry and agriculture pamphlets that said it should
be plowed under. All agreed that the pamphlets should urge
practices about which there was no question and which were
possible of attainment in this county. Finally it was decided to
omit the leaflet on sedge burning and to substitute one showing the principal causes of fire. *Be Careful With Fire* was
agreed on as its title.

Once the facts to be presented were decided, the staff
members who had to get ready final copy sought advice on
some emotional or dramatic approach. Discussion brought out
the point that the one thing that had made the most lasting
impression during the fires of the preceding year was a court
prosecution of a prominent citizen who had set a fire before
four o'clock in the afternoon contrary to the state law. The
other thing that had aroused people to the tragedy of forest
fires was the destruction of several homes the preceding year.
Saying that $80,000 worth of timber burned, it was felt, would
make less impression than saying that a home burned and a
family was left without shelter or possessions.

With these suggestions, the staff went to work again on
the leaflets. It had been agreed that they should be distributed
in February and early March—the dangerous season for fires.
This gave scant time for preparation of pictorial material, for
the committee had not thought of the idea until late January.
Then considerable time had been spent in studying and attempting to select from available materials.

The state forester had taken some pictures showing the
devastation from the fires of the preceding spring. He was
most generous in offering these and the use of any cuts he had
had prepared for his own publications. He also urged that the

com~~ittee feel perfectly~~ free to use facts, figures, sentences, or paragraphs from his material. He was wholeheartedly behind the experiment. He agreed with us that too many "credit lines" on a simple leaflet might distract attention from the main purpose, and that local names and organizations were more important than names of agencies and institutions remote from the people addressed. The second set of dummies, when prepared, was submitted to him for approval as well as to the local committee. The simplicity of the product is indicated in copies of the first two leaflets reproduced on the following pages.

Louisa County Citizens' Council Bulletin

It was in Louisa County that this idea had originated. Because Louisa was one of the three experimental areas in which the Special Projects were working and because the experiment in locally prepared materials was one we wished to carry further, we asked the Louisa County Citizens' Council to cooperate with the Extension Division not only in the publication of the forestry series but also of similar leaflets to be prepared by council committees on subjects of importance to the county.

The Extension Division's suggestions to the Council follow:

1. *Purpose*—To reach all citizens of the county but especially those in the less privileged groups who do not have easy access to information or ideas important to the welfare of the county as a whole.

2. *General Plan*—The plan is to issue a series of brief, simple leaflets dealing with the subjects being considered by the general committees—forestry, soil conservation, health, nutrition, recreation, etc.

3. *The Form*—The leaflets will be attractively printed in large type.

   Each subject will have a distinctive color as well as serial number—for example, forestry might be printed on green paper; nutrition might be on yellow paper.

   All leaflets will be uniform in size and shape for convenience in filing.

   They will be punched so that they can be bound easily in dime store loose-leaf covers.

STOP FOREST FIRES!!   STOP FOREST FIRES!!

BURN BRUSH EARLY!

JANUARY and FEBRUARY
are the best months for burning brush and trash

BUT

if you MUST burn brush later than February
the LAW says

YOU MUST NOT START A FIRE
UNTIL AFTER FOUR O'CLOCK IN THE AFTERNOON
from MARCH 1 to MAY 15

We Must Be More Careful With Fire

CARE WITH FIRE will prevent this Court room scene

Virginia Forest Service

Louisa County Citizens' Council

Prepared by
Rotary Committee On Forestry
W. Earl Crank, Chairman

FORESTRY LEAFLET NO. 1
February, 1943

STOP FOREST FIRES!! **STOP FOREST FIRES!!**

BURN BRUSH SAFELY

PILE BRUSH IN SMALL PILES AND FAR APART

BEFORE STARTING A FIRE
  rake a wide, well-cleared PATH or FIRE LINE around the
  place burned

**NEVER START A FIRE WHEN A STRONG WIND IS BLOW-
  ING**

**ALWAYS: BURN AGAINST THE WIND . . . BURN DOWN
  HILL**

**BEFORE YOU LEAVE THE PLACE YOU HAVE BURNED
  MAKE SURE THE FIRE IS OUT . . . DEAD OUT!**

The Ghost of a Home—Don't let this happen in Louisa

Louisa County Citizens' Council

Prepared by
Rotary Committee On Forestry
W. Earl Crank, Chairman

FORESTRY LEAFLET NO. 2
February, 1943

On each, credit will be given to the committees and the
special group which has helped prepare the material
4. *Preparation of Material*—Determining the content of each
leaflet will be the responsibility of the sub-committee
on that topic (forestry, nutrition, etc.).

These sub-committees may ask civic clubs, high school
social studies classes, or other groups to prepare some
of the leaflets.

All leaflets will clear through a publications committee
under the general committee.

Final writing or editing and printing will be cared for by
the Extension Division.

The council approved the publication of the suggested
leaflets on forest fires and the sending out of leaflets on the several subjects of interest to it, provided "in each case the copy
be approved by the committee concerned."

Discussion of methods of distribution resulted in the decision that the people most in need of the information would
be more impressed by something received by mail than by
something received in a more casual way. The forestry committee agreed to prepare a mailing list including all the families in the county, and the Extension Division agreed to take
responsibility for mailing for the present. It also agreed to
finance the bulletins for the first year with the understanding
that if they proved effective the council would then find a way
to finance future issues.

The four leaflets in the series *Stop Forest Fires* were mailed out one at a time at intervals of about a week. Credit for
preparation was given to the Rotary committee on forestry at
the request of the council committee since both groups had
worked on it, and it was thought that the older organization
was better known and might carry more weight in the county.

Before the forest fires leaflets had all been mailed out, the
local Ruritan Club had asked the council to cooperate with
it in circularizing the county with a bulletin to promote
better gardens and more canning. (This was the spring of
1943 when food production was being stressed.) This request
was approved by the executive committee of the council and
referred to the nutrition committee. That committee felt
that *two* bulletins were indicated if the council were to follow

the policy of *saying one thing at a time in brief and simple form*. The bulletin urging gardens should go out immediately, for March was the time for planting; the one on canning should come later or people would have forgotten about it by the canning season.

A member of the Ruritan Club met with the nutrition committee and the county farm and home demonstration agents. They adapted to Louisa County material published by the Agricultural Extension Service but not available for general distribution. To the suggestions of what to plant, and when to plant the various vegetables best suited to local gardens, they added the suggestion: "Consult your county farm and home demonstration agents for further information on gardening."

Thus five bulletins were distributed between the February and April meetings of the council. It had approved the idea of the bulletin just about a year after these citizens had first come together at the invitation of the Extension Division to consider their county. The effect of the bulletins was immediately apparent not only in the county but in the council itself. The April meeting was the largest, most eager, and most wide-awake it had held. An entirely new spirit seemed to have resulted from the tangible achievement of having circularized the county on forest fires and gardens. A report was given on the preparation and distribution of the five leaflets. Enthusiastic approval of both content and form of the *Bulletin* was expressed and it was suggested that the form of the one on gardening be regularly used with the title *Louisa County Citizens' Council Bulletin*. It provided special space for credit to the committee or other group participating in its preparation. The name of the Extension Division or the University did not appear on the *Bulletin*. Because of the amount of time the staff gave to preparation, the council felt that credit should be given them. Discussion brought out the facts content was determined by council committees or local organizations in consultation with local professional workers; that the Extension Division was really concerned with discovering the effectiveness of local material locally sponsored; and that it expected to withdraw and leave the *Bulletin* entirely to local groups after the experimental period. Hence the policy of giving credit to the council and participating local groups seemed, in no sense, unfair or dishonest.

At the same meeting the question was raised as to how many bulletins each committee could send out. Committee chairmen were now eager to have as many as possible. The chairman of the nutrition committee clamored loudest, saying that right now food production and conservation was one of the most important national problems, and that, during the summer at least, stress should be placed here. It was suggested that careful thought and study should go into the planning and the timing of the bulletins and that it might be well for the executive committee to consider the needs of the county and the relative importance of subjects and to lay out the year's program for the bulletins in view of the over-all needs of the county. This suggestion was accepted by the chairman.

The bulletins issued prior to the April, 1943, meeting had originated in groups outside the council. At this meeting the council decided that careful planning was preferable to opportunism. The nutrition committee insisted that information on pest control should follow the information on planting gardens if people rather than bugs were to eat the produce. The women on the committee said they needed the help of the men on pests and asked that a special committee be appointed.

The process followed in the preparation of this next bulletin set the pattern for preparing subsequent issues. It is a process that resulted (1) in getting the right thing said in the right way for the community concerned and (2) in training local people to be increasingly adept at preparing their own bulletins. There was a by-product of the process that was also of value: the committee educated itself pretty thoroughly in its efforts to study existing materials, to analyze local conditions, to select what was applicable, and to say it simply and effectively. Studying for the purpose of producing a bulletin seemed more effective motivation for committees than just studying.

We have adapted to other groups the same procedures in preparing materials. Experiments with the Virginia Federation of Women's Clubs and the Thomas Jefferson Soil Conservation District are referred to in chapter 12.

Evaluation

To date seventeen issues of the Bulletin, in addition to the *Stop Forest Fires* Series, have been prepared and distributed. These have included such subjects as canning, buying baby chicks, raising healthy chicks, soil conservation, frozen food lockers, education, and medical care. Exactly one year after the distribution of the one which described frozen food lockers in elementary terms for people who knew nothing of frozen foods, a second one on the subject announced the opening of the Louisa plant. The one on medical care likewise opened a campaign for a medical care center for which $50,000 toward a $75,000 goal has been raised.

The bulletins themselves as the first tangible achievements had been stimulating to the council. They were even more so when neighboring counties began to ask whether they might use the material. Five Virginia counties and one in Georgia used the first one on frozen food lockers. A large national commercial concern asked for permission to reprint. An Alabama community asked for the one on medical care to use as a model. The North Carolina State Planning Board somehow came by copies and wrote: "These bulletins are very interesting. We plan to suggest that a number of our community planning committees follow similar procedures." The one on soil conservation received wide attention. It was copied or adapted in many states. Locally it resulted in a request for help in preparation of similar material for five counties.

No attempt had been made to bring these bulletins to the attention of people outside the county. It was by chance that other people came upon them. The chairman of the council referred requests to the Extension Division because of the experimental nature of the program. Always in sending any of the leaflets in response to a request we urged that they be used only as models since the chief value was in the process of analyzing local needs and selecting material that applied directly. *The process, not the product, was of primary importance.*

Yet locally we attempted to evaluate the effectiveness of the product. Though no objective measures could be applied we knew that the council, its committees, and individuals who had worked on the bulletins had profited greatly. To find out how generally they were being read throughout the county we devised the following simple questionnaire toward the end of the first year of publication:

Louisa County Citizens' Council

You need not sign your name. But please check two of the following:

...........Male   ....Female

.....Under 20 .....Over 20

BULLETIN

What is your post-office? ....Route No.?......................

Does your family receive the BULLETIN? Yes..........................No..........................

Who reads it? Check ONE or MORE:

................Mother   ....Grandma

................Father   ....Grandpa

................Daughter   ....The Cook

................Son   ....Nobody

Write in any others..

....

Following are the subjects of the BULLETINS published from March to October, 1943. Check those that have been helpful to you or to some member of your family:

................Burn Brush Early   ....Your Canning Program

................Burn Brush Safely   (with chart)

................Be Careful with Fire   ....Simple Wartime Canning

................In Case of Fire   ....Fall and Winter Gardens

................Your Garden Program   ....Make Your Winter Garden
    (with planting chart)   Serve All Winter (storage
................Pest Control Program   ideas)

................Stop Forest Fires!

Now look at the list again. If you think any BULLETINS were of no use, draw a line through the titles of those.

SUGGESTIONS or COMMENTS may be written on back of page.

We did not send these by mail but asked to have them filled out in groups such as home demonstration clubs, home economics and agriculture classes, Ruritan, Rotary, and Grange. The 735 returns were a representative cross section of the population. Returns indicated that the mailing list was still incomplete and inaccurate. More than 200 reported that they did not receive the *Bulletin* and most of them asked to be placed on the list. Checking replies against mailing list showed that only three who claimed not to get it were actually on the list. In the case of one of these it was addressed to the husband's office and apparently not carried home. Of the more than 500 who reported that they did receive it, only two reported that no one in the family read it. The average number of readers reported to a family was three.

The other kind of check we tried was to bring the *Bulletin* into conversation whenever there was opportunity. Committee members also did this and reported results. All reports indicated that the *Bulletin* was making an impression and was helping to influence attitudes and habits in the spheres touched upon. The three that brought most comment locally were the first on frozen food lockers, one on medical care, and one on soil conservation.

The first of these gave specific information about a service of importance to people having little refrigeration. It answered direct questions about a locker plant, such as: "What is it for? What is it like? Who may use it? What does it cost the individual user? What is it worth to the farmer, to townsfolk, to sportsmen, to the community?" It was popular because it anticipated questions people would have been hesitant about asking.

The other two were the most specifically related to Louisa County. Farms using good soil practices were located on a map, and the names of farmers who would welcome visitors to inspect their farms were listed. The one on medical care listed facts and figures not only for rural Virginia but for Louisa County. It stirred people to action in their own behalf.

Cooperation with Committee on Southern Regional Studies

In August, 1943, the director of the Extension Division attended a work conference of the Committee on Southern Regional Studies and Education. The subject of the conference was *Channeling Research into Education.* By this time the Special Projects had been experimenting for two years with *New Dominion Series,* community stories with accent on process; and for six months with locally prepared bulletins interpreting community needs and resources. Both experiments had direct relation to the subject under consideration. They were described in the conference report as "pioneer efforts in Southern research education" representing "a unique effort on the part of the university to become more of a service and stimulating agency to the people of the state."[1] The following summer when this regional group again met, it was to work specifically on the problems of preparing materials on southern resource-use education. Mr. Zehmer served as chairman of the committee on resource-use education for non-school groups which made the following recommendations:

a. That instructional materials for non-school agencies on resources and their use be prepared in all of the media of instruction, including those of the motion picture, film strip and slide, radio script, charts, cartoons, exhibitions, etc., as well as that of print.

b. That materials in these several media be prepared (1) for general purposes and for general consumption throughout the South, (2) for more specific purposes and for more restricted areas of the South, and, (3) also, for different educational levels.

c. That criteria as guides to the preparation of materials of instruction be established.

d. That steps be taken to assist in identifying persons and institutions qualified to prepare the materials needed.

e. That assistance be given in the distribution of materials with special reference to disseminating information on materials available, on effective methods being used in the distribution of materials.

-----

[1] John H. Ivey, Jr., *Channeling Research into Education.* American Council on Education Studies. Series 1, No. 19. Washington, D. C. August, 1944.

In the intervening year the Special Projects had not only continued the two experiments with specially prepared materials but had extended the program through countywide and community workshops begun in the winter of 1943-44 in three different areas. In these workshops, committees analyzed local resources—natural, economic, human, and institutional—and tried to relate them to meeting local problems. In each community, need was felt for finding more effective ways of giving people information about resources available, helping to bring about a realization of their significance, and planning for their more intelligent utilization and conservation.

The Extension Division had planned for the extension of local workshops with the help of additional staff members made available through a special grant. Hence it seemed possible to extend the experiment in preparation of materials in relation to these actual study groups. An additional grant was requested for the purpose of engaging someone to "prepare materials in close collaboration with interested adults who are actively engaged in community study, thus getting the advice and help of local people which we think is highly desirable—in fact almost essential—in order to be sure that we will prepare material on subjects of interest to the ultimate consumers and write in a language with which they are familiar and which they will understand."[2]

This request had the backing of the Committee on Southern Regional Studies and Education expressed by its chairman, Dr. Maurice Seay, Director, Bureau of School Service, University of Kentucky, as follows:

1. The project planned by the University of Virginia is closely related to the interests expressed in the two Gatlinburg Conferences.
2. The proposed project also relates very closely to the interests expressed in different meetings of our Committee on Southern Regional Studies and Education.
3. If the program planned in this project is carried out our committee, and the South in general, will have a demonstration the need

---

[2]This experiment with resource education for adults by the University of Virginia Extension Division paralleled one for schools sponsored by the State Board of Education.

for which has been carefully defined in our rep¹   ʻChanneling Research into Education."

4. The Committee on Southern Regional Stu-lies and Education has not been informed of any institution, other than the University of Virginia, which has a specific interest in translating materials at the adult level and which has a broad and valuable experience in working in the field of adult and community education.

5. I am sure that the Committee on Southern Regional Studies and Education would follow with interest the progress of the project planned at the University of Virginia and that, upon request, we would be glad to give consultative service either by members of the committee or by our executive secretary.

6. The Committee on Southern Regional Studies and Education expects to be in a position to take materials produced by such projects as the one planned at the University of Virginia and secure "tryouts" under various circumstances in different places in the South.

7. Our committee is especially interested in knowing of the value of certain procedures of translation; the University of Virginia project would provide an opportunity to discover and evaluate definite techniques in translation.

8. The program planned at the University of Virginia would provide a "training ground" for those who participate in it, giving to them valuable experience in translating and in the conduct of workshops; the plan might also provide a place where students of resource-use education could visit for observation and instruction.

In September, 1945, Miss Margaret Snyder joined the staff to undertake this work. The request for help which had come from the Thomas Jefferson Soil Conservation District (see chapter 12) as a result of the Louisa County *Bulletin* suggested a natural starting place. Materials of interest to other groups and dealing with other resources are getting under way. The policy of "collaboration" with the persons whose lives are affected slows down the process in its initial stages but, we are convinced from experience, makes it really effective. The next two years for which this program has been planned should yield rich returns.

This matter of "telling the people" which is so fundamental to desirable social change is not simple. The "telling" inevitably involves getting them to see it for themselves in terms of their own experience and in relation to their own values. To be sure, the process may enrich their experience and change their values. *But it must start with a recognition of both as they are at the moment and not as wishful thinking would have them.*

There is evidence in our experience that the educational process worked out locally is effective. Adult education is the sure foundation on which such a program can be built. Yet the persons who study most searchingly the needs of their communities and seek ways of meeting them seldom think they are being "educated" or that they are "educating" others.

From a county adjoining Louisa, a farmer having heard of the program there has written: "We are desperately in need of that kind of help. We are fighting an uphill battle for the soils of Goochland . . . . as these same soils are fiercely charging *down hill.*"

His battle, like ours, is in final analysis an uphill fight against ignorance and resistance to change. *Telling the people in a way that is meaningful to them is the only effective weapon.*

CHAPTER 15

Experiment in Pamphleteering

"The *New Dominion Series* published by the Extension Division of the University of Virginia is doing some of the most interesting pamphleteering that has been done in this state in years."

It was exactly one year after the beginning of publication of the *Series* that these words appeared in an editorial in the Richmond *Times-Dispatch*. "Pamphleteering" was a startling term. Yet, objectively considered, it seemed to be correctly applied to the *Series* and it might even be interpreted as implying some measure of success in relation to one of its objectives: *to tell the stories of selected programs in such a way as to stimulate other communities to action and show them something of the processes involved.*

About the same time that the *Times-Dispatch* editorial quoted above appeared, one in the Richmond *News Leader* made rather extravagant claims for the potentialities of the *Series* in relation to the attainment of this same purpose:

No, you do not have to count George B. Zehmer among the prophets. He would disclaim that distinction. Modestly he would say that when he began in September, 1941, the publication of the *New Dominion Series* the dim outline of a changed society was shadowed on his desk. The second World War had been two years in progress then. Although America had not become belligerent, it was manifest she soon would be. War spending was on a basis that was burning billions. The Old Dominion never again could be "old" in the sense so often and so affectionately voiced. Ahead was a New Dominion.

The director of Extension at the University of Virginia correctly sensed this and chose the appropriate title for his fine folders. The excellence of *New Dominion Series* is not in appropriate title only but also—and even more—in the treatment. The aim is to describe "experimental approaches to democratic living that are being tried effectively in various communities." Some of these experiments are startling, some are novel. What most will strengthen the hope of the Virginian who reads the *Series* is the evidence of vitality, leadership, and initiative in Virginia rural districts and small towns. If we must build a "new Jerusalem," these folders show that we can do it!

Such editorial comment after a year of publication was encouraging. So were the requests that came in every day's mail from persons who wished to be placed on the mailing list, to receive complete sets of all stories published to date, or to have additional copies of a particular story for a group or study club. Experimental publication of the *Series* was continued for another three years. Toward the end of its fourth year of publication, one issue asked advice as to its future. Opinion that the *Series* should be continued along much the same lines was positive and strong.

Of more than 900 individual responses, only one said, "No. Save the money for the war effort." All others indicated that the contribution made by the *Series* to the peace effort warranted its continuance.

Two editorials again presented a fair summary of the replies. Excerpts are quoted below:

> On August 15, the University of Virginia Extension Division's *New Dominion Series* will complete four years of publication and in a recent number, the editors have called for suggestions from "the consumer" as to the *Series'* future.
>
> We hope that this does not imply any questioning of the project's continuance, for this has been a truly extraordinary series of leaflets. Devoted entirely to accounts of effective cooperative effort in small towns and rural communities of the Southeast . . . . they have given us ample evidence that there are almost no community problems that have not been solved, no community needs that have not been met, in some manner, in some of the communities that are covered in this series.
>
> These little stories have done much to brighten the war darkened years. They have renewed our faith in the ability of people living at the "grass roots" to develop new patterns of cooperation, new ways of bettering their community life together. Individually modest and unassuming, they are wonderfully impressive when viewed collectively. In community efforts like these—living proof that people can work and plan together in solving their common problems—lie the hope and the promise of democracy.—*Adult Education Journal.*
>
> *The News Leader* suggestion is unhesitating: By all means the *New Dominion Series* should be continued in its present form and scope. It is one of the few publications of its kind that started out correctly and continued intelligently and informatively on the proper line. It ought not change editorial policy. Anything that modifies will mar.—*Richmond News Leader.*

Purpose and Plan

The *Series* had been undertaken for a dual purpose: (1) to muster and record experiences of others demonstrating effective ways of improving some aspects of community life:

(2) to tell the stories of selected programs in such a way as to stimulate other communities to action and show them something of the process involved.

A summary of results related to the first of these purposes has been attempted in chapter 4, "Finding and Telling Success Stories." Evaluation in relation to the second or "pamphleteering" purpose is undertaken here in an analysis of distribution, of requests for sets or specific issues, of use made of the bulletin, of reactions of readers as expressed in letters and in the press, of programs known to have been stimulated by the *Series*, and of replies to the questionnaire sent to readers at the end of the four-year experimental period.

The plan for the *Series* had provided for (1) the publication of eighteen bulletins a year, four to sixteen pages in length, each telling the story of a single successful community program; (2) printing the bulletins in a simple but attractive format with paper, type, and size of page all designed for easy reading in order to encourage the indifferent; (3) telling each story *interestingly* and *briefly* with primary emphasis on the method rather than on the achievements or personalities of a program; (4) a positive approach through recounting tales of success rather than of failure—with recognition always of the difficulties encountered; (5) an informal style of writing and vocabulary free from the jargon of the professional educator or social worker; (6) a minimum of theory or philosophy except as it was self-evident in the story.

In selecting a story for inclusion in the *Series*, the first test was always its workability. If the process was one that would not have fairly general usefulness, the story—though good in itself—was not published. Methods of finding, investigating, evaluating, and writing the stories are described in chapter 4.

Finding the Audience

Finding the right audience was the next problem. It presented even greater difficulties than finding and telling the stories. There were no ready-made lists of citizens who were leaders or potential leaders in their communities, and these were the people to be reached.

The first issues of *New Dominion Series* were sent to 1,200 Virginians and 40 persons in other states. The former were primarily school principals, agricultural agents, welfare superintendents, and similar professional workers whose names were already on the Extension Division mailing list. The latter consisted chiefly of directors of extension. This original mailing list was specially selected but not specially prepared for its purpose. Members of the staff added names of citizens active in community affairs as they became acquainted with them. Each bulletin carried the announcement:

To receive without cost the leaflets in *New Dominion Series* describing experimental approaches to democratic living that are being tried effectively in various communities, send your name and address to the Extension Division, University of Virginia, Charlottesville, Virginia.

The Extension Division did not seek wide publicity for the *Series*, on the basis that it was more important that it reach the right people than that it reach large numbers. Waiting for personal requests or personal suggestions, therefore, seemed better than general circularizing or advertising. City and county papers were on the mailing list. The very first issue received an editorial in the Richmond *Times-Dispatch* with the challenging title "New Dominion in Virginia?" From that time on, Virginia newspapers were generous in giving favorable notice to the stories, and usually such notice was accompanied by the announcement that the *Series* would be sent without cost to those requesting it. Each editorial, news item, or reprint in a county paper brought in new names.

Inclusion on general lists of pamphlets published (such as in the New York *Times Book Review*) was not sought because the audience reached by such notices was more general than we were aiming at. Moreover, many persons who read such notices habitually ask for anything that is free. Unsolicited listings that came later justified our original decision. They brought requests from many persons to whom we sent a sample copy with explanation of purpose and scope and a statement that if they were interested after seeing the publication we would add their names to the list. "Planning Tomorrow's Community," for example, listed without annotation, brought many requests from schools of architecture and similar groups. Only one of these replied to our explanation. He said that the publication was not what he expected but it interested him *avocationally* and please keep sending it. "Put It in the Paper," listed in the *Postwar Bulletin*, brought scores of requests from metropolitan settlement houses and social agencies that could have no possible concern with the use of the county weekly dealt with in the pamphlet.

On the other hand, careful reviews, accurately defining the publication, in such periodicals as *Adult Education Journal, Survey, National University Extension Bulletin, Rural Electrification News*, resulted in requests that extended not only the mailing list but also the usefulness of the *Series*. The same was true of reviews in *Community Coordination* (Los Angeles) and *Community Service News* (Yellow Springs, Ohio). Regional publications such as *Mountain Life and Work* and the *Southern Patriot* likewise reached an important regional audience. The last named seemed to reach as many laymen as professional workers. Its notice, which brought in a record number of requests from persons mentioning it as the source of their information, follows:

One of the most interesting publications in the South is the *New Dominion Series*, published by the University of Virginia. The various copies, issued twice monthly, describe experimental approaches to democratic living that are being tried effectively in various communities.

The subjects have ranged from how citizens of a small town organized to get a free public library to the formation of a youth club; two of the best issues described the Carroll County, Georgia, Cooperative Project.

You may receive the magazine regularly without cost by writing the Extension Division, University of Virginia in Charlottesville.

When our own workshops got under way in 1943, participants added many names of leaders and potential leaders in their communities who would benefit from the *Series*. These suggestions and word-of-mouth publicity seem to us to have been the most useful in reaching the desired audience, second only, perhaps, to those lists sent in by community leaders whose projects were described in the *Series*.

Response—Numerical and Geographical

Requests to be placed on the mailing list began coming in almost immediately after the first issue. They have continued up to the present, reaching a peak in October and November, 1944, after three years of publication.

Analysis of the mailing list at the end of the four-year experimental period is recorded in the tables that follow. Names added and later dropped for some reason are not included in the figures since the *permanent increase* is what seems significant.

Table 10. Increase in NDS Mailing List—September, 1941-
September, 1945

Original list, September, 1941
    Virginia 1200
    Other states 40
    Foreign 0

       Total 1240

Added by request to September, 1945
    Virginia 1224
    Other states 1373
    Foreign 54

       Total 2651

Total list, September, 1945..3891

Table 11. NDS Circulation by States and Foreign Countries,
September, 1945

Total circulation...3891
    Virginia 2424

Other southern states:
    Maryland 46
    North Carolina 114
    South Carolina 24
    Tennessee 134
    Florida 77
    Georgia 99
    Alabama 55
    Mississippi 12
    Louisiana 23
    Kentucky 93

       Total 677

Non-southern states 672
Washington, D. C. 64
Foreign:
  England 5
  Canada 28
  Australia 7
  Chile 2
  Cuba 2
  Puerto Rico 5
  India 1
  British West Indies... 2
  New Zealand 2

  Total 54

As indicated in the figures there was no state to which the *Series* did not go by the end of the fourth year. Since our interest was first in Virginia communities and then in those of other southeastern states, there is satisfaction in noting that "added by request" in Virginia (1224) almost equals the total for other states (1373); and that those for the other southeastern states (677) is approximately the same as the total for non-southern states (672). Washington, D. C., figures have been tabulated separately because most readers there are workers in federal agencies and are not identified with any one state or community. The circulation figures may be interpreted as indicating that the *Series* has been most successful in reaching the regional audience (Virginia and the Southeast) at which it was aimed.

The ten states outside Virginia having the largest circulation and the ten having the lowest appear in the following tables:

Table 12. Ten States with Highest Circulation—Outside Virginia

Tennessee 134
North Carolina 114
New York 111
Georgia 99
Kentucky 93
Florida 77
Ohio 68
Alabama 55
Michigan 53
Pennsylvania and Maryland... 46

Table 13. Ten States with Lowest Circulation

Nevada	1
Wyoming	1
South Dakota	1
Delaware	1
Vermont	1
Idaho	2
Utah	2
New Mexico	2
New Hampshire	3
Rhode Island	3

That Tennessee and North Carolina should head the list in Table 12 is not surprising, for in both states many agencies are at work helping communities to help themselves. The four non-southern states in that table also have strong community and adult education programs, and their basic problems do not differ from those in southern communities. Verification of this comes from the New York State Bureau of Planning:

[These stories] rank high in being invaluable to those interested in community programs and activities. Although there are a great many differences between communities of Virginia and those of our state, still the suggestions carried by the *Series* are so fundamental that their application is truly universal.

To have expressions of this kind and at the same time to have evidence that the region aimed at was the most responsive was gratifying.

Response—Professional Workers and Laymen

The audience, however, had been even more specifically defined as the *laymen in the community* rather than professional workers and officials.

The original 1,200 to whom the *Series* was sent were almost entirely professional workers and public officials. Through them we hoped to reach laymen. Many of them have seen the importance of this and have reacted with enthusiasm. One school principal sent a list of sixty patrons; another, a list of forty. Each wrote that if this were asking asking too much, he would try to pass on the one copy sent to him. One said he preferred not to do this because the social science teachers made use of the stories and he wished to keep a complete file for the library. A county agent sent names of more than one hundred lay leaders in his county. Welfare workers and school principals and superintendents were especially eager to have members of their boards added to the list. "If individual mailing costs too much," one superintendent of public welfare wrote, "you could send all the copies to me and I would give them to board members. But if it could come direct, rather than from me, I think it would carry more weight." One county agent asked whether it would be possible to send every family in his county issues on food production and preservation.

These are typical responses from professional workers and officials. Many, of course, have never been heard from. But they have been kept on the list *because we think they should be interested*—and someday, if exposed long enough, they may become so.

That this does happen was proved in a workshop conducted by Dr. Hayes. A member of the board of supervisors suddenly remembered he "had been getting those things for years." He had never read them but had saved them all feeling sure that if the University sent them out they must be worth saving. He began to read them and to see their relation to the job at hand. He has since become an enthusiastic reader and promoter of the *Series*.

Only one from the 1,200 on the original list reacted unfavorably. His reaction came on a postal card written by his wife. We can only assume he subscribed to her sentiments!

"My husband," she wrote, "has for years been getting literature (*New Dominion Series*) as chairman of the board of supervisors. Why not take money *you waste* on this and similar printed matter and put an enthusiastic leader in the field of rural affairs to do something besides talk and write?"

A reply to her explaining the program of Special Projects and the availability of field workers whose job was *to help citizens to work out their community problems* and offering the services of such a field worker to her community if citizens wished "to do something" brought no response. We decided she was looking for that enemy of democracy—the superman to whom the citizen can delegate his job.

The additions to the mailing list as a result of individual requests include a large number of laymen — exact figures cannot be determined because some requests are from persons who do not tell us much about themselves. A careful analysis of 552 requests made during the second year of publication, preceding the beginning of our workshops, indicated that about 10 per cent were unquestionably from laymen. General distribution of these requests is shown in the following table.

Table 14. Analysis of 552 Requests over Period of Several Months

Educators 192
    (Curriculum supervisors; teachers; principals; professors of sociology, agriculture, education; administrative officials and state departments; students)
Libraries 110
    (High school, college, foundation, legislative reference, curriculum, home economics, public)
Health and welfare supervisors.. 47
Federal agencies.. 70
    (Social Security, U. S. Department of Agriculture, REA, Office of Education, Department of Labor, TVA)
Agricultural agents and supervisors.. 14
    (County and state)
Planning agencies.. 41
    (State and community)
Recreation and conservation commissions... 11
Religious leaders.. 5
Industry 5
Publishers and newspapers... 4
Just people.. 53
                                              —————
    Total 552

Since the above analysis was made, we feel certain that the percentage of requests from laymen has increased. Occasionally one asks, "May a mere citizen be put on the list?" Such questions indicate a diffidence that the *Series* and other activities of the Special Projects have been attempting to overcome. The layman in the community is not yet entirely convinced that the University of Virginia wishes to serve him.

In analyzing distribution by area, communities, and individuals, so far as we can identify them, we are forced to admit that in general the *Series* like the preacher's sermons, seems to reach those who are already on the road to salvation. That they think it will help others is indicated in such requests as the following:

"Please send this publication to my brother. He needs it. I have never been able to do him much good, but perhaps you can."

"Please add the following names to the mailing list. If copies are limited, send it to them instead of me. I already know about cooperatives and things, but they don't."

Unsolicited comments from readers (25 inches in a file drawer by actual measure) indicate that the stories have opened the way to some who were seeking, have made it clearer to many who were already upon it, and have encouraged the faint of heart.

Effectiveness of Individual Stories

Each story is, of course, complete in itself. Some have had fairly general appeal whereas others have appealed to special interest groups. Requests from individuals for single copies of stories from Nos. 1 through 72 continue to come in daily though all the early issues have been out of print for some time. The Kingsport, Tennessee, young people's program, "Putting Christianity to Work" (No. 63) heads the list in ' number of requests from individuals. The Jordan Area story, "A Planned Rural Community" (No. 11) holds second place. Requests for this story, which have have come in steadily since its publication, showed a revival of interest immediately after publication of "Programs Revisited" (No. 55) in which the progress of the community during three years was described. The third on the list of individual requests is the Pulaski recreation story, "From Gangs to Boys' Club." Its popularity is undoubtedly accounted for, at least in part, by the wartime search for cures for juvenile delinquency. Requests for single copies of a story are frequently accompanied by the explanation that a reader has passed his on to an interested friend and wishes to keep his file complete.

In addition to individual requests, 68 of the 72 issues included in this report have been requested in quantities ranging from 10 to 3,000 for various purposes. Mere numbers of requests are not necessarily proof of effectiveness of a story.

Yet figures in the following tables bear some relation to use. They have been divided into single and group requests. Some explanation of typical use of bulk orders follows the tables.

Table 15. Ten NDS Stories Bringing Largest Number of Requests in Addition to Regular Mailing of Approximately 4000

Title	Single Requests	Requests in lots of 10 or more	Total
We the Citizens (No. 53)	139	3000	3139
Putting Christianity to Work (No. 63)	356	2000	2356
A Planned Rural Community (No. 11)	239	1172	1411
The Community and Health (No. 71)	24	1249	1273
Lights of Tyrrell (No. 57)	76	1164	1240
For All Mothers (No. 36)	14	1130	1144
Letting People Know (No. 56)	67	1018	1085
Facing Facts (No. 49)	46	1000	1046
Recreation Meets a Challenge (No. 12)	175	546	721
Abilities and Possibilities (No. 44)	122	515	637

Note: Figures in this table and those which follow do not include requests for complete sets of which several hundred have been filled and an almost equal number unfilled because the bulletins were out of print.

Table 16. Ten NDS Stories Bringing Lowest Number of Requests in Addition to Regular Mailing of Approximately 4000

Title	Single Requests	Requests in lots of 10 or more	Total
Emphasis on Marketing (No. 42)	17	0	17
The Trees Are There (No. 66)	9	12	21
Self- Help Through Gardens (No. 28)	25	10	35
Handing on Their Heritage (No. 34)	13	30	43
United Efforts and United Funds (No. 31)	15	30	45
How Well Are They Served? (No. 64)	39	20	59
Citizens Consider Their County (No. 69)	45	16	61
Still Sits the Schoolhouse (No. 54)	49	12	61
Church and School Cooperate (No. 32)	25	37	62
It's a Fine Thing to Sing (No. 52)	23	44	67

Stories asked for in quantity have been used in many ways, including study in adult groups, college and high school classes, CPS camps, community councils and the like; and distribution to a club, a board of supervisors, field workers in some agency, or the citizens of a county. Below are typical statements selected from 380 requests for numbers of copies of specific issues.

The Champion Paper and Fibre Company writes, "So much interest has been taken in your little pamphlet "Boys Become Foresters" (No. 35) that our supply is completely depleted. We hope you will be able to send us 100 more."

Another request for the same bulletin comes from the Kansas Association of Municipal Utilities asking for 25 copies to be distributed at its annual convention. "The major portion of the program will be devoted to *Anticipating Peacetime Needs*. After reading the article on the municipally owned forest of Canton, North Carolina, I see no reason on earth why every city should not develop a forest."

A club woman in Maine sends a rush order for several stories, saying, "The urgency at this time is prompted by the fact that I am addressing a district meeting of Federated Club women to whom I am to have the opportunity of showing some factual approaches to solving community problems."

A Ruritan Club president writes for 35 copies each of "Planning Tomorrow's Community" (No 4) and "From Gangs to Boys' Club" (No. 8) to distribute to members of his club to arouse their interest in similar undertakings.

A school board chairman asks for 25 copies of "Recreation Meets a Challenge" (No. 12) to distribute to school trustees in Virginia "who are concerned about need for recreation programs."

A county agent in northern Virginia writes, "We can use a couple hundred copies of your recent publication 'Frozen Food Lockers' (No. 43) in developing interest in this project." From a Southside county comes a request for the same bulletin: "It would be a great help to place one of these bulletins in the hands of each family in the county. However, we would greatly appreciate any copies you could send us."

A request from a worker in a federal agency for 100 copies of "By the Youngsters" (No. 45) is explained as follows: "There are many communities in western Virginia and West Virginia where I work to which this bulletin would prove an incentive to set up a youth recreation program."

From the University of Toronto comes this request: "I am in receipt of pamphlet No. 44 ("Abilities and Possibilities"). It is of much interest. I am wondering whether it would be possible to purchase 100 copies of this for distribution in Ontario?"

A request for 200 copies of "Pioneering in Food Preservation" (No. 37) from Yellow Springs, Ohio, states: "We have under consideration a cooperative locker plant for our village and would like to distribute your pamphlet in an educational program."

From the United States Office of Education comes this request: "I have just finished reading with much interest the latest pamphlet in the *New Dominion Series,* 'The Mountain Comes to the School.' This has some material in it that I think would be very helpful in the Obion County, Tennessee, program. Would it be possible for you to send copies to the following . . . We hope that you will be able to keep on preparing and distributing these leaflets indefinitely. I don't know any material that compares with this in value for helping people see the possibilities in community organization."

A teacher at Hampton Institute asking for 50 copies of "The Mountain Comes to the School" (No. 46) for distribution to seniors writes: "A major part of our endeavor is directed to training of teachers for rural areas in the South. Such publications as this should be both inspiration and challenge to the aspiring teacher . . . Our seniors before many months will be part of the fabric of community relationships in many rural areas in the South."

The director of extension in a southern university writes: "This material ought to be very valuable to alert teachers who are serious in their study . . . It occurred to me that it might be possible for you to supply me with additional copies of the *Series* to place in the libraries which go along with the various extension centers. I am anxious to have as many as ten copies of each of the *Series* so that I could place one in each library. Will you kindly let me know whether you could supply these and what will be the cost?"

The educational director of the CIO for the Southeastern region writes: "Bulletin No. 48 (By Popular Vote) is down my alley exactly. Could I purchase 50 copies to send to these my good friends [local union officials in Virginia]?"

A public health committee in Winchester, Virginia, asks for 30 copies of "Toward Better Health" (No. 50) for distribution to a "local postwar planning organization."

An order for 1,000 copies of "Letting People Know" (No. 56) from the educational director of Rural Electrification Administration says he plans to "send one to each borrower and have a reserve for the new cooperatives we may finance in the future. It is exactly what I want them to know and understand."

The Warwick County (Virginia) Improvement Association asked to purchase 3,000 copies of "We the Citizens" (No. 53) for distribution to all voters in the county. "Warwick County is voting on whether to adopt a county manager form of government. One of the arguments used against the change is that it will cost more more. [We] believe it (No. 53) will aid us in overcoming this question." A later letter brought this statement: "I am glad to advise you that the county voted to adopt the county manager form of government and I believe these pamphlets were most helpful. They were distributed throughout the county and certain information in them was also used in at least two editorials."

Demand for Complete Sets Exceeds Supply

More than 300 complete sets were supplied, while copies were still available, for use in study groups, classes, and community development workshops. Following the May, 1945, questionnaire which stated that the experimental period of publication was drawing to a close and asking advice as to future plans for the *Series*, many requests came for complete sets or for certain numbers to fill in sets. These came from libraries, schools, civic organizations, and individuals. Most of them could not be filled because supplies of 40 of the 72 stories were completely exhausted. Many persons in asking for sets or missing numbers for their files commented on the cumulative effect of the stories and expressed the hope that they might become available in a bound volume.

"I am tremendously impressed," wrote a Wisconsin professor, "with what is happening down there, and I have long been telling my classes that the civic leadership has passed to the South because of such work."

It was from the South itself that the following comment came: "As one with four generations of contact with your university, I should like to express my delight in the *New Dominion Series*. The will and understanding that are obviously back of these leaflets I believe to be the most precious ingredient in a sound program of construction for the South. In wide travel, I find these leaflets read and discussed with unusual interest."

Organizations Using Series

We have, of course, only such information as happens to come to us about uses to which the *Series* is put. Our files indicate that it is being used in 146 colleges, universities, and teacher-training institutions in 39 states and 3 foreign countries. Organizations using it in relation to their programs include community councils; state and local planning boards; credit unions; League of Women Voters; women's clubs; men's service clubs; Chambers of Commerce (including the Netherlands); state departments of health, welfare, and education; U. S. Department of Agriculture; United States Office of Education; Tennessee Valley Authority; university extension divisions; Rural Electrification Administration; Cooperative League of the U. S. A.; Community Service, Inc.; Brethren Service Committee; International Council of Religious Education; Agricultural Extension Service.

Reprints in Papers and Magazines

It was three months after *New Dominion Series* had begun publication that Arthur E. Morgan, director of Community Service, Inc., wrote: "May we have the privilege of quoting from the *New Dominion Series* in stories we are writing of community achievements? We are preparing a newspaper column for country papers, describing significant community activities."

Even before this, county papers in Virginia had begun to reprint the stories. The *Blue Ridge Herald* (Loudoun County) used the caption *New Dominion Series* with the sub-head: *With Ideas Perhaps for Loudoun.*

We have had no way of checking on the extent of such use of the stories. We do know definitely that 19 of the first 72 leaflets have been reprinted in 15 different newspapers and magazines with or without our permission. One reprinted in *Recreation* ("New Plans in Old Communities," No. 68) was also distributed by National Recreation Association in reprints numbering 3,000. Hence our figure of 4,500 copies of this story distributed within three months of its publication in no sense represents its use. The same is true of others. One of the stories for which we have had fewest requests ("The Trees Are There," No. 66) was reprinted in *The Bridge* and attracted considerable attention there.

None of the ten stories which our figures indicate as most popular has, to our knowledge, been reprinted. One of the ten on the least popular list (Table 16) was reprinted twice. Of the middle 52, that is those that we rated as moderately popular, 18 were reprinted in this country and Canada.

The stories have also been used as the basis of articles in magazines and newspapers (as far afield as the St. Louis *Post-Dispatch*). Occasionally the author has sent us a copy or reported such use. More frequently we have known about it because we happened upon the story. In one instance, the editor of a magazine sent us a sample of what could be done with material such as ours, saying he frequently used a *New Dominion* story as the basis of an article and suggesting that we "jazz up" the story as he had. Facts were garbled, individuals were misquoted, accuracy was sacrificed to dramatic interest, and the result was a story we should not have recognized. In this case, we were glad no credit was given to the *Series* as the source!

Other Publications Inspired

The *Series* has inspired similar publications elsewhere. Kentucky was the first to ask whether we had any objection to a similar series there. We do not know that one was ever started. In January, 1943, five attractive little leaflets published by the Tennessee State Planning Commission came with a letter which stated: "I got the idea of these from your *New Dominion Series* and I have copied your idea to a considerable extent." There was similarity in both form and content, though the latter was definitely restricted to stories of community planning in various areas of interest.

Much more recently came copies of studies from the Agricultural and Industrial Development Board of Georgia with the information, "You may be interested to know that various copies of the *New Dominion Series* have been used extensively in this program of planning in this state."

Others have asked, "Do you mind if we copy your idea?" And still others seem to have done so without asking. Our response is always, "More power to you!"

Advice from the Consumer

In the May, 1945, issue the following announcement was made:

Future of *New Dominion Series*

The experimental program of which *New Dominion Series* is a part is drawing to a close. The *Series* will complete four years of publication August 15. We hope to continue in some form. Length, style, points of emphasis, and frequency of publication may be changed.

We have told only success stories. Our purpose has been to stimulate other communities to action. We have, therefore, told each story in detail in order to give emphasis to *why* and *how* as well as *what*. We have chosen primarily small town and rural communities in the Southeast. Various aspects of community life have received attention—economics, social welfare, health, recreation, education, coordination, planning. Possibly we should give attention to one type of community or one aspect of development over a period of time (say six or eight issues) and then attempt to draw some generalizations (as we have done for techniques in Nos. 56, 58, 60, 62). This is one of *many* possibilities.

We want suggestions from the consumer.

If you wish to write us, we shall be delighted.

But if time is scarce, please at least detach and return the card below with your comments.

We shall report results in a later issue.—*The Editors.*

Have you found the stories in *New Dominion Series* stimulating?...............

Do you know of community activities stimulated or encouraged by the *Series*? ....

Have you used the stories in classes or study groups?............................

Have the stories already published sufficiently demonstrated the possibilities of community development so that the *Series* should be
discontinued? ....
    Or radically changed?..
WOULD YOU LIKE TO CONTINUE TO RECEIVE THE SERIES
    1) With no change in general plan?...
    2) With a new emphasis?........................For example: ....
    3) Even if it were necessary to pay a small subscription fee?.............
COMMENTS:
        NAME ....
        ADDRESS ....

Of those who replied, 992 said they found the *Series*
stimulating. One answered the question with an unqualified
"no." Of those who replied to the question in the affirmative,
more than 500 added a qualifying statement, such as:

"*Inspiring* is a better word."

"So stimulating that I read it out of 2 feet of daily mail."

"They are always helpful. My blessings on you."

"I use them frequently in my sermons."

"Most encouraging in a war-torn world."

"Very helpful. Use regularly in club work."

"News of constructive group action is most welcome in
world where there is so much destruction. It renews one's
faith in man."

"They emphasize problems and opportunities generally
overlooked and resources now neglected."

"They are simply swell! I have literally carried them all
over the United States."

"They are forward-looking and practical as well as inspiring."

In reply to the question "Should the *Series* be continued?"
there was again one "no" against 992 affirmative votes, most
of them bolstered with reasons for its continuance.

Two readers thought radical changes might be in order
such as detailed studies of all aspects of one community
extending over a period of time and described in eight or ten
consecutive issues. Five others thought there might be minor
changes such as "more generalizations" or "a critical evaluation or interpretive paragraph each time." But 985 voted for
no change at all, many adding such comments as:

"Stick to the small community. Too many are trying to save the world."

"Do not try to improve on perfection."

"It has been a unique and valuable means of encouraging community cooperation and action."

"The *details* are most important. Whatever you change, *keep the details*."

"My opinion is that they will do the most good just as they are. Any fresh efforts should be directed toward reaching more people. How can I get a complete file?"

The strongest expression against change brought out by this question was in the editorial already quoted in this chapter, ending "anything that modifies will mar."

Six other newspaper editors sent in replies urging continuance of the *Series* in its present form. Four of these were in Virginia, one in St. Petersburg, Florida, and one in St. Louis, Missouri.

In reply to the question about willingness to pay a subscription fee, 618 said they would be more than willing; 318 said they would pay "if necessary to keep the *Series* going;" 13 said "no."

One of the thirteen said, "I do not need it that much but I would be willing to pay so some of my friends could get it." Another, who was identified as a county treasurer, explained his unwillingness to pay by saying, "The University is a State institution. It owes this service to the State. Increase your budget to cover cost. *Please punch bulletins for convenience in filing*."

Three offered to contribute to a fund, if necessary, to assure continuance of the *Series*. One of these was a Virginia newspaper editor, one a Virginia professor, and the third a Wisconsin professor.

In response to the question, "Do you know of activities stimulated by the *Series*?" 187 were reported. These included old programs revitalized as well as new ones inspired and begun.

A few answers were general, such as:

"Tangible results have accrued in many of our communities."

"Many activities have been stimulated throughout Alabama."

Many others named specific programs now under way which received their initial spur from the *Series*. These included the Greenville (Va.) Council; Kingsport (Tennessee) recreation program; Washington County Development Association; Louisa, Prince William, and Chesterfield frozen-food locker plants; Farmville recreation program; Emporia cannery; Edonton (North Carolina) consumers mutual.

The letter which came from this last named group was one of the most inspiring received:

Dear Sirs:

I have enjoyed reading the *Series*. Please continue to send it. It has been the cause of the organization named in this letterhead. It has been incorporated for $25,000. Started 8th of Jan. 1945.

Yours in Christ,

W. H. A. STALLINGS.

In addition to the 187, several who admitted they had nothing as yet to report were optimistic as to the future:

"As we get under way in Nebraska, programs will be stimulated by these stories."

"It is stirring the imagination with results that will show up for years to come. Four years is too short a time to show tangible results."

"Try again to estimate results after twenty-five years."

Suggestions for the Series

Many interesting suggestions came in on the questionnaires:

"Do the same thing for other regions of the United States."

"Include stories of big urban areas."

"Would like to see reports on commercial enterprises operated either by individuals or groups as a *paying business* that could be duplicated elsewhere."

"Tell of several approaches to the same problem by different communities, with analytical interpretation."

"Are there some stories of old programs that have been revitalized?"

"Telling of failures would encourage those of us who try and keep trying without spectacular results."

"Have you found ideas for a relatively prosperous and too-content farm community?"

"Can you find a way to make sure some key person in every Virginia community receives the *Series*?"

"Continue to report progress of programs already described. There is good cheer in the freshness of the morning; there is courage in the sight of endurance on a dusty road under the noonday sun."

One suggestion was in itself a declaration of faith: "Why not now describe parallel programs stimulated by the *Series*?" Not only was it a moving expression of faith in the efficacy of the stories, it was in itself a good idea. Replies had indicated that there was ample material. It seemed especially fitting that the first story published under the regular rather than the experimental program (October, 1945) should be one of these inspired by the *Series*. After other programs have had more time to take root, we may follow the suggestion of *a series stimulated by The Series*. There could be no more satisfying way of mustering the evidence of the success of our experiment in pamphleteering.

CHAPTER 16

Summer Residence Workshops

The experimental program of the Extension Division had been under way for two years when the first "workshop in community development" was announced as part of the University of Virginia Summer Quarter in 1943. Two considerations influenced the decision to offer such a workshop: (1) the time seemed appropriate for beginning to pass on to others some of the results of two years' intensive exploration of and experimentation in community programs in the Southeast; and (2) an experiment with summer employment of high school principals, undertaken in cooperation with the State Board of Education, could be given an excellent start in such a work conference.[1]

The printed announcement of that first workshop explains its purpose, scope, and general plan as follows:[2]

ANNOUNCEMENT OF WORKSHOP IN COMMUNITY DEVELOPMENT
June 21 to July 10, 1943

Why Community Development in 1943

With the world in turmoil and democracy on trial, there is more than ever reason for every community to analyze its own problems and muster its resources for solving them. It must be ready to meet not only emergency needs arising from the present crisis but also the inevitable problems of adjustment and rehabilitation following the war.

Why a Workshop

A workshop affords the kind of study group where experienced adults can come together; talk over practical problems; study the literature in the field; hear and ask questions about the experience of others; divide themselves into working units according to the problems they have in common; and, day after day, consider ways of tackling these problems in their own communities.

Why the University of Virginia

For the past two years the Extension Division of the University of Virginia has been exploring problems of community development through its Special Projects in Adult Education. Its purpose has been

---

[1] See chapter 11.
[2] *Summer Quarter Bulletin,* April, 1943. Vol. XVII, No. 4.

to discover techniques for helping communities to plan their own programs in terms of local needs and resources. It has studied existing programs, has investigated a large number in the Southeast, and has reported thirty of these to date in the *New Dominion Series*. In addition, staff members have conducted experimental work in three selected rural areas.

Requests for information and advice on community projects from various agencies and individuals indicate an active and widespread interest in community planning and development.

The Workshop Program

The workshop program will include the following: (1) a study of the theory and practice of community development through a survey of the literature and unpublished reports under the guidance of practical and experienced leaders in the field; (2) opportunity for informal discussion with a number of persons who have had firsthand contact with outstanding programs in their own communities; (3) continuous exchange of ideas and analysis of problems by the participants themselves; and (4) opportunity for each participant to work out detailed plans for his own community in consultation with the staff and those persons invited to discuss special community programs.

Procedure

There will be two class periods daily, the first devoted to a general survey of the field and the second to consideration of specific programs as presented by visiting community leaders.   Afternoons will be kept free for study and for individual or small group conferences on proposed projects of participants.   Four evenings a week will be spent in informal discussion which will serve as a general clearinghouse and afford opportunity for more intimate questioning of and discussion with the morning speakers.

Who May Attend

The group will be limited to fifteen in order that there may be ample opportunity for individual participation and attention to pre-planning of the local projects in which the participants are interested.

Six high school principals have already been accepted.   They will take part in an experiment in school-community relations in which the Extension Division is cooperating with the State Board of Education.   These principals will return to their communities to work on their programs during the remainder of the summer under the guidance and supervision of staff members of the Extension Division.

Three more places are reserved at the request of the Department of Public Welfare for members selected because of their opportunity to participate in local programs of community development.

The remaining six places are open to either professional or lay workers who are not only interested in community prblems in general but also have specific local programs they would like to help in developing.

Planning Becomes a Group Process

The plan had not "sprung full-grown" from the head of any one person. It was the outgrowth of numerous discussions by members of the staff of Special Projects and the Extension Division; of several conferences between the staff and members of the State Board of Education and the State Department of Public Welfare; of consultations with members of the faculty at the University of Virginia; and finally of a conference in March with those participants who had already been selected. *The principles of group planning and exchange of experience were considered basic to this type of workshop process from its very beginning.*

For, in a sense, the workshop was to be in itself *a demonstration of what we considered the best procedures in adult education* which is a necessary part of any community program. No one had *A Plan.* No one knew all the answers. In fact, no one knew all the problems. Each participant, whether staff member or student, could contribute from his experience not only to the consideration of community development but also to the best method of utilizing the three weeks set aside for study and planning. Hence, preliminary discussions and conferences influenced the content of the tentative schedule and calendar that had to be set up before the opening of the workshop in order that additional staff members and guest speakers could be procured.

Mature Group—Adult Method

The workshop was planned on the graduate level and might be taken for credit if desired. All participants were mature adults with years of professional experience. Their greatest need was for an opportunity to reconstruct their experience into a working philosohy in relation to the entire community rather than only that segment for which their jobs made them directly responsible. In addition they needed to acquire some understanding of and skill in using methods of working with other adults on community affairs. Program was planned and staff selected with these needs in mind.

In spite of the maturity of the group and the desire of the staff to establish a situation in which experience subjected to group analysis would be basic rather than a teacher-student relationship or a classroom approach, there were difficulties to be overcome. These were largely habits and attitudes resulting from many years of formal education. Like the legendary child-victim of progressive education who "did not want to do what he wanted to do," these adults were inclined to resist "being developed." They wanted to be told *by teachers* rather than to be helped to figure things out under the guidance of other adults with somewhat more experience in the special field of community programs but equally concerned in the search for more effective ways of working. These difficulties decreased as the days passed and had almost entirely disappeared long before the end of the three weeks, for everyone, to a greater or lesser degree determined largely by temperament, was caught up in the process of working things out and began to enjoy it.

Staff and Students All Learners

There were two important factors in establishing the necessary *rapport* and in covering an unusual amount of ground in a short period of time.

The first of these was that each participant gave his entire attention during the three-week period to the workshop. No one was permitted to take another course in the summer session. Even the living arrangements contributed to this end. It was possible to have the entire group live and work in one of the fraternity houses and have their meals at a nearby boarding house. This fact was not unrelated to the education process, for it resulted in a close working relationship that would have been difficult, if not impossible, under other circumstances.

The second important factor was that a large staff worked with a small number of students and *every member of the entire group was in a learning state of mind*. Each person was sincerely seeking to find the best ways of initiating and carrying through programs that would enrich community living in some of its many aspects. Three staff members (two workers from Special Projects and a professor engaged for the workshop) attended all sessions, whether or not directly responsible for them, and took part in discussion along with workshop participants. The same three staff members were available throughout the afternoon and evening for consultations with individuals or conferences with small groups. Thus any one of the three was ready at any moment to help in relating immediate or previous discussion to questions or problems that had been raised by individuals. In addition to these three instructors, an assistant who had also worked the preceding year with Special Projects was a regular part of the group doubling in the roles of helper and learner. Her full notes on all lectures and discussions were valuable for reference during the three-week period as well as for a permanent record showing the progress of the group. Thus twelve students had four persons whose entire time and attention were at their disposal. Besides the full-time staff members, the director and other members of the Extension Division staff were with the group as often as possible and contributed from their experience. Eight leaders in good community programs were invited for periods ranging from one to three days. Most of them were skillful at identifying themselves with the workshop and some of them asked to stay beyond the time they were on the program because they, too, had a practical interest in working out community programs. One of them who had spent three days in the workshop wrote afterward: "You are one of those rare groups that are privileged to get together all too seldom. If such groups could get together in a few more places, we would be a long way toward understanding the nature of our problems and their solutions."

Then there were many visitors some of whom stayed a short time and were puzzled by the small segment of the process they saw; and others of whom were real assets to the group. Two of the latter were a professor of sociology who attended most of the evening meetings and an officer in the School of Military Government, then in session at the University, who had had long experience in community work.

Of course, exposure to so many and so much in so short a period at first resulted in confusion on the part of many students in the group. It was, however, a healthy confusion that was necessary to shaking them out of established patterns in order that they might draft new patterns for broader community programs.

A Working Philosophy Developed

Mere exposure to many ideas was not enough. The ideas must all be analyzed and built into the working philosophy of each individual. The purpose was one of *stirring* rather than *stuffing*. Without the three staff members who worked continuously on showing relationships, on clearing up apparent contradictions, and on helping each individual to select those things he especially needed, the program would have been hopelessly packed. As it was, the plaintive *"I am confused!"* reiterated by one member throughout the first week became a by-word of the group used as indication of real enjoyment of working themselves both into and out of the confusion. The summing-up discussions of the last few days indicated pretty clear thinking through of knotty problems of both philosophy and methodology.

The Program as Planned

A tentative program, set up and mimeographed before the opening of the workshop, divided the morning into two "class" periods of an hour and a half each. An afternoon period of two hours and a half was set aside for individual and small group conferences with staff members, for reading in general background materials bearing on specific problems of individuals, or for pre-planning work to be carried out later in the individual's own community. Four evenings a week were also scheduled for exploration of special "techniques" and procedures, with the guest speaker of the morning or some other "expert" invited to participate in the discussion.

The first morning period was the most formal of the day. "Theory and Practice of Community Development" was the formidable sounding subject assigned. During the first week it was attacked from the point of view of the sociologist by Dr. Wayland Hayes, professor of sociology at Vanderbilt University; and during the last two from the point of view of educational philosophy by Dr. Morris Mitchell of the Macedonia Cooperative Community who has had wide experience in education. Getting a background on the basis of which to plan and evaluate future activities was the purpose of this part of the program.

The second morning period was for discussion of "community programs in action." The staff of Special Projects carried chief responsibility for continuity, bringing in from various communities two or three persons each week who had worked in good programs. Relating their reports to the background material and to the tentative plans of the "students" required not only class time but also afternoon and evening conferences with individuals and small groups. Whenever the guest speaker of the morning could stay through for two or three days, the results were much more satisfactory, for in this way he and the group began really to understand each other.

In the informal afternoon and evening sessions much of the digesting and relating of ideas took place. The introduction of new personalities in the evening session was one of the most questionable parts of the program, and the group recommended its elimination from future programs.

A copy of the three-week tentative calendar as set up following preliminary discussions but preceding the opening of the workshop is reproduced on the pages that follow.

UNIVERSITY OF VIRGINIA WORKSHOP
CALENDAR—FIRST WEEK

PERIOD	MONDAY June 21	TUESDAY June 22	WEDNESDAY June 23	THURSDAY June 24	FRIDAY June 25	SATURDAY June 26
9:00 to 10:30	Theory and Practice in Community Development — Mr. Hayes	Theory and Practice — Mr. Hayes	Theory and Practice — Mr. Hayes	Theory and Practice — Mr. Hayes	Theory and Practice — Mr. Hayes	Theory and Practice — Mr. Hayes
11:00 to 12:30	General Survey of community programs in the South: Types, leadership, sponsorship, etc. — Mrs. Ogden	The Holland Community: From Survey to Action — Mr. Savage	Greene County: Hollows and one-room schools — The Ogdens	The Louisa Council: A Program in process — Mr. Zehmer	Charlotte County: Strengthening Consolidation through an adult program — Mr. Bobbitt	Recent Developments in the Charlotte County Program — Mr. Bobbitt
—LUNCHEON—						
2:00 to 4:30	Workshop, study, and individual and small group conferences — The Staff	Workshop and conferences	Workshop and conferences	Workshop and conferences	Workshop and conferences	
—DINNER—						
7:30 to 9:00	Informal discussions: Getting acquainted with each other's communities — Leader: Mr. Ogden	Informal discussions: The survey as a technique for starting a program — Leader: Mr. Ogden — Resources: Mr. Savage		Informal discussions: Utilizing community agencies for better planning — Leader: Mr. Ogden — Resources: Mr. Gee, Mr. Cummings, Mr. O'Neill, Dr. Daniel	Informal discussions: Taking inventory of workshop program and procedures to date — Leader: Mr. Ogden — Resources: The Group, The Staff	

UNIVERSITY OF VIRGINIA WORKSHOP

CALENDAR—SECOND WEEK

PERIOD	MONDAY June 28	TUESDAY June 29	WEDNESDAY June 30	THURSDAY July 1	FRIDAY July 2	SATURDAY July 3
9:00 to 10:30	Theory and Practice Mr. Mitchell	Theory and Practice Mr. Mitchell	Theory and Practice Mr. Mitchell	Theory and Practice Mr. Mitchell	Theory and Practice Mr. Mitchell	Theory and Practice Mr. Mitchell
11:00 to 12:30	The Harrisonburg Community Council Mrs. Logsden	The Jordan Area and Greenville County Council Mr. Verdin	The Jordan Area and Greenville County Council Mr. Verdin	Nebraska Health Program Miss Anderson	Meeting Wartime Health Needs Miss Anderson	Evaluation by group of programs with special attention to professional and lay workers Mrs. Ogden
—LUNCHEON—						
2:00 to 4:30	Workshop and conferences	Workshop and conferences	Workshop and conferences	Workshop and conferences	Workshop and conferences	
—DINNER—						
7:30 to 9:00	Benefits to school from principal's participation in community affairs Speaker: Mr. Oliver Chairman: Mr. Smithey	Informal discussions: Getting citizens to take responsibility Leader: Mr. Ogden Resources: Mr. Verdin Mr. Wygal		Panel discussion: Getting a community behind a health program Leader: Mr. Zehmer Members: Miss Anderson Mrs. Fletcher Dr. Roper Dr. Lee	Utilizing emergency programs for permanent community planning Speaker: Dr. Lancaster Chairman: Dr. Manahan	

UNIVERSITY OF VIRGINIA WORKSHOP
CALENDAR—THIRD WEEK

PERIOD	MONDAY July 5	TUESDAY July 6	WEDNESDAY July 7	THURSDAY July 8	FRIDAY July 9	SATURDAY July 10
9:00 to 10:30	Theory and Practice Mr. Mitchell	Theory and Practice Mr. Mitchell	Theory and Practice Mr. Mitchell	Reports by members of the group on proposed programs	Recapitulation and evaluation of workshop by entire group	Continuation of evaluation
11:00 to 12:30	Getting official support for community projects Mr. Goldsmith	A statewide planning program Mr. Long	Volunteers in the Community Miss Marks	Reports by members of the group on proposed programs	Recapitulation and evaluation of workshop by entire group	Conclusions
—LUNCHEON—						
2:00 to 4:30	Workshop and conferences	Workshop and conferences	Workshop and conferences	Workshop and final conferences	Final conferences	
—DINNER—						
7:30 to 9:00	The welfare worker as a citizen of the community Mr. Stauffer Miss Wert	Drama and recreation in a community program Miss Faulkner Mr. Ogden		The use of movies and other visual aids Mr. Rorer	The study group as a technique Mr. Seeber	

Adapting the Program to the Group

Our subsequent criticism of this program was that it was too crowded. There was too little "accordion pleating" to allow for addition of discussions especially requested by the group. At the end of the first week, this came out in the "evaluation" discussion set for Friday night. Also, there was a feeling that students had too little time to read, to digest, and to think through their own plans. Yet attempts to eliminate anything from the programs planned for the next two weeks was met with strong resistance by the group. They felt they needed everything that was there. The afternoon consultation period of two hours and a half, they decided, they could use to better advantage than they had been doing. During the first week whenever a small group had met at that time on a special problem, everyone wanted to listen in, fearing he might miss some words of wisdom. So the period had tended to become just another discussion. Perhaps this was inevitable at first. For the last two weeks, however, each individual was better able to settle down to his own job of reading or planning during the afternoon period.

The other chief modifications in the program as set up in advance was a salvaging of more time at the end of the three weeks for recapitulation and evaluation of the entire workshop by the group. It was during these final discussions that things began to fall into place for most people—and the workshop ended with the feeling, "Now, we are really ready to begin." To the staff, this seemed a good stopping place, for they knew that the real beginning had to be made back in each person's community. *If the workshop had prepared for a beginning and had given each individual control of processes of continued growth, it had served its purpose.*

A Participant Sums It Up

Excerpts from a report submitted by one member of the group to the State Department of Public Welfare, which had made it possible for him to attend, threw interesting sidelights on the program as interpreted by a student:

The day was divided into four periods with the first period each morning devoted to theory. For the first week in these morning discussions Mr. Hayes who is a professor at Vanderbilt gave us a background for community development with a good many of what he considered the basic principles underlying democratic development. From him we gained the feeling that most social development must come from our small communities and that to be at all successful any such program if superimposed must be acceptable to the community and adapted by it to fill community needs. This first period discussion was carried on for the next two weeks by Mr. Morris Mitchell who gave us the privilege of seeing with him the development of his philosophy through taking us with him through a number of educational projects to which he had given direction.

From the experiences he related we gained the feeling of what could be done through concerted community action or democracy applied to the economic and social life as well as to government. At first I, at least, had the idea that Mr. Mitchell was a theorist and not too practical but as his experiences grew I had the feeling that, to use a slang expression, "he had something" and that his philosophy of community development was the thing to build on.

. . . .

The second hour each morning was devoted to the stories of different community projects all of which were very interesting. Mrs. Ogden gave us the story of the organization of the Greene County project with—since I had also worked there—many, many interruptions from me. Mr. Verdin gave the story of the Jordan Community of Greenville County, South Carolina. Mr. Zehmer told of the community development in Louisa, this being another county in which he and the Ogdens have been working. Mr. Savage [then] high school principal of the Holland High School, Nansemond County,[3] told us the story of a program designed to take adult education back into the home communities surrounding a consolidated school. Mr. Bobbitt, the school superintendent from Charlotte County, gave us a similar story. Miss Andersen who had organized a health program in Nebraska on a cooperative basis gave us a most interesting story—and one that can, we hope, be developed into one of practical value for our welfare clients. Mr. Wygal and Mr. Goldsmith gave a very interesting story of community development in Radford, including a municipal forest, recreational project, and other community developments. They spoke at different times and from entirely different angles, Mr. Wygal being former school superintendent, and Mr. Goldsmith commonwealth's attorney. Mr. Goldsmith's presentation was chuck full of politics but brought a very realistic picture that added a good deal to our thinking. All of these speakers gave us a chance to ask questions. *In fact this was literally a workshop.*

The afternoons were devoted to reading, small group conferences, conferences with the leaders, and many just plain "bull sessions." There was much literature available for use at this time. The Ogdens opened their files on all phases of community development to us. These files will be available to all of us, as we need materials, through the Extension Division of the University of Virginia.

———
[3]The third experimental area of the Special Projects.

In the evening we always had more visitors and an attempt had been made to secure leaders of the discussion who would tell us of the work of their agencies. School men, welfare representatives, public health, visual education, were all included. In my estimation most of these people failed to sense just what we were trying to do and did not present their programs as well as they could have with a better understanding of the workshop method.

It was very interesting to watch the change in one's thinking as the weeks went by—and if very little else grows out of the workshop than the change in our individual philosophies regarding democratic community growth and its relationship to our own lives, it will be well worth while. Most of us had very definite plans for some sort of community organization to take home with us and we had developed criteria for judging these attempts at organization.

. . . .

The two things that stand out in my mind as I look back at the workshop are: (1) Mrs. Ogden's summary in which we all concurred —that change is inevitable, that we cannot stop if we would, but that we may with skill be able to direct it into community growth along democratic lines rather than leave it to run its own course; and (2) Miss Anderson's statement that after our plans are started, the hardest thing for us will be to wait a natural development and that we may spoil everything by too much and too rapid pushing.

Criteria for Judging Community Programs

The criteria for evaluating community programs referred to in the above report were worked out by members of the group. They were first presented in response to an assignment at the end of the first week. At that time they were in the form of more or less dogmatic statements as to what a program should be and do. No one felt satisfied. It was decided to keep thinking about criteria during the succeeding two weeks and to restate them later. The final statement came out in the form of questions to be kept in mind rather than any hard-and-fast standards. It is quoted in full:

Some Questions Suggested for Consideration in Evaluating Community Development Programs

(Prepared by the Workshop Committee on Criteria appointed by Mr. Hayes June 26, 1943, and reconsidered by the entire group during the succeeding weeks.)

A. CONCERNING A SINGLE (OR ISOLATED) PROJECT which may be or may become a part of a broader program
    1. Does the project grow out of informal conversations relative to an area of difficulty or concern?

2. Do these informal conversations develop into formal meetings where additional insight is gained and where the ramifications of the issue are perceived?
3. Are these ramifications which are perceived attacked by the project, and do the solutions arrived at lead to a democratic county, state, national, and world government?
4. Is there a good cross section of the people interested?
5. Is formal organization called for? If so, does it furnish ways for spreading information?
6. Are natural and institutional resources being adapted and utilized?
7. Are young people being brought in as a natural part of the process without patronizing toleration?

B. CONCERNING A CHAIN OF PROJECTS (OR PROGRAM)
1. Are undertakings set in motion in order of strategic significance and demonstrability of success in the briefest time?
2. Is the program so set up that it can profit by difficulties which arise and become stronger for each experience?
3. Do definite satisfaction and a growing self-confidence accompany the efforts?

C. CONCERNING THE COMMUNITY
1. Does the program articulate around a cultural background?
2. Are the feelings of happiness, friendliness, appreciation, and understanding increasing in the group or community?
3. Is the community spirit growing to the extent that individuals or small groups are willing to sacrifice their personal desires for the good of the community?
4. Is participation in voting, religious expression, sociability, and recreation increasing?
5. Are economic opportunities and employment increasing?

D. CONCERNING COMMUNITY LEADERSHIP
1. Are there effective leadership, personal talents, and capabilities emerging and developing so that the "professional" worker can fade out of the program and eventually it can move on under its own power?
2. Is the leader focusing attention on the job at hand and its relation to community growth?
3. To what extent are the leaders getting the community to evaluate the program in process?

Evaluation of Workshop by Members

At the request of the staff, the group attempted to evaluate their workshop experience and to make recommendations that might serve as a guide in planning subsequent workshops in community development. This had a dual purpose. Not only would it be useful to the staff but also the careful analysis would clarify the process for the participants. They made the following suggestions:

1. We suggest that the day continue to be set up in four periods as it has been, but that somehow more time be allowed for reading and planning individual programs.

2. We suggest that Mr. Ogden serve regularly as chairman of all evening meetings since it is important that these be related to the other sessions and this can be done only by someone who is in constant contact with the group.

3. We suggest a more diversified group to include public health workers, agricultural agents and teachers, ministers, etc. But the total should not exceed fifteen members.

4. We feel that stories of how a few communities have gone about their jobs have been most valuable and should be retained as a part of any future workshop program. Even the stories of declining interest in programs and the deductions from them have important implications for us in setting up our programs.

5. We feel that we have gained much from discussions of specific techniques and methods of approach.

6. We feel that the vast amount of material on community programs gathered by the Extension Division is of great value and should continue to be made available to us and to others interested in community development.

In addition to the recommendations for others, they asked for themselves opportunity "to further our study and evaluate our work in the light of what we are able to accomplish." To implement this request, they suggested specifically: (1) a week-end conference to be called in October; (2) a second-year workshop the following summer with a few (not more than four) new members from other fields of community interest; and (3) "when travel becomes possible a conducted tour to those communities where theories discussed here are being put into practice."

Used as Basis for Subsequent Workshops

The first summer workshop has been described in some detail because it set the pattern for those held in the summers of 1944 and 1945. Modifications were made on the basis of the recommendations of the first group and the needs of subsequent groups as these needs emerged. Circumstances never again permitted the amount of group participation in preliminary planning that had been possible in 1943. This was a definite loss which was reflected in the time it took in 1944 and 1945 to define objectives and get to work on individual projects. The differences that emerged in later workshops are commented on below as evidence of the fact that plans must be adapted to each group and the process must continue to be a creative one.

Workshop—1944 Model

For 1944 a more diversified group was recruited in accordance with the 1943 recommendation. In 1943 there had been school principals and welfare superintendents. In 1944 there were, in addition, teachers and supervisors of agriculture, a school board clerk, a minister, a supervisor of instruction for county schools, a public health doctor, a county administrator, and the secretary of a textile workers union. This diversity meant fewer specific common problems and approaches to programs. On the other hand, it made for a more comprehensive consideration of the community as a whole.

During this second summer, several persons had been allowed to enroll for only a part of the time because they could not leave their regular duties for three weeks. There was general agreement that this procedure was unsatisfactory for all concerned. The cumulative effect of the discussions makes it important that everyone stay through to the end. Those who left after the first week must have had something of a feeling of futility about it all because so many questions had been raised and so few answers arrived at. Those who came in during the second and third weeks found it difficult to become a part of a group that was already a working unit. Moreover, they slowed up the process and were irritating to other members because of their insistence on covering ground that had already been covered. In its recommendations for future workshops, this group included the suggestion "that future workshops be planned so that members be required to attend full time."

The staff heartily concurred in this recommendation since it seemed to them that the short-time participant could have gained little understanding of the workshop process. This conviction, however, was shaken by the fact that the program of Ruritan-sponsored local workshops (described in chapter

12) was initiated and promoted by one of the short-time participants who felt the workshop approach was of such value that it should be extended to more people in the communities where they live.

Not all the recommendations of the first group applied to the second. The need for more time for reading and planning individual projects, for example, was strongly urged by the 1943 workshop. The 1944 schedule made provision for it. It developed, however, that the 1944 participants lacked an urge for individual studious application and liked to have the talk flow on throughout the afternoon though the conference period had been reduced from two hours and a half to one hour and a half. Fewer members of this group left at the end of three weeks with definitely formulated plans. Yet almost all had a feeling of real accomplishment, and subsequent activities have proved that plans were made and carried out.

Test of Time to Be Applied

The "evaluation statement" of the 1944 group differs widely in both form and content from that of the 1943:

Because most of the true values lie in the future, the group believes that a true and realistic evaluation of the workshop cannot be made at the present time; however, we submit the following evaluating statements:

1. We feel that the workshop has been highly satisfactory and justified in that it has provided stimulation that will affect the coordination of agencies in our respective communities.
2. The workshop has increased in us an awareness of our responsibility as professional and institutional workers and as individual citizens.
3. The workshop has afforded an opportunity for the representatives of the various agencies to become more closely associated in recognizing their responsibilities in developing leadership.
4. The selection of participants from a wide variety of communities and from a wide variety of professional and occupational fields has broadened our concept of community problems.
5. The dynamic personalities of the workshop staff during the morning sessions supplemented by the reports of people from programs in action have provided the real core of the workshop.
6. The physical setup of the workshop has provided an atmosphere most conducive to the type of work we have undertaken. The mutual understanding and sociability of staff and workshop members have been a valuable contributing factor towards the success of the workshop.

Two of the distinguishing characteristics of the 1944 group were (1) the strong *esprit de corps* that developed among those who were present throughout the three weeks and (2) their ability to laugh at themselves when they began to regard too seriously their roles as saviors of mankind. Both were reflected in their organizing themselves into the "Shackle Shakers" at the end of the session.

Recreation Develops from Sociability

For neither group had it been necessary to have a planned recreation program. An atmosphere of informal sociability was established from the beginning, and a picnic was planned for the middle of the first week for each group. Thereafter the group became its own recreation director and was the dispenser rather than the recipient of hospitality.

Further Modification for 1945

In planning for the 1945 summer workshop, the staff again modified the original pattern in terms of experiences of two preceding summers. Again they found that they faced an entirely different kind of group. In the first two years men had been far in the majority. In the third, women outnumbered them. The proportion of persons in administrative positions was increased. Experience with three groups convinced us that, though a general pattern may be used for many groups, it must undergo continuous modification.

Two things worked together to give this third group less cohesion than either of the preceding. The ideal housing arrangements and provisions for eating together as a group which had been possible in preceding years could not be planned in 1945 because of crowded conditions in Charlottesville. For the group this proved to be unfortunate. For evaluation of it as part of the workshop it was perhaps fortunate. Without the 1945 experience of having the group divided for housing and scattered for meals, we could never have been sure we were not overestimating the importance of the residence situation. This experience convinced us that it is an extremely important part of such an educational process.

The other thing that made this group less of a working unit was, at the same time, its unique educational feature so far as our summer workshops were concerned. Several members worked as a unit on a special project set up in advance in cooperation with the Virginia Federation of Women's Clubs. The club women attended regular morning sessions but at other times withdrew to their own room in the library to work on their special project under the guidance of one of the staff members. This fact not only divided the group but also made available fewer staff members for individual conferences.

The special project was the study guide in community affairs for local club programs discussed in chapter 12.[4] When the president had asked the Extension Division in the winter of 1945 to prepare such a guide, its preparation by the club women themselves with guidance from the staff was suggested. There were several preliminary conferences of club women with Dr. Hayes who was then conducting local workshops. Together they set up a general outline. Then the plan was to have a small group attend the summer workshop and complete the study guide with the assistance of any others who might be interested. This method was a further application of the approach used in writing the Louisa County Citizens' Council Bulletins described in chapter 14. The persons whose lives were affected were to select and phrase the materials to be used.

The ministers, welfare workers, and school people in the workshop contributed generously from their experience to the study guide. Experts from the various departments of the University (political science, rural sociology, Bureau of Public Administration, etc.) and from state agencies were invited in to the afternoon work sessions. By the end of the three-week period a rough draft of "Community Quiz" was completed with lists of pertinent questions and references (both printed and human) on aspects of community life including resources, economics, government, education, health, religion, recreation, aesthetics, and planning.

---

[4]*Community Quiz: Some $64 Questions. A Study Guide on Community Development.* Prepared in collaboration with and published for the Virginia Federation of Womens Clubs. Extension Division, University of Virginia. October, 1945. 60 pages.

Dr. Hayes was the staff member who had given most time to this part of the workshop program. Unfortunately he had to return to his duties at Vanderbilt before the editorial process was complete. The final editing was ably done by Miss Margaret Snyder when she joined the staff in September. Thus the "Community Quiz" became even more a "group creation."

This type of project can be a valuable part of a summer workshop program and, with careful planning, may serve as a cohesive rather than a divisive force. In this situation, the club women who participated probably had insufficient understanding of the fact that they were to be a part of a larger group. Again the problem of part-time attendance presented itself. Yet before the three weeks ended the relationship of the club group to the workshop had been clarified and their contribution to the whole as well as to their special project was important. Two of the four who attended have expressed the desire to attend another workshop later. A third has written:

> Through the workshop I discovered brand new avenues of thought. It certainly takes one out of the groove that everyone slips into. There is danger even of finding oneself alone, misunderstood, frustrated by inactivity, and in a constant state of discontent. But seriously, it was a grand experience to be a part of a group such as the workshop and to have this unusual opportunity of exploring new channels. I am ever so grateful to those of you who planned the sessions. I have done nothing but sing the praises of the University since I left.

The experiment with the club women was a decided success from the point of view of the staff. The problems are mentioned merely because of the conviction that they could be obviated by more careful preliminary planning related to the whole rather than to only a special project that was to be a part of the whole.

The third workshop, like the two preceding, attempted a group evaluation. It was very like those already quoted. But, as the 1944 group pointed out, the real evaluation must take place later in terms of what happens to the individual in his community.

Trying to Keep in Touch

The staff felt that it was important to keep in touch with members of the groups and to keep them in touch with each other. Following the 1943 workshop, this was possible because the group was small. As the numbers increased and the work of Special Projects kept expanding, it became more difficult. A newsletter planned at the close of the 1944 workshop never materialized because the staff did not have time to prepare and get it out. This is a serious admission of failure to use a simple technique which we know can be effective.

Making a specialist available to those communities that wished to plan local workshops was a part of the follow-up program. Its value is discussed in chapter 18.

There have been many personal visits by staff members when invited for a special occasion or when chance took them into the community of one of the workshoppers. Books and pamphlet materials have been supplied whenever requested —and advice has been given freely. Yet a more comprehensive plan for sustaining the feeling of fellowship and cooperative thinking on common problems which developed in each workshop could have been followed to the mutual advantage of staff and participants.

A midwinter conference of the 1943 and 1944 groups provided for an exchange of experience that was both helpful and inspiring. During the 1945 session, several members of preceding workshops returned for a day or two to take part in the discussions and to get acquainted with the new group. At a picnic held at that time came the suggestion that we form a "Workshop Alumni Association." This was, of course, in jest but it indicated that the feeling of fellowship which developed in each group extended to all those who had participated in this experience. It also was further evidence of the need expressed in the letter quoted above to continue to have a channel of communication with those who have like purposes.

Follow-up by Questionnaire

In the late fall of 1945, an attempt was made to get individual evaluations of the workshop process in relation to effective participation in community affairs and personal gains. Each participant in the three groups received the following appeal:

To the Workshoppers of '43, '44, and '45—Greetings!

The Ogdens had hoped to visit you all before this time to get some answers to questions in order to do a better job of evaluating workshops in the report of the five-year experimental program which is now nearing completion. Said report plus an expanding program in new areas have made visits impossible. So this is a cry for help.

Could you take a few minutes out of your life, which we know is just as busy as ours, to answer whatever questions on the enclosed pages you have any answers to?

If you prefer to write a letter or a general statement disregarding the questions, that will be quite all right. We have no intention of "tabulating" the replies. But we need both facts and opinions upon which to base any generalizations we make about workshops as a "technique."

We promise to send you a summary of the replies so that each can know what others are doing and thinking.

Really exciting things are happening in the program of community development in Virginia of which this is a part. Before too long, we hope to send you a newsletter about it.

In the meantime, help please————!

The questionnaire which accompanied the letter included the following questions:

A. THE COMMUNITY

1. Are there tangible evidences or achievements in your community that have a direct or indirect relation to your workshop experience? (Do not be modest in listing any you consider belong here even though you moved so indirectly toward them that some other individual, agency, or group takes the credit. We shall be impersonal in our reporting.)

2. Did any plans you made in the workshop materialize? *If so,* what modifications did you have to make in face of the actual situation? *If not,* did the process of analyzing and planning in the workshop make it easier for you to analyze and plan afterward?

3. Is there evidence of a change or improvement in community spirit and/or understanding? If so, what steps helped to bring it about?

B. YOU PERSONALLY

1. Have you found yourself more sensitive to goings-on in your community?

2. Have you been more eager to put a shoulder to the wheel when something is started?

3. Have you been better able to think in terms of the *community as a whole* and to see your job in relation to it?

4. Has your professional work been strengthened by the addition of increased knowledge of people and resources at your disposal?

5. Have you found yourself more deft in the carrying out of your job?

6. Aside from the fellowship and comradeship we enjoyed together (and we do not underestimate its value) was the experience worth enough that you would choose it now knowing as much about it as you do? (Be honest, please. Remember we are being impersonal about this.)

Replies were prompt and helpful. They were unanimous in their enthusiasm for the workshop as a technique both for stimulating an intelligent interest in community affairs and for contributing to personal growth.

In Terms of the Community

With reference to tangible evidences in the community were listed such things as organization of a women's club, of boys' and teen-age clubs, of coordinating councils, of recreation programs; making of community surveys and studies leading to improved services and industrial growth; development of health programs, clinics, and hospital facilities; development of a library; cooperation with schools in extending their farm-machinery-repair and food-preservation programs; revitalization of civic clubs, Parent-Teacher Associations, and similar community organizations; initiation of continuous study of community problems by citizens in local workshop and study groups.

One reply to this question about "tangible evidences" stated: "I know a number of steps have been taken to build a more unified community. It is hard to list specific items but the results are obvious to all who live here. Everyone seems to be working together for a *good* community. Is that a 'tangible' thing?"

In relation to the second question—the usefulness of pre-planning community activities while in the workshop—the repeated warnings of the staff that such plans must be regarded as *tentative* seem to have borne fruit. Only one person reported that he had followed his plan without modification. All those, however, who had worked out careful plans reported that the *process of planning had been of great help to them.* There was no feeling that it had been time wasted. One said, "Planning, (though I have not been able to get the jobs done) helped me more than anything else in formulating a philosophy and point of view."

"Evidence of change or improvement in community spirit" was difficult to state. Many reported that they felt it was there but could give no evidence. Others reported better attendance at meetings, readiness of persons to serve on working committees, and a feeling of increased friendliness. As steps to attaining the improved spirit, several mentioned, as of perhaps greatest importance, working together on a program and carrying through to completion a specific plan—e. g., a recreation program or a community cannery. The satisfaction of *having done something* seemed to serve both as a morale builder and as a springboard to the next job. One person thought he found a better spirit and increased interest because he now looked for it whereas before he had assumed that he must do the whole job himself.

In Terms of the Individual

Personal effects of the experience were even more startlingly stated. Several intimated that their personal comfort had been disturbed as a result of increased awareness of community needs and potentialities and realization of their own responsibility for doing something about them.

"I sometimes feel quite helpless in the face of needs of which I was formerly not aware," said one. "But most times I tackle things one at a time and see them not as problems but as opportunities for greater usefulness."

Ability to think in terms of the community as a whole was the one evidence of personal growth most frequently mentioned. "For this reason," said one welfare worker, "the workshop experience has been more helpful to me in my job than any other training I have ever had. I not only *see the community as a whole but I see my job in relation to it.*"

Another said: "Perhaps the main value of the workshop for me has been seeing the *total* community. My ministry has been broadened and strengthened thereby. The experience has been invaluable to me both in my professional life and in my philosophy of life. *For me it has opened up a way of Christian expression."*

The 1945 group had had, of course, too short a time in which to achieve much that was tangible. But it was from one of them that the following statement came:

I do not know when I have enjoyed anything more than the workshop. And I can't recall a class or group meeting or conference from which I derived more help. As the days pass, I become more and more fully aware of just what I did get. *First,* I got tremendous stimulation. The meeting of minds *and hearts* there did a lot to awaken me to the real challenge which is before us in our communities. *Second,* I got a great deal of information— so much in so short a time that often my head seemed to reel under its impact. This information will be valuable all my life. *Third,* I got perspective which I needed. Since, I have been able to lift up my eyes to behold a broader view of our work. I believe I see community development from the standpoint of the whole community and not just the church. I know I see it as a cooperative affair. And that is important to one who was a little too much inclined to be a "churchman." *Fourth,* I received understanding. I still see through a glass darkly to be sure. But I understand more of what this is all about. All in all I am sold completely on the workshop. I think it one of the best things that ever hit "Ye Olde Dominion."

Basic Principles Same for All Workshops

The kind of summer workshop in community development described in this chapter is, of course, only one of many types that could be planned. All three included here were of the same type: *a resident workshop for mature adults* (primarily professional workers) *already engaged in some kind of community activity and in need of seeing it in relation to the total community as it is and as it might be.*

The basic principles, however, in this type of workshop can be applied to any adult group. From our experience in these and our observation of other workshops, we offer a few generalizations.

Definition of Term

The term *workshop* has come to be so generally used for types of informal study groups that it needs to be clearly defined—or possibly discarded for a more exact word. The method of learning discussed in this chapter might, perhaps, better be called a work conference except that it is more intensive and extensive than the connotation of that word implies. Then, too, there is another difference: In the conference, one thinks of the group as working cooperatively on a common problem or project. In the workshop there are common interests; group participation; and, to a degree, group creation. *Yet each individual has his own specific job to do in the light of the common experience and under guidance of workshop associates.*

The student's workshop project is of an immediately practical nature. He must do intensive individual work and planning in relation to a program in which he expects to apply the plans. Application is to a situation with which he is familiar.

The accent is on the *concrete* rather than the *abstract*. The student begins with the concrete as related to himself and uses theory and background information for its interpretation, thus reversing the usual direction of the formal organization of subject matter.

The workshop idea is not new. It is merely an attempt to popularize the seminar and to indicate its practical nature through the use of a term that has a non-academic connotation. For many so-called workshops, the formal class or seminar might serve the purpose more effectively. *A workshop is important only when participants have some workaday, already-recognized problems or situations to work out.*

Adult Methods for Adults

The workshop is a method for use with adults. It implies some facility in self-education and a desire to become increasingly capable of self-direction in relating knowledge and philosophy to living. It is the best method we have found for a practical, down-to-earth, in-service training program for adult leaders of adults.

Only those should participate who are committed to seeking solutions to problems through a sincere personal effort to relate theory to practice. Readiness for such an experience implies maturity and, at the same time, that humbleness and dissatisfaction with self which characterize any sincere seeker after truth.

The staff must be "leaders in learning" rather than teachers or preachers. They must be willing and able to put their knowledge, skills, and experience at the disposal of the group. They must be sensitive to individual needs and ready to help individuals to see relations. Presumably they have more background or experience in specialized fields than do the participants. Yet they, too, must be learners. Giving—or learning— *The Answers* has no place in the workshop process. Increasing each individual's awareness and his ability to analyze situations and arrive at *tentative answers to be revised in the light of more knowledge or subsequent experience is the process.*

Guest Speakers and Visiting Experts

Selection of guest speakers and experts in various fields must be made with the leader-in-learning idea in mind. Our experience has been that successful practitioners in community programs pretty generally fit into the plan without difficulty. Their ability to be "leaders in learning" is undoubtedly related to the fact that they have been leaders in successful programs. Then, too, most of them are still seeking better ways of doing the job just as members of the workshop are. Administrators of state departments and specialists from state and national levels have been more difficult to incorporate into the workshop process.

Participation in Planning

The more participation in planning there can be in advance by all members of the group, the more quickly the workshop can get under way. Such participation is not just a way of "getting people interested." It is an important part of building exactly the right kind of program. It is based on a sincere belief that in adult education every individual in a group has an important contribution to make and that the sum of group planning is greater than its parts. It is a method that is implicit in this philosophy.

Group analysis of process and group planning of program should not stop when the workshop gets under way or even when it has ended. The process should become continuous and automatic. Here it is frequently necessary to break down strong student-teacher attitudes and to convince participants that honest evaluation rather than polite platitudes are desired.

The Physical Setup

To achieve the maximum results so far as total group planning and learning are concerned, the right atmosphere must be established in the beginning. An informal and comfortable physical setup contributes to this. Sitting around a table or even in comfortable chairs around a room helps to break down the schoolroom attitude. The degree of informality may vary to suit the temperament of a particular leader or the material that is being presented. The formal lecture and other classroom procedures may, at times, be legitimate parts of the workshop. These may require somewhat more formal physical arrangements. For morning "class periods" in our three resident groups we found a large table, straight chairs, and a blackboard generally helpful. During the second period, however, if it seemed more suitable or desirable, the group frequently settled in the lounge rather than the classroom. This happened naturally, during the first summer for example, when Morris Mitchell's talks assumed the nature of telling friends about things that had happened rather than giving formal lectures.

The advantages of having the group housed together in the place in which meetings are held have been commented on before. The "post mortems" and "bull sessions" that naturally develop in a residence situation are an important part of the process of digestion and assimilation of ideas. Eating together as a group with pleasant table conversation is also important. The group that did not have these advantages never acquired the effective group-attack on problems that the others did. Moreover, playing together naturally develops when the group lives and eats together, and the tendency to become too serious disappears. Jack is less likely to become the dull boy produced by an all-work-no-play atmosphere. Yet nobody has to promote an artificially stimulated recreation program.

Having a selected library and pamphlet files in the place where the group regularly meets and is housed is also impor-

tant. If one can reach for a book at the moment an idea occurs to him or a discussion arises, he is more likely to pursue
it than if he has to go to a library and find a reference jotted
down in his notebook or mimeographed on a reading list.

The Less Tangible Matter of Atmosphere

Just as important as the right physical setup is the building
of a feeling of fellowship. One workshop member tried to express his reaction to this in a letter to the staff following the
workshop:

> The fellowship was wonderful. I believe your technique in that
> is the outstanding thing you do. I like the way you bring the group
> together. That "togetherness" lends so much to the atmosphere. The
> workshop represents a lot of thinking, working, and planning.. But
> even more important it represents a willingness on the part of the
> staff to give of their *personality* as well as their knowledge and skill.
> And just this is one of the biggest secrets of the success of the
> endeavor.

Important though this technique is, to analyze it is difficult. A few small matters that have helped can be mentioned,
though they might not work elsewhere. The staff can learn
everyone's name, locale, and job before the workshop starts.
Fitting names to persons then becomes easy. Everyone likes
to feel that his personality has registered. Moreover, he feels
more responsible when known by name and position.
Anonymity encourages irresponsibility. Providing a time on
the program the first day for everyone to tell the group
something about himself furthers this process of getting acquainted. *Everyone* means staff as well as students. Just "sitting around" to talk between classes or in the afternoon and
evening is also helpful.

In each of the first two groups included in this chapter, it
just happened that there was one person who believed that
use of first names was important. The first year it was a staff
member; the second year, a student. The idea was accepted
with some diffidence by many in the group, particularly when
applied to staff. But, after the first few days, the practice had
become fairly general and, strange to say, it did something important in the building of fellowship. The third year there
was no one with conviction in this matter. To have forced

the issue would have been artificial and awkward. But dignity or pompousness which have been assumed as a cloak to hide inadequacy must be laid aside. An atmosphere of mutual respect and confidence makes this possible. The first-name habit may help to create it.

But more important than any specific "techniques" is the attitude of those responsible for the workshop. If they are sincerely interested in the participants as people rather than as students (and the two are by no means mutually exclusive); if they are willing to give unstintingly of themselves in their desire to have the experience a rich one for all concerned, there will be no problem. Without such an attitude, all the techniques in the world will not do the job. Though the staff must at first carry chief responsibility for creating such an atmosphere, it quickly spreads to the group as guest speakers and visitors come in. The growth in a group's ability really to include these guests (and make them a part of the whole) is one of the most interesting developments to watch. To the degree each individual can carry this over to his community, his work as a leader will be strengthened.

The Workshop in Education

Like every educational "fad," workshops have enjoyed a kind of mushroom growth. The use—and misuse—of the term has caused some concern among administrators and schools of education. They have attempted to define and formalize the workshop in such a way as to make it fit into the academic pattern.

Though sound educational standards are necessary if the workshop is to have a place in the academic world, *standardization* would defeat the very purpose behind the workshop idea. The workshop must be adapted to the background and needs of the group, and no two groups are the same. Therefore no standards should be set up which tend toward standardization of procedure, content, or techniques.

If participants and leaders are sincerely *looking for ways* in the light of all available knowledge and experience, the quality of the work will inevitably be of a standard that the most formal academic mind could not question.

But there is nothing in the term *workshop* that makes this inevitable. That it has become the newest white magic in educational jargon is unfortunate. As a matter of fact, it is neither new nor magic. On the other hand, there must be elements of newness in each adaptation of the method. It is in its adaptability and capacity for variation to suit all kinds of groups that its unique value as an educational method lies. And like any educational process which really helps individuals to realize their potentialities, it is the *Open Sesame* to an unbelievably richer life.

CHAPTER 17

Workshops on Wheels

When the staff of the Special Projects in Adult Education began to plan ways of stimulating community programs, one way kept suggesting itself. This was taking community leaders to visit good programs and to talk with persons responsible for them.

It was necessary first to find the programs and to become acquainted with their leaders in order to make sure that our visitors would not only see something worthwhile but would also have it explained to them in a way that would be really helpful. This was one reason for the exploration that resulted in *New Dominion Series*. That exploration began in the summer of 1941. It was November before we visited the Jordan Area and discovered the first total community program that seemed just right for persons with whom we were working in rural Virginia counties. It was a long way from Charlottesville, but the following summer between the time they planted and harvested their crops we hoped to be able to take some community leaders from our experimental counties to see what that area had done. A month after our first visit to the Jordan Area came Pearl Harbor—and war. By summer the emphasis in the communities in which we were working had shifted to meeting emergency needs. People could not take time from their farms because of shortage of labor and pressure for increased production. The need for conservation of gas and rubber had become urgent. The idea of traveling several hundred miles to see even so good a program as that of the Jordan Area was not to be considered.

Approach from a New Direction

But the idea persisted. Exploration of programs was continued. Many more were found that were excellent for visits. Meantime we must content ourselves with talking and writing about them. Finally for the summer workshop of 1943, a compromise plan was made. We could not take the group to visit communities but we could bring leaders from good community programs to visit the summer workshop and discuss what they had done and how.

This discussion of "community programs in action" was one of the best aspects of the workshop program. It led to something we had not anticipated. Members of the group began to say, "We ought to go to see these things for ourselves." At the end of the session, they recommended that when conditions made travel possible the Extension Division plan a trip for them to visit several of the best programs.

In October, after about four months of trying things in their own communities, members of the 1943 workshop returned to the University for a conference. It was then that their desire to visit programs was urgently expressed. They had tried things themselves. Some ways had not worked as they had in the stories. Were the stories perhaps better than the programs on which they were based? Or were there elements in these other situations that had not been made clear? Or (perish the thought!) did these leaders have something we lacked? The general attitude was, "If they can do it, we can. But *what have they really done?* Are we perhaps reading too much success into their stories and being discouraged when our own results are less spectacular?"

It seemed as if an almost ideal situation now existed from an educational point of view. There was strong motivation for seeing and background for understanding what was seen on the part of each individual. To all of us a trip seemed to offer much greater possibilities for further growth in understanding community development than a second summer workshop with a few new members added to the group as had been proposed at the end of the 1943 session. Moreover, such a plan offered opportunity to test, before the end of the experimental program, the soundness of our original idea about the value of visits to other communities. We were as eager to try it as were members of the group.

The Idea Becomes Reality

The gas stringency was less acute by this time. The fact that regular Extension Division activities decreased during summer months would make it possible to plan a trip without additional allotments of gasoline. Planning for peace was assuming increasing importance in everyone's mind. The time seemed right. A small grant from a foundation was procured to finance a trip, and plans were made.

The program was announced in the summer Quarter *Bulletin* as follows:[1]

Education 3W104L: Workshop in Community Programs in Action:

During the first ten days visits will be made to ten successful community projects of various types. These will include food preservation centers, recreation programs, libraries, public health and medical care programs, rural cooperatives, and school-centered community programs.

Preliminary study of each project and discussion group meetings with local leaders have been provided for.

The last four days will be devoted to evaluation of the projects visited; discussion of possible application of techniques to local situations; and pre-planning of their summer programs by the participants in this workshop.

Registration is definitely restricted to participants in last summer's Workshop in Community Development and selected members of the local winter workshops which followed it.

About the same time, members of the group were notified and each received a copy of the following proposed itinerary and calendar:

Saturday, June 10 (or June 17)
    Leave Charlottesville 8:00 A.M.
    Montgomery County Library (afternoon)
    Radford Recreation Program —NDS No. 12 at night and overnight in Radford

Sunday
    Leave Radford 9:00 A.M.
    Drive to Clayton, Ga. (376 miles)
    Overnight at Clayton

Monday
    Clayton Health Center, Maternity Program, Bookmobile— NDS No. 36

Rabun Gap Homesteads
    Overnight at Macedonia (25 miles)

Tuesday
    Clarkesville school-centered food preservation program —NDS No. 37
    Drive to Carrollton, Georgia (162 miles)

Wednesday
    Cooperative projects in Carroll County sponsored by West Georgia Teachers College and the public schools—NDS No. 39 and 40
    Carrollton overnight

[1]*University of Virginia Summer Quarter Bulletin,* Vol. XVIII, No. 4. March 15, 1944.

Thursday

Drive to Greenville, S. C. (166 miles)

P. M. Discussion with Furman University people

Overnight in Greenville

Friday

The Jordan Area —NDS No. 11

P.M. Drive to Charlotte, N. C. (102 miles)

Overnight Charlotte

Saturday

Start 9:00 A.M. for Raleigh, N. C. (154 miles)

Raleigh Teen-Age Club —NDS No. 45

Chapel Hill overnight

Sunday

Back to Charlottesville (185 miles)

OR

Drive to Lawrenceville, Va. (114 miles)

Monday

Tri-County Health Program —NDS No. 14

To Charlottesville (140 miles) in evening

Tuesday, Wednesday, Thursday, Friday at University of Virginia. Discussion of trip and making of new community plans.

This itinerary had been planned by the staff on the basis of: (1) their intimate knowledge of the group, and of the needs and interests of the individual members; (2) their acquaintance with the programs proposed for visit and with the leadership in the various communities; (3) the conviction that every mile traveled should be made to count to the fullest extent.

Everyone was invited to comment and everyone did. Most of the comments, however, were merely enthusiastic approbation. Minor modifications were made later but not on the basis of suggestions from the group.

Careful Advance Planning

The next step was to work out detailed plans for each visit with local leaders. They had been consulted before the announcement went out. But between March and June dozens of letters were exchanged, for, if the trip were to run on schedule, everything had to be planned in advance. The staff members who were to accompany the group had previously visited all the programs and had reported most of them in *New Dominion Series*. They knew the local situations and leaders. They felt that they were working with old friends in making arrangements. Yet they felt they had no right to expect the wholehearted cooperation they received from everyone. This went a long way toward assuring the success of the trip. The importance of knowing what you are going to see and of doing careful planning in advance for each visit cannot be over-emphasized for those conducting such a tour.

On May 9, just a month before the trip was to start, plans were reported to the group in the letter quoted below. The breezy informality of the letter is typical of the spirit which was to make a really strenuous trip enjoyable as well as profitable.

To the Prospective Intrepid Wayfarers:

Plans have gone far enough to merit a report to all of you at this date and to prepare you for your final instructions which will get to you sometime the first week in June.

First of all, with two exceptions, last year's gang will be 100 per cent strong. Jean and I will be the two who start from here because George and Alex have to get ready for the Summer Quarter. They will be on hand to meet us when we pull back into Charlottesville in the late afternoon of Monday, June 19. From that time until Saturday morning, we will be hard at work reconstructing our experiences and making definite plans for our summer's work.

So, first thing, start the calendar of the itinerary for Saturday, June 10, nine o'clock at the absolute latest. We will probably pick up such rugged individualists as Jack Hyatt and Elizabeth Divers *en route,* but we have a luncheon date either in Radford or Christiansburg Saturday noon and it will be up to us to get there. Saturday night we are hoping to meet several interested and interesting officials of the Radford area for dinner and then take a good look at the Radford recreation center. We will stop overnight at the Governor Tyler Inn and set out on the long trek south very early Sunday morning.

A bit of luck has made it possible for us to stay Sunday night at High Hampton Inn (quite the loveliest spot Jean and I have run across in all our travels—high in the Smokies—you're in for a treat). Monday morning finds us in Clayton—where we will be met by the one and only Morris Mitchell. Frank Smith, Ordinary of Rabun County, and his Health and Welfare Council will have lunch with us and discuss their program which we are to visit in the afternoon. Monday evening we will spend at Macedonia at Morris' invitation. We have planned a picnic supper on the top of the mountain which Morris' labor with us last summer purchased. That means, especially for Elizabeth and Jean, hiking shoes, and, for the rest of us, minds steeled for a mile-and-a-half hike.

Tuesday morning we look over Clarkesville and then set sail for Carrollton, Georgia. Morris and Barbara are coming along. At Carrollton we will be met by Ed Yeomans and whatsoever members of the exceptional teaching group at West Georgia College can be rallied around at that date. We will stay two nights at their Log Cabin, and I can testify personally that you're in for another treat. All day Wednesday will be spent in looking over Carroll County and talking with Ed Yeomans and the others at West Georgia Teachers College.

Wayland Hayes may join us at this spot—that hasn't been worked out yet. At any rate, we start for Greenville, South Carolina, Thursday—one car dropping Morris and Barbara at Macedonia, but the rest of us meeting Tom Verdin, Tom Nelson, Pete Hollis, *et al,* in Greenville for a gabfest at dinner. Friday, Verdin will retread the Jordan Area with us.

We shall spend Saturday night and Sunday at Chapel Hill talking with Lee Brooks and some of the North Carolina group who have been so influential in the South. Somewhere along the line we will get a glimpse at the Raleigh Teen-Age Club and its sponsors as well as the Junior Board which actually does all the work for that interesting organization. Monday, early, we will look over what projects of the Tri-County Health Program (Brunswick-Greensville-Mecklenburg) Dr. Valentine feels we should see.

Then boots and saddles, and away for Charlottesville. You will all work; so will the Ogdens—but it will be fun and profitable.

Now, let me put in a plea. We will have four in each of three cars the whole trip. Some stretches there will be five in a car. That means baggage at an *absolute*—and I *mean absolute* — minimum. Otherwise our bones will creak even more than is necessary. There is not one dressup occasion in the whole plan. We will have to limit everyone to one bag each. The smaller the bag the more considerate.

If you are getting as much fun out of anticipating the trip as I am, you are probably finding it hard to keep your feet on the ground.

The general response to this letter can be summed up by an excerpt from one letter: "Hey! Wait a minute! It's a whole month yet, and your letter has me counting the days, with no mind to put on my job, like a kid waiting for Santa Claus."

The letter with final instructions went out on June 1. It covered such matters as finances, type of clothes needed, baggage, exact times and places of meeting for those who were to be picked up along the way, and addresses at which mail would be most likely to reach the group *en route.*

Observations on the First Traveling Workshop

On Saturday morning, June 10, 1944, the workshop on wheels started from the University of Virginia. There were twelve persons (two women and ten men) in three cars. Professionally the group was made up as follows: seven principals of consolidated high schools serving rural areas, two county superintendents of public welfare, one county agricultural agent. They came from eight different counties of Virginia extending from Nansemond in the tidewater to Tazewell in the extreme southwest. Two counties had two representatives each.

The two staff members had worked with the 1943 summer workshop and had planned this trip. Nine members of the group had been in the 1943 workshop, and the tenth had been in a local winter workshop organized by a principal from the 1943 summer group and conducted by the same staff members. This meant that the group had a considerable common background for the new venture. Moreover they had been closely associated over a period of time and could look forward to ten days of even closer association with full knowledge of each other's vagaries.

In preparation for the visits, everyone had been urged to reread the *New Dominion* stories concerned with the programs. These had been noted on the original itinerary. The staff had made up a folder on each program for the trip and planned to review each with the group just preceding the visit. This was found to be difficult for, once started, the group found so much of interest along the way that there was little time for reading. Discussion never stopped but it was likely to be concerned with what had just been seen and heard rather than with what was going to be seen next. The background acquired preceding the trip became especially important in view of this development. The group became so conscious of this that they urged even more preparation as a prerequisite for future traveling workshops.

The inestimable contribution of the preliminary planning within the communities visted also became clear as the trip progressed. Local leaders had planned community meetings, had organized tours, and had done everything possible to facilitate the progress of the group without in any way hampering its opportunity to see the entire community and talk with average citizens as well as with program enthusiasts. Under other circumstances visits to ten widely separated programs in ten days might well have resulted in little but confusion.

An important contribution to the educational value for everyone had been neither planned nor anticipated by the

leaders. The people we visited were eager to know what we
had seen and to have our suggestions for their own programs.
This necessitated keen and continuous analysis as we went
along. The twelve visiting Virginians were regarded as
people of importance, and this put us on our mettle. It helped
also to clinch the realization that the leaders in these programs that were pointed out as successful were not supermen.
They did not have glib answers to all problems. They were
ordinary people like us. They, too, were seeking to find better
ways of tackling community problems. What was seen on the
trip was important but probably nothing was more important
than the morale-building effect of the mutual exchange that
took place everywhere. Almost everyone in the group realized more and more that he, too, had a contribution to make
and he could look back on his own community with a new
perspective.

At West Georgia Teachers College a workshop on
school-community relations was in progress. Here we were
plied with questions not only about what we were seeing on
the trip but also about school-community programs where we
lived. In Greenville, Mr. Verdin (former superintendent of
schools in the Jordan Area) met us on our arrival and spent
an evening asking searching and challenging questions. He
had come to our workshop the preceding summer to tell about
the Jordan program and was, therefore, an old friend. What
he wanted to know about the programs we had seen required
exactly the kind of analysis the group needed to make for
digestion and assimilation. Again at Chapel Hill, after a full
week of travel, we had the privilege of telling our tale to another and genuinely interested audience. Here there was a
workshop of social studies teachers meeting with Dr. Gordon
Blackwell. Again our process of sorting out and evaluating
was given a push forward. This time it was facilitated by the
sociability of a delightfully informal breakfast which this
workshop group prepared for us.

Details of the trip are not given here because they are
recorded (at least those they deemed suitable for publication) in the groups' own report, *We Went to See for Our-*

selves.[2] This report was prepared at the suggestion of the faculty members who gathered at the University to hear the report on the trip.

Reporting and Summing Up Impressions

In planning the traveling workshop the staff had felt that after ten days of talking with each other we would need a fresh audience. They had not realized that there would be fresh audiences all along the way eager to hear our tales. By the time we left Chapel Hill we began to have apprehensions that the story might have become too old to tell again in Charlottesville. But not so. It seemed as if so much had been seen and heard that the group could keep reporting with infinite variety. We had not even tired of listening to each other!

So each one chose the program he liked best and organized his material for a group of University of Virginia faculty members. The latter considered the report so impressive that they urged its publication together with some tentative conclusions that had been formulated. It was one of them who reported in the University of Virginia *Alumni News*:

Vision Down to Earth—Practical

June 21, the Extension Division held an unusual meeting at the University. It was attended by a group of high school principals, social workers, and county agents. Anyone who happened to drop in at that meeting heard some interesting talk. It was more than that; it was exciting and inspiring. At the same time, it was down to earth and extremely practical. The talk demonstrated just how useful adult education can be as a force for making democracy work. These schoolmen reported on a tour they had made at the instigation of the University of Virginia Extension Division, to look at some of the projects described in the *New Dominion Series*. They had been and seen; they weren't conquered but they had found out a lot about how to conquer certain problems in their own rural communities where democracy is not working on the beam to produce the best possible living for the largest number of people. These were the educators who attended the workshop at the University last year. The Community Workshop is an idea packed full of fine practical possibilities. More will, and should be heard from it. It is another example of the University serving the state, of which there are many, and about which the public does not know enough.

---

[2]*We Went to See for Ourselves* . . . . . *The Account of an Itinerant Workshop in Community Programs in Action.* University of Virginia Extension Division. Vol. XXII, No. 8. January 1, 1945.

The report was not written until the following fall because at the moment everyone had to get back to his own
community and begin to do rather than to talk. When time
for writing came no one was "able to recapture that first fine
qareless rapture." But everyone retained his enthusiasm
about the programs visited and about the itinerant workshop
as a potent educational technique. They conclude their report
thus:

> The value to us individually and as a group working together to-
> ward more effective living in Virginia communities makes us recom-
> mend with enthusiasm the itinerant workshop as an educational
> method.
>
> The following admonitions we should like to pass on to any
> others considering the idea: Get all the background of each project
> that you possibly can in advance. Know as much as possible about
> how school organization, governmental setup, etc., differ from yours
> in order to be able to understand the programs in relation to their
> settings. Travel, if possible, with a group which has already become
> a working unit through previous workshop or community program.
>
> The resident workshop in 1943 was good preparation for the
> itinerant workshop of 1944. A third step in the process suggested it-
> self to us as, one after another, we found programs that touched our
> special interests. We found we were remarking in turn, "What I
> want to do is to come back here for a week . . . " or "for a month," or
> "for a whole summer." That is, each seemed to be suggesting a kind
> of internship in the program of his choice. We still think it has possi-
> bilities. Its practicality we have yet to explore.

Plans for a Second Experimental Tour

The next year there was no money available for a traveling workshop, yet we hoped to be able to try a second one to
make sure that the success of the first had not been one of
those happy chances that come only once in a lifetime. The
1944 summer resident workshop had followed hard on the
heels of the itinerant workshop just described. Inevitably the
staff members talked about the trip which was still fresh in
their minds. Some of the trippers visited the new group
and they talked. So before the 1944 session ended members
of that group had begun to say, "We want to see, too."

By midwinter they had not forgotten. From all sides
were murmurs, "What about the trip?" The staff wanted to
break the news of no money gently and yet not to close the
door on the possibility of a second attempt. So on February

9, the following letter went out from the most flippant and the most courageous of the staff:

To the Shackle-Shakers and Associates—individual and collective:

"The time has come," to quote the well-known Walrus, ". . . . . to talk of many things," including, for the nonce, the proposed, projected and infinitely-to-be-desired trip to see for YOURselves what some of the folks we talked about last summer are doing. This letter is in the nature of a feeler-outer.

For the sad and brutal truth is that no such munificent sums of money as we wangled last year are discernible. The Powers-That-Be are all for the trip, but have nothing in the way of the wherewithal. Gas, yes (if we can get it by that time); a couple of us to act as guides, philosophers, and friends, yes (I shall be the philosopher); and whatsoever trimmings as are deemed essential, such as arranging meetings with Interested Citizens and all that, yes, But He Who and She Who will have to Bear the Brunt.

It really isn't TOO much of a brunt, and we'll all of us work hard to pare down to a minimum, keeping in mind the extent of the travel and the intensiveness of the job. Last year's trip came to an average of $3.90 a day for the ten days. Well, there you are. A maximum, say, of forty bucks. We *didn't* stint last year; nor yet did we splurge, as you can easily see. The trip this year would be much the same as to time and the *number* of places visited, although we would take in two or three new communities and drop some of the old. Expenses definitely would not be greater.

As I say, this is a trial balloon. If you are interested or even on the fence, drop me a line and I'll work up a suggested itinerary, with dates and all the rest. Tell me such things as:
Can't think of it...............
Can't go if it will cost more than $...............
Tell me some more; I'm listening! ....
My school closes...............................(or I can get off on...)
I think you are a so-and-so, but I still love you...........................
                    (and sign your name!)

Next letter (if there is a next letter, and I think there will be) I'll tell you more about trip plans, and I'll also have a report on the follow-up of our winter meeting, including the progress of the workshops Wayland is leading. The Lunenburg and the Rustburg groups are definitely Something.

Replies came back. Many had checked the last statement but all at least wanted to hear more. So again an itinerary and calendar were planned on the basis of the individuals involved and the experience of the preceding summer. Carrollton was omitted because of the two extra days involved and the necessity of retracing that part of the trip to get on to the next stop. Kingsport was added because of the interest on the part of members of this group in the church in the total community and in health facilities. This would take the group through Knoxville and make possible a "one-day tour of the TVA." This would provide opportunity to relate local and state planning to regional. Omission of any such program had been felt as a weakness in the first trip. Gatlinburg would serve as a bit of relaxation as High Hampton had the preceding year. The proposed itinerary follows:

Saturday, June 16

7:30 a.m.—Leave Charlottesville (Jess Ogden and Jim Orser at the wheels)

10:00 a.m.—Hotel Virginian, Lynchburg, to pick up Fay Moorman and Sam Crockett

12:00 noon—Roanoke lunch S & W Cafeteria—Pick up Georgia Carter and E. Lowe

Evening—Discussion with George Eutsler, director of Holston Valley Community Hospital

Overnight at Kingsport Inn

Sunday, June 17

8:00 a.m.—Visit to hospital and discussion of prepaid medical care programs with George Eutsler

Church (of your own choosing)

2:00 p.m.—Meeting with members of Christian Youth Association (*New Dominion Series No.* 63)

Evening—Attend some one of young people's church groups (if desired)

Overnight at Kingsport Inn

Monday, June 18

Leave Kingsport *early.* Lunch with several of the TVA people and discussion of TVA program.

Monday night in Gatlinburg—a perfectly gorgeous spot in the middle of the Smokies and the home of Pi Beta Phi Settlement School. We shall plan a meeting with some of the handcraft specialists and the Weavers Guild for Monday night (see *New Dominion Series* No. 34). They are beginning a handcraft workshop there that week.

Overnight at New Gatlinburg Inn, Gatlinburg, Tennessee.

Tuesday, June 19

To Clayton, Georgia. Lunch with Frank Smith (County Ordinary) and some members of his Health and Welfare Council. See WE WENT TO SEE FOR OUSELVES Pages 11-14.)

Visit to maternity center (*New Dominion Series* No. 36 and 55) and the really noteworthy traveling library.

Overnight at Rabun Gap-Nacoochee School, Clayton, Georgia

Wednesday, June 20

Discuss Rabun Gap School and its rotating homestead plan (*New Dominion Series* No. 51 and WE WENT TO SEE FOR OUR-

SELVES, pages 8-10) with Dr. Bellingrath and the agriculture teacher. Visit some of the farm families.

Brief stop at Clarkesville to see most complete high school food preservation center we have found anywhere. (*New Dominion Series* No. 37)

To Greenville, S. C., Wednesday night

Overnight at Hotel Ottaray, Greenville, S. C.

Thursday, June 21

Visit the Jordan community with Tom Verdin, the school superintendent who started the program there. (*New Dominion Series* Nos. 11 and 55. Also WE WENT TO SEE FOR OURSELVES, pages 19-22)

Visit the Parker School District and meet with the superintendent and some of the people there who have tried to work out plans for a school-community program where industry and rural problems meet.

Overnight at Hotel Ottaray, Greenville, S. C.

Friday, June 22

Discussion with Dr. Lee Brooks and Dr. Gordon Blackwell who are concerned with community development programs in North Carolina, and with Dr. Harold Meyer who is head of the North Carolina Recreation Commission.

Overnight at Carolina Inn, Chapel Hill, N. C.

Saturday, June 23

Visit to programs in Chapel Hill area sponsored by the "Health Educators" under Dr. Lucy Morgan.

Overnight at Carolina Inn, Chapel Hill, N. C.

Sunday, June 24

Return to Charlottesville.

Monday and Tuesday, June 25 and 26

Remain in Charlottesville as guests of the University to report the trip and discuss our observations with interested members of the faculty here.

Seven reported interest in the proposed itinerary and admitted readiness and ability to pay. With one staff member, this would make a good group. So the die was cast. Later two members had to withdraw but it was decided to go with the six who remained. On June 9, the last instructions went out, and on June 16, the second traveling workshop was on its way.

More Observations Based on Experience

Again the group was predominantly male — two women and four men. There were three school principals, one minister, one superintendent of public welfare, and one school board clerk. The staff member who accompanied them had been with them in the workshop the preceding summer and had worked with some of them throughout the winter. The group was, if possible, an even closer working unit than the 1944 traveling workshop had been. Moreover, the trip was neater and smoother because the staff had learned much from the first experience. One of the trippers expressed the group's feeling about this in a letter to the director of the Extension Division later in the summer:

I want to tell you how very much we appreciate the way the trip was arranged and handled. It could not have been more efficiently done. *Everything clicked.* And yet we did not have the feeling of being rushed along. Of course, we wanted to stay longer in most of the places but that was because we liked the people so much and were having such a good time. The whole trip was perfect. I certainly caught a larger vision of the program you are trying to carry out, and it is a very worthwhile experience to have even a tiny part in such a program.

The staff member would have passed the ball back to the fine spirit of the entire group. He would have given the credit to their punctuality for all appointments—in spite of some individual temperaments to which this was foreign; to their ability to subordinate immediate personal wishes and minor comforts to the pleasure of the group; to the true community of interest which they were able to sustain through eight days of careful adherence to a close schedule planned in advance and of enforced association with each other during long days of travel and investigation and short nights which never allowed quite enough hours for sleep.

Not only the staff had become more deft as a result of the first experience but also groups visited were more certain of what we wanted. Those to whom we made "repeat" visits had organized time and mustered people in such a way as to make the most of every minute. They had also mustered their own questions and, even more than the preceding year, we were made to feel like a group of visiting experts. The session at Chapel Hill with Dr. Morgan's health educators and lay committee members was one of the most challenging of the entire experience because they knew exactly what they wanted to know as well as what they had to offer.

As in the residence workshops, we found, that the 1944 and 1945 groups were entirely dissimilar. Both groups had had the same type of experience under much the same circumstances and leadership. Yet results were not the same. Each gained tremendously from the trip, but their needs and, as a result, their emphases were different. The members of the second group, perhaps, started with more clearly formulated personal philosophies. As they saw programs and talked with leaders along the way, they tried to translate what they saw and heard into personal and practical terms to an even greater degree than the first group. On their return to the University, it was in terms of such application that they discussed the trip. They were impatient to get back home to begin trying things out. Their decision was that they did not wish to take time to theorize about programs they had seen or to make a complete report. Perhaps the fact that they came back between terms when there was a smaller group to hear their reports than there had been the preceding year was partly responsible for this. Possibly the facility with which a small group could discuss things as it went along had made a difference. Certainly, there was no lack of enthusiasm and eagerness to apply ideas. But the second group produced no such generalizations based on their experience as the decalogue of the first group. Yet they were equally enthusiastic in their endorsement of the method and recommended that a trip be planned for subsequent workshops if possible.

Recollected in Tranquility

An attempt was made to get an evaluation from members of both groups after they had lost the first flush of enthusiasm. On the questionnaire that went to all workshop participants in the late fall of 1945 was this question: "If you were in either of the groups that went on the traveling workshop, what do you think of the relative value of the two types of experience [residence and traveling workshops]?"

Fifteen had participated. Fifteen replied that both were of greater value than could be reported in concrete terms.

Only one said that if he had to choose between the two, he thought he would choose the trip rather than the residence workshop. All the others said, in one way or another, that both were essential to a complete understanding.

"I am not able to separate one from the other. The summer workshop was essential from the viewpoint of theory. The trip fitted the theory and proved the case. In the first, we grasped community life in the mind; in the second we experienced it emotionally. The combination adds up to *reality*."

"I think that, as valuable as the trip was, it would have had less value had it not been for the 'common mooring' provided by the summer workshop. To me, the one without the other is a job only partly done."

"I think the summer workshop important as a basis for the trip. I think the trip *absolutely necessary* to fulfill the teachings of the first year. In fact it crystallized the things taught."

"I think the two types are complementary. Each becomes more valuable for having had the other. I would subscribe to the first summer without the second, but I doubt the wisdom of the second without having gone through the first experience. Personally I am glad I was able to participate in both and, I believe, they came in the proper sequence."

"The first workshop was essential. *Seeing is believing*. But we would not have been able to see what was right before our eyes if we had not already studied the theory and methods of community development. The traveling workshop is ideal *after study and work in one's own community*. One comes back with the feeling: *it has been done; it can be done; we can do it, too, if we organize on a common objective to meet a definite need*. Not only were my ideas strengthened by conversing with people on the spot, but also, to my surprise, my influence at home was strengthened. People like to hear one say 'I saw' rather than 'We were told at the University.' "

One person suggested tentatively that both experiences might be had in the one summer with, perhaps, ten days of study followed by ten days of travel. He felt, however, that the digestion period of the intervening year and the chance to try applying theories had been of great value to him and had made him more eager to see how others worked. The combination would be definitely second choice.

The reaction of the staff to that suggestion is that it could be done but that three weeks is a pretty short time for the combination. One or two field trips may be put into a short-time program to advantage. But anyone who has tried this knows that it takes time to prepare for and to interpret the field trips in relation to the whole and that, unless this is done, they are likely to be disruptive. To a totally inexperienced group they doubtless have more value than to a group trying to interpret experience already provided by their own situations. The greatest value to our groups was in the cumulative effect of each of these experiments in adult education methods. Education must proceed at a rate compatible with the capacity of human beings to assimilate new ideas and relate them to experience. Just how much can be done in a given period depends upon the previous background and experience of the group. And no two are alike.

Some Suggestions for Ourselves and Others

In relation to traveling workshops, as to other techniques, there are certain conclusions that may have general application.

Careful preparation is essential. Whether this be done in a study group or by some other method may be determined by circumstances. But the process is too costly in time, energy, and money, and too disturbing to the programs visited to be lightly and generally undertaken. *A traveling workshop differs widely from a sightseeing tour.*

With careful preparation and planning both among the members of the group and with leaders in those programs to be visited, the process can have value for all concerned. The visiting group can give as well as get. To the degree that they fail to do this, they are imposing on the good nature of the groups they visit. Leaders in community activities are invariably the busiest people. On the other hand, they are never too busy to want to find out more about how to do the job better. There is, we have found, a real bond among persons engaged in such programs whether they be in South Carolina, Tennessee, Georgia, or Virginia; and whether they be schoolmen, farmers, or health educators. The degree to which the educational process on our trips became a mutual exchange surprised us all—though theoretically we accept the fact that *education is a two-way process*. It was another bit of evidence that seeing is necessary to really believing.

Having physical arrangements, time schedules, and similar mundane matters carefully planned in advance and adhered to throughout the trip makes for absence of friction which can do so much to dull one's sensitivity to real values. Even the most punctilious adherence can be free of unpleasant rigidity and irritating infringement of personal freedom.

"We found evidence," said the first group in their conclusions, "that democracy can function at a high degree of efficiency." And they maintained that they found that evidence within their own group on the trip as well as in the programs visited. But their interpretation of *democracy* was not the too common one which insists on individual rights with no regard for responsibilities. In fact, its emphasis was on the latter.

Creating such a group spirit cannot be left entirely to chance. It is too important to the success of the venture. Yet no formula can be given for bringing about the *rapport* necessary if a group is to be ready for the vicissitudes of travel and continuous companionship. Having such *rapport* established in advance obviates the need for pouring oil on troubled waters along the way.

The size of any visiting group should be kept small both for its own best interests and out of consideration for the programs visited. We found that the group of twelve just stopped short of being unwieldy. The group of six seemed an ideal size in many respects. Yet arguments can be mustered from this report in favor of the larger group.

At any rate, the group should be small enough for visiting individuals to chat with local individuals. This becomes impossible if the group assumes the proportions of a sightseeing

tour. Sightseers seldom see anything but externals. They
may even see a show put on for their special benefit. This
does not serve the purpose of the traveling workshop which
must study and evaluate as well as see.

.   As our groups went along, they began to comment on the
amount of "twosing" that had developed as an indication of
the success of a particular visit. By this they meant spontaneous and informal discussion between individual visitors
and individual hosts. On those rare occasions when our group
stuck together throughout a visit and the local people did
the same, there was a feeling of unfinished business on our
part.

A carefully organized meeting or presentation of material
by a local group can expedite the process of getting the necessary background and lead to more purposeful discussion among
members of the two groups. If no informal and spontaneous
discussion follows, there is indication that it has all been too
carefully organized and, perhaps, too superficial. There must
be provision for a flow of reason and a feast of souls if the
process is really to work.

Selecting programs to be visited requires intimate knowledge of both the programs and the group. In 1943, before we
had had the first workshop on wheels, an enthusiastic reader
of *New Dominion Series* suggested that we publish a list of
good programs to visit. It seemed to us an excellent idea. We
spent some time planning such a list. Fortunately, before we
published it, we were faced with planning a trip for a specific
group. It was different from making lists in a vacuum. We
found that programs are not good to visit in and of themselves.
They are good only in terms of the interests and needs of the
visitors concerned. Schoolmen naturally are interested in
school-centered programs, but some individuals among them
may be already too school-centered. Their need may be for a
broader perspective. The same is true of ministers, welfare
workers, and others. In selecting the right programs for our
traveling workshops, considerable thought went into the needs
of each individual. At the same time, there was an attempt
to have a variety and to maintain a balance so that the whole
trip might add up to something like the total community.

This would be relatively simple if one could use a magic carpet and flit quickly and easily about the country. It is not so simple when economy of miles and hours must be considered. A swing around a circle is, of course, the ideal shape of a trip. Retraversing miles is tiresome and unprofitable. Location of programs in relation to a practicable route must be considered. Planning the trip is a kind of jigsaw puzzle. The pieces are many and varied. They include individual and group interests and needs; programs with emphasis, approach, and leadership that will meet these needs; routes that lead from one program to the next with just about the right distance between and that return to the starting place in the number of miles and days allowed for the trip; overnight stops and mealtimes that will assure the rest and food necessary to continuous travel without upset dispositions and stomachs; schedules that make possible keeping appointments but, at the same time, do not result in long waits because too much time has been allowed. Fitting all these together to get a pleasing and profitable total is as fascinating as any game we have ever played. But it is one in which little can be left to chance. And it is one which has convinced us that every trip must be tailor-made. Those who have visited programs can, perhaps, serve as consultants, but only those who have the total picture in mind can do the actual planning.

CHAPTER 18

The Workshop in the Community

In the two-year period ending December, 1945, the Extension Division conducted eleven local workshops as a part of the experimental program for finding ways to help communities to help themselves. The local workshop in community development has proved to be an excellent means of extending the program of Special Projects without losing the intensive quality necessary to its becoming an integral part of community living. To describe the process covered by the term *workshop* as applied to local groups is not easy, for no two have been the same.

In the first place, the communities differed from each other and the areas varied in size from a community served by one consolidated elementary school to an entire county. Sponsorship varied from the county school board to the Parent-Teacher Association of a school or a local service club. Participants were determined in part by the sponsoring agency. In six cases there were from one to four persons in the local group who had attended a summer workshop at the University. In five, the local group started without such a nucleus of already interested members. Two of the groups were composed entirely of men; one was composed entirely of school teachers and principals; and the others of fairly representative cross sections of their communities.

They differed also in outside leadership. All were conducted by the Extension Division. Its director and Special Projects staff assisted in planning and kept closely in touch with each as it progressed. Direct leadership, however, was furnished by several different persons. The first three workshops were conducted by the staff of Special Projects with assistance from other members of the Extension Division staff. Dr. Hayes carried primary responsibility for the next four while on leave from Vanderbilt University to give full time to the program of Special Projects for eight months. The next four were conducted by Dr. Jones of the University of Tennessee who joined the staff for a four-month period. In all cases regular staff members attempted to know the groups and the ground covered well enough to do what follow-up work was necessary and possible without disrupting the continuity of the process begun in the local workshop.

For each workshop the purpose was the same: ". . . . . to encourage and stimulate community groups to consider the resources and assets of their counties against the needs, wishes, and desires of the group for their communities. Then, to think and plan concretely, if so desired, to create a more satisfying personal and community life by using and organizing their resources within the framework of tested and workable principles and practices of community organization."[1]

Likewise the general pattern established during the first three was followed with only such modifications as were necessary to suit the composition of the group and the personality of the leader. Frequent staff conferences assured continuous exchange of experience among all who had participated in this part of the program. Dr. Jones had been associated previously with Dr. Hayes. He had a similar philosophy and approach to community programs. Moreover, before he actually joined the staff, he was able to attend several meetings of workshops then in session.

Out of this variety in type of community, in sponsoring agencies, in composition of groups and in outside leadership, grew a wealth of experience on which to base some generalizations. More than in any other aspect of the experimental program, there was evidence that the technique was not dependent for its success on a particular personality or a special circumstance. It worked well under different leaders and widely varying circumstances. We are, therefore, convinced it can be even more widely applied.

Summing up the experience is not easy. One member of

[1]W. B. Jones, Jr., *Report on Four Workshops Conducted for the Extension Division, University of Virginia. September 15, 1945—December 23, 1945.*

the staff, in commenting on his part in the program, prefaced his report with the following statement:[2]

The ideal or model for such a report would be the Acts of the Apostles and the Letters of St. Paul. These contained a full account of the Acts themselves with a continual interweaving of the philosophy which motivated the whole movement. There was a continual communication between the early groups and those who visited them. In these communications there was a recurrent opportunity to state the principles of group life which were to be emphasized. Then, too, there was a continuance of the personal relation between the initial leadership and emergent groups.

Far be it from me to suggest that I aim to follow any such ideal in my report to you. About as close as I shall come is to use the form of a letter, and I could have hit upon that notion without reference to the Scriptures. I merely mention the Acts and the Letters because I think there are some parallels between the development of early church groups and local community workshops. I think, for instance, that the leader who goes into a strange community from the outside "must have a message." And I think he must develop relations of such a character as to be incorporated into the group and the group process. But "the message" must dominate both him and the group so that he can withdraw and the work go on.

"So that he can withdraw and the work go on" was implicit in the purpose of the workshops. It determined, to a large extent, both content and method. The "message" was one of faith in democratic processes and conviction that the role of the outside leader is to revitalize these processes on the local level where the individual must live his life and make his direct contribution. The test of the skill of the leader lay in the degree to which the groups acquired control over the direction of their own affairs and in the quality of the "continuance of the personal relation between the initial leadership and the emergent groups."

Even had we the skill, there is neither time nor space in this report for a play-by-play description of each of the eleven workshops "with a continual interweaving of the philosophy which motivated the whole movement." Keeping in mind the philosophy and purpose already indicated, the reader can, perhaps, do his own interweaving in relation to the general description which follows.

---

[2]Letter from Wayland J. Hayes to George B. Zehmer, August 1, 1945.

What the Extension Division Offered

In setting up the local workshop program, the Extension Division was simply making its services available to communities that had a few citizens who were aware of their need for help. It had no idea of promoting through general advertising, or of superimposing on any community, a program for which there was not a felt need.

The plan was made because requests came from members of the first summer workshop for help in extending ideas of community development. (See chapter 11.) When it became evident that the demand was greater than could be met by the regular staff, a foundation grant was sought to make available additional persons for a two-year period. This grant paid salary only. Each local community had to finance expenses of staff travel and living in the field when that was necessary. The statement about cost which was sent to interested community leaders follows:[3]

Where no question of degree credit is involved, the Extension Division is concerned only that the expense of the worker, or workers, in the field be met. Probably each study group should receive separate consideration. The number of meetings involved, the distances to be covered, and the like, are the factors that would determine cost. Under most circumstances, the cost to the community would be $10 a meeting. Thus a program of eight meetings would cost $80; one of twelve meetings, $120. Some saving could be effected if groups were formed in neighboring communities. The Extension Division will welcome inquiry and will be glad to work out an estimate of the exact cost to any community.

The policy of asking the community to pay the cost was in line with the general purpose. Communities do not learn to help themselves by having everything done for them. In the workshops which preceded the foundation grant, each person had paid a fee as he would for any extension class. The plan outlined above left the method of payment up to the community. In most cases the entire amount was paid by the sponsoring agency; in some, the individuals in the group all contributed. But where this was done, responsibility for

---

[3]*An Opportunity to Take Stock of Your Community and Plan for Its Further Development.* Extension Division, University of Virginia. January, 1945.

collecting the money from individuals was taken by the local group rather than by the Extension Division. Having to pay for the service seems to have deterred no community that was ready for a workshop.

Although requests from participants in summer workshops were to be met first, a general announcement[4] went out to school people, civic club officers, and other leading citizens. It read in part as follows:

. . . . Many citizens, hitherto concerned only with their own personal problems, have been forced to the conclusion that the solution for even their own problems depends largely upon the combined efforts of all agencies and all individuals within their own community. Recognizing the growth of such awareness, and desiring to make its contribution to Virginia communities, the Extension Division of the University of Virginia has secured the loan of Dr. Wayland J. Hayes from Vanderbilt University. It is offering to communities his services and those of the Extension Division staff who have for four years been concerned with the organizing of community citizens and the mustering of community resources. Because every community differs from every other in details of social and economic life, each community must analyze its own situations; must make its own plans; and must assume the responsibility of carrying them out. There are, however, certain general procedures and recognized techniques which will enable interested citizens to function more effectively. It is in giving an understanding of these as well as in helping to analyze the local situation that the Extension Division has a contribution to make.

Organizing the Local Group

Selecting members for local groups was entirely the responsibility of the sponsoring agency. The Extension Division announcement offered the following suggestions:[5]

Professional workers, teachers, service club members, representatives of church organizations, and individuals who wish to play their part but who may have no special group through which to work might well be included in such a study-for-action group. The more representative of the entire community the group can be, the more likely it is to make a plan that will fit the realities of the situation. On the other hand, a small group of not more than twenty is usually more effective than a large one. With a small group working, it will be important to find ways of informing and stimulating the entire community.

Whenever members of the staff were consulted, they urged that every effort be made to have a group truly representative

---

[4]*Ibid.*
[5]*Ibid.*

of the community and that as much opportunity for participation be given to laymen as to officials and professional workers. Each experience strengthened their conviction of the importance of this. In counties where participation was largely of those living in or near the county seat, or largest town where meetings were held, jealousies and petty divisions continued to exist or were even strengthened. Planning inevitably was focused on this one center with a more or less perfunctory bow to other community, neighborhood, or countywide needs. On the other hand, widespread representation tended to break this down. In two counties, the local persons responsible for, getting the groups together gave special attention to the divisions that tended to keep the counties from working as units. Through planning representation for each section and by alternating the meeting place between the two areas of rivalry, spectacular results were achieved. In a third county, the technique of holding alternate meetings in rival centers was tried without the careful preliminary planning for it by the group. Here the result was that meetings in each center were attended primarily by those who lived there. Only a few hardy souls crossed over into enemy territory. There was little progress here toward unifying the county.

Six of the eleven groups were recruited by and built around one to four persons who had participated in the summer workshops. The group which, in many ways, seems to have made the most progress had two members who had been in the 1943 summer residence workshop and in the 1944 traveling workshop, one who had been in the 1944 residence workshop, and one who had spent several days visiting the summer workshops and had attended all conferences of workshop members. There is little doublt that the careful preliminary work of these four men and their continuous interpretation of the program played an important part in the success of this local group.

On the other hand, two of the best groups, from the point of view of carrying study into an action program, had no one with previous workshop experience. One of these dealt with a relatively small area and had a definite goal set up when it asked for help. The sponsoring agency was the Parent-Teacher Association of a consolidated elementary school. The group had about equal numbers of teachers and patrons. Their concern was primarily in finding ways of consolidating the several communities composing the new school district. They discovered several ways of working toward this end and, incidentally, found other community problems needing their attention.

The second was in a county whose citizens had had several years' experience in tackling their own problems. In fact, their community program had progressed far enough to be reported in *New Dominion Series* as long ago as 1941.[6] They heard of the workshop in a neighboring county and saw it as a way of revitalizing their program. This group, like the PTA workshop, had previous experience in working together that most of the other local workshops lacked.

One of the five that had neither previous experience in working as a group, nor members who had attended summer workshops, took almost the entire period to become a working unit. Without careful follow-up there will probably be little future progress there.

On the whole, the staff would agree with Dr. Hayes' summary based on the four workshops with which he worked directly:[7]

The workshops in Lunenburg and Campbell were built around persons who had attended summer workshops whereas those in Augusta and Rockingham were brought together by Ruritans. In general, the latter basis of formation is less satisfactory. But the experience in Augusta demonstrates to me that with proper preliminary contact a workshop may be just as effective when initiated by citizens as by professionals who have had some preliminary experience. It is even possible for it to be more effective for the very reason that it is initiated by a widely representative civic organization with no particular professional, commercial, or political axe to grind. The Ruritan groups were fairly representative of all groups in the county; and if they had included some representative women and one or two additional professional interests, they would have had a very satisfactory membership.

---

[6]"New Plans in Old Communities." *New Dominion Series*, No. 2. September 15, 1941.

[7]Letter from Wayland J. Hayes to George B. Zehmer, August 1, 1945.

I say this because I was at first somewhat doubtful about working with a group "from scratch" rather than one built around a "conditioned nucleus." But my experience convinced me that all that is
needed for a good workshop is a nucleus of intelligent, socially minded
persons who are highly respected and know the local situation.

Evolution of a Pattern

The general pattern evolved in the first three local workshops. The groups met for three or four hours one evening a
week for ten or twelve weeks. The first hour was devoted to
a lecture on and discussion of the sociology of the community.
The second hour afforded a more informal time used during
early meetings for mastering some technique such as leading
singing, directing games, or using educational films. As problems began to emerge and interests to crystallize, this hour
was used for meetings of the small committees into which the
groups had been divided. These analyzed economic, institutional, and human resources of the area in an attempt to relate
available resources to emerging problems. Then, for the third
hour, the group came together again for discussion of community programs in action using stories from *New Dominion
Series* as basic material.

From the beginning, an attempt was made by the staff to
establish an atmosphere in which a group of mature individuals could work at their common problems, getting what
background they needed for interpreting them but finding
ways of attacking them through use of their own thought
processes. There was no book of problems with answers in
the back. The problems and the answers were in the community. The job of the workshop was to dig them both out
of the confusion of present-day living and fit them together.

As the small committees worked at analyzing natural resources, economic needs and resources, and agencies available
for help in specific jobs, the need for consultation with specialists began to emerge. A few were invited in to give the group
experience in conferring with such specialists. Because the
ten-week period was approaching its end before the committees knew what kind of specialists they needed, only a few
could be used. Others on local, state, and regional levels were
listed, however, and ways in which they might be helpful to
the group in the future were discussed.

The pattern of these first local workshops had been influenced by experience in summer residence workshops. When a staff member was assigned to give full time to local workshops in January, 1945, the experience of these three experimental groups was added to that of two summers. Necessity for varying the pattern to suit each situation was the first premise in planning. The second was the importance of participation in planning by citizens as well as by staff members.

Preliminary Planning

To assure the latter, participants in summer workshops of 1943 and 1944 were invited by the director of the Extension Division to attend a week-end conference at the University to assist in "planning the most effective way or ways in which to make use of a specialist in community study and development."[8] Many helpful suggestions came out of this conference. Specific plans were made for workshops for two communities having several representatives present. A third plan was offered by four public welfare workers which resulted in the Hungry Mother Park workshop described in chapter 12.

In addition to the conference, there were preliminary planning visits to the communities that had asked for workshops. The director of Extension and the staff of Special Projects assisted in this preliminary work in order that the experience of the entire group might be drawn upon in planning each workshop.

The announcement of local workshops made the following suggestions about organization and procedure growing out of the previous experience and preliminary planning:[9]

There are many ways in which groups could be organized for study and work. Here again the greatest attention must be paid to the local situation. However, experience has proved that a series of from eight to sixteen meetings, convening once a week or twice a month, is the most fruitful. These meetings usually last from one and one-half hours to three hours and include: First, a discussion by the

---

[8]Letter to participants in 1943 and 1944 Workshops in Community Development from George B. Zehmer. November 21, 1944.

[9]*An Opportunity to Take Stock of Your Community and Plan for Its Further Development.* Extension Division, University of Virginia. January, 1945.

leader of some major problem of community life; next, a discussion by the group of the problem as it pertains to their own community; and, third, a study of successful achievements in other communities.

Procedures in the meetings are informal and quite unlike those associated with the traditional class. The plan is to proceed simply and in a forthright and commonsense way. Perhaps the method most nearly approaches the corner drugstore and fireside discussion technique. Everyone feels at home and is eager to contribute his ideas and suggestions to the common pool.

Adaptations of the Pattern

In the eight workshops held between January and December, 1945, the general pattern was redrafted to suit each community and to fit the personality and temperament of the leaders, each of whom was responsible for four workshops.

One of these leaders liked to begin each session with a more or less informal talk followed by a period of questions from the floor and answers by the leader. After three or four meetings at which background was given for understanding community processes, he suggested that small committees might like to do intensive "research" on specific problems that were emerging. The committees, as they progressed, made practical application of ideas thrown out in lectures and discussions.

The second leader placed emphasis from the beginning on the working committee. After one or two preliminary meetings at which he helped the group to define its objectives and interests, committees went to work on such subjects as health, recreation, county government, and industry. Sociological background was then furnished in relation to problems that arose in committees. Both approaches seemed to get about the same results in plans for action and in background material covered.

In the first three workshops there had been systematic study of community programs in action. This was partly because summer workshops had found such study of both inspirational and practical value. It was also partly because the staff of Special Projects wished to test further for study groups the value of stories reported in the *New Dominion Series*. The use of selected stories as case studies by the entire group proved very effective both in broadening the concept of community activities and in furnishing practical ideas for local programs. Selection was made with both purposes in mind.

In the eight later workshops there was less systematic use of case stories. They were referred to when pertinent to discussions and were recommended to individuals for reading. Members of all workshops were added to the mailing list to receive *New Dominion Series.* But the stories did not become the basis of discussion for one hour of the workshop period as in the first three groups.

This difference in emphasis is mentioned as another indication that details of a pattern may be changed to fit interests and background of the leader as well as to meet needs of a group, without fundamentally changing the approach.

Variations in Pattern Necessitate Individual Reports

In commenting on the variations in the pattern as they developed in his workshops, Dr. Jones says:[10]

While the objectives and general procedure were the same for each group or workshop, the workshops, from the very outset, departed from the general pattern; or, to be more exact, from the expected pattern. Though deviations were expected, such immediate deviations and individuality were not anticipated but were not considered undesirable. The leader could have exercised controls and followed a more rigid program of lectures and controlled discussion, but he consciously and continuously attempted to relate sociological principles and instruction of community structure and organization to the groups' discussions of community needs and problems and ways of meeting these needs. This willingness to depart from the planned and controlled lectures and discussions originally set up for the twelve meetings, and the practice of making the presentation of theoretical material secondary to the groups' interests and spontaneous discussions of needs and ways of meeting future needs, resulted in complete individuality for each workshop. It is impossible to describe the nature or do justice to the dynamics of each in a composite report.

The deviations were especially apparent, Dr. Jones continues, in (1) sponsorship and leaders; (2) membership and attendance; (3) procedure and content; (4) community activities evolving from the workshop. He illustrates this in the

---

[10]W. B. Jones, Jr., *Report of Four Workshops Conducted for the Extension Division, University of Virginia.* March, 1946.

individual reports[11] of four workshops, from two of which the excerpts which follow have been selected.

Charlotte County Workshop

The Charlotte County workshop was sponsored and arranged by Mr. R. W. Bobbitt, division superintendent of public schools. Mr. Bobbitt is a long-time resident of the county and has an intimate knowledge of the county's problems and needs. He has extraordinary leadership ability which he exercises with untiring zeal. He is widely respected and his judgment and opinions are generally followed. A number of other persons were active in developing the workshop. . . . This group is *rich in experienced leadership.*

Thirty-four people attended the first meeting at Randolph-Henry High School on September 24. These persons represented six communities and included public officials from governmental, welfare, health, and educational agencies; the county planning board; county agent's office, and the county treasurer's office. Business and farming were well represented, as were private welfare agencies and various associations, such as the PTA. Attendance increased from meeting to meeting, with most of the persons at the first meeting attending all the sessions. The average attendance (excluding the final meeting, which was a countywide public meeting, and the countywide fun night on December 17, which was in addition to the twelve regular meetings) was over fifty. One of the meetings had an attendance of nearly ninety persons. This attendance was due to the efforts of one of the interest groups to have several representatives from every community of the county to discuss the county telephone problem.

The large attendance, while necessitating departure from the usual method, still permitted workshop activity and procedure, for the workshop was subdivided into four interest groups which, in effect, constituted four workshops dealing with specialized interests.

Some of the major questions and principles of community development and organization were discussed for one hour of the two-hour period during the first meeting. . . . . Major interests and problems soon became apparent and more or less clearly defined, however, and at the third meeting the workshop organized into four interest groups: health; small industries; local government, housing and roads; and recreation. An extended meeting of the steering committee was held, resulting in the organization of these interest groups, a chairman and secretary being elected for each interest group by its members.

General topics of community organization were discussed at two other meetings. Special resource leaders were brought in from time to time by the several interest groups, or "committees" as they were called. These leaders discussed their specialty for half an hour before the entire workshop. Outside resource leaders who participated in the workshop were: Dr. D. C. Acker of Rockingham County, a leader in the cooperative movement in Virginia as well as in Rockingham County, who consulted with the industries committee about a mutual telephone system; Mr. Verben Kemp, state secretary of the Chamber of Commerce, who talked to the industries committee about

[11]*Ibid.*

developing industries in Charlotte County; Drs. Roper and Gardner of the state health department, who consulted with the health committee on obtaining a director of public health for the county health unit, and extending health services for school children; and Dr. G. W. Spicer, who discussed the county manager form of government with the local government group. This group, incidentally, made an intensive study of the Extension Division's recent publication, *Ten Years of County Manager Government in Virginia*. Mr. Jess Ogden, of the Extension Division, advised with the recreation committee one evening and participated in the fun night which was arranged by the recreation committee as a demonstration of community recreation. . . . . One unique feature of this workshop was the participation of a number of high school students, upon invitation of the recreation committee, in the discussions of that committee.

Each of the four committees engaged in intensive study and investigation pointed toward some specific problem or problems. Their work resulted in recommendations presented at the final meeting of the workshop. Despite inclement weather, an estimated three hundred people attended the meeting. Specific recommendations were made which called for further activity by specific groups and agencies in the community and by the community at large, leading to the realization of plans and meeting of needs which had been discussed in the workshop. . . . .

It is easy to present resolutions and have them officially passed. Frequently no action eventuates. This may occur in Charlotte County; however, the extraordinary general interest, the hours of work of the steering committee, and the rich and interested leadership operating in this workshop, lend encouragement to the belief that community life will be bettered and enriched in Charlotte County by realization of the workshop committees' suggestions for community action.

Chesterfield County Workshop

Mr. S. C. Peck, cashier of an insurance company in Richmond but a resident of Chesterfield County, was mainly responsible for the Chesterfield County workshop. He recruited most of the members of the group from the Ruritan Club, for which he was acting in promoting the workshop. . . . .

His active interest and zeal in county problems and community work have extended over a period of years. Earlier he was a leader in the movement within the county to obtain more efficient local government, and his efforts were in no small way responsible for the present form of county government, which includes a full-time executive secretary for the county board of supervisors.

Twenty-seven people attended the first meeting of the workshop in the Manchester High School. The group soon settled down to twenty regular members. These folks were very faithful in attending, some driving over thirty miles to the meetings. Included among the membership were farmers, business men, industrial employees, the executive secretary of the county board of supervisors, a member of the county planning board, an attorney, a high school principal, and several housewives. The smaller number facilitated group discussion and more individual participation than was possible in Charlotte County.

The first five meetings consisted of a study of some of the major questions and principles of community organization and development. The discussions of these meetings centered about such topics as the wants and needs of persons, what do persons need and want in community living, what is a community, how does a community function in meeting the needs and desires of persons, how may persons study and take stock of their community to ascertain how well the community is meeting their needs, and what is needed in the way of community organization or reorganization to better individual and community life.

The group participated freely in the discussion of these topics. As the members of the group began thinking in terms of their own needs and desires, and of their respective local communities and larger community (the county), they became increasingly aware of their almost total ignorance of the institutional structure and practices of their community. They found they knew so little about the educational, welfare, health, and governmental agencies, services, and practices in Chesterfield County that they could not consider intelligently the part those agencies were playing in meeting the needs and problems of which they had now become aware. They wanted information first, and felt that they should find out about these agencies first hand from the persons who were directing them.

The chairman and leader, therefore, arranged that the superintendent of public welfare, the superintendent of schools, the director of public health, and the executive secretary of the board of supervisors meet with the group, one official at each meeting for the next four consecutive meetings, and inform them of the work of their respective agencies.

These officials came as planned and discussed the work and problems of their agencies in a surprisingly frank, realistic, and informal manner. No one attempted to make a formal speech, but, had he done so, the numerous questions and continuous discussion from the group would have prevented it.

Following these meetings, some of the members of the workshop felt that similar presentations and discussions should be made before all public and private organizations in the county. It was interesting to note the genuine interest displayed by these citizens in their public services and the quick and ready application they made of their newly gained knowledge to the needs and problems they had discussed in the earlier meetings.

Following these four meetings, two of the three remaining workshop meetings were given over to a discussion of what action might be taken to develop better community living. The leader talked briefly of effecting community action. A coordinating council and county council were discussed. Some of the group had heard of councils but most had not, and the county council idea so impressed the group that they decided to attempt to organize one in Chesterfield County. Plans were made for a countywide meeting in the court house at Chesterfield on December 20 for the presentation of the county council idea to a representative countywide group and to propose at that time that a council be organized.

The pre-organizational meeting was held on December 20 as planned. Despite exceedingly bad weather—cold, snow, and ice — some thirty to thirty-five persons were present. In addition to the workshop members there were representatives of various public and private organizations who had been invited by letter to come and consider the organization of a county council.

Mr. Peck, chairman of the workshop, presided and did an excellent job in explaining the workshop's findings and opinion about a county council. Comment from each person showed an unanimous opinion and support for such an organization, and a committee was appointed to draft a proposed constitution and by-laws. The constitution was duly prepared somewhat later, and the first meeting of the Chesterfield County Council will be held on April 8, 1946.

Use of Visiting Specialists

There is, perhaps, no one workshop which can be pointed to as "typical." The two reported above, however, can serve as examples of specific procedures from which the report may again turn to the general.

In all groups, specialists were brought in to help in the consideration of certain aspects of community life. These included persons from the State Board of Education, the State Department of Public Health, the Bureau for Industrial Research, the State Forestry Service, the Department of Political Science at the University; specialists in recreation or use of visual materials; and persons who had successfully engineered the development of a frozen food locker plant or similar service in other communities.

All agreed that use of such specialists served two important purposes: (1) the immediate problem could be attacked in the light of their specialized knowledge; (2) the community became acquainted with resources for help in future planning. Both purposes are reflected in one statement in the evaluation of their workshop by members of a group: "We feel that the method used in the workshop of bringing in specialists in particular lines has been most advantageous to our county and that this should be continued in the future."

In one of the workshops described above, it will be noted, local specialists, with whose work the members of the group were not familiar, were used to good effect. In fact, the group recommended "similar presentations and discussions before all organizations in the county." In other groups, specialists from state or regional levels or from other communities were more often used. The experience of the staff was that, like every phase of the workshop process, *the use of specialists must be planned with the greatest care.*

First, the kind of specialist must be chosen who could readily adapt himself to the group-thinking (or even group-groping) process. "A representative" of a department or bureau would not do. Yet to convey this idea tactfully to the persons concerned was not always easy. "If I can't go myself, I'll send someone" was the kind of offer that was politely but firmly declined. A few experiences with "someone" who was sent could have been disastrous had the members of the workshops been less understanding.

Second, the leader must orient the specialist before the meeting and must keep him on the right track as the meeting progressed. The speech the visitor wanted to give might be a good one but it might not be what was needed to throw light on a specific problem faced by a specific community. Using the specialist to advantage required skill on the part of the leader. On the part of the specialist, it required unusual sensitivity to a group and unusual deftness in relating his specialized information to the problem at hand. He had usually only one meeting with each group and thus had to hit the bullseye the first time. In the course of meeting with several workshops, the leader and the specialist began to master the technique. Groups, too, became more adept at using the specialists after a few experiences.

By-Approaches and By-Products

Because of the conviction that the leader must know the community as intimately as possible, considerable time was spent there preceding or following the meetings by each staff member who conducted workshops. Chatting with people on the street or in their places of business, calling on officials and professional workers in their offices, or enjoying a dinner party with friends in the community could not be thought of as a part of the workshop proper. Yet these visits, formal and informal, professional and social, constituted an important part of the process of "developing relations of such a character as to be incorporated into the group and the group process." In commenting on these by-approaches and by-products of the workshop, Dr. Hayes says:

> Many activities and relationships develop during the workshop process which are not recorded in any way. In fact a ferment is introduced which spreads to all sorts of formal and informal situations. Conversations on the street are provided with new substance and home visits are flooded with things to talk about. Committees not only work at the workshop meetings but at different times through the week. [Examples of these are] in one county formation of a ministerial association, holding of inter-racial meetings of social science teachers, and a series of meetings to develop a more satisfactory program for a youth center.

The Working Committees

Transfer from study to action is the crucial point of any study-for-action program. In the workshops, the concrete plans for this transfer were made in the special interest groups or working committees. These differed from one community to another. One group reports, "The members of the workshop found that their interest crystallized into five general lines, namely: recreation, education, industry, postwar planning, and religion." In another, "committees reported on recreation, health, county government, and industry—the subjects selected for special attention by the study group." In another, roads and transportation received attention; and, in another, where the local telephone system was woefully inadequate, a committee on communication studied the situation and made recommendations for action. Whatever the subject, the committee approach was in terms of doing something about it.

Interest in these matters was not theoretical. It arose from a conviction that the welfare of the community demanded that citizens give their attention to doing something about local problems in those areas of interest. Behind that conviction was one even more fundamental to the success of the study program: *The study-action approach was based on the assumption that communities can help themselves through the efforts of their own citizens.*

Not every member of every workshop, to be sure, accepted this point of view or wanted to work on a committee. A contributor to the local paper in one county commented on this as follows:

Some of the group members, chiefly public officials, are said to take a dim view of the whole idea of a community survey, adopting the attitude of "who says there is anything wrong with the community?" And others, while admitting they have enjoyed the meetings, say they are too busy to do any research work as committee members. Could it be that the need for a survey is occasioned by the fact that some of these folks have been too busy too long? Could be.

So far as we are presently informed, this is the first time such a study has been attempted in the county within the memory of those living, and certainly once in a lifetime is not too often to take an inventory. Even though nothing is done as a result, it will afford an interesting basis for comparison with other communities and what they are doing, and it might disclose some remediable defects even to those who are now satisfied with conditions as they are.

In this county, a coordinating council which grew out of the workshop is basing its program on some of the "remediable defects" discovered by the "research work of committee members." Moreover some of those reputed to have taken a "dim view of the whole idea" are active in the council program.

Emphasis on Local Leadership

In order to underline the facts that the workshop was a local affair and that the member of the Extension staff was there as a consultant rather than as a teacher, the plan of having a local presiding officer was suggested and, in most cases, followed. In some places one chairman was elected to preside throughout the series of ten or twelve meetings. In others a rotating chairmanship was adopted. The latter seemed better both for getting total participation and for uncovering potential leadership. In at least two communities, committee chairmen worked so efficiently that each committee became a miniature workshop. To the degree that this could be accomplished, an indirect job of leadership training became an integral part of the workshop process.

Evaluating the Educational Process

One group had a secretary whose job it was to summarize the discussion of each meeting and have it mimeographed before the next. This was done at the suggestion of the group for their convenience. Actually it proved more helpful to the leader than to the group, for it afforded him a glimpse of what at least one person thought the discussion added up to Misapprehensions could be corrected and gaps filled.

Newspaper reports, which in some places were pretty detailed, served a like purpose. Dr. Hayes comments on this in his report after quoting stories of the same meeting from three different papers:

Thus, it took three newspapers to approximate the whole idea. This raises the interesting question about what individual members of the workshops may have derived from these sessions. It also makes clear that too much may be attempted in one workshop meeting. We have little idea how rapidly laymen may be able to go with basic ideas.

Yet, Dr. Hayes points out later in his report, the "secret of the workshop procedure is the education or enlightenment of laymen. Their organization and action can go no further than their understanding."

In relation to the learning that took place, Dr. Jones makes these observations:

It was both refreshing and stimulating, to one who is more or less forced by institutional practices and conventions to teach within the somewhat rigid academic procedures and techniques, to try the workshop procedure and techniques in teaching adults community organization. They are interested in learning and they learn.

Particularly is the workshop method valuable in teaching adults who are the community leaders and who may not otherwise learn of the tried and tested procedures and some of the newer methods and practices in community organization. The workshop method is likewise conducive to an immediate application of these principles. Learning is immediately related to social behavior in a manner which benefits others in the community as well as the individual. One aspect in this learning process has been particularly impressive. It is the degree to which self-interest is widened and expanded into group-interest.

The combination of learning the principles of social behavior in real life situations by considering needs, wants, and desires of individuals and groups which are immediately related to resources, and the pointed thinking and planning for use of the available resources, is sound. The validity of the philosophy underlying the workshop procedure has been demonstrated in this experiment.

After the Workshop

Just as no two of the eleven workshops were alike in spite of similarity of purpose and approach on the part of the staff, so no two communities have exactly the same program as a result of their workshops. Each is carrying on in its own way. Two have asked for second workshops with some former and many new participants in order that, while a program of action gets under way, still more people may be drawn into planning. Two have formed countywide coordinating councils, but an examination of their constitutions shows that local needs and attitudes have determined the form. The councils have little similarity. One group is in process of forming a countywide development association to carry out recommendations of the several workshop committees. One has organized monthly forums to continue to discuss local problems with leadership from its own members. Another which started on a countywide basis is now working in smaller community groups in an effort to work out some of the problems that threaten to divide rather than unify the larger community.

Staff members who have participated in workshops agree that the whole program must be conducted in such a way that they "can withdraw with assurance that the work will go on." Yet they have learned from experience with the groups included in this report that the termination of relationship between staff and community usually cannot be coincidental with the termination of the ten or twelve meetings set for the workshop. Having stimulated members of a community to an awareness of responsibility for guiding social change, they must continue to give them the help they have just begun to know they need.

"I am convinced," says Dr. Jones, "that, even in those communities where councils are organized as part of the workshop activity or following a workshop, such groups should be nurtured by the Extension staff."

Such belief on the part of those in the communities is reflected in their requests:

"We want to organize a coordinating council. Can you send us sample constitutions from already organized communities?"

"Can some of you people come down for a planning meeting for putting some of the ideas discussed in the workshop into action?"

"We are planning a newsletter to inform all the people of the county of plans of the council. Have you suggestions or samples of similar publications? What is the experience of other communities with methods of distribution? Could some of you meet with us to discuss the idea?"

"Will you look over the proposed constitution for our new County Council and let me have your reactions?"

Such requests come to the individual staff members who were directly responsible for the workshops or to the Extension Division. They are relatively easy to meet. Something more of a problem lies in discovering needs about which communities are less articulate but which may be effectively blocking the desirable next steps. A staff member has been assigned to visit all communities that have had workshops, to evaluate progress and help to meet problems that are continuously arising. It is too soon yet to report on such evaluation or service.

The Extension Division is, in no sense, fostering dependence so far as those communities are concerned. Yet it wishes to help them avoid the feeling of frustration that comes of knowing what should be done and lacking the skills or knowledge necessary to achieve it. The more citizens know about the possibilities of community development and the more determined they become to have the best possible community through their own efforts, the more demands they are likely to make on institutions and agencies set up to serve them.

"I am convinced," says Dr. Hayes, "that the Extension Division will make a serious error if it continues to foster short workshops without plans for careful follow-up. It should be the job of the University to so plan that further education is demanded and provided."

Communities are demanding it. The Extension Division continues to seek the best methods for providing it.

CONCLUSION

We Pause To Rally Our Forces

To write *finis* to this report is difficult. It marks the end of a five-year experimental period, but not the end of the program started during that period. Nothing has really ended nor even been interrupted. Activities started in a few communities for the purpose of "discovering techniques" are continuing because they are meeting real needs there. Other activities have grown out of them and have spread to many communities.

Hence it is not possible to say that this report marks the end of exploration and experimentation and the beginning of application of what has been learned. Application began as exploration and experimentation indicated that certain approaches and techniques were worth extended use. Among the activities that have thus begun and are now in progress are summer workshops at the University for training professional and lay leaders in the philosophy and techniques of community development; local workshops for the purpose of helping citizens to take stock of community resources in relation to community needs and, on this basis, to plan programs of action and of community organization; workshops or work conferences for special groups (e.g. social workers or high school principals) for helping these groups see their programs in relation to the community as a whole; maintenance of pamphlet files and a film library for use of study groups, committees, community councils, or other adult groups; monthly reports in *New Dominion Series* of successful programs of various kinds in communities throughout the Southeast; and continuous contact of the staff *with people where they live, working directly with them rather than accepting the easier but less significant role of working only with leaders of organized community groups and agencies and hence touching people's lives only indirectly.*

Through such activities, exploration of the experiences of others and experimentation in our programs continue. Old techniques are being continuously tested and refined; new techniques, or new ways of using old, are being discovered and applied. There has been no ending of an experiment and launching of a program. Rather a program has evolved from the experiment and has led in turn to fresh experimentation. The laboratory which at first had to be created by choosing "experimental communities" is now established not only in those areas selected but in the many others that have been added as the program has developed and still others that are asking for help.

In fact, Special Projects must now be ever alert to the importance of working in all parts of this extended laboratory. *People in the communities where they live are the group tending to be touched only indirectly unless they are consciously included.* Leaders of organized groups and agencies set up to serve the people are much more articulate than are just plain citizens. Their requests for help are more insistent. Staff time and energy are limited. In a sense, the same amount of staff leadership can be made to go further if the staff works through such leaders. Yet the experience of the Special Projects indicates that the staff can help leaders in community organizations and agencies to the degree that they continue a close relationship with the people these groups serve. It also indicates that the more "successful" a program becomes, the more opportunity there is, and hence the greater the temptation, to work at levels once or twice removed from the people. The present continuing activities as listed above provide opportunities for work on all levels.

With an extensive program in progress, we cannot *conclude.* We can only pause to clarify our thinking; to take stock of what is happening; to make sure that we are profiting from our own experience to the fullest degree; to share the results of our experience, in so far as possible, with others who are interested in the question, "How can an educational agency help communities to help themselves through the efforts of their own citizens?"

To this end we attempt a brief recapitulation and summary with some explicit statements concerning the point of view which is implicit in this entire report.

Philosophy and Approach

The program was based on a firm belief in the democratic way of life. Its purpose was to find ways of strengthening democratic procedures to the end of better communities created through the efforts of citizens and in their turn creating better citizens.

Such a program must provide for widespread participation in planning. It must make clear distinction between *planning for* and *planning with the people whose lives are affected.* Real progress could be measured only by "the extent that individuals participate in the formulation of any plan affecting them and apply their energies and intelligence to its execution."[1]

Implicit in such an approach was provision for wide variation in patterns or programs adopted by communities concerned. Hence neither the Extension Division nor members of the staff had a formula by which a group should proceed nor specific goals or objectives other than the general one of making people (and hence communities) increasingly masters of their own destinies. To decide what a community should do or have and find clever ways of getting the people to cooperate was contrary to the philosophy on which the program was based. It must so develop as to help individuals and communities learn to choose their ways of living in the light of the best information available, and, having made the choice, to achieve the desired results.

Approach and method were implicit in the philosophy and purpose. Individuals (and communities) become adept at self-development through having opportunity to practice it. *Doing for* has no more place in such a program than *planning for* those whose lives are affected. *They must plan and do for themselves.* The job of the adult educator, in such a situation, becomes one of giving the persons involved mastery of the

[1]William A. Smith, "How People Can Educate Themselves to Help Themselves."

tools of social progress and helping them to plan opportunities to use these tools.

This involved starting where the individuals (or communities) had arrived in their own development and helping them move forward from there. Neither the starting point nor the goal could be known in advance. Only the direction was fixed. Starting points varied. Rate of progress was uneven. But to the extent that citizens did start and did move in the direction of the good community, to the extent they became increasingly able to keep moving in that direction even though slowly, the program was achieving its purposes. In measuring results, as in setting up plans, there could be no rigid standards generally applied. What indicated very real progress in one community might leave it still far behind the starting point of another.

Such a program is the direct antithesis of that of the social engineer with a blueprint. It allows the blueprint for each community to evolve in the process of working with the citizens. The persons guiding the process could, perhaps, have made a prettier blueprint in the beginning than the one which evolved. They would, however, have had to depend on something other than democratic processes to make it reality.

This does not mean that guiding the evolving community can be trusted to persons incapable of blueprinting "the good community." They must have their own blueprint, based on the very best that the scientists and the social scientists have to offer. But they must not be mastered by it. They must make it serve them and those with whom they plan and work. Only thus can be retained the flexibility that is the foundation and the safeguard of democracy.

Learned from Looking at Others

In looking ahead, five years ago, two main approaches were agreed upon in the search for techniques to help communities to help themselves—exploration of what was being done and experimentation in what might be done. Both were of great value during the so-called experimental period and each must continue to supplement the other as long as a program of community service is offered to citizens' groups and public agencies.

In exploring programs, it was discovered that there was in existence much printed material dealing with many aspects of community life. Some of it was ready for use; much of it had to be adapted to the needs of special groups. Even when the material collected was good for general use, we found that making it available was not enough. *A need had to be stimulated through work with study groups or committees before the available materials could be channeled into community programs.*

The same was true of research materials that needed to be translated into popular or simplified form. Translation alone still left a gap to be filled. Direct contact must be made with the ultimate consumer. *He must be made aware not only that such material was ready for him but also that he had need of it in relation to some activity that was important to him.*

Materials became most useful when the translation or adaptation was truly the result of a two-way process—that is, when the staff tried to meet a felt need in a community or organization, when the group found that existing materials did not meet the need, and when the two (Extension Division and consumer) joined forces, drawing on research agencies in the field, to produce just what was needed. In a very real sense *the staff served as middlemen between research reports or agencies and the citizens who must make the application in the community.*

Exploration also uncovered many excellent approaches to better communities that had not been reported anywhere and a few that had not even been recognized as having value beyond the immediate situation they had been set up to serve. Investigating, evaluating, and reporting such programs, likewise, was found to be a two-way process. In trying to interpret a program, those who had participated in it subjected it to searching analysis. Very often their objectives were clarified and their techniques refined as a result. The report (in *New Dominion Series*) often served to interpret a program *not only to other communities but also to the community of which it was a part. Again the staff served as middlemen.*

Reporting the programs was not enough. Reports must not only be made easily and attractively available; they must be sought by citizens in relation to a need. Getting the stories into the hands of educators, workers in public agencies, members of organizations in search of a program, and citizens who had evinced an interest proved effective. Sending them merely to those who knew enough about what they were looking for to ask for them stopped short of making them as generally useful as they should be. Yet it was found that they were used primarily by those who were seeking, and that if they were to stimulate others the process of *stirring must go on simultaneously and continuously with that of stuffing.*

The exploratory, or "looking at others," part of the program was undertaken for the education of ourselves and of the experimental groups we were working with. It has contributed generously to that. It has, to our surprise, afforded opportunity for us and our groups to contribute to others. In many instances a kind of continuous interchange has been set up. What may have been started by a note in a newspaper about a program, or a letter of inquiry from a citizen or a casual conversation, has been carried forward in a visit to the community by the staff to see for themselves. They have frequently found it difficult "to see" because the persons they were visiting were so eager to know how others were approaching similar problems. Later these bonds have been strengthened by sending materials from the files, by subsequent visits from the staff or by traveling workshops, and by participation of persons from these communities in summer workshops. *This interchange, resulting as it has in the feeling of a fellowship based on common interests, is a valuable technique discovered entirely as a by-product of "looking at others." It can be consciously and more systematically applied.*

From Trying Things Ourselves

Special approaches and techniques have been analyzed in detail in preceding sections and an attempt has been made to evaluate each in its place. A few generalizations emerge from the total program.

One of the strengths of Special Projects has resulted from the fact that the program throughout has been a group process. In retrospect it is impossible to discover who deserves credit for initiating specific ideas or plans. Credit to the individual has never been a factor to be reckoned with. In a like manner, in work in communities and in cooperation with other agencies, credit to the Extension Division or to the University has been subordinate to getting the job done. *The entire program has been a demonstration of the ability of a group to work effectively toward a goal which transcends individual (or institutional) interests and to get results that clearly indicate that the whole is greater than the sum of its parts.*

A second strength of the program lay in the conviction that the individuals and communities had a contribution to make to the educational process. They were helping the staff in the search for ways that would work as surely as the staff was helping them. Our experience has proved that this process of collaboration between adults in their communities and agencies for adult education has even greater possibilities than was realized in the beginning. But *it will get results only when the collaboration is sincere, when staff members are frankly learners along with those to whom they would give guidance in the process.*

The policy of adapting the program to community needs and of keeping it continuously flexible was put to an unusual test. Less than a year after the experimental work in communities had started, the country entered the war. Emergency problems must be met in every community. A few months before the experimental period ended, hostilities ceased and communities were facing peacetime problems that, in some ways, made the homefront problems of the war seem simple by comparison.

The war presented problems of shifting populations, suspension of programs because men and materials were urgently needed elsewhere, difficulties of travel, loss of leadership, preoccupation of those leaders who remained with filling the gaps left by those who had gone from the communities. Ways in which the program was affected by these problems have been commented on in relation to the work in the experimental counties and elsewhere in the report. *But the program as a whole met this test of adaptability and flexibility. In so doing it had unforeseen opportunities for trying varied techniques under unusual circumstances.*

With the second adjustment made necessary by the ending of the war, Special Projects faced the questions: Are there peacetime goals around which citizens will rally? Are there strong enough motivations to replace those inherent in the situation during the emergency? Are the same techniques valid in the postwar world?

The time has been too short to furnish conclusive proof. There, is, however, strong evidence that all three questions can be answered in the affirmative. The emphasis in most communities during the latter years of the war on "postwar planning" built a bridge before the time had come to cross it. Consciousness of the need made it possible for them to prepare for the transition. "We are winning the war," said a statement sent out by a citizens' council, "as a result of careful plans, aggressive action, and a determination to win. With this same approach—*planning, action, and determination*—we can be ready for the peace." In another community what started as an emotional drive for a "living war memorial" has developed into careful planning for a health center to serve peacetime needs. Its "memorial" aspects are almost lost sight of. Yet could there be a more fitting monument to those who fought for the democratic way of life than the perpetuation of a process for getting such services in a community through the planning and efforts of its citizens?

Undoubtedly the war was, in part, responsible for the need for prolongation of the experimental period. At the same time, it seems certain that even under normal conditions two years would have been too short a period to yield evidence of the soundness of the approach. Self-education that leads to action that leads to more self-education and more action is a slow process. It can undoubtedly be expedited by the application of tested procedures. But, even so, time alone can tell whether or not it has become a continuous process.

Some activities, started during the first two years of the program, have continued without subsequent attention. More, however, have required a longer period of nurturing before help could be withdrawn. Education that changes communities must allow for "reaction" time of the individuals concerned, for life-long habits and attitudes must be changed in the process.

Time is also essential to that broadening of the base of participation and leadership which are important factors in assuring the continuation of the process set in motion. Undoubtedly the wartime situation resulted in more than normal shifting of persons from one community to another. Thus the mortality was high in both professional and lay leaders. This underlined the danger, merely from the standpoint of survival of a program, of placing too much dependence on a few persons in a community. From the point of view of continued vigor and vitality of a program, widespread leadership was found to be even more important. Acceptance of leadership by the individuals fitted for it by temperament and training, but unaccustomed to it as a result of status in the community, is a slow process. Acceptance of such leaders by a community accustomed to "hereditary leaders" may be even slower. *Patterns and folkways of communities as well as habits of individuals must have time to change.*

Just as provision must be made for widespread leadership, so must it be made for widespread participation of the many agencies and interest groups to be found in any community. Participation in planning is just as essential for representatives of these groups as for lay citizens, *but, on the other hand, the planning is not their prerogative.* Unwillingness of some agencies, institutions, or individuals to accept their place as only one of many participants is a stumbling block in the development of many communities.

In considering the three types of approaches to stimulating community programs in the three experimental counties, it is not possible to say that any one of them is *best*. An attempt has been made to evaluate each in the chapters dealing with the counties. One thing seems clear: whatever the approach, there must, at some place in the program, *be provision for careful stock taking and planning in relation to resources as well as needs, and for a program of action which grows out of careful study of the situation.*

Local workshops in which the best techniques emerging from the experimental program have been applied, have been found an excellent means of analyzing resources in relation to needs and for planning a program of action on the basis of study. In such a situation, survey and planning go on simultaneously. Organization and action are directly related to both. This affords opportunity to combine the best aspects of surveys, planning, community councils, and action programs or "projects." Some such combination of all into an integrated whole is essential to well-rounded community development. So long as workshop procedure and organization can be kept flexible and leaders are sensitive to community differences, it is a good approach—perhaps the best. Yet we would not offer it as the only one nor as infallibly right for every community.

It may be considered as a technique which combines many techniques. Like its component parts, whether it works depends on why and how it is used.

The program described in this report had for its purpose to "discover techniques." Many were tried and found to get results. But techniques alone will do very little. They are merely tools that become effective when used creatively, painstakingly, and with untiring patience by skilled craftsmen to express something which they know unerringly and feel deeply. These tools can help to build the *Good Community* and make the democratic dream reality only as they give expression to "inherent faith in the ability of the common man to improve his conditions and environment if helped to help himself."[2]

---

[2]*Ibid.*

The Process Works

Because the program reported in these pages has been based on the philosophy and approach described above, *it must deal with processes rather than products.*

As has already been pointed out, tangible results are by-products and are important only as they prove the soundness of the procedures. We reiterate this for that person of literal mind who wants "to see results" and who persists in asking, "But what have you to show for the time and energy expended?"

The answer is *a process* which once started is, we believe, self-perpetuating. Tangible results such as libraries, canneries, locker refrigeration plants, health centers, recreation programs, and other services assuring more abundant life to communities mark the way of this process. But the process itself consists in the cooperative deliberations and planned action of citizens who are discharging their civic obligations to the best of their ability. *And the process works.*

Education as a means of implementing democracy through the creation of a continuously alert citizenry has been too often sterile. Hence adult education has a job to do in this field. This becomes the more difficult because of the need of breaking the habits of inertia and indifference that have been built up during many years of living. Only as a program of education to this end permeates communities, will citizens bestir themselves to accept the responsibilities that the rights of citizens in a democracy imply. To the degree that citizens shake off their lethargy, inform themselves in matters of public concern, and take action based on information and understanding—to that degree, communities will become better socially, economically, and culturally. And what happens to the community and to the citizen where he lives has important implications for the wider communities of the state, the nation, and the world of which he is an inescapable part.

APPENDIX A

Publications of the Special Projects

I. ANNOTATED LIST OF NEW DOMINION SERIES, Nos. 1-72.[1]

1. *Albemarle Considers County Affairs.* September 1, 1941.
   Albemarle County conducts a forum. 4 pages.
2. *New Plans for Old Programs.* September 15, 1941.
   Charlotte County agencies cooperate to plan a countywide program. 6 pages.
3. *Building Morale While Feeding Children.* October 1, 1941.
   Mecklenburg schools experiment with school lunches as a morale builder. 4 pages.
4. *Planning Tomorrow's Community.* October 15, 1941.
   School and community organizations conduct a survey as a basis for future planning. 6 pages.
5. *Welcoming Young Voters.* November 1, 1941.
   The Pittsylvania Citizenship League educates young voters. 4 pages.
6. *Coordinating Community Efforts.* November 15, 1941.
   Community organizations in Harrisonburg organize a council. 6 pages.
7. *The Community Builds A Home.* December 1, 1941.
   Women in Dinwiddie County build a community house. 4 pages.
8. *From Gangs to Boys' Club.* December 15, 1941.
   A boys' gang becomes a club in Pulaski. 8 pages.
9. *Supplementing Farm Income.* January 1, 1942.
   The stories of two producers' cooperatives that help Virginia farm families supplement cash income. 8 pages.
10. *Prince William's Five-Point Program.* February 1, 1942.
    The Negroes of Prince William County plan a better community.
11. *A Planned Rural Community.* March 1, 1942.
    A South Carolina school community improves its living through cooperative efforts. 12 pages. Illustrated.
12. *Recreation Meets a Challenge.* April 1, 1942.
    Radford plans a recreation program. 8 pages.
13. *Ironto Cooperative Cannery.* May 1, 1942.
    Farmers increase their cash income through a cooperative enterprise. 8 pages. Illustrated.
14. *A Rural Health Program.* June 1, 1942.
    Three Virginia counties pool their resources for a public health program. 8 pages. Illustrated.
15. *Farm Women Go to Market.* July 1, 1942.
    Farm women in Augusta County organize to sell the products of their kitchens in town. 8 pages Illustrated.

---

1. A selection from these *New Dominion* stories with interpretive material was published by Harper and Brothers under the title *Small Communities in Action.*

16. *Wanted—Diversified Farming.* July 15, 1942.
Farmers of Southside Virginia decide in vocational classes to form a cooperative as a means of attacking problems inherent in single-crop farming. 4 pages.

17. *Adventures in Joint Ownership.* August 1, 1942.
Planning and pooling of resources among neighbors enables low income families in Prince Edward County to buy pressure cookers and washing machines, stock hogs and lime spreaders that they could not afford to buy separately. 8 pages. Illustrated.

18. *Maximum Good with Minimum Effort.* August 15, 1942.
To avoid duplication of effort and to help in planning community programs of all kinds the people of a rural county create a council of community organizations. 4 pages.

19. *Communities Carry On.* September 1, 1942.
The first year's stories brought up to date. 12 pages.

20. *New Machines from Old.* September 15, 1942.
Farmers of Fauquier, with the help of a teacher of vocational agriculture and the school shops, keep their own farm machinery in good working order. 4 pages.

21. *Poultry for Profit.* October 1, 1942.
Cooperative marketing converts poultry raising in Rockingham County from a liability to a most definite asset. 8 pages.

22. *Pine Grove Health Program.* October 15, 1942.
A curative clinic makes it possible for the people of an isolated rural community to have medical care. 4 pages.

23. *Ruritan in Action.* November 1, 1942.
A civic club proves that it is possible to help improve a community without incurring large club expense. 4 pages.

24. *A Home-Grown Library.* November 15, 1942.
School and townspeople working together develop a library to serve both school and community. 6 pages.

25. *Democracy Applied to Serving Children.* December 1, 1942.
Through a lenten study group, Lynchburg women learn of a need to care for the children of working mothers and fill the need by establishing community centers. 8 pages.

26. *Ravenscroft Discovers the Land.* December 15, 1942. Unemployed miners of an abandoned mining community in Tennessee recreate their lives and their fortunes through farming. 8 pages.

27. *A Museum Begins at Home.* January 1, 1943.
Big Stone Gap builds a museum of local history. 8 pages. Illustrated.

28. *Self-Help through Gardens.* February 1, 1943.
In Wythe County people formerly dependent on public help win for themselves self-respect and self-support through gardens. 8 pages.

29. *Farmers Study for Action.* March 1, 1943.
    Study clubs among farmers develop a community from
    a collection of families and lead to improved living con-
    ditions in a Tennessee mountain area. 6 pages.
30. *Substituting We for They: Result a Clinic.* April 1, 1943.
    A successful effort by a few women in Lexington to have
    diseased tonsils of school children removed leads to the
    establishment of a children's clinic by the whole com-
    munity. 6 pages.
31. *United Efforts and United Funds.* May 1, 1943.
    A farmers' cooperative provides cheap lime for soil and
    improves livestock in Clarke County. 4 pages.
32. *Church and School Cooperate.* June 1, 1943.
    A church and a school in Rockbridge County work to-
    gether to solve community problems and improve com-
    munity living standards. 8 pages.
33. *Children Serve Their Own Community.* July 1, 1943.
    A Negro community near Newport News trains its chil-
    dren for more intelligent citizenship in the Aberdeen
    Gardens School Cooperative. 8 pages.
34. *Handing on Their Heritage.* July 15, 1943.
    The Weavers' Guild of Gatlinburg, Tennessee, records a
    disappearing way of life in dramatic form. 8 pages.
35. *Boys Become Foresters.* August 1, 1943.
    High school boys, under expert supervision, assume re-
    sponsibility for a community forest at Canton, N. C. 4
    pages.
36. *For All Mothers.* August 15, 1943.
    A rural community in Georgia maintains a maternity
    center to provide medical services and education on in-
    fant care. 6 pages.
37. *Pioneering in Food Preservation.* September 1, 1943.
    The people of Clarkesville, Georgia, build for their com-
    munity a complete plant to preserve their food surpluses.
    8 pages.
38. *Children of Mothers Who Work.* September 15, 1943.
    A Negro day nursery in Charlottesville develops through
    cooperation and community responsibility. 6 pages.
39. *Carroll County Cooperative Project.* Part I; October 1, 1943.
&   Part II; October 15, 1943. Small cooperatives built up
40.   around rural schools grow into countywide program. 16
      pages.
41. *Actual Needs and Practicable Solutions.* November 1, 1943.
    A school in Williamsburg uses its resources for all mem-
    bers of the Negro community which it serves. 8 pages.
42. *Emphasis on Marketing.* November 15, 1943.
    Farmers of Buckingham County establish a cooperative
    cannery and develop a second cash crop. 4 pages.
43. *Frozen Food Lockers.* December 1, 1943.
    A community, working cooperatively, creates a service to
    meet individual needs at Staunton. 4 pages.

44. *Abilities and Possibilities.* December 15, 1943.
    The State Board of Education in Virginia provides voca-
    tional advice for people in school and out. 8 pages.
45. *By the Youngsters.* January 1, 1944.
    Raleigh's boys and girls have their own club. 8 pages.
46. *The Mountain Comes to the School.* February 1, 1944.
    A rural school in Cullman County, Alabama, relates edu-
    cation to community life. 12 pages.
47. *Electricity Down on the Farm.* March 1, 1944.
    Through REA the Northern Neck of Virginia finds new
    ways of living and earning a living. 8 pages.
48. *By Popular Vote.* April 1, 1944.
    Citizens of Montgomery County, Virginia, demand and
    get a free public library. 8 pages.
49. *Facing Facts.* May 1, 1944.
    Citizens of Georgia establish the Fact-Finding Movement
    to appraise their state as a basis for action. 12 pages.
50. *Toward Better Health.* June 1, 1944.
    Citizens of Charles City County form their own health
    committee. 8 pages.
51. *Education—Family Style.* July 1, 1944.
    Rotating Homesteads at the Rabun Gap-Nacoochee School
    provide education for farming and citizenship. 8 pages.
52. *"It's A Fine Thing to Sing. . "* July 15, 1944.
    A small Maryland community pools its musical resources.
    4 pages.
53. *We the Citizens.* August 1, 1944.
    How Albemarle County came to adopt a new plan of
    county government. 8 pages.
54. *"Still Sits The Schoolhouse."* August 15, 1944.
    An abandoned rural school continues as a community
    center. 4 pages.
55. *Programs Revisited.* September 1, 1944.
    A second look at a few programs described in *New
    Dominion Series.* 8 pages.
56. *Letting People Know.* September 15, 1944.
    This is the first of several midmonthly issues of the *New
    Dominion Series* telling of devices used by communities
    to make their programs more effective. It tells how sev-
    eral communities have used newsletters and locally pre-
    pared bulletins. 8 pages.
57. *Lights of Tyrrell.* October 1, 1944.
    A credit union in Columbia, N. C., lights the way to a
    better life. 8 pages.
58. *Put It in the Paper.* October 15, 1944.
    In this second issue telling of devices used to make pro-
    grams more effective are stories of how some commun-
    ities have used their local papers. 6 pages.
59. *Substance of Things Hoped for.* November 1, 1944.
    A community center grows out of high school social
    studies class work. 8 pages.

60. *Study the Situation.* November 15, 1944.
 The third issue telling of devices used to make programs
 more effective gives accounts of study groups in several
 communities. 8 pages.
61. *Using Nature's Surplus.* December 1, 1944.
 Patrick County picks its wild berries and establishes an
 industry. 4 pages.
62. *Mustering Community Resources.* December 15, 1944.
 The fourth issue telling of devices to make programs
 more effective describes several kinds of community
 councils. 8 pages.
63. *Putting Christianity to Work.* January 1, 1945.
 Young people apply Christian principles to their community in Kingsport, Tennessee. 8 pages.
64. *How Well Are They Served?* February 1, 1945.
 A coordinating council in Cumberland, Maryland, studies
 the county's youth. 8 pages.
65. *Plans without People.* March 1, 1945.
 Fluvanna gets a cannery and learns about tactics. 6 pages.
66. *"The Trees Are There."* April 1, 1945.
 Neighbors get together to harvest and market black walnuts. 4 pages.
67. *Council of Forty-Nine.* May 1, 1945.
 Seven committees of seven each work for "seven betters"
 in the Negro Organization Society. 8 pages.
68. *New Plans in Old Communities.* June 1, 1945.
 Recreation becomes a reality in Fairfax County. 8 pages.
69. *Citizens Consider Their County.* July 15, 1945.
 The Louisa County Citizens' Council is stimulated by
 university extension. 8 pages.
70. *To Meet or Not to Meet.* July 15, 1945.
 The fifth issue telling of devices used by communities to
 make their programs more effective discusses meetings—
 good and bad. 6 pages.
71. *The Community and Health.* August 1, 1945.
 Health educators develop a broad community program
 with the Negroes of Hillsboro, N. C. 8 pages.
72. *Finding the Leaders.* August 15, 1945.
 The sixth issue telling of devices used to make programs
 more effective discusses leadership as found in *New
 Dominion* programs. 12 pages.

II. ANNOTATED LIST OF LOUISA COUNTY CITIZENS' COUNCIL BULLETIN.

The **Forest Fires Series.** February—March, 1943.
 Prepared by the Rotary committee on forestry with assis-
 tance of Special Projects staff. Published and distributed
 by Extension Division in cooperation with Louisa County
 Citizens' Council.
 Burn Brush Early
 Burn Brush Safely

Be Careful with Fire
In Case of Fire
>   (Note: These four one-page broadsides were prepared by the forestry committee and mailed to citizens of the county at intervals of one week during the spring fire season, 1943. Out of this series the *Bulletin* developed.)

The **Bulletin,** Nos. 1-17.

Published and distributed to all families in the county by the Louisa County Citizens' Council in cooperation with the Extension Division of the University of Virginia:

1. *Victory Food Supply Campaign:* Your Garden Program. April 1, 1943.
   >   Prepared by the nutrition committee of the council in collaboration with staff. 4 pages.
2. *Victory Food Supply Campaign:* Pest Control Program. May 1, 1943.
   >   Prepared by a special committee of the council in collaboration with staff. 4 pages.
3. *Victory Food Supply Campaign:* Your Canning Program (with chart for record). June 1, 1943.
   >   Prepared by nutrition committee of the council in collaboration with staff. 4 pages.
4. *Victory Food Supply Campaign:* Simple Wartime Canning for school lunch program. July 1, 1943.
   >   Prepared by nutrition committee of the council in collaboration with staff. 4 pages. Supplement 1 page.
5. *Victory Food Supply Campaign:* Wartime Fall and Winter Gardens. August 1, 1943.
   >   Prepared by nutrition committee of the council in collaboration with staff. 4 pages.
6. *Victory Food Supply Campaign:* Make Your Victory Garden Serve You All Winter. September 1, 1943.
   >   Prepared by nutrition committee of the council in collaboration with staff. 4 pages.
7. *Stop Forest Fires!* October 1, 1943.
   >   Prepared by the forestry committee of the council in collaboration with staff. 4 pages.
8. *Cut Pulpwood Now.* November 1, 1943.
   >   Prepared by the forestry committee of the council in collaboration with staff. 2 pages.
9. *Facts About A Frozen Food Locker Plant.*[2] December 1, 1943.
   >   Prepared by a special committee of the council at the suggestion of the soil conservation committee and in collaboration with staff. 4 pages.

---

2. Reprinted in special editions for Fluvanna and Buckingham Counties and permission for reprints given to one other state and commercial concern.

10. *Choose Chicks with Care.* February 1, 1944.
>   Prepared by a special committee of the council at
>   the request of the county agent and in collaboration
>   with staff. 2 pages. Illustrated.

11. *Be Careful with Fire.* March 1, 1944.
>   Prepared by forestry committee of the council in
>   collaboration with staff. 2 pages.

12, *Grow Healthy Chicks.* March 15, 1944.
>   Prepared by a special committee of the council at
>   the request of the county agent and in collaboration
>   with staff. 2 pages. Illustrated.

13. *"Take It or Leave It."*[3] Soil Conservation Quiz. June 1,
    1944.
>   Prepared by the soil conservation committee of the
>   council in collaboration with the publicity commit-
>   tee and the staff. 4 pages plus map insert locating
>   farms to be visited.

14. *"Go" Sign For Home Canning.* July 1, 1944.
>   Prepared by the nutrition committee of the council
>   in collaboration with the publicity committee and
>   the staff. 4 pages plus insert chart for recording
>   quantities canned. Illustrated.

15. *That Frozen Food Locker Plant.* January 15, 1945.
>   Prepared by the publications committee of the
>   council in collaboration with the staff. Printed and
>   distributed with the cooperation of Southern States
>   Cooperative. Announcing opening of locker plant
>   suggested in *Bulletin* No. 9. 4 pages.

16. *Have You Heard The News?* A Plan for Medical Care
    in Louisa. July 1, 1945.
>   Prepared by the publications committee of the
>   council at the request of the publicity committee
>   for the medical care center and living war memorial
>   in collaboration with the staff. 4 pages.

17. *A Primer For Parents.* October 1, 1945.
>   Need for cooperation of parents and schools.
>   Prepared by publications committee of the council
>   in collaboration with the staff at the request of the
>   Ruritan education committee from material gathered
>   by the Ruritan committee. 4 pages.

Questionnaire—to check on the effectiveness of the *Bulletin.*
November, 1943. 2 pages.

III. WE WENT TO SEE FOR OURSELVES. January, 1945.

The Account of an Itinerant Workshop in Community Programs in Action. Written by the Participants. Extension
Division, University of Virginia. 32 pages.

---

3. This bulletin was the forerunner of the *Soil Saver* and the cooperation with
the Thomas Jefferson Soil Conservation District.

**IV. COMMUNITY QUIZ: SOME $64 QUESTIONS. A Study Guide
on Community Development.** October, 1945.

Prepared in collaboration with and published for the Virginia Federation of Women's Clubs. Foreword by George B. Zehmer. Introduction by Etta Belle Northington. Extension Division, University of Virginia. 60 pages.

V. THE SOIL SAVER. Some Modern Talk for Some Modern
Farmers.

A monthly bulletin prepared in collaboration with and published for the Thomas Jefferson Soil Conservation District and distributed to the farmers of five counties through the courtesy of the local banks.

No. 1 *Food Factory.* January 1, 1946.
4 pages.

**VI. TEN YEARS OF COUNTY MANAGER GOVERNMENT IN VIR-
GINIA. An Experiment in Local Government.** September 1,
1945.

By George W. Spicer, Professor of Political Science, University of Virginia. Foreword by George B. Zehmer. Extension Division, University of Virginia. 94 pages.

APPENDIX B

Articles About Work of the Special Projects

Virginia Community Experiment. J. N. G. Finley. Journal of Adult Education. April, 1941.

Opportunity for Choice. Jean and Jess Ogden. Adult Education Journal. April, 1942.

Back of the Yards and Back in the Mountains. Per Stensland. The American-Scandinavian Review. Summer, 1942.

Clubbing Together to Get Things Done. William H. Wranek. Richmond Times-Dispatch. February 28, 1943.

Toward Better Use of Southern Resources George B. Zehmer. Virginia Journal of Education. October, 1943.

Report from Virginia. Donald Slesinger. Film News. January, 1944.

New Dominion Series. Jean and Jess Ogden. University of Virginia Alumni News. March, 1944.

Helping to Build a New Dominion. George B. Zehmer. The Commonwealth. April, 1944.

Techniques of Community Organization. Jean and Jess Ogden. Proceedings of Seventeenth Annual Meeting of the Virginia Social Science Association. May, 1944.

Describing Effective Patterns of Community Action. John E. Ivey, Jr. Channeling Research into Education. Pages 70-75. American Council on Education Studies. Series I. No. 19. August, 1944.

A University Aids Community Development. L. F. Addington. Virginia Journal of Education. October, 1944.

Up from the South. Jean and Jess Ogden. Adult Education Journal. January, 1945.

Success Stories. Glen Burch. Journal of Adult Education. July, 1945.

Citizens Consider Their County. New Dominion Series. Extension Division, University of Virginia. July, 1945.

Records of Community Progress. Paul Greer. St. Louis Post-Dispatch. August 15, 1945.

Interaction of School and Community. Jean and Jess Ogden. The National Elementary School Principal. Twenty-Fourth Yearbook. September, 1945.

Education That Changes Communities. Jean and Jess Ogden. The Journal of Educational Sociology. September, 1945.

Experiment with Principals. New Dominion Series. Extension Division, University of Virginia. December, 1945.

Taking Stock of the Community. New Dominion Series. Extension Division, University of Virginia. January, 1946.

APPENDIX C

Unpublished Reports and Records
Referred to or Used in This Report

Southern Readings Project
Correspondence, reports of conferences, outlines of proposed plans and administrative setup. George B. Zehmer. November, 1937—April, 1939.

How People Can Educate Themselves To Help Themselves.
A Program of Action to Stimulate and Develop Individual Initiative for the Economic and Social Betterment of Individuals, Neighborhoods and Communities. William A. Smith. 1940. 1941-June, 1945.
Typed. 59 pages.

Memoranda on conferences with southern educators and others concerning the proposals of William A. Smith and ways of implementing them through the Special Projects in Adult Education at the University of Virginia. George B. Zehmer.

Memoranda and Reports to President Newcomb and the Advisory Committee. George B. Zehmer. December, 1940-June, 1941.

Memoranda on Investigation of and Visits to Proposed Experimental Areas by Mr. Zehmer and members of the staff of the Extension Division and the Special Projects. December, 1940-July, 1941

Comments and Suggestions on Work in Greene County. Submitted to George B. Zehmer by Jess Ogden. October 1, 1941. Typed. 53 pages. Maps and charts.

Progress Reports on Greene. April 1942, April 1943, April 1944.

A Village Consolidated School in Relationship to Its Community. William Richard Savage, Jr. A thesis submitted in partial fulfillment of the requirements for the degree of Master of Education in the Graduate School of Arts and Sciences of Duke University. (Background on *Nansemond* County). Typed. 117 pages.

Nansemond County Correspondence and Progress Reports. George B. Zehmer, William R. Savage, Jr., and members of the staff. June, 1941-March, 1945.

Background and Statistical Material on Louisa County. Collected May, 1941-September, 1943.

Minutes and Reports. Louisa County Citizens' Council. January, 1942-March, 1945. 70 pages.

Progress Reports to Advisory Committee and/or included in Annual Reports of the Extension Division. George B. Zehmer. October, 1941-June, 1945.

Summer Workshop, 1943. Verbatim reports of all regular sessions and
   summaries of less formal meetings. Recorded by Anne I.
   Faulkner. Typed. 226 pages.

Wanted More and Better Movies. A complete report of use of films
   in Greene and Louisa Counties showing need and outlining a
   program for a New Dominion Series of Educational films.
   January, 1944. Typed. 69 pages. Illustrated by maps and
   charts.

Scrapbook (2). Clippings on and reprints of *New Dominion Series.*
   September, 1941-September, 1945.

INDEX

Louisa *Bulletin*, 254, 307; Louisa committee, 268

Soil Saver, 256

Southampton County, Virginia, in workshop, 241

South Carolina, State of, 7

Southern Appalachians, 5, 100; Greene, 102ff.

Southern Readings Project, 12, 36

Specialists (Experts), use of, 290, 357, 396

Special Projects in Adult Education, iii; approach, 3; beginning, 2; consultants, v; exploratory steps, 3; limitation of, 231; philosophy of, ix, 2ff., 140, 250; purpose of, 250; raising funds, iv; relation of Grundy program, 235; staff, v

Spicer, George W., 253, 394

Spotsylvania County, Virginia, experiment with principals, 238

Staff, conferences, 22, 235; demands on, 242, 246; for local workshops, 245, 246, 382; for summer workshops, 21, 334; list of, ii; part-time, 21; philosophy of, 8; qualifications of, 19ff.; selection of, 20; Special Projects, ii, v; working directly with people, 403

St. Louis *Post-Dispatch*, 325

Stop Forest Fires Series, 294ff.

Study for action, evolution, 197; interest of Extension Division in, 172

Study groups, local, 254; materials for, 26; Scandinavian, 22; study-action approach, 399; use of materials, 35ff.; variety in, 89

Suffolk, Virginia, 117

"Supplementing Farm Income," (NDS # 9), 52

Surveys, Holy Neck District, 116, 198ff.; not always expedient, 22; of experimental counties, 101ff.; recommendations, 120ff.; resistance to, 172

Tate, Leland B., 232ff.

Tazewell County, Virginia, in workshop, 241, 247

Techniques in adult education, delay in beginning often effective, 151; in experimental counties, 134-37, 196; learning from mistakes, 168; limitations of, 412; serving other agencies, 153;

should have been tested, 197; staff demonstrations, 183ff., 197; study for action group, 172, 258ff.; variety of, 7

"Telling the people," 91, 191, 256, 307

Tennessee, State of, 7, 326; University of, 245, 382

Tennessee Valley Authority, 12, 20, 324

Ten Years of County Manager Government in Virginia, 394

"The Mountain Comes to the School" (NDS # 46), 322

"The Trees Are There" (NDS # 66), 325

Thomas Jefferson Soil Conservation District, 133, 190, 254ff., 269, 302, 307

Thompson, Lorin A., v, 253

Time analysis, in Greene, 166; in Louisa, 194, 195

Time element, effect of war on, 139, 410; optimistic estimate, 22; relation to community patterns, 410, 411; underestimation of, 166, 197, 210

Toronto, University of, 322

"Toward Better Health" (NDS # 50), 323

U. S. Office of Education, 322, 324

"Using Nature's Surplus" (NDS # 61), 60

Vanderbilt University, iii, 245, 336, 382

Verdin, Tom, 342, 367

Virginia Federation of Women's Clubs, cooperation and financing, viii; extension of program, 251ff., 302; in workshop, 349

Virginia Forestry Service, 396

Virginia Polytechnic Institute, 205, 232ff., 253

Virginia State Board of Education, cooperation with, 6, 100, 235; provision for summer employment of principals, 240, 241; specialists from, 396; sponsor program (NDS), 47

Virginia State Conservation Commission, 59

Virginia State Department of Public Health, 396

Virginia State Department of Welfare, 100; cooperation with, 6,

3-157